"This valuable volume brings the kind of broad perspective to mild cognitive impairment that has long been needed. Rather than basing conclusions on a single sample or framework, the editors have pulled together articles from leading research groups around the world. This is the kind of comprehensive approach that is needed for developing systematic and valid definitions of MCI and identifying better tools that make it possible to differentiate between benign memory changes in later life and the early signs of pathological processes."
—Steven H. Zarit, Department of Human Development and Family Studies, The Pennsylvania State University, USA

"This volume provides the most comprehensive overview of mild cognitive impairment currently available. The conceptual and methodological challenges for studying MCI are tackled with rigor, and the complexities of defining the syndrome are not underestimated. This book is certain to become a classic text for those studying or researching cognitive aging, MCI and dementia, and for clinicians seeking an authoritative reference on the clinical manifestations of MCI."
—Kaarin J. Anstey, Centre for Mental Health Research, Australian National University, Australia

"The editors of this book have done a great job. The description of the issues is laid out in a well-written introduction, making the descriptions of the research papers very accessible, even to the less well-informed reader. The conclusion likewise pulled together the various strands, including defining what still needs to be done to further refine the concept of MCI."
—Graham A. Jackson, Laverndale Hospital, Scotland.
In *Dementia*, August, 2008

Mild Cognitive Impairment

The Classic Edition of this foundational text includes a new preface from Holly A. Tuokko, examining how the field of Mild Cognitive Impairment (MCI) has developed since first publication. Bringing together research from multiple studies and perspectives from various countries, the volume identifies MCI as an important clinical transition between normal aging and the early stages of Alzheimer's disease (AD).

The up-to-date preface highlights the expansion in research, examining the benefits of various pharmacological, cognitive and behavioral approaches to intervention. Influenced by recent findings in neuroplasticity across the lifespan, the book recognizes the importance of intervention at the earliest stages of the decline trajectory. It revisits the contested diagnostic approaches for MCI as well as the varying prevalence of MCI internationally, yet points to the need for further longitudinal studies to fully understand the condition.

Mild Cognitive Impairment continues to provide a comprehensive resource for clinicians, researchers and students involved in the study, diagnosis, treatment and rehabilitation of people with MCI.

Holly A. Tuokko was a Professor in the Department of Psychology and Institute on Aging and Lifelong Health at the University of Victoria. She was awarded Senior Investigator status through the Canadian Institutes of Health Research, Institute of Aging (2002–2007), for her program of research on mental health and aging.

David F. Hultsch was a Professor of Psychology at the University of Victoria from 1984 onward, with a major research focus on cognition and aging. He was a founder of the journal *Aging, Neuropsychology, and Cognition*, serving as co-editor for 10 years.

Psychology Press and Routledge Classic Editions

The *Psychology Press and Routledge Classic Editions* series celebrates a commitment to excellence in scholarship, teaching, and learning within the field of Psychology. The books in this series are widely recognized as timeless classics, of continuing importance for both students and researchers. Each title contains a completely new introduction which explores what has changed since the books were first published, where the field might go from here, and why these books are as relevant now as ever. Written by recognized experts, and covering core areas of the subject, the *Psychology Press and Routledge Classic Editions* series presents fundamental ideas to a new generation.

Mild Cognitive Impairment: International Perspectives
Edited by Holly A. Tuokko and David F. Hultsch

Language Development and Social Interaction in Blind Children
Edited by Miguel Pérez-Pereira and Gina Conti-Ramsden

Hypothetical Thinking: Dual Processes in Reasoning and Judgement
By Jonathan St B. T. Evans

Models of Cognitive Development
By Ken Richardson

Children and Television
Edited by Barrie Gunter and Jill Gunter

Knowledge in Context: Representations, Community and Culture
By Sandra Jovchelovitch

The Psychology of Language and Communication
Edited by Geoffrey Beattie and Andrew Ellis

Family, Self, and Human Development Across Cultures: Theories and Applications (Classic Edition)
By Çigdem Kagitçibasi

Mild Cognitive Impairment
International Perspectives

Classic Edition
Edited by
Holly A. Tuokko & David F. Hultsch

NEW YORK AND LONDON

Classic Edition published 2020
by Routledge
52 Vanderbilt Avenue, New York, NY 10017

and by Routledge
2 Park Square, Milton Park, Abingdon, Oxon, OX14 4RN

Routledge is an imprint of the Taylor & Francis Group, an informa business

© 2020 Taylor & Francis

The right of Holly A. Tuokko & David F. Hultsch to be identified as the authors of the editorial material, and of the authors for their individual chapters, has been asserted in accordance with sections 77 and 78 of the Copyright, Designs and Patents Act 1988.

All rights reserved. No part of this book may be reprinted or reproduced or utilised in any form or by any electronic, mechanical, or other means, now known or hereafter invented, including photocopying and recording, or in any information storage or retrieval system, without permission in writing from the publishers.

First Edition published 2015 by Psychology Press

Trademark notice: Product or corporate names may be trademarks or registered trademarks, and are used only for identification and explanation without intent to infringe.

Library of Congress Cataloging-in-Publication Data
A catalog record for this title has been requested

ISBN: 978-0-367-89649-2 (hbk)
ISBN: 978-0-367-89646-1 (pbk)
ISBN: 978-1-003-02030-1 (ebk)

Typeset in Times New Roman
by codeMantra

Contents

About the editors	ix
List of contributors	xi
From the series editor	xiii
Introduction to the Classic Edition	xv

Part I
Introduction   1

1 An overview of mild cognitive impairment   3
   HOLLY A. TUOKKO AND IAN MCDOWELL

Part II
General Population Research on MCI   29

2 The PAQUID study   31
   COLETTE FABRIGOULE, PASCALE BARBERGER-GATEAU,
   AND JEAN-FRANÇOIS DARTIGUES

3 Cognitive impairment in elderly persons without dementia:
   Findings from the Kungsholmen Project   57
   KATIE PALMER, LARS BÄCKMAN, BRENT J. SMALL, AND
   LAURA FRATIGLIONI

4 Population levels of mild cognitive impairment in
   England and Wales   77
   JANE FLEMING, FIONA E. MATTHEWS, MARK CHATFIELD,
   AND CAROL BRAYNE

5 The Melbourne Aging Study   93
   ALEXANDER COLLIE, PAUL MARUFF, DAVID G. DARBY,
   COLIN MASTERS, AND JON CURRIE

Part III
Specific Samples — 115

6 Mild cognitive impairment in the Religious Orders Study — 117
ROBERT S. WILSON, NEELUM T. AGGARWAL, AND DAVID A. BENNETT

7 A perspective from the Mayo Clinic — 131
GLENN SMITH, MARY MACHULDA, AND KEJAL KANTARCI

8 Prediction of probable Alzheimer's disease: The Sunnybrook Memory Study — 163
MARY C. TIERNEY

9 Studies in the Leipzig Memory Clinic: Contribution to the concept of mild cognitive impairment — 181
HENRIKE WOLF AND HERMANN-JOSEF GERTZ

Part IV
Interventions — 215

10 Emerging pharmacological therapies for mild cognitive impairment — 217
HOWARD CHERTKOW

11 Cognition-based therapies and mild cognitive impairment — 245
ROBERT T. WOODS AND LINDA CLARE

12 Combined therapies in mild cognitive impairment — 265
KEVIN PETERS AND GORDON WINOCUR

Part V
Summary and Future Directions — 289

13 The future of mild cognitive impairment — 291
HOLLY A. TUOKKO AND DAVID F. HULTSCH

Author index — 305
Subject index — 315

About the editors

Holly A. Tuokko was a Professor in the Department of Psychology and the Centre on Aging at the University of Victoria. She has been awarded Senior Investigator status through the Canadian Institutes of Health Research, Institute of Aging (2002–2007) for her program of research on mental health and aging. Her research focuses on issues that are clinically informative and of practical concern (such as identification and management of people with MCI).

David F. Hultsch is a Professor of Psychology at the University of Victoria with a major research focus on cognition and aging. He is a co-investigator of the *Victoria Longitudinal Study*, and is also examining the role of short-term inconsistency in response speed as an indicator of cognitive aging. He was a founder of the journal *Aging, Neuropsychology, and Cognition*, serving as co-editor for 10 years.

List of contributors

Neelum T. Aggarwal, M.D., Rush University Medical Center, Chicago, USA

Lars Bäckman, Ph.D., Karolinska Institutet and Stockholm Gerontology Research Center, Stockholm, Sweden

Pascale Barberger-Gateau, M.D., Ph.D., Université Victor Segalen Bordeaux, 2, Bordeaux, France

David A. Bennett, M.D., Rush University Medical Center, Chicago, USA

Carol Brayne, Ph.D., University of Cambridge, Cambridge, United Kingdom

Mark Chatfield, Ph.D., University of Cambridge, Cambridge, United Kingdom

Howard Chertkow, M.D., FRCB(C), McGill University, Montreal, Canada

Linda Clare, Ph.D., University of Wales, Bangor, United Kingdom

Alexander Collie, Ph.D., The University of Melbourne, Melbourne, Australia

Jon Currie, MD, Ph.D., Westmead Hospital, Sydney, Australia

David G. Darby, Ph.D., The University of Melbourne, Melbourne, Australia

Jean-François Dartigues, M.D., Ph.D., INSERM U593, Bordeaux, France

Colette Fabrigoule, Ph.D., Université Victor Segalen Bordeaux, 2, Bordeaux, France

Jane Fleming, Ph.D., University of Cambridge, Cambridge, United Kingdom

Laura Fratiglioni, Ph.D., Karolinska Institutet and Stockholm Gerontology Research Center, Stockholm, Sweden

Hermann-Josef Gertz, M.D., Ph.D., Universität Leipzig, Leipzig, Germany

David F. Hultsch, Ph.D., University of Victoria, Victoria, Canada

Kejal Kantarci, M.D., Mayo Clinic College of Medicine, Rochester, USA

Mary Machulda, Ph.D., Mayo Clinic College of Medicine, Rochester, USA

Paul Maruff, Ph.D., La Trobe University, Melbourne, Australia

xii *List of contributors*

Colin Masters, Ph.D., The University of Melbourne, Melbourne, Australia

Fiona E. Matthews, Ph.D., University of Cambridge, Cambridge, United Kingdom

Ian McDowell, Ph.D., University of Ottawa, Ottawa, Canada

Katie Palmer, Ph.D., Karolinska Institutet and Stockholm Gerontology Research Center, Stockholm, Sweden

Kevin Peters, Ph.D., Trent University, Peterborough, Canada

Brent J. Small, Ph.D., University of South Florida, Tampa, USA

Glenn Smith, Ph.D., Mayo Clinic College of Medicine, Rochester, USA

Mary C. Tierney, Ph.D., University of Toronto, Toronto, Canada

Holly A. Tuokko, Ph.D., University of Victoria, Victoria, Canada

Robert S. Wilson, Ph.D., Rush University Medical Center, Chicago, USA

Gordon Winocur, Ph.D., Trent University, Peterborough, Canada

Henrike Wolf, M.D., Ph.D., Universität Leipzig, Leipzig, Germany

Robert T. Woods, Ph.D., University of Wales, Bangor, United Kingdom

From the series editor

Mild Cognitive Impairment (MCI) has been a controversial concept ever since its designation in the early 1990s. Whether it is truly a form of incipient dementia or a variant of normal cognitive aging is the subject of numerous studies, articles, book chapters, and even an annual conference such as the "Mild Cognitive Impairment (MCI) Symposium" held each year at the Mount Sinai Medical Center in Miami Beach. *Mild Cognitive Impairment: International Perspectives*, edited by Holly Tuokko and David Hultsch, is a truly remarkable volume which covers not only the many issues surrounding the classification and prognostic implications of MCI, but findings from the many national and international studies of cohorts of aging populations. Chapters range from an incisive overview of these salient issues, to aging studies from France, Australia, Sweden, the UK, Australia, Canada, Germany, and the USA.

With rapidly aging populations around the world, the implications of cognitive change in aging are indeed profound. If, as some maintain, MCI is a harbinger of dementia, then large portions (up to 30% prevalence of MCI noted in the first chapter) of older individuals are at risk. If, on the other hand, MCI is not necessarily such a portent, what are the implications for what is termed "normal" functioning with older age? And, can MCI be treated? Tuokko and Hultsch include chapters on pharmacological and behavioral treatments for MCI and their potential benefits as well as implications and guidance for future research. *Mild Cognitive Impairment: International Perspectives* clearly meets the need for a concise summary of the wide range of international work addressing these important issues and is a stellar addition to our series. I commend it to you highly.

Linas A. Bieliauskas
February, 2006

Introduction to the Classic Edition

Introduction

The aim of this chapter is to provide an update to the information on mild cognitive impairment (MCI) that was provided in 2006 from multiple studies and perspectives from various countries. At that time, a number of challenges confronting researchers were identified, such as base rate differences among different samples and evolving conceptions of cognitive change in later life. Most notably, MCI was observed to be a heterogeneous classification, regardless of how it was defined (i.e., narrow to broad definitions), possibly associated with various underlying pathological processes and expected outcomes (i.e., revert to normal, stable MCI, progression to dementia). At that time, there was substantial controversy concerning whether MCI was associated with a specific disease process (e.g., most notably Alzheimer's Disease – AD) or whether it was best used as a descriptor of current functioning. Interventions, both pharmacological and behavioral, for those with MCI were beginning to emerge but were limited by the complexities of the MCI construct. As with diagnostic implications, it was noted that approaches to intervention differed in terms of intention. Pharmacological approaches sought to slow, stop, or even reverse the underlying pathological process, whereas behavioral interventions sought to optimize well-being, minimize disability, and prevent dysfunctional family and social functioning. In this chapter, these lines of investigation will be revisited.

Current Understanding of MCI

Over the past 10–15 years, there has been a movement away from efforts to establish the existence of MCI toward the acceptance of the condition. While efforts to clarify subtypes (i.e., amnestic, non-amnestic; single domain, multiple domain) of MCI and associate these with presumed underlying disorders (Petersen, 2004) have generated much research, the construct continues to evolve, with new sets of criteria emerging. Most recently, criteria for MCI have been articulated by the National Institute of Aging – Alzheimer's Association (NIA-AA) workgroups on diagnostic guidelines for AD (Albert et al., 2011) and the *Diagnostic and statistical manual of mental disorders: DSM-5™* (5th ed.) (American Psychiatric Association, 2013). Of note, the NIA-AA core clinical criteria are specific to MCI presumed to be associated with AD pathology, which was the predominant position in the past. The NIA-AA have also proposed research criteria for MCI that incorporate biomarkers. Until biomarkers become better understood and more accessible, these research criteria are intended for use only in research settings (Petersen et al., 2014). Other new sets of criteria acknowledge that MCI defined in particular ways may be indicative of other neurological conditions. For example, the 2019 edition of *International classification of diseases – 10th edition – Clinical modification* (ICD-10-CM, effective on October 1, 2018; World Health Organization) codes MCI (G31.84) as a synonym for mild neurocognitive disorder and may be descriptive of the present level of cognitive impairment. Other codes denote MCI related to specific etiologies (e.g., cerebral degeneration G31.9, following cerebral hemorrhage I69.01, due to intracranial or head injury S06) and specific cognitive impairment, such as mild memory disturbance (F06.8).

Significant changes from previous editions of the Diagnostic and Statistical Manual (DSM) have emerged in the manner in which the 5th edition (DSM-5; APA, 2013) addresses MCI. Here too, the term mild neurocognitive disorder (i.e., mild NCD or mNCD) is used, and the understanding of this condition arises almost exclusively from previous research on MCI (Sachs-Ericsson & Blazer, 2015). Unlike the NIA-AA criteria, the DSM-5 acknowledges that mNCD may be associated with a variety of potential etiologies (e.g., AD, Lewy Bodies, and others). However, mNCDs associated with these presumptive etiologies are all coded as 331.83 (G31.84) in the DSM-5 as the links to these conditions remain uncertain. This is in contrast to the DSM-5 convention to code *known* etiologies of major NCD into subtypes. Within the diagnostic criteria for these subtypes of major NCDs, descriptions for the associated mNCD presentations are provided. Other sets of criteria similar to Albert's (2011) have emerged describing MCI related to specific non-AD pathologies, such as vascular cognitive impairment (Skrobot et al., 2017) and Parkinson's-related cognitive impairment (e.g., Goldman et al., 2018; Litvan et al., 2012).

In Table 1, the domains of relevance for the NIA-AA and DSM-5 sets of diagnostic criteria are listed. Of note, these sets of criteria differ with respect to the specific cognitive domains identified but are similar with respect to the necessary number of cognitive domains where impairment is evident (i.e., one or more). In keeping with the potential for various etiologies, memory impairment has been removed as an essential criterion in the DSM-5, and specification of behavioral deficits has been improved. Memory impairment remains as an areas of impairment typically seen for MCI due to AD (Albert et al., 2011). Both the NIA-AA and DSM-5 strongly support the use of objective neurocognitive assessments, when available. Albert et al. (2011) provide guidelines for the identification of impairment as 1–1.5 standard deviations below the mean for age and education matched peers on culturally appropriate normative data. The DSM-5 notes

Table 1 Summary of NIA-AA and DSM-5 criteria associated with MCI

Criteria	Albert et al. (2011)	DSM-5 (APA, 2013)
Identification	Concern regarding a change in cognition from the patient, an informant who knows the patient well, or a skilled clinician	Concern of the patient, a knowledgeable informant, or clinician about mild decline in cognitive function
Cognition	Impairment in one or more cognitive domains, including memory, executive function, attention, language, and visuospatial skills	Modest decrement in cognitive functioning from a previous level in one or more cognitive domains (complex attention, executive function, learning and memory, language, perceptual motor, or social cognition)
Daily activities	Mild problems performing complex functional tasks may be present, but there is general preservation of independence in functional abilities	Typically does not interfere with independence in daily functioning; however, the use of new compensatory strategies and accommodations may be evident
Medical conditions	Not demented. All other causes for cognitive impairment ruled out (e.g., vascular, traumatic, medical)	Not part of a delirium and not better explained by another medical condition (e.g., schizophrenia)
Prognosis	Indicative of subsequent cognitive decline associated with AD	May signal subsequent cognitive decline, resulting in diagnosis of major NCD, but not necessarily the case

that performance typically lies 1–2 standard deviations below appropriate norms, with performance being evaluated in relation to the person's prior level of functioning.

Subtypes of MCI

MCI was originally proposed in a diagnostic capacity to herald the onset of greater cognitive decline associated with AD pathology (e.g., Petersen et al., 1999). Many longitudinal studies since have examined conversion rates from MCI to dementia, and, regardless of how it is defined, MCI remains heterogeneous in terms of expected outcomes (i.e., revert to normal, stable MCI, progression to specific forms of dementia). For example, Mitchell and Shiri-Feshki (2009) examined 41 robust longitudinal cohort studies using MCI defined at baseline with the criteria of Petersen et al. (1997) or Petersen et al. (2004). They observed that most people with MCI did not progress to dementia, even after ten years. More recently, Marcos et al. (2016) examined conversion rates after 4.5 years using Petersen et al.'s (1999) and DSM-5 MCI criteria. Approximately 10% and 15% of MCI individuals identified with Petersen et al.'s (1999) and DSM-5 criteria, respectively, were diagnosed with dementia. This suggests that the DSM-5 criteria may be an improvement on previous sets of criteria. However, as was seen in the past, most individuals with MCI do not progress to dementia.

A number of approaches have been proposed as ways to enhance classification within MCI with respect to anticipated outcomes. These include (1) a focus on biological events thought to be reflective of underlying pathological processes (i.e., biomarkers), (2) a further clarification of differing cognitive profiles within the MCI construct, and (3) combining information on biological events and cognitive profiles.

Biomarkers

As noted above, the NIA-AA research criteria (Albert et al., 2011) includes information concerning biomarkers relevant to the diagnosis of AD-related MCI. Two groups of biomarkers are identified that may increase the likelihood that the MCI clinical profile is due to AD pathophysiology: (1) indicators of key protein deposition, such as beta amyloid, and tau resulting in (2) neuronal injury. Markers of deposits of beta-amyloid protein and tau can be found within cerebral spinal fluid, and evidence of amyloid deposition may be shown on positron-emission tomography (PET). Less specific neuronal injury, such as brain atrophy, hypometabolism, or hypoperfusion, may be demonstrated with various measures of structure or function (e.g., PET, magnetic resonance imaging). While neither of these protein depositions or the observed neuronal injuries are unique to AD pathology, their use in combination may be particularly informative. These biomarkers, taken in conjunction with MCI cases with memory impairment, may then support a diagnosis of prodromal AD (Petersen et al., 2014). However, at this point in time, it must be noted that the application of these biomarkers is currently limited, not just by the availability of these resources in clinical settings but by the reliability of measurement due to issues of standardization, test accuracy, and interpretation (Albert et al., 2011; Smailagic, Lafortune, Kelly, Hyde, & Brayne, 2018).

When biomarkers associated with MCI outside the context of AD are considered, the neuropathological profile is complex (Stephan, Hunter, et al., 2012; Stephan, Matthews, et al., 2012). This might be expected, given that MCI may be reflective of a variety of underlying conditions. Observed pathological changes in MCI include vascular pathology, inflammation, mitochondrial changes, disrupted metabolic homeostasis, as well as other biological characteristics (Stephan, Matthews, et al., 2012). Moreover, it has long been shown that considerable pathology may be evident in the absence of clinical cognitive impairment (Petersen et al., 2014).

As yet, clear associations between cognitive impairment and brain pathology continue to be hampered by operational definitions of MCI, types of studies undertaken (e.g., cross-sectional, longitudinal), samples studied (e.g., clinical samples, population-based samples), measurement of cognitive impairment, and length of follow-up (Petersen et al., 2014; Tuokko & McDowell, 2006). Additional research on the links between cognitive impairment and brain pathology are needed to determine which early biological events are indicative of a progressive neurocognitive disorder and which biological events may be secondary.

Cognitive Profiles within MCI

Over the past decade, it has become generally accepted that objective evidence of cognitive impairment, using measures with appropriate normative (i.e., relevant age, education, and culturally appropriate) data, be employed when defining MCI. While there has been increasing clarity with respect to how cognitive impairment has been operationalized, there remains no accepted standard in this regard. Even the newest sets of criteria (Albert et al., 2011, DSM-5) do not fully agree (see Table 1 and above). Certainly, the use of consistent and appropriate neuropsychometric test data will improve the reliability of the MCI diagnosis. It has been demonstrated that applying different neuropsychometric criteria results in differences in the prevalence of MCI (Jak et al., 2009). Jak and her colleagues (2009) applied five sets of neuropsychometrically based criteria that differed with respect to their characterization of objective cognitive impairment (see Table 2).

Table 2 Five sets of neuropsychometrically based criteria of Jak et al. (2009)

Criteria	Neuropsychometric impairment	Normal classification
Historical (Petersen et al., 1999)	Memory performance more than 1.5 SD below age appropriate norms on WMS-Revised Logical Memory subtest*	Normal if not impaired
Typical/Conventional (Petersen & Morris, 2005)	Impairment more than 1.5 SD below age appropriate norms on only one test within a domain	Normal if no scores more than 1.5 SD below age appropriate norms
Comprehensive	Impairment more than 1 SD below norms on at least two performances within a cognitive domain	Normal if one measure within one or two cognitive domains more than 1 SD below norms
Liberal	Impairment more than 1 SD below norms on one measure within domain	Normal if no measure more than 1 SD below norms in any domain
Conservative	Impairment 1.5 SD below norms on two measures within a domain	Normal if one measure more than 1.5 SD below norms within one or two domains

NB – * only measure administered.

When applied to 90 non-demented volunteers enrolled in a longitudinal study of normal aging, marked differences in the prevalence on MCI was seen at baseline and over 17 months. The percentage of those identified as MCI at baseline ranged from 10–74%, depending on the criteria used. Over time, substantial diagnostic instability was observed. The authors observed that the 'comprehensive' criteria struck the greatest balance between sensitivity and specificity, and showed acceptable stability over time.

Subsequently, Clark et al. (2013) examined the conventional (Petersen & Morris, 2005) and comprehensive (Jak et al., 2009) criteria for MCI, and applied cluster analysis using neuropsychometric scores to determine how empirically derived subtypes corresponded with these sets of criteria. Amnestic and mixed subtypes emerged in relation to either set of criteria. Dysexecutive and visuospatial subtypes were seen in relation to the comprehensive criteria, whereas the conventional criteria yielded a subtype performing within the unimpaired range. Post hoc analyses indicated that the cluster-derived normal group did not differ from the normal control group with respect to neuropsychometric test performance, age, gender, or educational attainment. Further analyses on a subset of the cluster-derived normal group for whom MRI scans were available demonstrated that they did not differ from the normal controls with respect to cortical thickness in areas associated with MCI and AD. Edmonds et al. (2015) also applied cluster analysis on neuropsychometric scores with 825 individuals who met conventional MCI criteria from the longitudinal, multi-center Alzheimer's Disease Neuroimaging Initiative (ADNI) study. Once again, a cluster-derived normal group emerged in addition to amnestic, dysnomic, and dysexecutive groups. When biomarkers and clinical outcomes were compared across these cluster-derived groups, fewer members of the normal group progressed to dementia at follow-up (mean 22.9 months), and AD biomarker profiles did not differ from those of the normal control group. These findings call into question the utility of the conventional criteria for MCI, suggesting susceptibility to false-positive diagnostic errors.

Other research from the ADNI study (Jessen, Wolfsgruber, et al., 2014) has examined MCI distinguishing subtypes based on the level of observed impairment on the Consortium to Establish a Registry for Alzheimer's Disease (CERAD) verbal memory delayed recall task. Those classified with early MCI (EMCI) scored between 1.0 and 1.5 SD below the normative mean for the CERAD task, whereas the performance of those with late MCI (LMCI) fell more than 1.5 SD below the normative mean. In addition, they identified those who performed less than 1.0 SD below the normative mean as exhibiting subjective memory impairment (SMI). Self-report of concerns (worries) about memory impairment was solicited from all groups as previous risk has suggested that those reporting concern (worries) about memory impairment are at increased risk for developing AD (Jessen et al., 2010). These individuals were followed for six years, and risk for AD was assessed. Risk for developing AD was greatest in the LMCI group. For the

EMCI and SMI groups, those reporting concerns about memory showed a similar level of risk. For those reporting no concerns about memory, EMCI continued to be at increased risk for AD, whereas SMI was not (Jessen, Wolfsgruber, et al., 2014).

Subjective Cognitive Decline (SCD)

The observation that perceived concern regarding cognitive functioning, even prior to the emergence of subtle cognitive impairment, may hold prognostic value (Amieva et al., 2008; Jessen, Wolfsgruber, et al., 2014; Reisberg et al., 2008) has prompted an emerging field of research on subjective cognitive decline (SCD) (Tales et al., 2015). Like MCI, interest in SCD has initially focused on its utility in relation to the onset of AD. However, also like MCI, SCD appears to be a complex construct that needs to be dissociated from memory complaints associated with normal aging and may be associated with various emerging conditions, including vascular dementia (Slot et al., 2019). Regardless of the underlying cause of the condition, it has become apparent that SCD can adversely affect quality of life (Tales et al., 2015). In response to the challenge posed by this evolving construct, the Subjective Cognitive Decline Initiative (SCD-I) Working Group, an international group of scientist-clinicians, was established in 2012 (Jessen, Amariglio, et al., 2014). Needless to say, many of the challenges confronting SCD researchers are similar to those faced by MCI researchers: the operational definition including specific relevant cognitive domains (i.e., memory versus others domains) and measurement of self-reports, samples involved (e.g., clinic settings versus community-based), and timing of the sampling window (i.e., when it occurs in the developmental trajectory).

One of the early steps taken by the SCD-I was to create consensus criteria for use in the study of SCD (Jessen, Amariglio, et al., 2014). The resulting Jessen criteria for pre-MCI SCD require self-reported persistent decline in cognitive capacity in relation to previous levels of functioning and unrelated to an acute event or better accounted for by other medical conditions or medication/substance use. In addition, neuropsychometric performance must fall within the normal range in relation to appropriate normative data. Moreover, 'SCD plus' criteria are specified for preclinical AD that require the self-reported decline to be in memory, with specific concerns/worries about this memory decline relative to same-aged peers and an age of onset of SCD greater than 60 years. Confirmation of cognitive decline by a knowledgeable informant, the presence of apolipoprotein ε4 (APOE ε4), and/or biomarker evidence of AD support the identification of 'SCD plus'. Molinuevo et al. (2017) later provided guidelines on how to operationalize and implement the Jessen criteria for research purposes and recommended that the following information be provided in SCD research reports: (1) measurement approach, including research environment (e.g., memory clinic, population-based cohort), names and properties of measures, respondent category (e.g., self, informant, clinician), mode of administration (e.g., telephone interview), timeframe and reference group (e.g., comparison with oneself at earlier time point, comparison to age-related peers), and cognitive domains assessed; (2) defined cutoffs on subjective report measures or other approaches used (with explanations of how derived); and (3) defined cutoffs on objective report measures or other approaches used (with explanations of how derived). It is hoped that these efforts will promote harmonization of SCD measurement across studies and enhance comparability.

While these SCD criteria have been developed only recently, research has begun to examine the rates of incident dementia (Slot et al., 2019). Earlier research yielded estimates of non-normal cognitive decline to be substantial. For example, a recent meta-analysis found that people with subjective memory complaints were at twice the risk for developing dementia over a four-year period (Mitchell, Beaumont, Ferguson, Yadegarfar, & Stubbs, 2014). In a recent multicenter study of SCD, dementia incidence was 17.7%, compared with 14.2% in controls (Slot et al., 2019). The risk for developing AD was higher than non-AD (11.5 versus 6.1) in the SCD group, and a higher risk was associated with memory clinic setting, higher age, and the presence of APOE ε4. A variety of earlier studies have also noted associations of SCD with biomarkers, particularly those associated with AD, but findings have been mixed, perhaps due to differences in operational definitions (Buckley et al., 2013, 2016; van Harten et al., 2013). Moreover, biomarker research can often be expensive and/or invasive, with limited availability outside specialty academic medical research centers.

It has been proposed that a more cost-effective approach to clarifying which people with SCD are likely to progress into dementia may be the novel application of neuropsychometric measures. By definition, people with SCD show no deficits on standard neuropsychometric tests. Yet the use of experimental cognitive paradigms may reveal the earliest stages of non-normal decline. For example, Koppara et al. (2015) showed subtle deficits on a short-term memory binding task in people with SCD whose standardized memory performance did not differ from normal controls. Similarly, people with SCD have been shown to have higher rates of discounting than healthy controls on a delayed discounting task where people weigh future outcomes less heavily than immediate ones (Hu et al., 2017). Evidence that people with SCD may be more likely than healthy controls to discount prior outcomes in favor of temporally contiguous ones when making decisions has also been demonstrated by Smart and Krawitz (2015) using a more advanced statistical analysis (i.e., Bayesian parameter estimation) of performance on the Iowa Gambling Task (Bechara, Damasio, Damasio, & Anderson, 1994). Additional evidence of such subtle cognitive decline has been provided by Rabin et al. (2014), who observed that people with SCD scored lower than healthy controls on specific elements of a prospective memory task. Prospective memory tasks assess memory for future intentions and are considered far more complex than other forms of memory assessment. Mulligan, Smart, and Ali (2016) noted that, in addition to over-reporting cognitive complaints relative to informant-reports of cognitive functions, people with SCD were less accurate and more variable on a computerized experimental multi-source interference task. These studies suggest that it may be possible to demonstrate very subtle cognitive deficits in those people highly sensitive to their own change in cognitive functions (i.e., SCD).

Interventions

While the primary interest in MCI (and now SCD) has historically been as an indicator of progressive neurodegenerative diseases, such as AD and other dementias, pharmacological efforts to slow, stop, or even reverse the pathological changes have shown limited efficacy. Conversely, much recent research suggests that neuroplasticity, and particularly experience-dependent neuroplasticity (EDP), is possible in later life as well as at other points in the lifespan. This has led to a rapid proliferation of research on non-pharmacological interventions that may, in fact, lead to adaptive brain changes (Greenwood & Parasuraman, 2010) or serve as primary and secondary prevention strategies at the earliest stages of the decline trajectory (Imtiaz, Tolppanen, Kivipelto, & Soininen, 2014). That said, a comprehensive multimodal approach to intervention may best address the complexity of developmental factors that affect cognitive functioning in later life (Tuokko & Smart, 2018).

Pharmacological Interventions

There is no doubt that medications may be required to ease symptoms for those people with MCI or SCD who have comorbid conditions, such as physical health concerns or disorders of mood or anxiety. The ways in which these medications affect cognitive and emotional functioning, and their side-effects, need to be well understood by clinicians. On the other hand, the use of cognitive-enhancing medications designed to delay or slow the rate of cognitive decline, as yet, has not been demonstrated to be effective. In two recent reviews, no strong evidence for a beneficial effect of acetylcholinesterase inhibitors (AChEIs) on risk of progression to dementia or on measures of cognition has been shown (Fitzpatrick-Lewis, Warren, Ali, Sherifali, & Raina, 2015). Presumably, this compound was selected for investigation in relation to MCI being viewed as a prodrome for AD. That said, methodological issues, such as heterogeneity of MCI inclusion criteria and lack of sensitivity of cognitive measures employed, continue to limit progress in this field. The use of cognitive-enhancing medications for people with SCD remains highly controversial as these people, unlike those with MCI, present with normal neuropsychological functioning, and until there is a way to reliably identify those destined to decline, treatment raises ethical concerns.

Non-Pharmacological Interventions

Until relatively recently, it was believed that damage to the brain sustained in middle and older adulthood had limited capacity for recovery of function (Jellinger & Attems, 2013). However, both animal and human research has shown that the brain can continue to change and adapt in response to training well into older adulthood (Greenwood & Parasuraman, 2010). Both structural and functional plasticity can occur in response to structured interventions. That is, changes to the underlying structure of the brain can occur (e.g., Smart, Segalowitz, Mulligan, Koudys, & Gawryluk, 2016; van Paasschen et al., 2013), as can changes to the functional organization of the brain, with or without structural change (Park & McDonough, 2013). These observations have prompted much emerging cognitive and behavioral research with older adults. Clare and Woods (2004) described three main types of intervention for use with older adults: cognitive training (guided practice on standardized tasks targeting specific cognitive functions at a range of levels of difficulty), cognitive stimulation (a range of pleasurable activities that provide general stimulation for thinking, concentrating, and memory, most typically applied with people with dementia), and cognitive rehabilitation (enhancement of everyday functioning by incorporating the use of compensatory practices rather than restitution of function).

Since various outcomes may be expected for people with MCI, both cognitive training (restitution) and cognitive rehabilitation (compensation) approaches have been investigated. A meta-analysis of 17 studies of computerized cognitive training applied to people with MCI showed that the overall efficacy of cognitive outcomes were moderate and statistically significant, (Hill et al., 2017). Positive effects were seen for some cognitive domains (e.g., attention, working memory, verbal learning) but not others (e.g., processing speed, executive functions, visuospatial skills), and most studies focused on short-term effects. No information on rates of decline to dementia were obtained. Huckans et al. (2013) attempted to examine conversion rates of MCI to dementia in 14 randomized controlled trials of various cognitive rehabilitation therapies (CRTs), but follow-up intervals were insufficient, ranging from 6 weeks to 6 months. However, a positive impact on objective cognitive performance was observed for seven life-style interventions, with mixed effects for other specific CRTs. While the authors considered the evidence to be encouraging, several methodological concerns limited the confidence with which strong conclusions could be drawn. Chandler, Parks, Marsiske, Rotblatt, and Smith (2016) examined studies expressly concerned with the impact of cognitive interventions on everyday functions in people with MCI. The overall meta-analysis of the 24 viable studies suggested a small positive effect on everyday outcomes (i.e., mood, activities of daily living, and metacognition), though significant heterogeneity in methods and outcomes made specific, firm conclusions difficult.

Some studies examining the effects of cognitive and behavioral interventions with SCD have begun to emerge (Canevelli et al., 2013; Metternich,

Kosch, Kriston, Härter, & Hüll, 2009; Smart et al., 2017). Methodological challenges continue to limit the conclusions that can be drawn, but these studies provide cautious optimism that cognitive and behavioral interventions are worthy of further investigation in terms of effectiveness and long-term preventive benefits.

Psychological Interventions

Given the lack of prognostic clarity about the meaning of a diagnosis of MCI (or SCD), it is not surprising that there may be psychological and psychosocial implications when providing people with this diagnosis. Ethically, feedback provided about these conditions must note the lack of precision concerning future outcomes: improvement, stability, or possibly decline. Such ambiguity may lead individuals to have difficulty accepting or adjusting to their new level of functioning and fear that MCI necessarily foreshadows subsequent decline (Corner & Bond, 2004). The psychological experiences of individuals diagnosed with MCI have been studied through qualitative methods, revealing themes of ambiguity, change in social and family roles, embarrassment and shame, emotionality, and loss of aspects of one's identity (Beard & Neary, 2013; Frank et al., 2006).

Particularly in the context of diagnosing conditions of prognostic uncertainty, such as MCI and SCD, the manner in which the information is conveyed is of the utmost importance. A sensitive and supportive approach that acknowledges the limitations of diagnostic opinion may help to allay fears and concerns about future decline. In addition, it is important to assess for past history or current depression or anxiety and provide appropriate interventions aimed at management of such symptoms. These may include pharmacological (i.e., medications) as well as psychological supports, such as psychotherapy or supportive counselling with respect to grief and loss. Even when there is no evidence of marked mood concerns, it is prudent to emphasize the person's strengths and provide illustrations of steps that can be taken to maintain active engagement to the fullest extent possible. It may also be prudent to begin discussions about the practical implications of the impact MCI may have on complex decision-making over time. Before engaging in such discussions, the risks associated with doing so (i.e., reduce hope, precipitate fear) must be weighed and considered (Werner & Korczyn, 2008).

Summary

While much additional information and many sets of diagnostic criteria have been generated concerning MCI as a diagnostic entity, no consensus has yet been reached. MCI is now accepted as a heterogeneous classification possibly associated with various underlying pathological processes and expected outcomes. A variety of approaches have been proposed to enhance classification within MCI with respect to anticipated outcomes (e.g., biomarkers and/or cognitive profiles within the MCI construct).

Not much progress has been made with respect to pharmacological interventions designed to slow, stop, or reverse the underlying pathological process. However, research examining the benefits of various cognitive and behavioral approaches to intervention has expanded rapidly. While previously, the intentions for these types of intervention were to optimize well-being, minimize disability, and prevent dysfunctional family and social functioning, recent research identifying neuroplasticity across the lifespan has recognized that these types of experience may lead to adaptive brain changes or serve as primary and secondary prevention strategies at the earliest stages of the decline trajectory. Many encouraging findings from the application of cognitive and behavioral approaches to intervention have emerged, but the impact of these interventions on changes in rates of decline must await further longitudinal studies. It appears, then, that, even now, after decades of research, the meaning of an MCI diagnosis might best be viewed as descriptive, with a focus on interventions to minimize the psychological impact and optimize social functioning and well-being, which we now know may well have benefits to underlying brain health.

References

Albert, M. S., DeKosky, S. T., Dickson, D., Dubois, B., Feldman, H. H., Fox, N. C., ... Phelps, C. H. (2011). The diagnosis of mild cognitive impairment due to Alzheimer's disease: Recommendations from the National Institute on Aging-Alzheimer's Association workgroups on diagnostic guidelines for Alzheimer's disease. *Alzheimers Dement, 7*(3), 270–279. doi:10.1016/j.jalz.2011.03.008

American Psychiatric Association (2012). *Diagnostic and statistical manual of mental disorders: DSM-5™* (5th ed.). (2013). Arlington, VA: Author.

Amieva, H., Le Goff, M., Millet, X., Orgogozo, J. M., Pérès, K., Barberger-Gateau, P., ... Dartigues, J. F. (2008). Prodromal Alzheimer's disease: Successive emergence of the clinical symptoms. *Annals of Neurology, 64*(5), 492–498. doi:10.1002/ana.21509

Beard, R. L., & Neary, T. M. (2013). Making sense of nonsense: Experiences of mild cognitive impairment. *Sociology of Health & Illness, 35*(1), 130–146. doi:10.1111/j.1467-9566.2012.01481.x

Bechara, A., Damasio, A. R., Damasio, H., & Anderson, S. W. (1994). Insensitivity to future consequences following damage to human prefrontal cortex. *Cognition, 50*(1–3), 7–15. doi:10.1016/0010-0277(94)90018-3

Buckley, R. F., Maruff, P., Ames, D., Bourgeat, P., Martins, R. N., Masters, C. L., ... Ellis, K. A. (2016). Subjective memory decline predicts greater rates of clinical progression in preclinical Alzheimer's disease. *Alzheimer's & Dementia: The Journal of the Alzheimer's Association, 12*(7), 796–804. doi:10.1016/j.jalz.2015.12.013

Buckley, R., Saling, M. M., Ames, D., Rowe, C. C., Lautenschlager, N. T., Macaulay, S. L., ... Ellis, K. A. (2013). Factors affecting subjective memory complaints in the AIBL aging study: Biomarkers, memory, affect, and age. *International Psychogeriatrics, 25*(8), 1307–1315. doi:10.1017/S1041610213000665

Canevelli, M., Adali, N., Tainturier, C., Bruno, G., Cesari, M., & Vellas, B. (2013). Cognitive interventions targeting subjective cognitive complaints. *American Journal of Alzheimer's Disease and Other Dementias, 28*(6), 560–567. doi:10.1177/1533317513494441

Chandler, M. J., Parks, A. C., Marsiske, M., Rotblatt, L. J., & Smith, G. E. (2016). Everyday impact of cognitive interventions in mild cognitive impairment: A systematic review and meta-analysis. *Neuropsychology Review, 26*(3), 225–251. doi:10.1007/s11065-016-9330-4

Clare, L., & Woods, R. T. (2004). Cognitive training and cognitive rehabilitation for people with early-stage Alzheimer's disease: A review. *Neuropsychological Rehabilitation, 14*(4), 385–401. doi:10.1080/09602010443000074

Clark, L. R., Delano-Wood, L., Libon, D. J., McDonald, C. R., Nation, D. A., Bangen, K. J., ... Bondi, M. W. (2013). Are empirically-derived subtypes of mild cognitive impairment consistent with conventional subtypes? *Journal of the International Neuropsychological Society, 19*(6), 635–645. doi:10.1017/S1355617713000313

Corner, L., & Bond, J. (2004). Being at risk of dementia: Fears and anxieties of older adults. *Journal of Aging Studies, 18*(2), 143–155. doi:10.1016/j.jaging.2004.01.007

Edmonds, E. C., Delano-Wood, L., Clark, L. R., Jak, A. J., Nation, D. A., McDonald, C. R., ... Bondi, M. W. (2015). Susceptibility of the conventional criteria for mild cognitive impairment to false-positive diagnostic errors. *Alzheimer's & Dementia: The Journal of the Alzheimer's Association, 11*(4), 415–424. doi:10.1016/j.jalz.2014.03.005

Fitzpatrick-Lewis, D., Warren, R., Ali, M. U., Sherifali, D., & Raina, P. (2015). Treatment for mild cognitive impairment: A systematic review and meta-analysis. *CMAJ Open, 3*(4), E419–427. doi:10.9778/cmajo.20150057

Frank, L., Lloyd, A., Flynn, J. A., Kleinman, L., Matza, L. S., Margolis, M. K., ... Bullock, R. (2006). Impact of cognitive impairment on mild dementia patients and mild cognitive impairment patients and their informants. *International Psychogeriatrics, 18*(1), 151–162. doi:10.1017/S1041610205002450

Goldman, J. G., Holden, S. K., Litvan, I., McKeith, I., Stebbins, G. T., & Taylor, J. P. (2018). Evolution of diagnostic criteria and assessments for Parkinson's disease mild cognitive impairment. *Movement Disorders, 33*(4), 503–510. doi:10.1002/mds.27323

Greenwood, P. M., & Parasuraman, R. (2010). Neuronal and cognitive plasticity: A neurocognitive framework for ameliorating cognitive aging. *Frontiers in Aging Neuroscience, 2*. doi:10.3389/fnagi.2010.00150

Hill, N. T. M., Mowszowski, L., Naismith, S. L., Chadwick, V. L., Valenzuela, M., & Lampit, A. (2017). Computerized cognitive training in older adults with mild cognitive impairment or dementia: A systematic review and meta-analysis. *The American Journal of Psychiatry, 174*(4), 329–340. doi:10.1176/appi.ajp.2016.16030360

Hu, X., Uhle, F., Fliessbach, K., Wagner, M., Han, Y., Weber, B., & Jessen, F. (2017). Reduced future-oriented decision making in individuals with subjective cognitive decline: A functional MRI study. *Alzheimer's & Dementia (Amst), 6*, 222–231. doi:10.1016/j.dadm.2017.02.005

Huckans, M., Hutson, L., Twamley, E., Jak, A., Kaye, J., & Storzbach, D. (2013). Efficacy of cognitive rehabilitation therapies for mild cognitive impairment (MCI) in older adults: Working toward a theoretical model and evidence-based interventions. *Neuropsychology Review, 23*(1), 63–80. doi:10.1007/s11065-013-9230-9

Imtiaz, B., Tolppanen, A. M., Kivipelto, M., & Soininen, H. (2014). Future directions in Alzheimer's disease from risk factors to prevention. *Biochemical Pharmacology, 88*(4), 661–670. doi:10.1016/j.bcp.2014.01.003

Jak, A. J., Bondi, M. W., Delano-Wood, L., Wierenga, C., Corey-Bloom, J., Salmon, D. P., & Delis, D. C. (2009). Quantification of five neuropsychological approaches to defining mild cognitive impairment. *The American Journal of Geriatric Psychiatry, 17*(5), 368–375. doi:10.1097/JGP.0b013e31819431d5

Jellinger, K. A., & Attems, J. (2013). Neuropathological approaches to cerebral aging and neuroplasticity. *Dialogues in Clinical Neuroscience, 15*(1), 29–43.

Jessen, F., Amariglio, R. E., van Boxtel, M., Breteler, M., Ceccaldi, M., Chételat, G., ... Wagner, M. (2014). A conceptual framework for research on subjective cognitive decline in preclinical Alzheimer's disease. *Alzheimer's & Dementia: The Journal of the Alzheimer's Association, 10*(6), 844–852. doi:10.1016/j.jalz.2014.01.001

Jessen, F., Wiese, B., Bachmann, C., Eifflaender-Gorfer, S., Haller, F., Kölsch, H., ... Bickel, H. (2010). Prediction of dementia by subjective memory impairment. *Archives of General Psychiatry, 67*(4), 414–422. doi:10.1001/archgenpsychiatry.2010.30

Jessen, F., Wolfsgruber, S., Wiese, B., Bickel, H., Mösch, E., Kaduszkiewicz, H., ... Wagner, M. (2014). AD dementia risk in late MCI, in early MCI, and in subjective memory impairment. *Alzheimer's & Dementia: The Journal of the Alzheimer's Association, 10*(1), 76–83. doi:10.1016/j.jalz.2012.09.017

Koppara, A., Frommann, I., Polcher, A., Parra, M. A., Maier, W., Jessen, F., ... Wagner, M. (2015). Feature binding deficits in subjective cognitive decline and in mild cognitive impairment. *Journal of Alzheimer's Disease, 48*(Suppl 1), S161–S170. doi:10.3233/JAD-150105

Litvan, I., Goldman, J. G., Troster, A. I., Schmand, B. A., Weintraub, D., Petersen, R. C., ... Emre, M. (2012). Diagnostic criteria for mild cognitive impairment in Parkinson's disease: Movement disorder society task force guidelines. *Movement Disorders, 27*(3), 349–356. doi:10.1002/mds.24893

Marcos, G., Santabárbara, J., Lopez-Anton, R., De-la-Cámara, C., Gracia-García, P., Lobo, E., ... Lobo, A. (2016). Conversion to dementia in mild cognitive impairment diagnosed with DSM-5 criteria and with Petersen's criteria. *Acta Psychiatrica Scandinavica, 133*(5), 378–385. doi:10.1111/acps.12543

Metternich, B., Kosch, D., Kriston, L., Härter, M., & Hüll, M. (2009). The effects of nonpharmacological interventions on subjective memory complaints: A systematic review and meta-analysis. *Psychotherapy and Psychosomatics, 79*(1), 6–19. doi:10.1159/000254901

Mitchell, A. J., Beaumont, H., Ferguson, D., Yadegarfar, M., & Stubbs, B. (2014). Risk of dementia and mild cognitive impairment in older people with subjective memory complaints: Meta-analysis. *Acta Psychiatrica Scandinavica, 130*(6), 439–451. doi:10.1111/acps.12336

Mitchell, A. J., & Shiri-Feshki, M. (2009). Rate of progression of mild cognitive impairment to dementia—Meta-analysis of 41 robust inception cohort studies. *Acta Psychiatrica Scandinavica, 119*(4), 252–265. doi:10.1111/j.1600-0447.2008.01326.x

Molinuevo, J. L., Rabin, L. A., Amariglio, R., Buckley, R., Dubois, B., Ellis, K. A., ... Jessen, F. (2017). Implementation of subjective cognitive decline criteria in research studies. *Alzheimer's & Dementia: The Journal of the Alzheimer's Association, 13*(3), 296–311. doi:10.1016/j.jalz.2016.09.012

Mulligan, B. P., Smart, C. M., & Ali, J. I. (2016). Relationship of subjective and objective performance indicators in subjective cognitive decline. *Psychology & Neuroscience, 9*(3), 362–378. doi:10.1037/pne0000061

Park, D. C., & McDonough, I. M. (2013). The dynamic aging mind: Revelations from functional neuroimaging research. *Perspectives on Psychological Science, 8*(1), 62–67. doi:10.1177/1745691612469034

Petersen, R. C. (2004). Mild cognitive impairment as a diagnostic entity. *The Journal of Internal Medicine, 256*(3), 183–194. doi:10.1111/j.1365-2796.2004.01388.x

Petersen, R. C., Caracciolo, B., Brayne, C., Gauthier, S., Jelic, V., & Fratiglioni, L. (2014). Mild cognitive impairment: A concept in evolution. *The Journal of Internal Medicine, 275*(3), 214–228. doi:10.1111/joim.12190

Petersen, R. C., & Morris, J. C. (2005). Mild cognitive impairment as a clinical entity and treatment target. *Archives of Neurology, 62*(7), 1160–1163; discussion 1167. doi:10.1001/archneur.62.7.1160

Petersen, R. C., Smith, G. E., Waring, S. C., Ivnik, R. J., Kokmen, E., & Tangalos, E. G. (1997). Aging, memory, and mild cognitive impairment. *International Psychogeriatrics, 9,* 65–69.

Petersen, R. C., Smith, G. E., Waring, S. C., Ivnik, R. J., Tangalos, E. G., & Kokmen, E. (1999). Mild cognitive impairment: Clinical characterization and outcome. *Archives of Neurology, 56*(3), 303–308. doi:10.1001/archneur.56.3.303

Rabin, L. A., Chi, S. Y., Wang, C., Fogel, J., Kann, S. J., & Aronov, A. (2014). Prospective memory on a novel clinical task in older adults with mild cognitive impairment and subjective cognitive decline. *Neuropsychological Rehabilitation, 24*(6), 868–893. doi:10.1080/09602011.2014.915855

Reisberg, B., Prichep, L., Mosconi, L., John, E. R., Glodzik-Sobanska, L., Boksay, I., ... de Leon, M. J. (2008). The pre-mild cognitive impairment, subjective cognitive impairment stage of Alzheimer's disease. *Alzheimer's & Dementia: The Journal of the Alzheimer's Association, 4*(1, Suppl 1), S98–S108. doi:10.1016/j.jalz.2007.11.017

Sachs-Ericsson, N., & Blazer, D. G. (2015). The new DSM-5 diagnosis of mild neurocognitive disorder and its relation to research in mild cognitive impairment. *Aging & Mental Health, 19*(1), 2–12. doi:10.1080/13607863.2014.920303

Skrobot, O. A., O'Brien, J., Black, S., Chen, C., DeCarli, C., Erkinjuntti, T., ... Kehoe, P. G. (2017). The vascular impairment of cognition classification consensus study. *Alzheimer's Dementia: The Journal of the Alzheimer's Association, 13*(6), 624–633. doi:10.1016/j.jalz.2016.10.007

Slot, R. E. R., Sikkes, S. A. M., Berkhof, J., Brodaty, H., Buckley, R., Cavedo, E., ... van der Flier, W. M. (2019). Subjective cognitive decline and rates of incident Alzheimer's disease and non–Alzheimer's disease dementia. *Alzheimer's & Dementia: The Journal of the Alzheimer's Association, 15*(3), 465–476. doi:10.1016/j.jalz.2018.10.003

Smailagic, N., Lafortune, L., Kelly, S., Hyde, C., & Brayne, C. (2018). ^{18}F-FDG PET for prediction of conversion to Alzheimer's disease dementia in people with mild cognitive impairment: An updated systematic review of test accuracy. *Journal of Alzheimer's Disease, 64*(4), 1175–1194. doi:10.3233/JAD-171125

Smart, C. M., Karr, J. E., Areshenkoff, C. N., Rabin, L. A., Hudon, C., Gates, N., ... Wesselman, L. (2017). Non-pharmacologic interventions for older adults with subjective cognitive decline: Systematic review, meta-analysis, and preliminary recommendations. *Neuropsychology Review, 27*(3), 245–257. doi:10.1007/s11065-017-9342-8

Smart, C. M., & Krawitz, A. (2015). The impact of subjective cognitive decline on Iowa Gambling Task performance. *Neuropsychology, 29*(6), 971–987. doi:10.1037/neu0000204

Smart, C. M., Segalowitz, S. J., Mulligan, B. P., Koudys, J., & Gawryluk, J. R. (2016). Mindfulness training for older adults with subjective cognitive decline: Results from a pilot randomized controlled trial. *Journal of Alzheimer's Disease, 52*(2), 757–774. doi:10.3233/JAD-150992

Stephan, B. C. M., Hunter, S., Harris, D., Llewellyn, D. J., Siervo, M., Matthews, F. E., & Brayne, C. (2012). The neuropathological profile of mild cognitive impairment (MCI): A systematic review. *Molecular Psychiatry, 17*(11), 1056–1076. doi:10.1038/mp.2011.147

Stephan, B. C. M., Matthews, F. E., Hunter, S., Savva, G. M., Bond, J., McKeith, I. G., ... Brayne, C. (2012). Neuropathological profile of mild cognitive impairment from a population perspective. *Alzheimer Disease and Associated Disorders, 26*(3), 205–212. doi:10.1097/WAD.0b013e31822fc24d

Tales, A., Jessen, F., Butler, C., Wilcock, G., Phillips, J., & Bayer, T. (2015). Subjective cognitive decline. *Journal of Alzheimer's Disease, 48*(Suppl 1), S1–S3. doi:10.3233/JAD-150719

Tuokko, H. A., & McDowell, I. (2006). An overview of mild cognitive impairment. In H. A. Tuokko & D. F. Hultsch (Eds.), *Mild cognitive impairment: International perspectives* (pp. 3–28). Philadelphia, PA: Taylor & Francis.

Tuokko, H. A., & Smart, C. M. (2018). *Neuropsychology of cognitive decline: A developmental approach to assessment and intervention*. New York, NY: The Guilford Press.

van Harten, A. C., Visser, P. J., Pijnenburg, Y. A. L., Teunissen, C. E., Blankenstein, M. A., Scheltens, P., & van der Flier, W. M. (2013). Cerebrospinal fluid Aβ42 is the best predictor of clinical progression in patients with subjective complaints. *Alzheimer's & Dementia: The Journal of the Alzheimer's Association, 9*(5), 481–487. doi:10.1016/j.jalz.2012.08.004

van Paasschen, J., Clare, L., Yuen, K. S. L., Woods, R. T., Evans, S. J., Parkinson, C. H., ...Linden, D. E. J. (2013). Cognitive rehabilitation changes memory-related brain activity in people with Alzheimer disease. *Neurorehabilitation and Neural Repair, 27*(5), 448–459. doi:10.1177/1545968312471902

Werner, P., & Korczyn, A. D. (2008). Mild cognitive impairment: Conceptual, assessment, ethical, and social issues. *Clinical Interventions in Aging, 3*(3), 413–420.

World Health Organization. (2019). *International classification of diseases – 10th edition – Clinical modification*. Geneva, Switzerland: Author. Retrieved from https://www.icd10data.com/ICD10CM/Codes/G00-G99/G30-G32/G31-/G31.84.

Part I

Introduction

1 An overview of mild cognitive impairment

Holly A. Tuokko and Ian McDowell

The aim of this book is to provide a comprehensive examination, from multiple perspectives, of the concept of mild cognitive impairment (MCI) in old age. As interest in MCI has grown, the utility of the concept has been investigated in both clinical and population-based samples in many countries. Findings have varied widely. Although the differences observed between samples may reflect "legitimate variations" (Petersen & Morris, 2003), there has been little attempt to integrate what we have learned about MCI from each of these perspectives. This book aims to summarize the current understanding of MCI, to identify key findings and technical issues arising from the study of MCI, and to propose future directions for research. This introductory chapter provides an overview of the evolving conceptions of cognitive change in later life. Empirical studies of MCI are summarized and methodological issues influencing this research are then discussed. Finally, we review the implications of different conceptions of MCI for interventions. Subsequent chapters present perspectives on MCI taken by researchers around the world. In the final chapter of the book, we summarize findings from these various perspectives and highlight promising areas for future research.

Overview of the evolving conceptions of cognitive change in later life

It has long been recognized that while changes in memory are a normal part of aging, some forms of memory change may indicate an underlying neurodegenerative disease (Kral, 1962). It is this latter, abnormal, form of memory change that has stimulated the interest of clinicians and researchers in anticipation of the universal rise in the proportion of the population that will live well beyond 65 years of age. Age-associated neurodegenerative disorders of cognitive function such as Alzheimer's disease (AD) and vascular forms of dementia (VaD) produce devastating effects on the patient, their family, and society. Over the past 25 years, many studies have described the impact of these disorders; more modest advances have been made in developing interventions to slow or delay their progression. With the prospect of increasingly effective interventions, however, attention has focused on early identification of cognitive disorders under the assumption that earlier intervention will lead to better outcomes.

Attempts to identify those at risk of developing dementia have led to many proposals for ways to classify milder late life cognitive impairment—impairment that is insufficient to warrant a diagnosis of dementia. The early classifications were dichotomous, postulating the existence of discrete categories of normal and pathological aging. For example, Kral (1962) proposed the terms benign and malignant senescent forgetfulness to describe forms of cognitive decline distinguishable on the basis of symptoms, course, and prognosis. As more and more terms and classifications were introduced (Table 1.1), it was initially unclear which were intended merely to describe presenting cognitive symptoms and which carried implications regarding underlying pathology and eventual outcome. In several of the more recent classifications, however, formal sets of criteria were introduced and their links to pathology and eventual outcome were made explicit. In an attempt to integrate the various approaches for categorizing early cognitive decline, Rediess and Caine (1996) arrayed them along a spectrum of function from optimal cognitive aging through dementia. Rediess and Caine identified five broad clusters in the spectrum of cognitive function (Table 1.2), including (1) successful or optimal cognitive aging; (2) age-related cognitive decline (ARCD; American Psychiatric Association, 1994) or age-associated memory impairment (AAMI; Crook, Bartus, Ferris, Whitehouse, Cohen, & Gershon, 1986); (3) age-associated cognitive decline (AACD; Levy, 1994) and MCI (Smith, Petersen, Parisi, & Ivnik, 1996; Zaudig, 1992); (4) questionable dementia and mild neurocognitive disorder (MND; American Psychiatric Association, 1994); and (5) dementia (ranging from mild to severe). Differences along this spectrum of cognitive function are viewed as quantitative in nature with a substantial overlap between stages in terms of both biological and psychological variables (Brayne & Calloway, 1988; Von Dras & Blumenthal, 1992). Cluster 2 includes people with subjective cognitive complaints and/or age-*consistent* cognitive function where decline is not necessarily anticipated: their cognition is on a plateau. In contrast, Clusters 3 and 4 exhibit objective evidence of cognitive impairment and form a heterogeneous group, including people who have always occupied the lower end of the normal distribution in terms of memory performance as well as those considered likely to progress to dementia over time. We shall here apply the term "MCI" in a generic sense to identify these groups, and extend it to include people identified with MCI by specific criteria such as those developed at the Mayo Clinic (Petersen, Smith, Waring, Ivnik, Tangalos, & Kokmen, 1999; Smith et al., 1996), or by Zaudig (1992).

With so many options and uncertainties in the definition of MCI, it is not surprising that many rival approaches have been proposed. None of the approaches identified in Table 1.1 is generally accepted or consistently applied in the research literature, and the collection of empirical evidence on their

Table 1.1 Some terms and definitional criteria sets used to describe cognitive impairment not sufficient to meet criteria for dementia

	Inclusion criteria	
MCI from DSM-III-R (Zaudig, 1992)	Type 1	Short- and long-term memory impairment only with no functional disabilities
	Type 2	Short- and long-term memory impairment, no functional disabilities, and at least one of the following: Impairment in abstract thinking, impaired judgment, disturbance of higher cortical function (e.g., aphasia, apraxia, agnosia), or personality change
MCI from ICD-10 (Zaudig, 1992)	Type 1	Short- or long-term memory impairment only with no functional decline
	Type 2	Short- or long-term memory impairment and a decline in intellectual abilities with no functional decline
	Type 3	Short- or long-term memory impairment with a decline in intellectual abilities, a personality change, and with no functional decline
Late-life forgetfulness (Blackford & La Rue, 1989)		Perceived decreases in day-to-day memory functioning in 50- to 79-year-old individuals were verified by a standardized self-report memory questionnaire. Individuals required verbal and performance IQ scores between 90 and 130. Performance between 1 and 2SDs below the mean established for age on 50% or more of the tests that were administered
AACD (Levy, 1994)		Gradual decline in any one cognitive area that was present for at least 6 months and performance at least 1SD below norms for age on relevant neuropsychlogical tests
MND (American Psychiatric Association, 1994)		Presence of two or more areas of cognitive impairment lasting most of the time for at least 2 weeks (reported by person or informant). Objective evidence of cognitive abnormality or decline
MCI—Mayo Clinic Group (Petersen et al., 1999)		Memory complaint identified by person, family, or physician in the presence of normal everyday functioning. Objective evidence of memory or other area of cognitive functioning as evidenced by scores 1.5SD below age-appropriate mean
Mild cognitive disorder—ICD-10 (World Health Organization, 1993)		Objective evidence of decline in cognitive performance not attributable to other mental or behavioral disorders identified in ICD-10. May be reversible
Malignant senescent forgetfulness (Kral, 1962)		A progressive form of memory loss associated with disorientation, confabulation, and poor memory performance
Limited cognitive disturbance (Gurland, Dean, Copeland, Gurland, & Golden, 1982)		Person reports memory decline and shows mild memory impairment but may perform everyday tasks adequately

Table 1.2 Spectrum of cognitive functioning in later life

	1. Successful cognitive aging	2. ARCD or AAMI	3. MCI	4. MND	5. Mild to severe dementia
Description	Minimal cognitive changes	Normal age-related cognitive changes	Below average for age peers without functional impairment	Below average for age peers with functional impairment; deficit in at least two cognitive domains	Deficient memory and at least one other cognitive domain affected; associated functional impairment
Psychometric features	Above average compared to age peers; within the normal range for younger adults	Above or within the average range for age, but below mean for younger adults on selected tests	Memory or other cognitive function 1–1.5SD below age peers; impaired retention is most typical	Performance on tests of at least two cognitive areas 1–1.5SD below age peers	Performance on memory tests and tests of one other cognitive area 1–2SD below age peers
Functional status	Active, independent, working, or have active retirement	Active, independent, may work or have active retirement	Independent	Needs some assistance in daily activities or has discontinued some normal daily activities	Clearly impaired social and occupational functioning
Potential contributing factors	High baseline IQ; high education, active lifestyle; optimal health; this group may not develop dementia	Wider range of baseline IQ with decline referenced to estimated baseline level; good health	Wider range of baseline IQ with decline referenced to estimated baseline level; presence of AD risk factors	Wider range of baseline IQ with decline referenced to estimated baseline level; presence of AD risk factors; may include prodrome for atypical dementia syndromes	Appearance of clinically significant features of dementia may be influenced by premorbid level of functioning

Source: Modified from Rediess and Caine (1996)

predictive validity for identifying future progression to dementia faces a variety of methodological challenges. These contribute to uncertainty in establishing basic estimates of the incidence, prevalence, and speed of cognitive decline.

Empirical evidence concerning the prevalence of MCI and conversion to dementia

Virtually all commentators have noted the wide variation in estimates of the prevalence of early cognitive impairment (Bischkopf, Busse, & Angermeyer, 2002; Jonker, Geerlings, & Schmand, 2000; Luis, Loewenstein, Acevedo, Barker, & Duara, 2003). That there is variation between different syndromes, such as AAMI and MCI (Table 1.3), need not surprise us. However, there is also wide variation among prevalence estimates of apparently the same condition. Busse et al., for example, quoted figures for the prevalence of ostensibly the same definition of MCI ranging from 1 to 15% (Busse, Bischkopf, Riedel-Heller, & Angermeyer, 2003c); other estimates rise to over 30% (Busse, Bischkopf, Riedel-Heller, & Angermeyer, 2003a, 2003b).

Correspondingly, there is a wide variation in conversion rates from cognitive impairment to dementia. Bischkopf's review of 26 studies (Bischkopf et al., 2002) and Palmer's review of 17 (Palmer, Fratiglioni, & Winblad, 2003) showed annual conversion ranging from 1 to over 40%, varying by sample, diagnostic criterion, and severity of impairment. The majority of studies, however, report conversion rates between 10 and 20% per annum (Petersen, Stevens, Ganguli, Tangalos, Cummings, & DeKosky, 2001), although some findings are clearly higher. Flicker, for example, found about 72% conversion over 2 years, or 36% over 1 year (Flicker, Ferris, & Reisberg, 1991). To develop a mathematical model, Yesavage, O'Hara, Kraemer, Noda, Taylor, and Ferris (2002) needed to choose a representative conversion rate from MCI to AD, and they selected 10% per year, regardless of age.

Accounting for the variations

Some of the variation in estimates of prevalence and conversion merely reflects different ways of presenting the results. Some studies, for example, report crude conversion rates while others adjust for variables such as age or education, which helps to correct for demographic differences in the samples. Comparisons are also made difficult as the statistic used varies according to study design: case-control studies typically report relative odds of conversion (Bennett et al., 2002), while longitudinal studies report percentages converting to dementia (Petersen et al., 2001). Because the time period for longitudinal studies varies, results are often averaged to an annual rate. However, it may be difficult to compare conversion rates based on different time periods, as longer studies tend to suffer greater attrition, and those lost to follow-up have greater cognitive impairment (Hänninen, Hallikainen, Tuomainen, Vanhanen, & Soininen, 2002).

Table 1.3 Studies of early cognitive impairment, showing prevalence, incidence, and rates of conversion to dementia

Author	Dx. Criterion	Prevalence	Incidence	Progression to dementia	Institutional admission	Mortality
DiCarlo et al. (2000)	ARCD	7.5%				
Ritchie, Artero, and Touchon (2001)	AACD	19.3%		28.6% in 3 years (RR 2.1)		
Schroder, Kratz, Pantel, Minnemann, Lehr, and Sauer (1998)	AAMI ACMI LLF AACD	13.5% 6.5% 1.5% 23.5%				
Tuokko et al. (2003)	CIND			47% in 5 years	29% vs. 14% in 5 years	49% vs. 30% in 5 years
Larrabee, Levin, and High (1986)	BSF	10–20%				
Kumamoto et al. (2000)	CIND	10.8				
DiCarlo et al. (2000)	CIND	10.7				
Tuokko and Frerichs (2000)	CIND			50% in 5 years		
Graham et al. (1997)	CIND	16.8			3 × higher	
Unverzagt et al. (2001)	CIND	22.9%		26% in 18 months		
Low et al. (2004)	CIND (>1.49SD below mean in one test)	33.3%				
Low et al. (2004)	a-MCI (>1.49SD + low self-assessed memory)	9.5%				
Ritchie et al. (2001)	MCI	3.2		11.1% in 3 years		
Larrieu et al. (2002)	MCI		9.9/1000 per year	8.3% per year		

Amieva et al. (2004)	MCI		32.2% in 2 years
Fisk et al. (2003)	MCI (four different definitions) (CSHA)	1.03%	71% over 5 years (RR 19.7)	RR 5.2	RR1.3
Fisk et al. (2003)	MCI redefined	3.02	50% (RR 9.3)	RR 2.8	RR1.4
Fisk and Rockwood (2005)	MCI (four definitions)		78–38%	RR 1.1–1.3	RR 2–1.5
Busse et al. (2003c)	MCI	1–15%	10–55% over 2–6 years		
Bowen, Teri, Kukull, McCormick, McCurry, and Larson (1997)	Isolated memory loss		48% in 31 months		
Bozoki et al. (2001)	Isolated memory impairment (IMI) only (=amnestic)		6% in 2 years; 24% in 4 years		
Bozoki et al. (2001)	IMI + other cognitive impairments		48% in 2 years; 77% in 4 years		
DeCarli et al. (2004)	MCI (CDR 0.5)		33% in 3 years		
Ganguli, Dodge, Shen, and DeKosky (2004)	a-MCI	3–4%	27% in 10 years		
Korf, Wahlund, Visser, and Scheltens (2004)	MRI medial temporal lobe atrophy		49% in 34 months	HR of 3.1	
Meguro et al. (2004)	MCI	4.9%			
Meguro et al. (2004)	CDR 0.5	30.2%			
Qiu et al. (2003)	MCI (Petersen)	2.4%			

(Contd)

Table 1.3 (Contd)

Author	Dx. Criterion	Prevalence	Incidence	Progression to dementia	Institutional admission	Mortality
Tervo et al. (2004)	MCI		25.9/1000 per year			
Ritchie, Ledesert, and Touchon (2000)	MCI			18% in 3 years		
Lopez et al. (2003)	a-MCI	6%				
Lopez et al. (2003)	MCI (multiple cognitive deficits)	16%				
Busse et al. (2003b)	MCI (various definitions)	3–36%		23–47% in 2.6 years		
Busse et al. (2003a)	MCI (various definitions)	3–20%	8–77/1000 per year			
Hänninen et al. (2002)	a-MCI	5.3%				
Meyer, Xu, Thornby, Chowdhury, and Quach (2002a, 2002b)	MCI		47.9% AD + 20.5% VaD over 3.72 years	25.1% in 3.72 years		
Bennett et al. (2002)	MCI		34% (HR 3.17) in 4.5 years			30% in 4.5 years (HR 1.74)
Stump, Callahan, and Hendrie (2001)	SPMSQ CI	10.5% mild + 5.2% severe				40.8% vs. 21.5% (HR 1.7)

Study	Measure	Result
Morris et al. (2001)	MCI (CDR 0.5 DAT)	60.5% in 5 years to CDR 1
Morris et al. (2001)	MCI (CDR 0.5 incipient DAT)	35.7% in 5 years to CDR 1
Morris et al. (2001)	MCI (CDR 0.5 uncertain dementia)	19.9% in 5 years to CDR 1
Ritchie et al. (2001)	MCI	3.2%
Jack et al. (1999)	MCI	11.1% in 3 years
		33.75% in 32.6 months
Nguyen, Black, Ray, Espino, and Markides (2003)	Cognitive decline (MMSE)	HR 2.4 for severe cog. imp; HR 1.5 for MCI
Meyer, Rauch, Rauch, and Haque (2000)	CCSE scores	9.8% in 5.8 years
Frisoni, Fratiglioni, Fastbom, Guo, Viitanen, and Winblad (2000)	MMSE scores below norms, age-sex adjusted	15.9%

Note: AACD, age-associated cognitive decline; AAMI, age-associated memory impairment; ACMI, age-consistent memory impairment; AD, Alzheimer's disease; a-MCI, amnestic MCI; ARCD, age-related cognitive decline; BSF, benign senescent forgetfulness; CCSE, Cognitive Capacity Screening Examination; CDR, Clinical Dementia Rating scale; CIND, cognitive impairment with no dementia; CSHA, Canadian Study of Health and Aging; DAT, dementia of the Alzheimer's type; HR, hazard ratio; LLF, late-life forgetfulness; MCI, mild cognitive impairment; MMSE, Mini-Mental State Examination; MRI, magnetic resonance imaging; RR, relative risk; SPMSQ CI, short portable mental status questionnaire defined cognitive impairment; VaD, vascular dementia.

It is self-evident that the way cognitive impairment is defined will affect prevalence and rates of conversion, but factors such as study design and the sample can also affect results. The choice of definition and study design reflects the implicit model of the natural history of cognitive decline that underlies the study and this can also affect the findings. These sources of variation will be discussed in turn.

The operational definition of MCI

Collie and Maruff (2002) listed 17 different classifications of early cognitive impairment, yet their list is not complete. Divergences between the classifications include questions such as whether both objective and subjective memory problems are required, whether or not evidence for decline is required as opposed to merely impairment, whether or not other deficits beyond memory are required, and whether or not impairments in daily function are considered in the definition. Even minor differences in classification systems can exert large effects on the results (Morris et al., 2001). For example, Fisk, Merry, and Rockwood (2003) showed that removing the requirement for subjective memory complaints doubled the prevalence estimate. And, the definition of subjective memory complaints is variable: it can refer to a spontaneous comment during the clinical examination, or can be based on a formal interview (Jonker et al., 2000).

Most recently, it has been proposed that there are several clinical subtypes of MCI: amnestic MCI (a-MCI), single nonmemory domain MCI (sd-MCI), and multiple domains MCI (md-MCI). The latter can occur with memory impairment (md-MCI + a) or without (md-MCI − a) (Petersen, 2004b). These clinical subtypes may reflect distinct etiologies and vice versa. For example, a-MCI may represent a prodromal form of AD or may be related to depression; a-MCI and md-MCI + a both have a high likelihood of progressing to AD. Those subtypes affecting primarily nonmemory cognitive domains, such as executive functions and visuospatial skills, are thought to reflect the pathology of non-AD dementias such as Lewy body or frontotemporal forms.

Whatever subtypes are specified, there are three basic approaches to operationally defining MCI: norm-based, criterion-based, and via clinical judgment. Norm-based definitions classify the individual's performance relative to a known distribution of scores, such as defining scores $\geq 1.5SD$ below the mean of a cognitively normal sample as being impaired. This approach corresponds to the assumption of a single continuum of cognition, with impaired people showing quantitative differences rather than differences of kind. Hence, a purely statistical criterion is appropriate, with the choice of a particular threshold (e.g., $1.5SD$) determined empirically. An advantage to this approach is that no matter how difficult the memory test is, roughly the same number of people will be identified. The disadvantage is that there will almost always be an overlap in scores between the normal population and the group with cognitive impairment. If the distribution is based on a normal sample, roughly 7% of the normal population will fall below $-1.5SD$ and be falsely classified as impaired. It is also meaningless to use this approach in estimating prevalence: the choice of cutting-point in terms of standard deviations will largely determine the prevalence of MCI obtained.

Alternatively, MCI can be defined via a criterion, either by selecting a particular score on a reference test to designate a "significant" impairment, or in terms of a level of cognitive impairment that corresponds to a handicap such as not being able to live independently. The criterion approach has the advantage of permitting a fair assessment of prevalence, but of course this will vary according to the (essentially arbitrary) criterion used, as seen in Table 1.3. Furthermore, the problem lies in deciding what test to use as the criterion, and whether the criterion threshold should be constant for all groups. If the criterion threshold is adjusted for age, the absolute criterion is effectively turned into a relative one (Hänninen et al., 2002). Ultimately, both the norm- and criterion-based approaches are arbitrary: why 1 or $1.5SD$, and why choose a particular test as the defining criterion?

The idea of using an external criterion, such as living independently, seems conceptually relevant but may be impractical owing to the insensitivity of standard instrumental activities of daily living (IADL) questions to the very early stages of cognitive decline. It also runs counter to many definitions of MCI, which do precisely the reverse, and require that the person has *no* ADL or IADL problems, as a way of excluding dementia. Aside from the obvious problem of classifying people who have both MCI and a physical illness that restricts their daily function, there are significant measurement issues. Nygard (2003) argued that subtle IADL changes are valuable in identifying early MCI, yet existing scales are insensitive and do not include contemporary activities such as accessing the internet or remembering numerical codes. Nor do existing scales distinguish between motor and process limitations in function. Some studies suggest that everyday tasks that are particularly heavily cognitively mediated, such as handling finances or driving, may be affected in those people with MCI (Barberger-Gateau, Fabrigoule, Rouch, Letenneur, & Dartigues, 1999; Whelihan, DiCarlo, & Paul, 2005), so these might form useful criteria for classifying MCI.

The third option for classifying MCI is to use clinical judgment (Petersen, 2004a). Instead of relying on a set threshold on a particular test, Petersen's criteria involve clinical judgment based on an overall impression from several memory tests. This provides a broader picture of any deficits and permits higher scores on some tests to compensate for low scores on others (Petersen et al., 1999). Petersen argued that using only the recall of three items is not sufficiently sensitive to early deficits, not being challenging enough. Hence, by the time that people fall $1.5SD$ below the mean for such tests, they probably also have other cognitive impairments and are likely already in the early stages of dementia. "Typically, multiple more challenging memory instruments are required to detect the subtle memory deficits seen in early MCI" (Petersen, 2004a). None of this, however, strictly requires clinical judgment, as such rules could be formed into a computer algorithm. Instead, clinical judgment may become a shorthand for avoiding the specification of precise criteria. The difficulty with relying on clinical judgment is that a thorough and broad understanding of brain–behavior relations is required and a number of factors need to be taken into consideration. Factors that can influence the reliability with which cognitive impairment is identified fall into three broad categories: patient characteristics (e.g., their vision, hearing, health status), measurement issues (e.g., level and types of information available), and rater characteristics (e.g., experience, training, confidence levels) (Tuokko, Gabriel, & the Canadian Study of Health and Aging Neuropsychology Working Group, 2006). Conversely, the more clearly the inclusion and exclusion criteria are articulated, the more likely clinicians will agree on the presence of cognitive impairment (Graham, Rockwood, Beattie, McDowell, Eastwood, & Gauthier, 1996; O'Connor et al., 1996).

A critical issue in defining MCI lies in setting the lower threshold for inclusion. Evidently, raising the threshold to select only people with more advanced MCI will reduce prevalence but increase the proportion converting to AD in a given time period. Fisk et al. (2003) demonstrated this: using a severe definition of MCI produced a prevalence of only 1%, most of whom were clear cases who had a high rate of progression (70% over 5 years). As the inclusion criteria were expanded, the proportion of people meeting the criteria rose (3% in Fisk's illustration); the severity fell and, along with this, the annual proportion who progressed to dementia (50%). The rate of reversion to no cognitive impairment on reassessment also rose as the criteria were broadened. Many authors use conversion rates to indicate the success of a classification of MCI. This is misleading, however, for as the definition is narrowed (e.g., from MCI to a-MCI), specificity increases and with it the conversion rate, but this occurs at the expense of sensitivity, meaning that growing numbers of the eventual cases of AD are missed by the narrow definition.

Having argued that the critical issue lies in setting the lower threshold for defining MCI, it must be noted that the upper limit is set by the onset of ADL or IADL problems or by the definition of dementia. Here too, differing definitions have been used, and very different results, in terms of conversion rates for MCI, may be expected depending on the definition used (DeCarli, 2003).

Study design

Different study designs shed light on different aspects of a phenomenon, and gaining a comprehensive picture requires studies of several types. As with all epidemiological research, the study of early cognitive impairment began with clinical samples and later progressed to population studies. Each serves a different and ideally complementary purpose. Clinical samples are suitable for providing detailed information on the mechanisms involved in cognitive decline; detailed study of individual change is the *forte* of clinical studies that are used to generate and test hypotheses under relatively controlled conditions. Population studies, in comparison, are mainly descriptive, providing counts of prevalence, incidence, and conversion rates, but they can also be used in an interchange with clinical studies. Where hypotheses are developed and initially tested in a clinical study, they may later be tested for generality in a population study; the population study can also translate associations such as odds ratios into population attributable risks. This moves beyond estimating the relative probability of disease in the clinical setting to an estimation of the absolute number of cases of disease in a population, which arise due to a risk factor. In turn, a population study may identify a new hypothesis, which is typically further investigated on a smaller scale but more tightly controlled clinical setting where links to underlying biological mechanisms may be more easily studied.

The advantages of clinical studies are that they provide easier access to cases than population studies and benefit from more complete follow-up; the clinical setting is also well suited for making research assessments. Clinical samples gain internal validity, but at the expense of generalizability; the samples include people who sought treatment and who may not be comparable to others in the general population who did not seek care for their memory loss. Where follow-up is required, clinical samples can be transformed into registry studies, again using selected and perhaps not representative samples, but benefiting from an organizational structure that can enhance long-term retention rates. As budgets are always finite, no study is ever ideal and design compromises have to be made. These are especially challenging in population studies, where budget dictates a number of trade-offs, for example, between the sample size, the overall duration of the study, and the frequency of follow-up assessments. Thus, it is seldom possible to fund a study that has both a large enough sample to study diagnostic subcategories and frequent follow-up assessments to give detailed documentation of change over time. The timing of follow-up assessments is also a compromise: wide spacing allows more cases to accrue for study, but increases gaps in information and losses to follow-up. Most of the population studies with very large samples have used few repeat assessments, giving insufficient detail to monitor individual change over time, but allowing for estimation of group averages. A choice also has to be made between collecting limited information on a wide range of topics and detailed information on fewer topics.

The net result is that a composite picture of cognitive decline must be assembled from a variety of study designs, each of which has had to make compromises that limit and may bias the data they produce. An illustration of this lies in the sample chosen for study.

Sampling

There are advantages and disadvantages to representative samples: external validity generally comes at the cost of internal validity. Representative population samples tend to generate a wide range of types, degrees, and causes of cognitive impairment; one result is that population samples tend to show high rates of remission from MCI to normality (Petersen, 2004b). Bozoki et al. showed how entry criteria can influence estimates of progression rates (Bozoki, Giordani, Heidebrink, Berent, & Foster, 2001). For example, should a study exclude subjects who turn out to have another explanation for their cognitive impairment? How are people with delirium to be handled? Representativeness is always relative: there may be a healthy study volunteer effect in population studies, and perhaps a vigilant consumer effect in clinical studies. For example, clinical samples tend to have a higher proportion of people with a positive family history, generating family concern (Petersen, 2004b). Likewise, the age of the sample will influence results: samples of younger, healthy participants will not produce a high incidence estimate (Jonker et al., 2000). The age of the sample will be influential, but not necessarily in a linear fashion: the prevalence of MCI tends to taper off at higher ages because so many people who formerly had MCI have developed dementia. This is especially true if the oldest age group is open-ended, and it depends critically on whether or not institutions are included in the sampling frame. Conceivably, the way the study is introduced to participants may also influence representativeness and the resulting estimates of prevalence. If it is presented as a study of memory or memory loss, participants with concerns over their memory may preferentially self-select to participate, and may consider some symptoms as pertinent that they might not have considered relevant if the study had been presented in a more neutral manner (Low et al., 2004).

Measurement

Inherent difficulties in measuring cognitive impairment have led to the use of different approaches, and these have contributed to the variability in empirical results. First, there is wide variation in test scores in the normal elderly population; this can generate both false-positive and false-negative impressions of impairment.

Second, we lack good norms for the oldest old and the choice of reference sample for defining "normal" is important. This can include a general population sample of people without dementia (but which presumably includes some with MCI), or it can aim to include only those who are aging optimally, or it can include younger people who may be presumed not to have yet developed cognitive impairments (Petersen, 2004b). Naturally, the more demanding the standards, the higher the proportion of elderly people who will be classified as "impaired".

Third, test scores can fluctuate over time (Correa, Perrault, & Wolfson, 2001; Frerichs & Tuokko, 2005), so single measurements of cognitive impairment form an unstable criterion. However, making repeated clinical assessments to track cognitive decline is generally not feasible and so recording decline is often based on repeated applications of a simple scale such as the

Mini-Mental State Examination (MMSE). This runs considerable risk of false classification. While most studies define MCI in cross-sectional terms, impairment can also be defined in terms of change within each individual: decline in scores. Single measures can identify static memory impairments but not progressive deterioration. In particular, Zaudig (2002) argued that serial measures of memory are necessary to detect the very early and subtle stages of cognitive decline; this is more feasible in clinical studies than in population-based studies. As the MCI progresses, however, it becomes more evident and can be detected both via subjective complaints and common memory tests. Memory loss is often the central cognitive domain of interest in MCI, but there is considerable variation in how memory loss is measured. Is a simple clinical assessment, such as impairment on a three-word recall, adequate? Or must it involve a formal comparison to norms for an age-appropriate population? If so, which memory tests are used and how should culturally and educationally heterogeneous populations be handled? As noted by Petersen (2004a, 2004b), these issues have sometimes been side-stepped by using a Clinical Dementia Rating (CDR) of 0.5 as equivalent to MCI, and yet the CDR is a severity scale rather than a diagnostic instrument. A CDR of 0.5 may include some individuals with a very mild AD, hence exaggerating the rates of progression to true dementia.

Finally, a practical issue is that as the criteria for defining cognitive impairment evolve, new criteria often have to be retrofitted to existing data. As the data may not contain precisely the variables required, the fit will be imperfect, leading to discrepant prevalence estimates. Petersen (2004a) cited the example of using a question on memory problems from the Geriatric Depression Scale as a proxy measure of subjective memory complaints.

Implications for interventions

Despite uncertainties over our estimates, it is clear that a significant subset of people identified with MCI eventually progresses to dementia. This might be expected to be particularly true for clinic-referred samples, in contrast to population random samples, as the initial prevalence and significance of MCI may be expected to be greater in the clinic. It is with these clinic-referred samples that interventions for MCI have already begun, so we must consider their applicability to broader population samples.

Pharmacological and behavioral interventions form the two major approaches that have been taken; they will be discussed in detail in the final section of this book. These have evolved from ongoing work that focuses on management for AD. The evaluation of these approaches for use with MCI is still in its infancy (Geula, Farlow, Cummings, Morris, Scheltens, & Anand, 2000; Nagaraja & Jayashree, 2001; Sramek, Veroff, & Cutler, 2001) and so there is little clear evidence to guide practice. Within each of these approaches, implicit or explicit assumptions are made that reflect the conceptual stance taken toward MCI. Furthermore, a number of factors need to be considered when deciding whether intervention for MCI is appropriate.

These factors will be addressed below, after the pharmacological and behavioral approaches, in general, are described.

The intent of pharmacological approaches is to slow, stop, or even reverse the underlying pathological changes. This type of intervention has most often been pursued where MCI is viewed as a prodrome to AD, but conceivably could be used for other conditions as well. Since, as discussed above, the identification of MCI is based on cognitive performance, pharmacological approaches necessarily rest on the assumption of a direct link between underlying pathology and the behavioral presentation. This assumption is also inherent in the typical choice of outcome measures (e.g., measures of cognitive functioning or psychosocial markers such as prolonging time to admission to residential care). However, the link between the underlying pathology and the manifest behavioral symptoms is not always clear, even in AD.

Findings from the Nun Study (Greiner, Snowdon, & Greiner, 1996; Riley, Snowdon, Desrosiers, & Markesbery, 2005; Snowdon, Kemper, Mortimer, Greiner, Wekstein, & Markesbery, 1996) show that there may not be a close correspondence between the underlying pathology and cognitive symptoms in AD. Pathology must occur before clinical symptoms become apparent, but it may be debated whether cases in which pathological changes do not produce symptoms or affect function do, in effect, represent disease. This is important as it holds implications for approaches to intervention and their evaluation: should we measure pathological changes or the associated clinical symptoms? Thus, psychopharmacologic interventions presumably target specific forms of neuropathology that may or may not be associated with particular cognitive or behavioral impairments. Using behavioral measures as outcome indicators in these studies may not adequately reflect underlying biological changes in brain function. As the link between the underlying pathology and the manifest behavioral symptoms is of even greater concern in MCI than AD, there is a need to demonstrate the impact of the intervention with biological markers such as neuroimages or biochemical markers (e.g., amyloid precursor protein). At present, the impact of pharmacological approaches for MCI is likely to be limited by the demonstration of the link between behavioral and biological markers.

In contrast to the pharmacological approaches, behavioral approaches to intervention for MCI address cognitive or behavioral symptoms that may or may not be associated with specific underlying neuropathology. The focus here is on optimizing functioning and well-being, minimizing the risk of disability, and preventing the development of dysfunctional family or social functioning (Clare & Woods, 2001). Behavioral interventions derive from the field of cognitive rehabilitation for people with nonprogressive acquired brain injury where enhancing self-efficacy and coping skills, combating threats to self-esteem, and helping the person make the best possible use of individual resources are central. A wide variety of cognitive rehabilitation models and methods have been developed, many of which focus on aspects of memory functioning (Sohlberg & Mateer, 2001), the cognitive area most commonly associated with MCI. Some of these strategies emphasize internal processes to enhance memory functions such as visual imagery, rhyming exercises, or other efforts to increase depth of processing. Others focus on using external strategies for cueing and reminding (e.g., posted reminders, memory notebooks, paging systems, electronic organizers, and internet cueing systems). The various theoretical and conceptual frameworks developed for the application of rehabilitation approaches for people with nonprogressive acquired brain injury are relevant to people with neurodegenerative disorders. Both the dialectical (Kitwood, 1997) and social constructionist models of dementia (Sabat, 1994, 1995) emphasize the importance of humanism or personhood and the social context in approaches to dementia care. Cognitive rehabilitation approaches may be of more, and longer, benefit to people with MCI than those with dementia because the cognitive deficits, by definition, are less severe. However, as with interventions for dementia, behavioral approaches for MCI need to be flexible and responsive to changes in the person (Clare & Woods, 2001).

Early behavioral intervention could possibly enhance cognitive reserve (CR) and delay the clinical and functional impairments associated with underlying brain pathology. The brain reserve capacity (BRC) model (Roth, 1971; Roth, Tomlinson, & Blessed, 1967; Satz, 1993) suggests that individuals differ with respect to their BRC and that the existence of greater BRC exerts a protective effect against dementia. Stern (2002) described a CR model that, in contrast to the BRC model, suggests people differ in how effectively cognitive paradigms are used to approach a problem (and thereby maintain function), rather than in how much brain capacity is available. People with greater CR can sustain a larger amount of neural damage before clinical or functional impairment becomes evident. CR does not protect against the development of pathology, but delays the expression of clinical and functional impairments associated with underlying brain pathology. Stern (2002) further distinguished between CR and *compensation*, a distinct change in the brain areas used in the performance of a task induced by brain damage. Cognitive rehabilitation could lead to *compensation*, in Stern's (2002) sense of the word, and result in a distinct change in the brain areas used in the performance of a task induced by neurodegenerative processes. That is, the experiences and activities undertaken through cognitive rehabilitation may dynamically influence the development and function of neural substrates (Stern, 2002). Here, as with the pharmacological approaches, it will be important to obtain both behavioral and biological outcome measures.

Before implementing an intervention for MCI, a number of practical challenges need to be considered. If, as is reported for some narrowly defined clinical samples, the base rate of conversion of the identified group from MCI to AD is very high (e.g., 80% or more), intervention would be appropriate for all cases. With lower conversion rates, other considerations guide the decision of whether to intervene. First is the identification of other promoting or protective factors that may modify the basic conversion rate. A second consideration is the accuracy and certainty of the MCI classification. Third, the cost, availability, and accessibility of interventions need to be determined and this must be considered within the context of the current known efficacy of the intervention for people with that form of MCI. For pharmacological interventions in particular, potential side effects must be considered, especially for those who may not actually have AD. This is of less concern for behavioral interventions and it could be argued that all people with MCI, regardless of whether or not it is a progressive form, may derive benefit from behavioral interventions. Finally, the preferences of the patients and their family must be ascertained and given due consideration. Family support can play a major role in ensuring that intervention protocols are implemented appropriately and in collecting relevant follow-up information.

Once an intervention approach to MCI is adopted, its evaluation would be expected to proceed in the same manner as for other conditions; initially efficacy studies would be conducted, followed by effectiveness studies. Efficacy studies place a high value on internal validity and include only well-defined clinical samples under ideal, tightly controlled, conditions. These studies are to be seen as a beginning, not an end (Liebowitz & Rudorfer, 1998). Effectiveness studies usually involve large representative populations, including patients with multiple conditions and less characteristic presentations. In either circumstance, outcome measures would ideally include biomarkers, cognitive/neuropsychological test results, and other behavioral or quality of life indicators to assess breadth of impact. In practice, however, biomarkers are rarely available. Moreover, common, simple cognitive measures such as the MMSE are inadequate for measuring change over time, as there is large error variance around each application (Correa et al., 2001). There is accumulating evidence that some neuropsychological measures may be particularly useful for monitoring change (Frerichs & Tuokko, 2005; Heaton et al., 2001) but there is a need for more psychometrically sound instruments to be developed for this purpose. Performance on repeated neuropsychological tests will typically serve as the primary outcome measure, with independence in everyday functioning serving as a secondary outcome.

Poised at the threshold of early interventions for mild cognitive decline, we would do well to acknowledge the possibility of adverse outcomes. While simple maneuvers such as using *aides-mémoire* are unlikely to cause harm, the potential impact of labeling people as cognitively impaired should be recognized. Behavioral interventions may best be prescribed not in the context of dealing with a pathology, but more in the manner of simple and practical ideas to assist an elderly person. If pharmacologic interventions become the norm, there is greater potential for harmful side-effects, and these may be discounted or may pass unnoticed if the patient is believed to be in cognitive decline. It will also be desirable to explore the benefits of first withdrawing current medications and perhaps exploring the benefits of complementary therapies. While it is likely to be in the financial interest of pharmaceutical manufacturers to prescribe medications as widely as possible, trials must be undertaken to ensure that they do more good than harm. These will be costly, but have to be undertaken. The lessons of early trials of cholesterol lowering agents (Davey, Smith, Song, & Sheldon, 1993; Lipid Research Clinics, 1984) issued a strong warning of the dangers of extrapolating from trials of medication for serious conditions (here, dementia) to milder forms (MCI); instead, specific trials of treatments for MCI have to be undertaken.

Summary

This brief overview has introduced a number of challenges in conceptualizing and studying MCI. First, the term MCI implies a descriptive, quantified, behavioral classification. Key stages in defining MCI involve specifying cognitive and behavioral functions to be considered, and the procedure for their quantification. Memory function is generally mentioned, but varying patterns of impairment across other domains of cognitive function may also be included in some definitions. The threshold for defining the lower limit for "impairment" has to be established; this may be done in relation to normative data, or according to a criterion that could be based on subjective complaints or objective cognitive scores. The upper boundary for "mild impairment" has also to be decided. Does this include all people who have documented cognitive impairment that does not reach the threshold for dementia, or is it restricted to the mildest end of this spectrum, for example excluding people with multiple forms of cognitive loss?

A second consideration is that MCI typically implies an underlying pathology and poor eventual outcome. Inherent in many definitions is the notion of decline or change in function; the issue becomes how to quantify this change. If the classification is prognostic, the manner in which MCI is defined operationally will differ according to the anticipated outcome (e.g., AD, VaD, or frontotemporal dementia). Other terms like cognitive impairment with no dementia (CIND) have been used (Graham et al., 1996) to capture cases where no assumptions are made concerning underlying pathology as well as all other forms of nondementia impairments, including those too severe to be called "mild".

A third issue that has stimulated much interest is how the behavioral definition (clinical symptoms) used to characterize MCI relates to the presumed underlying pathology. The link between the underlying pathology and the manifest behavioral symptoms remains unclear and is of even greater concern in MCI than in AD. Pharmacological approaches to intervention rest on the assumption that a direct link is demonstrable. Behavioral interventions promote the best possible use of individual's resources and this, in turn, may, or may not, have an impact on the underlying pathology. Moreover, other promoting or protective factors may affect the development of pathology, or the association between an underlying pathology and the clinical expression of cognitive impairment. For example, there is evidence that life experiences and activities such as exercise may dynamically influence the development and function of neural substrates (Stern, 2002).

This leads to a fourth consideration: how the natural history of MCI is conceptualized. Where the motivation for studying MCI is descriptive (e.g., incidence, prevalence, patterns of performance), no assumptions are made about future outcomes, and cognitive functioning over time may improve, remain stable, or decline. On the other hand, when cognitive decline is implicit within the MCI conceptualization, one representation proposes a single-dimensional model with stages across which people may or may not transition according to the balance between promoting and protective factors. Ultimately, cognitive decline would be viewed as a path leading from normality through to dementia, along which everyone would move if they only lived long enough. A relatively trivial variant of this distinction concerns whether decline is viewed as a continuous process (a dimensional model) or as a discrete process. The latter implies a series of steps down which the patient descends, spending more or less time on each (a categorical model). The latter view is plausible, as progression across all stages does not appear inevitable and several types of factor could distinguish who will progress to the next step among a set of people showing early signs of cognitive loss. An alternative metaphor might be that of rain falling on a hillside and trickling downward, taking different routes. Here, the different routes represent differing patterns of cognitive decline, some subtly different and others clearly different. Some of the rain sinks into the soil and continues downward but unseen, representing pathology in the brain that may not be reflected by cognitive losses seen at the surface. Unlike the steps, this metaphor shows how there are not only different patterns of the surface presentation of decline, but also different levels of decline (pathological and clinical), which may operate differently.

Where the motivation for studying MCI lies in identifying those who will progress to dementia, predictors of further decline can be of three broad types. Predictors could be drawn from the pattern of early losses (thus, a descriptive classification); predictors could also lie in genomic or phenotypic factors (i.e., susceptibilities); or they could lie in environmental circumstances that form triggers for activating the personal susceptibilities. The status of these variables is different. Neuropsychological tests cannot *explain* progression, but may describe the characteristics of those who will progress. Environmental factors could plausibly form the conditions to *initiate* a decline, and may (or may not) serve to promote the continuation to dementia. But because there do not seem to be any environmental factors so overwhelmingly damaging as to inevitably cause dementia, individual susceptibility factors must play a role. If environmental factors do not actually trigger continued decline, at least there must be a lack of protective factors that could inhibit such progression. These could be genetic or phenotypic factors. Plausibly, both are required, interacting with environmental triggers.

Conclusions

We have identified and summarized at least some of the challenges associated with the concept of MCI. We now turn to the perspectives on MCI taken by different research groups around the world. Each chapter focuses on the research of a specific research group. The intent and major emphases of the research differ between groups, as do the specific topics of their investigations concerning MCI. Our intent, in bringing these chapters together, is to provide a comprehensive examination of the concept of MCI from these varying perspectives. This introductory chapter provides the background, or framework, within which these perspectives can be viewed. In the final chapter to the book, we will summarize, from our perspective, the essential issues emerging from these views of MCI and directions for future research.

References

American Psychiatric Association. (1994). *Diagnostic and statistical manual of mental disorders* (4th ed.). Washington, DC: American Psychiatric Association.

Amieva, H., Letenneur, L., Dartigues, J. F., Rouch-Leroyer, I., Sourgen, C., D'Alchee-Biree, F., et al. (2004). Annual rate and predictors of conversion to dementia in subjects presenting mild cognitive impairment criteria defined according to a population-based study. *Dementia and Geriatric Cognitive Disorders, 18,* 87–93.

Barberger-Gateau, P., Fabrigoule, C., Rouch, I., Letenneur, L., & Dartigues, J. F. (1999). Neuropsychological correlates of self-reported performance in instrumental activities of daily living and prediction of dementia. *Journals of Gerontology: Psychological Sciences and Social Sciences, 54,* 293–303.

Bennett, D. A., Wilson, R. S., Schneider, J. A., Evans, D. A., Beckett, L. A., Aggarwal, N. T., et al. (2002). Natural history of mild cognitive impairment in older persons. *Neurology, 59,* 198–205.

Bischkopf, J., Busse, A., & Angermeyer, M. C. (2002). Mild cognitive impairment—A review of prevalence, incidence and outcome according to current approaches. *Acta Psychiatrica Scandinavica, 106,* 403–414.

Blackford, R. C., & La Rue, A. (1989). Criteria for diagnosing age-associated memory impairment: Proposed improvements from the field. *Developmental Neuropsychology, 5,* 295–306.

Bowen, J., Teri, L., Kukull, W., McCormick, W., McCurry, S. M., & Larson, E. B. (1997). Progression to dementia in patients with isolated memory loss. *Lancet, 349,* 763–765.

Bozoki, A., Giordani, B., Heidebrink, J. L., Berent, S., & Foster, N. L. (2001). Mild cognitive impairments predict dementia in nondemented elderly patients with memory loss. *Archives of Neurology, 58,* 411–416.

Brayne, C., & Calloway, P. (1988). Normal ageing, impaired cognitive function, and senile dementia of the Alzheimer's type: A continuum? *Lancet, 331,* 1265–1267.

Busse, A., Bischkopf, J., Riedel-Heller, S. G., & Angermeyer, M. C. (2003a). Mild cognitive impairment: Prevalence and incidence according to different diagnostic criteria. Results of the Leipzig Longitudinal Study of the Aged (LEILA75+). *British Journal of Psychiatry, 182,* 449–454.

Busse, A., Bischkopf, J., Riedel-Heller, S. G., & Angermeyer, M. C. (2003b). Mild cognitive impairment: Prevalence and predictive validity according to current approaches. *Acta Neurologica Scandinavica, 108*, 71–81.

Busse, A., Bischkopf, J., Riedel-Heller, S. G., & Angermeyer, M. C. (2003c). Subclassifications for mild cognitive impairment: Prevalence and predictive validity. *Psychological Medicine, 33*, 1029–1038.

Clare, L., & Woods, R. T. (2001). *Cognitive rehabilitation in dementia*. New York: Taylor & Francis, Inc.

Collie, A., & Maruff, P. (2002). An analysis of systems of classifying mild cognitive impairment in older people. *Australian and New Zealand Journal of Psychiatry, 36*, 133–140.

Correa, J. A., Perrault, A., & Wolfson, C. (2001). Reliable individual change scores on the 3MS in older persons with dementia: Results from the Canadian Study of Health and Aging. *International Psychogeriatrics, 13*(Suppl. 1), 71–78.

Crook, T., Bartus, R. T., Ferris, S. H., Whitehouse, P., Cohen, G. D., & Gershon, S. (1986). Age-associated memory impairment: Proposed criteria and measures of clinical change. Report of the National Institute of Mental Health Work Group. *Developmental Neuropsychology, 2*, 261–276.

Davey, Smith, G., Song, F., & Sheldon, T. A. (1993). Cholesterol lowering and mortality: The importance of considering initial level of risk. *British Medical Journal, 306*, 1367.

DeCarli, C. (2003). Mild cognitive impairment: Prevalence, prognosis, aetiology, and treatment. *Lancet Neurology, 2*, 15–21.

DeCarli, C., Mungas, D., Harvey, D., Reed, B., Weiner, M., Chui, H., et al. (2004). Memory impairment, but not cerebrovascular disease, predicts progression of MCI to dementia. *Neurology, 63*, 220–227.

DiCarlo, A., Baldereschi, M., Amaducci, L., Maggi, S., Grigiletto, F., Scarlato, G., et al. (2000). Cognitive impairment without dementia in older people: Prevalence, vascular risk factors, impact on disability. The Italian Longitudinal Study on Aging. *Journal of the American Geriatrics Society, 48*, 775–782.

Fisk, J. D., Merry, H. R., & Rockwood, K. (2003). Variations in case definition affect prevalence but not outcomes of mild cognitive impairment. *Neurology, 61*, 1179–1184.

Fisk, J. D., & Rockwood, K. (2005). Outcomes of incident mild cognitive impairment in relation to case definition. *Journal of Neurology, Neurosurgery & Psychiatry, 76*, 1175–1177.

Flicker, C., Ferris, S. H., & Reisberg, B. (1991). Mild cognitive impairment in the elderly: Predictors of dementia. *Neurology, 41*, 1006–1009.

Frerichs, R. J., & Tuokko, H. A. (2005). A comparison of methods for measuring cognitive change in older adults. *Archives of Clinical Neuropsychology, 20*, 321–333.

Frisoni, G. B., Fratiglioni, L., Fastbom, J., Guo, Z., Viitanen, M., & Winblad, B. (2000). Mild cognitive impairment in the population and physical health: Data on 1,435 individuals aged 75 to 95. *Journals of Gerontology: Biological Sciences & Medical Sciences, 55A*, M322–M328.

Ganguli, M., Dodge, H. H., Shen, C., & DeKosky, S. T. (2004). Mild cognitive impairment, amnestic type: An epidemiologic study. *Neurology, 63*, 115–121.

Geula, C., Farlow, M., Cummings, J., Morris, J., Scheltens, P., & Anand, R. (2000). Alzheimer's disease: Translating neurochemical insights into chemical benefits. *Journal of Clinical Psychiatry, 61*, 791–802.

Graham, J., Rockwood, K., Beattie, B. L., McDowell, I., Eastwood, R., & Gauthier, S. (1996). Standardization of the diagnosis of dementia in the Canadian Study of Health and Aging. *Neuroepidemiology, 15*, 246–256.

Graham, J. E., Rockwood, K., Beattie, B. L., Eastwood, R., Gauthier, S., Tuokko, H., et al. (1997). Prevalence and severity of cognitive impairment with and without dementia in an elderly population. *Lancet, 349*, 1793–1796.

Greiner, P. A., Snowdon, D. A., & Greiner, L. H. (1996). The relationship of self-rated function and self-rated health to concurrent functional ability, functional decline, and mortality: Findings from the nun study. *Journals of Gerontology: Psychological Sciences & Social Sciences, 51B*(5), S234–S241.

Gurland, B. J., Dean, L. L., Copeland, J., Gurland, R., & Golden, R. (1982). Criteria for the diagnosis of dementia in the community elderly. *The Gerontologist, 22*, 180–186.

Hänninen, T., Hallikainen, M., Tuomainen, S., Vanhanen, M., & Soininen, H. (2002). Prevalence of mild cognitive impairment: A population-based study in elderly subjects. *Acta Neurologica Scandinavica, 106*, 148–154.

Heaton, R. K., Temkin, N., Dikmen, S., Avitable, N., Taylor, M. J., Marcotte, T. D., et al. (2001). A comparison of three neuropsychological methods, using normal and clinical samples. *Archives of Clinical Neuropsychology, 16*, 75–91.

Jack, C. R., Petersen, R. C., Xu, Y. C., O'Brien, P. C., Smith, G. E., Ivnik, R. J., et al. (1999). Prediction of AD with MRI-based hippocampal volume in mild cognitive impairment. *Neurology, 52*, 1397–1403.

Jonker, C., Geerlings, M. I., & Schmand, B. (2000). Are memory complaints predictive for dementia? A review of clinical and population-based studies. *International Journal of Geriatric Psychiatry, 15*, 983–991.

Kitwood, T. (1997). *Dementia reconsidered: The person comes first.* Buckingham: Open University Press.

Korf, E. S. C., Wahlund, L.-O., Visser, P. J., & Scheltens, P. (2004). Medial temporal lobe atrophy on MRI predicts dementia in patients with mild cognitive impairment. *Neurology, 63*, 94–100.

Kral, V. A. (1962). Senescent forgetfulness: Benign and malignant. *Canadian Medical Association Journal, 86*, 257–260.

Kumamoto, T., Sannomiya, K., Ueyama, H., Aoki, K., Nakashima, T., Nalamura, R., et al. (2000). Neurological abnormalities in cognitively impaired but not demented elderly. *Acta Neurologica Scandinavica, 102*, 292–298.

Larrabee, G. J., Levin, H. S., & High, W. M. (1986). Senescent forgetfulness: A quantitative study. *Developmental Neuropsychology, 2*, 373–385.

Larrieu, S., Letenneur, L., Orgogozo, J. M., Fabrigoule, C., Amieva, H., Le Carret, N., et al. (2002). Incidence and outcome of mild cognitive impairment in a population-based prospective cohort. *Neurology, 59*, 1594–1599.

Levy, R. (1994). Aging-associated cognitive decline. *International Psychogeriatrics, 6*, 63–68.

Liebowitz, B. D., & Rudorfer, M. D. (1998). Treatment research at the millenium: From efficacy to effectiveness. *Journal of Clinical Psychopharmacology, 18*, 1.

Lipid Research Clinics. (1984). Coronary Primary Prevention Trial: I. Reduction in incidence of coronary heart disease. II. The relationship of reduction in incidence of coronary heart disease to cholesterol lowering. *Journal of the American Medical Association, 251*, 351.

Lopez, O. L., Jagust, W. J., DeKosky, S. T., Becker, J. T., Fitzpatrick, A., Dulberg, C., et al. (2003). Prevalence and classification of mild cognitive impairment in the Cardiovascular Health Study Cognition Study: Part 1. *Archives of Neurology, 60,* 1385–1389.

Low, L.-F., Brodaty, H., Edwards, R., Kochan, N., Draper, B., Trollor, J., et al. (2004). The prevalence of "cognitive impairment no dementia" in community-dwelling elderly: A pilot study. *Australian and New Zealand Journal of Psychiatry, 38,* 725–731.

Luis, C. A., Loewenstein, D. A., Acevedo, A., Barker, W. W., & Duara, R. (2003). Mild cognitive impairment: Directions for future research. *Neurology, 61*(4), 438–444.

Meguro, K., Ishii, H., Yamaguchi, S., Ishizaki, J., Sato, M., Hashimoto, R., et al. (2004). Prevalence and cognitive performances of clinical dementia rating 0.5 and mild cognitive impairment in Japan. The Tajiri project. *Alzheimer Disease and Associated Disorders, 18,* 3–10.

Meyer, J. S., Rauch, G., Rauch, R. A., & Haque, A. (2000). Risk factors for cerebral hypoperfusion, mild cognitive impairment, and dementia. *Neurobiology of Aging, 21,* 161–169.

Meyer, J. S., Xu, G., Thornby, J., Chowdhury, M. H., & Quach, M. (2002a). Longitudinal analysis of abnormal domains comprising mild cognitive impairment (MCI) during aging. *Journal of Neurological Sciences, 201,* 19–25.

Meyer, J. S., Xu, G., Thornby, J., Chowdhury, M. H., & Quach, M. (2002b). Is mild cognitive impairment prodromal for vascular dementia like Alzheimer's disease? *Stroke, 33,* 1981–1985.

Morris, J. C., Storandt, M., Miller, J. P., McKeel, D. W., Price, J. L., Rubin, E. H., et al. (2001). Mild cognitive impairment represents early-stage Alzheimer disease. *Archives of Neurology, 58,* 397–405.

Nagaraja, D., & Jayashree, S. (2001). Randomized study of the dopamine receptor agonist piribedil in the treatment of mild cognitive impairment. *American Journal of Psychiatry, 158,* 1517–1519.

Nguyen, H. T., Black, S. A., Ray, L. A., Espino, D. V., & Markides, K. S. (2003). Cognitive impairment and mortality in older Mexican Americans. *Journal of the American Geriatrics Society, 51,* 178–183.

Nygard, L. (2003). Instrumental activities of daily living: a stepping-stone towards Alzheimer's disease diagnosis in subjects with mild cognitive impairment? *Acta Neurologica Scandinavica, 107*(Suppl. 179), 42–46.

O'Connor, D. W., Blessed, G., Cooper, B., Jonker, C., Morris, J. C., Presnell, I. B., et al. (1996). Cross-national interrater reliability of dementia diagnosis in the elderly and factors associated with disagreement. *Neurology, 47,* 1194–1199.

Palmer, K., Fratiglioni, L., & Winblad, B. (2003). What is mild cognitive impairment? Variations in definitions and evolution of nondemented persons with cognitive impairment. *Acta Neurologica Scandinavica, 107*(Suppl. 179), 14–20.

Petersen, R. C. (2004a). Challenges of epidemiological studies of mild cognitive impairment. *Alzheimer Disease and Associated Disorders, 18*(1), 1–2.

Petersen, R. C. (2004b). Mild cognitive impairment as a diagnostic entity. *Journal of Internal Medicine, 256,* 183–194.

Petersen, R. C., & Morris, J. C. (2003). Clinical features. In R. C. Petersen (Ed.), *Mild cognitive impairment: Aging to Alzheimer's disease* (pp. 15–39). New York: Oxford University Press.

Petersen, R. C., Smith, G. E., Waring, S. C., Ivnik, R. J., Tangalos, E. G., & Kokmen, E. (1999). Mild cognitive impairment. *Archives of Neurology, 56,* 303–308.

Petersen, R. C., Stevens, J. C., Ganguli, M., Tangalos, E. G., Cummings, J. L., & DeKosky, S. T. (2001). Practice parameter: Early detection of dementia: Mild cognitive impairment (an evidence-based review). Report of the quality standards subcommittee of the American Academy of Neurology. *Neurology*, *56*, 1133–1142.

Qiu, C. J., Tang, M. N., Zhang, W., Han, H. Y., Dai, J., Lu, J., et al. (2003). The prevalence of mild cognitive impairment among residents aged 55 or over in Chengdu area. *Zhonghua Liu Xing Bing Xue Za Zhi*, *24*, 1104–1107.

Rediess, S., & Caine, E. D. (1996). Aging, cognition, and DSM-IV. *Aging, Neuropsychology, and Cognition*, *3*, 105–117.

Riley, K. P., Snowdon, D. A., Desrosiers, M. F., & Markesbery, W. R. (2005). Early life linguistic ability, late life cognitive function, and neuropathology: Findings from the Nun Study. *Neurobiology of Aging*, *26*, 341–347.

Ritchie, K., Artero, S., & Touchon, J. (2001). Classification criteria for mild cognitive impairment: A population-based validation study. *Neurology*, *56*, 37–42.

Ritchie, K., Ledesert, B., & Touchon, J. (2000). Subclinical cognitive impairment: Epidemiology and clinical characteristics. *Comprehensive Psychiatry*, *41*(Suppl. 1), 61–65.

Roth, M. (1971). Classification and etiology in mental disorders of old age: Some recent developments. *British Journal of Psychiatry, Special Publication, No.6*, 1–18.

Roth, M., Tomlinson, B. E., & Blessed, G. (1967). The relationship between quantitative measures of dementia and of degenerative changes in the cerebral grey matter of elderly subjects. *Proceedings of the Society of Medicine*, *60*, 254–259.

Sabat, S. (1994). Excess disability and malignant social psychology: A case study of Alzheimer's disease. *Journal of Community and Applied Social Psychology*, *4*, 157–166.

Sabat, S. (1995). The Alzheimer's disease sufferer as a semiotic subject. *Philosophy, Psychiatry, and Psychology*, *1*, 145–160.

Satz, P. (1993). Brain reserve capacity on symptom onset after brain injury: A formulation and review of evidence for threshold theory. *Neuropsychology*, *7*, 273–295.

Schroder, J., Kratz, B., Pantel, J., Minnemann, E., Lehr, U., & Sauer, H. (1998). Prevalence of mild cognitive impairment in an elderly community sample. *Journal of Neural Transmission*, *54*(Suppl.), 51–59.

Smith, G. E., Petersen, R. C., Parisi, J. E., & Ivnik, R. J. (1996). Definition, course, and outcome of mild cognitive impairment. *Aging, Neuropsychology, and Cognition*, *3*, 141–147.

Snowdon, D. A., Kemper, S. J., Mortimer, J. A., Greiner, L. H., Wekstein, D. R., & Markesbery, W. R. (1996). Linguistic ability in early life and cognitive function and Alzheimer's disease in late life. Findings from the Nun Study. *Journal of the American Medical Association*, *275*, 528–532.

Sohlberg, M. M., & Mateer, C. A. (2001). *Cognitive rehabilitation: An integrated neuropsychological approach*. New York: Guilford Press.

Sramek, J. J., Veroff, A. E., & Cutler, N. R. (2001). The status of ongoing trials for mild cognitive impairment. *Expert Opinion on Investigational Drugs*, *10*, 741–752.

Stern, Y. (2002). What is cognitive reserve? Theory and research application of the reserve concept. *Journal of the International Neuropsychological Society*, *8*, 448–460.

Stump, T. E., Callahan, C. M., & Hendrie, H. C. (2001). Cognitive impairment and mortality in older primary care patients. *Journal of the American Geriatric Society*, *49*, 934–940.

Tervo, S., Kivipelto, M., Hanninen, T., Vanhanen, M., Hallikainen, M., Mannermaa, A., et al. (2004). Incidence and risk factors for mild cognitive impairment: A population-based three-year follow-up study of cognitively healthy elderly subjects. *Dementia and Geriatric Cognitive Disorders, 17*, 196–203.

Tuokko, H., & Frerichs, R. J. (2000). Cognitive impairment with no dementia (CIND): Longitudinal studies, the findings, and the issues. *The Clinical Neuropsychologist, 14*, 504–525.

Tuokko, H., Frerichs, R., Graham, J., Rockwood, K., Kristjansson, E., Fisk, J., et al. (2003). Five year follow-up of cognitive impairment with no dementia. *Archives of Neurology, 60*(April), 577–582.

Tuokko, H. A., Gabriel, G., & the Canadian Study of Health and Aging Neuropsychology Working Group. (2006). Neuropsychological detection of cognitive impairment: Inter-rater agreement and factors affecting clinical decision-making. *Journal of the International Neuropsychological Society, 12*(1), 72–79.

Unverzagt, F. W., Gao, S., Baiyewu, O., Ogunniyi, A. O., Gureje, O., Perkins, A., et al. (2001). Prevalence of cognitive impairment. Data from the Indianapolis Study of Health and Aging. *Neurology, 57*, 1655–1662.

Von Dras, D. D., & Blumenthal, H. T. (1992). Dementia of the aged: Disease or atypical-accelerated aging? Biopathological and psychological perspectives. *Journal of the American Geriatrics Society, 40*, 285–294.

Whelihan, W. M., DiCarlo, M. A., & Paul, R. H. (2005). The relationship of neuropsychological functioning to driving competence in older persons with early cognitive decline. *Archives of Clinical Neuropsychology, 20*(2), 217–228.

World Health Organization. (1993). *The ICD-10 classification of mental and behavioural disorders: Diagnostic criteria for research.* Geneva: Author.

Yesavage, J. A., O'Hara, R., Kraemer, H., Noda, A., Taylor, J. L., & Ferris, S. (2002). Modeling the prevalence and incidence of Alzheimer's disease and mild cognitive impairment. *Journal of Psychiatric Research, 36*, 281–286.

Zaudig, M. (1992). A new systematic method of measurement and diagnosis of "mild cognitive impairment" and dementia according to ICD-10 and DSM-III-R criteria. *International Psychogeriatrics, 4*, 203–219.

Zaudig, M. (2002). Mild cognitive impairment in the elderly. *Current Opinions in Psychiatry, 15*, 387–393.

Part II

General Population Research on MCI

2 The PAQUID study

Colette Fabrigoule, Pascale Barberger-Gateau, and Jean-François Dartigues

The term "mild cognitive impairment" was introduced by Flicker, Ferris, and Reisberg (1991) and colleagues in a paper showing that patients with mild cognitive deficits, as determined by clinical evaluation and objective psychological testing, manifested the progressive mental deterioration characteristic of dementia. The mild cognitive impairment (MCI) concept was further developed by Petersen, Smith, Waring, Ivnik, Kokmen, and Tangalos (1997), using research in specialized clinical settings, to characterize people in transition from a normal state to the demented stage of Alzheimers' disease (AD). The definition of MCI has since become extended to describe people in a pre-demented stage of other types of dementia. Since most studies depend on people visiting memory centers, there is a definite need to analyze the validity of this theoretical construct in the population at large; this will prove particularly important when drugs that can stop the evolution of people at risk do finally become available. Such people will then have to be detected within the general population and not only among memory clinic patients.

Population-based epidemiological studies are particularly useful in determining what characterizes elderly people engaged in pathways leading to AD or other types of dementia. A longitudinal approach is needed to question the validity of the MCI concept, evaluating its ability to detect those who will attain a given dementia criterion within a few years. Clinical MCI longitudinal studies typically evaluate the "conversion rate" of patients recruited according to an a priori criterion. These studies are, however, affected by a selection bias, since in most countries people with a good level of education and income, for example, are over-represented in memory clinics. Equally, it is not really possible in clinical settings to determine whether the presence of a memory complaint is a risk factor of conversion, since the simple fact of going to a memory clinic may in itself be assimilated to making a complaint; nonetheless, at-risk people who do not go to memory clinics definitely exist in the population. Moreover, clinical MCI studies generally imply far fewer participants than in epidemiological studies. Longitudinal population-based epidemiological studies, however, involve numerous participants, recruited with much less selection bias, and who are much more representative of the population in all its diversity.

Epidemiological settings allow two strategies of analysis to be employed. The first strategy uses existing MCI criteria to study the prevalence and incidence of MCI types, their predictive value for the development of AD or other types of dementia, as well as the stability of the syndromes. An alternative strategy, however, allows individual characteristics associated with future dementia, such as cognitive performance, cognitive complaints, instrumental activities of daily living (IADL), magnetic resonance imaging (MRI) data, and depression, to be determined, independently of any a priori definition. The literature devoted to this alternative strategy has certainly not been sufficiently taken into account, even though, by determining the best predictors of evolution, it can certainly be used to improve existing MCI definitions.

In this chapter, we will present the French PAQUID (Personnes Agées QUID: what about elderly people?) epidemiological study, and the results we found relevant to the MCI topic. First we describe the general methodology of the PAQUID study. Then, using Petersen's definition, we examine the incidence of MCI in our population, as well as its conversion rate and stability. We also examine the nature of the cognitive deficits that best predict AD or other types of dementia, as well as their connection with a slight decline in the IADL. All of this provides arguments to help determine which components need to be considered in elaborating MCI criteria and consequently require further research.

Presentation of the PAQUID study

The PAQUID study (Dartigues et al., 1992) was undertaken to study prospectively a representative random sample of 3777 people aged 65 years and over, living at home in the communities of Gironde and Dordogne, two administrative areas around Bordeaux, in southern France. PAQUID was designed to analyze the prevalence, incidence, risk factors, and predictors of dementia and AD, and their impact on daily functioning. Participants were recruited in 1988 and 1989 and they have been followed up almost every 2 years since then. The study has been approved by the Ethics Committee of the "Centre Hospitalier Universitaire" of Bordeaux.

General methodology of the study

Sample and baseline collection phase

Participants were randomly chosen from the communal electoral lists. Three criteria had to be met for participants to be included: (1) to be at least 65 years of age by December 31, 1987; (2) to be living at home at the time of the initial data collection phase; and (3) to give their written informed consent to participating in the study. In order to obtain a representative sample of 4000 elderly residents of Gironde and Dordogne, 75 geographic units were randomly chosen (37 in Gironde and 38 in Dordogne). A three-step random procedure, using the electoral rolls stratified by age, sex, and size of the geographical unit, gave 5554 elderly participants living at home in Gironde (4050) and in Dordogne (1504). Participants were informed by mail that they had been chosen to participate in a study on the health status and living conditions of people aged 65 years and older. They were then contacted by phone or visited directly at home (when participants did not have a telephone). When participants agreed to participate in the study, an appointment was made for the visit of a psychologist specially formed for home interviews, in order to complete a questionnaire and a functional and neuropsychological evaluation. A random sample of 200 nonresponders was interviewed by phone to provide minimum information on their age, sex, educational level, and principal occupation during life, and the name of their general practitioner (GP).

Of the 4050 participants contacted in Gironde, 1258 (31.1%) refused to participate in the study and 2792 (68.9%) accepted. Of the 1504 participants contacted in Dordogne, 519 (34.5%) refused to participate in the study and 985 (65.5%) accepted. Ultimately, 3777 participants were interviewed during the first screening. Among the 200 refusals who were contacted, 154 (77%) agreed to give at least minimal information. The nonresponders were not significantly different from responders in age, sex, and educational level, but were different as regards their principal occupation during working life. Nonresponders were more often craftsmen and domestic service employees, and less often farmers, executives, and blue-collar workers.

Variables collected

Several variables, including identification of the subject and a key informant, and the name and address of their GP, were collected. The questionnaire included: demographic variables (such as age, sex, marital status, educational level, principal occupation during working life); social variables (number of visits received, leisure activities, perceived social support); subjective health measures; health measures (weight, blood pressure, dietary habits, tobacco and alcohol use, prescription drugs, age at menopause and number of children, presence of visual, dental, and hearing impairments); a depressive symptomatology scale (CESD: Center for Epidemiology Studies Depression); personal antecedents (head injury, fractures, hospitalization, thyroid disease, depression, psychiatric illness, major weight loss, and World War II concentration camp internment); symptoms and pathologies (joint and back pain, dyspnea, arthritis, cardio and cerebrovascular diseases, and diabetes); self-perceived symptoms of cognitive deficits and neurosensory symptoms.

Functional impairment

A functional assessment was realized using different scales: the Katz scale of activities of daily living (ADL), including six functions—bathing, dressing, toileting, transferring, continence, and eating (Katz, Downs, Cash, & Grotz, 1970); the Lawton and Brody (1969) IADL scale including telephone use, shopping, transportation, budget management, medication management, cooking, housekeeping, and laundry, the latter three items being used for the assessment of women only.

Neuropsychological assessment

The neuropsychological battery, administered by a psychologist, comprised six tests:

- A global scale, the Mini-Mental State Examination (MMSE; Folstein, Folstein, & McHugh, 1975), which can be considered as the sum of subscores that measure different cognitive components: orientation to time, orientation to place, registration of three words, attention and calculation, recall of three words, language and visual construction.
- A visual memory test, the multiple-choice form (Form F) of the Benton Visual Retention Test (BVRT; Benton, 1965), which consists of 15 stimulus cards and 15 multiple choice cards. After the presentation of a stimulus card for 10 s, the participants are asked to choose the initial figure among four options.
- A semantic verbal fluency test, the Isaacs Set Test (IST; Isaacs & Akhtar, 1972), which measures the ability to generate lists of words in four specific semantic categories (colors, animals, fruits, cities) in a limited time period. In our study, in accordance with Isaacs and Akhtar initial rules, the maximum number of words generated in each category was limited to 10; thus possible total scores range from 0 to 40.
- A selective attention test, the Zazzo's Cancellation Task (ZCT; Zazzo, 1974), which measures the ability to cross out as fast and as exactly as possible 125 target signs on a sheet of white paper containing 40 lines of signs.
- A test of analogical reasoning and visuospatial attention, the Digit Symbol Substitution Test (DSST; Wechsler, 1981), which consists of assigning the correct symbol to digits ranging from 1 to 9 using a code table displaying pairs of digits and symbols. The subject has to copy as many symbols as possible in a time period of 90 s.
- A conceptualization test, the Wechsler Similarities Test (WST; Wechsler, 1981), where the subject must explain in what way two things are alike (e.g., orange-banana). In our study, only the first five pairs of the WAIS similarities subtest were considered. Items score two points if an abstract generalization is given and one point if a response indicated is a specific concrete likeness.

Diagnosis of dementia

At the end of the interview, the psychologist applied the dementia criteria given in *Diagnostic and Statistical Manual of Mental Disorders* (DSM-III-R, American Psychiatric Association, 1987) to select participants suspected of being demented. Next, a senior neurologist went to these participants' homes to confirm and complete the DSM-III-R criteria for dementia and apply the NINCDS-ADRDA criteria (McKhann, Drachman, Folstein, Katzman, Price, & Stadlan, 1984) and the Hachinski score (Hachinski et al., 1975) in order to document the diagnosis of dementia and its etiology: i.e., probable or possible AD, vascular or other types of dementia. A consensus conference was held in order to classify each case.

Follow-up procedure

The participants were followed up regularly. In Gironde, follow-up visits were conducted at 1, 3, 5, 8, 10, 13, and 15 years after the initial visit. In Dordogne, follow-up visits were realized according to the same schedule, apart for the 1-year visit, which was not completed. During these follow-up visits a quasi-baseline screening procedure was used, with some minor changes in the composition of the neuropsychological battery. For the follow-up screenings, in addition to participants suspected of dementia on the basis of DSM-III-R criteria, participants with a decline of more than two points in the MMSE were seen by the neurologist.

MCI in the PAQUID study

In the Larrieu et al. (2002) study, we estimated the incidence of MCI in a population-based sample of participants aged 70 years and more living in the community and then studied the evolution of MCI towards dementia and AD. Our objective was to determine whether MCI could be considered as an early stage of AD or as a predictor for it in the general population. MCI characterization was very close to that of Petersen et al. (1997). Another inclusive category of "other cognitive impairment with no dementia" (OCIND) was also used to characterize those participants who were not normal, demented, or MCI.

Methods

Sample

Between 1988 and 1998, five follow-ups were performed, but the present study started with data gathered in 1993 to document the cognitive decline of the participants at least 5 years later, to both eliminate the initial learning effect on the tests, and obtain more homogeneous and reliable data for the incident cases of dementia. Even if the DSM-III-R criteria used by the psychologists for screening dementia and AD remained the same during the 15 years of follow-up, the increasing experience of the study staff ensured that the diagnosis was more likely to be made at an earlier stage of the disease, a trend further increased by the introduction of new treatments in 1993. The present study was, therefore, based on three assessments: 1993 (baseline for this analysis), 1995 (2 years after), and 1998 (5 years after). This resulted in a cohort of 2084 participants aged at least 70 years at baseline.

Categorization of participants

At each of the three visits, participants were classified as demented, cognitively normal, MCI, or OCIND. Four age strata were defined (70–74, 75–79, 80–84, 85 and over) for each of the two education strata. Participants were classified in the high educational group if they had passed the French primary school diploma (certificat d'études) or a higher school diploma, and in the low educational level group otherwise (Letenneur, Gilleron, Commenges, Helmer, Orgogozo, & Dartigues, 1999). The diagnosis of dementia was made according to the DSM-III-R criteria for dementia as described above.

The diagnosis of MCI was made according to the following criteria: (1) no dementia; (2) subjective memory complaint screened through two questions on self-perceived forgetfulness in daily activities or in recent events; (3) normal general cognitive functioning as assessed by the MMSE, i.e., with a score greater than $1SD$ below the mean of age-and-education-defined strata in this cohort, after exclusion of prevalent dementia at entry; (4) objective memory impairment as assessed by a performance on the BVRT lower than $1.5SD$ of the mean of age-and-education-defined strata; (5) autonomy in the basic activities of daily living, as measured by the Katz ADL scale.

The participants were considered as cognitively normal if they were not demented and scored higher than $1SD$ below the mean of age-and-education-defined strata on the MMSE, and higher than $1.5SD$ below the mean of age-and-education-defined strata on the BVRT. The OCIND category was applied to participants who could not be considered normal, MCI, or demented, once all the relevant data had been collected.

Statistical methods

To estimate the incidence of MCI, participants at risk were followed up for 5 years and assessed at 2 and 5 years. Six types of participants were excluded from the study for the estimation of incidence of MCI because they were no longer at risk of developing it at the next follow-up, i.e., participants: (1) classified as demented; (2) classified as MCI; (3) with low general cognitive performances measured by the MMSE; (4) with objective memory impairment associated with dependency in ADL since it was a criterion of exclusion for MCI; (5) cognitively normal but dependent in ADL; (6) who could not be classified because of missing data on one of the criteria for MCI. Incidence rates were computed using the person-years method, according to age group, gender, and educational level.

To describe the outcome of MCI over 5 years, the sample of nondemented participants at baseline was divided into three groups: normal, MCI, and OCIND, to compare the risk of developing dementia and AD in these different groups. As a subject could be assigned a different category during the follow-up, the amount of observation time contributing to a given group was calculated for each individual. Specific incidence rates and the risk ratio (RR) of AD and other type of dementia were then calculated with 95% confidence intervals (95% CI) for the MCI and the OCIND groups, the normal group being taken as the reference. The stability of MCI and OCIND over time was then observed by examining the frequency of participants who remained in their previous category at the next visit or who moved to another category (normal, MCI, OCIND, or demented).

Results

Incidence of MCI

Among the 3777 participants first included in the cohort in 1988, 2084 were seen in 1993. Among the participants who were excluded from the study for the estimation of incidence of MCI we found 154 classified as demented, 58 classified as MCI, 160 with a low score at the MMSE, 17 with an objective memory impairment associated with dependency in ADL, 154 cognitively normal but dependent for the ADL, and 276 who could not be classified because of missing data on one of the criteria for MCI. The resulting sample for the estimation of the incidence consisted therefore of 1265 participants.

During the 5-year follow-up, 40 new participants with MCI were identified with an estimated incidence rate of 9.9/1000 person-years (p-y). MCI incidence rate estimates did not increase with age. The global incidence rate was higher in participants with high educational level (10.3/1000 p-y) than in those with low educational level (8.6/1000 p-y). The global incidence rates showed that women tended to be at higher risk of MCI (11.6 vs. 8.0/1000 p-y), whatever the age group.

Course of MCI

Among the 2084 participants seen at the baseline visit, 154 (7.4%) demented participants and 276 (13.3%) participants who could not be classified because of missing data were excluded. The resulting sample consisted of 1654 participants who were followed up for 5 years. Among these participants, 1389 (84%) were normal, 58 (3.5%) were classified as MCI, and 207 (12.5%) as OCIND. The 207 OCIND participants could be classified neither as MCI, because they did not meet the five criteria, nor as demented, since they did not meet DSM-III-R criteria for dementia, nor normal: most (77.3%) had a score on the MMSE lower than the cut-off limit chosen and so could not be considered as either normal or as having MCI. The 47 others had objective memory impairment but were not considered as MCI, either because they did not complain of forgetfulness (30/47) or because they were dependent for at least one ADL (17/47).

During the follow-up, 120 new cases of AD and 33 cases of other dementias were identified. The specific incidence rates of AD (Table 2.1) were similar in the MCI and OCIND groups (respectively 8.3 and 7.1%) and were significantly higher than in the normal group (1.7%): the RR for MCI versus normal was 4.9 (95% CI = 2.7–9.2) and the RR for OCIND versus normal was 4.2 (95% CI = 2.9–6.3). The conversion rate to other types of dementia was significantly higher in OCIND participants than in normal participants (RR = 3.2; 95% CI = 1.4–6.9), but there was no difference between MCI and normal participants (RR = 1.4; 95% CI = 0.2–10.6).

The stability of the MCI and OCIND over time is given in Table 2.2. Of the 58 participants considered as MCI at the baseline visit, 24 (41.4%) were classified as normal, 6 (10.3%) as OCIND, and only 4 (6.9%) remained MCI 2 years later. Of the 37 MCI participants at the 2-year follow-up, 16 (43.2%) returned to normal, 7 (18.9%) became OCIND, and only 2 (5.4%) remained in the MCI group after 3 years.

Discussion

For MCI, the estimated incidence was around 1% per year in people aged 70 and over in this prospective population cohort. In the case of dementia for the same age category, the incidence is much higher: 3% per year (Letenneur, Commenges, Dartigues, & Barberger-Gateau, 1994). Sex-specific incidence estimates showed that, as for AD in the PAQUID cohort (Letenneur et al., 1994), women are at higher risk of MCI. Surprising results are the stability of the incidence with age and the lower risk of developing MCI in participants

Table 2.1 Incidence rates per 100 person-years of AD and other types of dementia in the three groups of nondemented participants (reproduced with permission from Larrieu, S. et al. (2002). Incidence and outcome of mild cognitive impairment in a population-based prospective cohort. *Neurology, 59*, 1594–1599)

Group of participants	Person-years at risk	Number of cases	Incidence rates (95% CI)	
Alzheimer's disease				
Normal	4540.2	75	1.7	(1.6–1.8)
MCI	132.7	11	8.3	(6.9–9.7)
OCIND	482.9	34	7.1	(6.4–7.7)
Total	5155.8	120	2.3	(2.2–2.3)
Other types of dementia				
Normal	4540.2	24	0.53	(0.52–0.54)
MCI	132.7	1	0.75	(0.62–0.88)
OCIND	482.9	8	1.7	(1.5–1.8)
Total	5155.8	33	0.64	(0.62–0.68)

Table 2.2 Evolution of the prevalent MCI and OCIND cases from baseline to the 2-year follow-up, and from the 2-year to the 5-year follow-up (reproduced with permission from Larrieu, S. et al. (2002). Incidence and outcome of mild cognitive impairment in a population-based prospective cohort. *Neurology, 59*, 1594–1599)

Group of participants followed	Normal (%)	MCI (%)	OCIND (%)	Demented (%)	Dead (%)	Missing and withdrawals (%)
MCI at baseline ($n = 58$)	41.4	6.9	10.3	3.5	8.6	29.3
MCI 2 years later ($n = 37$)	43.2	5.4	18.9	18.9	10.8	2.9
OCIND at baseline ($n = 207$)	32.4	2.4	23.2	9.7	16.4	15.9
OCIND 2 years later ($n = 107$)	32.7	2.8	22.4	15.9	22.4	3.8

MCI: mild cognitive impairment; OCIND: other cognitive impairment with no dementia.

with low educational level, notably in the 70–74 age group, whereas old age and low education were strong risk factors for AD in the PAQUID study (Letenneur et al., 1999) and in other studies (i.e., Geerlings, Schmand, Jonker, Lindeboom, & Bouter, 1999). A likely explanation is that age and education were taken into account to choose the cut-off scores that defined MCI. The hypothesis of a greater "cognitive reserve" in participants with high educational levels may also help explain the higher MCI rate in more educated people. If, despite memory impairment, they are able to preserve other aspects of cognitive functioning for a longer period than low educated participants, they may remain longer in the MCI stage, and may, therefore, be more likely to be diagnosed as MCI during an interim visit.

MCI participants showed a greater conversion rate to AD (8.3% per year) than normal participants (1.7% per year). These results agree with studies performed on clinical series (Petersen, Smith, Waring, Ivnik, Tangalos, & Kokmen, 1999). The OCIND group, however, was three to four times larger than the MCI group, and its AD conversion rate was similar to that of the MCI group. As for the other types of dementia, OCIND had a slightly higher conversion rate than the MCI and the normal groups. This indicates that even if their predictive value is similar, the MCI construct is a more specific predictor of AD than OCIND. A lack of stability was observed, both in the OCIND and the MCI group, with about one-third of OCIND prevalent cases and more than 40% of prevalent MCI cases returning to normal at the next follow-up, 2 or 3 years later. This finding, which is consistent with another study in which up to 40% of MCI cases also reverted to normal (Ritchie, Artero, & Touchon, 2001), underlines both the heterogeneity of MCI and

OCIND cases and the lack of specificity of these constructs. Moreover, although participants with MCI and OCIND showed a higher risk of developing AD than normal participants, most people who did develop AD (75/120) or other types of dementia (24/33) were classified as being cognitively normal at baseline. This underlines the lack of sensitivity of MCI and OCIND constructs in detecting people at risk of AD and other dementias within a few years. As regards the weakness in MCI predictive value, this may, in part, have been due to the fact that memory trouble was defined by a performance under $1.5SD$ of the same age and education normal population, as proposed earlier for a verbal memory test (Petersen et al., 1997). This cut-off, which only takes the lowest 10 percentile of normal participants' performance distribution into consideration, may, thus, have been far too restrictive. Some participants may well be at risk because they have already experienced a real memory decline even if their performance is not yet as low as this cut-off.

In conclusion, although MCI was associated with a greater risk of having AD within the next few years, this construct demonstrated a real lack of both sensitivity and specificity. In a recent review of 19 longitudinal studies addressing the conversion of MCI to dementia, Bruscoli and Lovestone (2004) found an overall annual conversion rate of 10%, ranging from 2 to 31%. The conversion rate for clinic attenders was twice that of the community participants (15.01 vs. 7.5%), which, according to the authors, suggests that participants seeking help for memory problems have a higher risk of dementia. Nonetheless, even in clinical settings, MCI criteria need to be improved if they are to reach a better predictive value for conversion to dementia and AD. Bruscoli and Lovestone pointed out that, in the 19 studies reviewed, it is the cognitive performance factor, above all, which best predicts conversion from MCI to dementia. Cognitive performances are certainly one of the key features to be considered for improving the construct. Memory has long been considered as the core of AD and "prodromal" AD cognitive deficits and, consequently, other cognitive functions have not been systematically looked for in MCI. They have, however, often been considered in epidemiological studies, whose results certainly need to be taken into consideration. Starting from the results of the PAQUID studies we will discuss the nature of cognitive deficits characterizing the predemented phase, arguing that, besides memory, other cognitive processes have to be looked for, especially components of executive control. We will also argue that slight impairments in the cognitively demanding IADL have to be considered, due to their close relationship with memory and executive decline.

The nature of cognitive deficits in the predemented phase of AD

The nature of cognitive components affected in the predemented phase of AD

Different analyses realized in the PAQUID study may help to determine what cognitive processes are affected in the predemented phase of AD. Fabrigoule,

Lafont, Letenneur, and Dartigues (1996) have shown that conceptualization performance assessed by the WST was associated with a risk of AD 2 years later. Dartigues et al. (1997) have shown that global cognitive level assessed by the MMSE, short-term visual memory assessed by the BVRT, and semantic verbal fluency assessed by the IST are independent predictors of dementia for a period of 1–3 years later. Moreover, the risk increased with the accumulation of test performances below the first distribution quartile. Thus not only a test of memory, but also tests of other functions were all associated with an increased risk of dementia within the next few years. Equally, in other population studies, measures of various cognitive processes had also been shown to be associated with the risk of dementia: episodic memory and verbal fluency tests in the Bronx cohort (Masur, Sliwinski, Lipton, Blau, & Crystal, 1994), abstract reasoning and confrontation naming in the North Manhattan Aging Project (Jacobs, Sano, Dooneief, Marder, Bell, & Stern, 1995), and verbal memory tests and immediate auditory attention in the Framingham cohort (Linn et al., 1995). We undertook an analysis (Fabrigoule et al., 1998) to determine whether different cognitive processes are really affected in the predemented phase of AD, or if this apparent heterogeneity is the result of common cognitive components being shared by different tests. First we analyzed the association between performances at each of seven neuropsychological tests taken at the first follow-up of the PAQUID study, and the risk of AD 2 years later. Afterwards, we used a multivariate approach with principal component analysis (PCA) to dissect the multicolinearity of these cognitive tests.

Methods

The analysis was limited to 1159 participants from Gironde who respected the following three criteria: to be considered as nondemented at the first year of follow-up of the cohort, to have performed the whole battery of tests, and to have accepted the visit 2 years later. The Wechsler Paired Associated Test (WPAT, Wechsler, 1945), which was added to the neuropsychological battery, involves the reading of 10 word pairs. After reading the list, the examiner gives the first word of each pair and the subject is asked to provide the second word. Three learning trials and a delayed recall are performed. Six of the word pairs are easy associates (e.g., baby-cries) and four are difficult (e.g., cabbage-pen). The easy pairs are given a score of 0.5 and the difficult ones a score of 1. We considered scores of the first learning trial (WPAT1) and the delayed recall (WPATr).

For each type of analysis we considered (1) the risk of AD, taking into account only the participants classified as AD, and (2) the risk of dementia, considering all the demented participants, whatever the type of dementia, including AD; the number of participants presenting another type of dementia did not justify being analyzed separately. The association between each test score performed at the first year of follow-up and the risk of either subsequent dementia or AD were assessed by calculating the odds ratio (OR) and its corresponding 95% confidence interval (95% CI). The model we used was a logistic regression model. Scores on the individual tests were subjected to a PCA. PCA is a multivariate statistical technique used to examine the relationships among a set of correlated variables, in this case neuropsychological performances across different tests. It transforms the original set of variables into a new and smaller set of uncorrelated variables called principal components. The new variables are ranked in decreasing order of importance so that the first principal components account for the maximum of the variation in the original data. Individual patient weightings on each of these new variables (principal components) were subsequently correlated with the risk of dementia and AD in the two following years, by logistic regression with backward stepwise and adjustment for age, gender, and educational level.

Results

A total of 645 women and 514 men were included in this study, with a mean age of 72.9 years at the baseline screening. Among the 1159 participants, 25 developed dementia 2 years later, 16 cases were classified as AD, 7 as vascular dementia, and 2 as Parkinson dementia. Using a univariate logistic regression analysis, all neuropsychological scores were strongly related to the subsequent risk of dementia and to the subsequent risk of AD. The PCA generated a one-factor solution with eigenvalue greater than 1, which accounted for 45.3% of the variance (Table 2.3) in test performance. With a cut-off of 0.75 for the eigenvalues, three more factors were generated, which accounted for 29.2% of the variance.

The patients' loadings on each of these four PCA factors were subsequently correlated with the risk of dementia and AD 2 years later, with adjustment for age and educational level. Four new variables corresponding to the four PCA factors were used. The logistic regression with backward stepwise selected only the first factor as both an independent predictor of dementia and of AD. For a decrease of one point of the PCA score the OR for the risk of dementia was 2.31 (95% CI: 1.82–2.95, $p < .00001$) and for the risk of AD was 3.25 (95% CI: 2.18–4.8, $p < .00001$). The other factors did not reach the significance level.

Discussion

The results of this paper confirmed that the clinical diagnosis of dementia or AD was preceded by a preclinical stage of at least 2 years, detectable by neuropsychological tests. As found in previous papers, various neuropsychological performances were associated with the subsequent risk of dementia as well as with the subsequent risk of AD. Despite this apparent heterogeneity, the clinical impairment of cognition seems to be homogeneous, since only one component of the neuropsychological pattern of the participants was found to be a strong independent predictor of dementia and AD.

Table 2.3 Principal component analysis for the neuropsychological tests (reproduced, by permission of Oxford University Press, from Fabrigoule, C. et al. (1998). Cognitive process in preclinical phase of dementia. *Brain*, *121*, 135–141)

	Factor				
Variable[a]	1	2	3	4	5
MMSE	0.67	−0.26	−0.07	−0.19	0.53
DSST	0.82	0.28	0.20	0.01	−0.12
BVRT	0.71	0.12	0.01	0.07	0.36
IST	0.74	0.16	0.19	0.09	0.08
WPAT1	0.71	−0.43	−0.06	0.20	−0.18
WPATr	0.66	−0.47	−0.15	0.33	−0.21
ZCTtot	0.35	0.47	−0.78	0.16	−0.03
ZCTspeed	0.71	0.37	0.38	0.01	−0.20
WST	0.58	−0.12	−0.20	−0.72	−0.26

[a]MMSE: Mini-Mental State Examination; DSST: Digit Symbol Substitution Test; BVRT: Benton Visual Retention Test; IST: Isaacs Set Test; WPAT1: Wechsler Paired Associates Test, first recall; WPATr: Wechsler Paired Associates Test, delayed recall; ZCTtot: Zazzo Cancellation Test total; ZCTspeed: Zazzo Cancellation Test speed; WST: Wechsler Similarities Test.

The major problem was, of course, to interpret what the first factor generated by the PCA represents. Eight neuropsychological scores among the eleven tested were highly correlated with this factor. DSST and IST scores characterize the PCA Factor 1 better than the other test scores, since their loadings on this factor were at least twice as large as their loadings on any other factor; BVRT and ZCT time scores are very close to fulfilling this criterion. The cognitive processes involved in these tests might well help to characterize this common component. Visuospatial perception, selective attention, response speed, visuomotor coordination, and incidental memory of digit-symbol pair association may play a role in DSST performances. In ZCT, visuospatial perception, selective attention, and response speed contribute to the subject's performances. This test shares many components with the DSST, but it is simpler in that a single target has to be detected among distracters and, unlike the DSST, it may, with practice, give way to automatization. Our score does, however, reflect the controlled part of the test because participants completed only the first eight lines, and at this stage the automatization process has only just begun (Amieva, Rouch-Leroyer, Letenneur, Dartigues, & Fabrigoule, 2004). The IST is a categorical fluency test in which production depends on the integrity of semantic memory networks as well as on the ability to initiate systematic search and retrieval strategies; it also involves working memory in keeping track of what words have already been said. Moreover, response speed contributes to the subject's performance as in the two previous tests. Besides these three timed tests, we find the BVRT, which may best be characterized by its memory component. This test, used in recognition, involves visuospatial perception, visual conceptualization, immediate memory span, recognition, and a form of selective attention, because the memorized stimulus has to be selected among three very similar distracters.

This description of the processes involved in the four tests which are the most specific of PCA Factor 1 shows that it has to do with processing speed and selective attention, as well as with the more controlled aspects of memory functioning, i.e., the "central executive" of working memory described in Baddeley's model (1987) and/or the strategic aspect of memory retrieval proposed by Moscovitch (1992). Therefore, there are good reasons to suspect that PCA Factor 1 represents a general factor corresponding to the executive or controlled aspects of the tasks used, and that the other factors of PCA, which correspond to other components of the same tasks, are more automated.

According to Schneider and Shiffrin (1977) controlled processes are described as slow, generally serial, requiring mental effort ("effortful" for Hasher & Zacks, 1979), regulated by the subject, and of limited capacity. In a review paper, Jorm (1986) hypothesized that relative deterioration of controlled processes, as opposed to preservation of automatic ones, constitutes one of the first signs of dementia. Following Jorm's hypothesis, our results seemed to show that the controlled/automatic distinction may be relevant in characterizing the early deterioration of cognitive functioning in the preclinical phase of dementia and AD.

Confirmation of the deterioration of executive control in the AD predemented phase

Because the hypothesis of a deterioration of controlled processes in the preclinical phase of dementia relied essentially on the interpretation of PCA factors, we undertook a specific analysis to test this interpretation (Amieva, Rouch-Leroyer, Fabrigoule, & Dartigues, 2000). One of the tests in the neuropsychological battery administered to participants was of particular interest for this. The WPAT consists of recalling ten word pairs, "six related pairs" being highly semantically or functionally related (north-south; fruit-apple; metal-iron; top-down; flower-rose; baby-cries), whereas four "unrelated pairs" are not readily related (school-grocery; crash-dark; cabbage-pen; obey-advance). It can be assumed that unrelated pairs which do not have semantic associations need a deliberate and sustained effort to be encoded and retrieved, and thus involve the more controlled, strategic, and executive aspects of memory functioning, whereas related pairs make use of semantic associations, so their access involves more automatic components of memory functioning. If our previous interpretation of PCA factors was correct, we advance the hypothesis that, when included separately in the analysis, the unrelated pairs score should have a higher loading on Factor 1, previously interpreted as the "controlled" factor, than the related pairs score which should have a high loading on another factor, assumed to correspond to more automated processes. Additionally, this "controlled" factor should remain the only component significantly associated with subsequent dementia.

Results and discussion

Using the same set of data as in the previous analysis, we first confirmed the respective difficulty of the so-called unrelated and related word pairs in normal elderly participants, since the percentages of success at the first trial of WPAT ranged from 79.6 to 94.9% for the retrieval of the six related pairs, and from 21.7 to 54.4% for the four unrelated pairs. We then tested our interpretation of the PCA factors, including the same neuropsychological tests, by introducing the WPAT, divided into two subscores of related and unrelated pairs, into the PCA. The amount of variance explained by the first two factors of this new PCA was reliably improved relative to the factors of the previous PCA (69.2 vs. 56.1%). Factor 1 was loaded by the same neuropsychological tests as in the previous study (DSST, IST, BVRT, and ZAZtime), suggesting that the underlying cognitive process is comparable in both studies. Additionally, the inspection of factor loadings of the new variables included showed that the unrelated pairs scores were clearly specific to Factor 1 (load of 0.7 for the third immediate recall and the delayed recall), since their factor loadings were twice as high on Factor 1 as on any other factor. Conversely, although moderately correlated with Factor 1 (0.46 and 0.52, respectively, for the third and delayed recall), the related pairs scores were by far the two test scores most strongly correlated to Factor 2 (0.61 and 0.58, respectively, for third immediate and delayed recall). Factor 1 also remained the only factor significantly associated with both a risk of subsequent dementia and of AD.

These results confirmed our previous PCA interpretation of Factor 1. It is widely accepted that neuropsychological tests are multidimensional, in that they rarely stand for a unique cognitive function such as memory or language, and that they are also carried out by complex mixtures of controlled and automatic processes used in combination (Jacoby, 1991). Our results strongly suggest that what is primarily deteriorated at the predemented stages of dementia and even AD may be the ability to deal with the more effortful and executive aspects of any task, whatever the primary function of the task, visuospatial, language, or memory.

Conclusion

In different analyses of PAQUID data we found various neuropsychological tests, not only memory tests, associated with the risk of dementia and AD. Besides memory tests, tests of other functions are also affected in the predemented phase. In a recent review, Bäckman, Jones, Berger, Laukka, and Small (2004) have also shown that multiple cognitive deficits exist during the transition to AD, measures of executive functioning, episodic memory, and perceptual speed being the most effective at identifying at-risk individuals. This pattern of deficits is certainly compatible with our pattern of results and with the hypotheses that the more controlled and executive aspects may be affected in this transitional stage to AD. Moreover, the authors underlined the fact that, in episodic memory, the preclinical deficit increases with increasing cognitive demand, which fits very well with our results on WPAT. It seems then quite clear that, in addition to decline in memory tests, decline in tests demanding high executive control has to be considered.

Trying to define an AD-specific syndrome by characterizing MCI purely on the basis of some isolated memory deficit, to the exclusion of other types of cognitive deficit, may well prove counterproductive. It seems preferable to combine memory and executive control deficits to improve the sensitivity of the syndrome; it will also help to select people who will attain the demented stage of AD more rapidly than people with an isolated memory trouble. Bäckman et al. (2004) underlined the fact that there is evidence from different fields that the aging brain possesses compensatory capabilities. Results obtained using functional MRI show positive associations between relatively preserved performances and recruitment of the pre-frontal dorso-lateral cortex (PFDLC) both in normal aging (for a review see Grady, 2000) and early AD (Grady, McIntosh, Beig, Keightley, Burian, & Black, 2003). Additionally, a lot of imaging experiments have underlined that PFDLC plays a crucial role in executive control (e.g., Duncan & Owen, 2000). All this suggests that executive control processes may be at the heart of compensatory ability. If so, this may explain why the presence of executive dysfunction, added to that of memory dysfunction in MCI, may help to select people at risk of conversion to AD in the short term. If this hypothesis of executive control processes being at the heart of compensatory abilities is confirmed, it also argues for the inclusion of a slight deterioration of highly cognitively loaded IADL in the MCI construct.

MCI and instrumental activities of daily living

Decline in professional and social functioning is one of the criteria for dementia. However, the course of disability is very progressive before this stage is reached. Petersen et al. (1999) in his definition of MCI stated that there should be no impairment in ADL. However, as pointed out by Ritchie et al. (2001) "no guidelines have been given as to what constitutes activities of daily living restriction in MCI," functional impairment being mainly focused on basic ADL. However, basic ADL, such as bathing or feeding, are affected late in the dementing process, whereas IADL may be affected much earlier (Gauthier, Gelinas, & Gauthier, 1997).

Further results of the PAQUID study may help in investigating the impact of MCI on IADL. Barberger-Gateau, Commenges, Gagnon, Letenneur, and Sauvel (1992) showed that a score summing the number of impairments at four activities (ability to use the telephone, mode of transportation, responsibility for own medication, and ability to handle finance), all selected from the Lawton and Brody (1969) IADL scale, showed a strong association with both the MMSE score and the diagnosis of dementia. This four IADL score was also a strong predictor of the risk of being diagnosed as demented 1 year

(Barberger-Gateau, Dartigues, & Letenneur, 1993) and 3 years (Barberger-Gateau, Fabrigoule, Helmer, Rouch, & Dartigues, 1999a) after baseline screening.

We will now describe the results of an analysis realized to determine how much the predictive value of the four IADL score is explained by its relation to cognitive performances (Barberger-Gateau, Fabrigoule, Rouch, Letenneur, & Dartigues, 1999b).

Methods

This analysis was realized, using the data collected at the 1-year follow-up of the PAQUID study, because this follow-up, to which the WPAT had been added, included more neuropsychological tests than other visits. The sample was restricted to Gironde, where the whole battery had been proposed and 1424 participants completed all the neuropsychological tests. Among MMSE items, we used the orientation score (ten time and space orientation items), the calculation score (five items of subtraction), and the recall score (delayed recall of the three words). To analyze the correlations between neuropsychological performances and IADL in nondemented participants, we performed stepwise logistic regression analyses on each of the four IADL items dichotomized (zero corresponding to the full autonomy level and one corresponding to at least the first level of restriction). These regressions were adjusted for age, sex, educational level, and visual and hearing impairment. In order to allow a better comparison of the OR measures we transformed all test scores into Z scores by subtracting their mean and dividing by their standard deviation.

Finally, PCA was conducted to take into account the colinearity between the various neuropsychological tests and to better identify the specific components of performance on each IADL. The factors of the PCA were then used as explanatory variables in a Cox proportional hazard model with delayed entry, adjusted for educational level and age at baseline. The end point was to have an incident dementia at 3- or 5-year follow-up visits, i.e., 2–4 years later.

Results

Each IADL item had specific associations with neuropsychological tests (Table 2.4). Speed of processing, as tested by Zazzo's cancellation time (ZCTtime), was the only common cognitive component significantly associated with a higher probability of being autonomous on each of the four IADL. In addition to processing speed, telephone use was associated with both conceptual abilities (WST) and orientation (subscore of the MMSE), and responsibility for medication was associated with memory (three-word recall subscore of the MMSE). Handling finances was related to processing speed, conceptual abilities, as well as orientation and memory. Mode of

Table 2.4 Final models of the stepwise logistic regressions on each dichotomized IADL item: odds ratios and 95% confidence intervals of being classified as "autonomous," with test scores expressed as Z scores (Barberger-Gateau et al., *Journal of Gerontology: Psychological Sciences*, 1999)

	Telephone	Transportation	Medication	Finances
Age		0.91 (0.88–0.93)***	(0.95–1.04)	0.99
Female sex		0.35 (0.24–0.51)***		
Education (at least CEP)	1.56 (0.62–3.97)	0.59 (0.39–0.88)**		0.90 (0.53–1.51)
Visual impairment		0.55 (0.35–0.86)**		0.54 (0.29–1.00)*
BVRT				
WPAT1				
WPATr				
DSST		1.58 (1.20–2.09)**		
IST				1.77 (1.30–2.42)***
ZCTtime	0.63 (0.48–0.83)***	0.66 (0.54–0.80)***	0.52 (0.40–0.68)***	0.74 (0.61–0.90)**
ZCTtot				
WST	2.04 (1.32–3.15)**			1.50 (1.20–1.89)***
MMSori	1.45 (1.18–1.79)***			1.27 (1.08–1.50)**
MMScal				
MMSrec			1.64 (1.04–2.59)*	1.34 (1.06–1.69)*

*$p < .05$; **$p < .01$; ***$p < .001$.

transportation was the most physical item, being significantly and independently influenced by age, sex, and visual impairment, but it was also correlated with two processing speed measures (selective attention for ZCTtime and visuospatial attention for DSST).

To reduce the number of variables, we used only the delayed recall for the WPAT test in the PCA (Table 2.5). The first three factors of the PCA explained 49.6% of variance and they all had eigenvalues greater than 1. The first factor explained 30.2% of variance. The neuropsychological test loadings on this first factor were the same as those previously identified in the PCA used in the Fabrigoule et al. (1998) study, although the previous PCA

Table 2.5 The first three factors of the principal component analysis: PAQUID study, 1-year follow-up, nondemented subjects (N = 1424) (Barberger-Gateau et al., *Journal of Gerontology: Psychological Sciences*, 1999)

	Factor 1	Factor 2	Factor 3
Eigenvalue	4.23	1.59	1.13
BVRT	0.68	−0.22	−0.05
WPATr	0.60	−0.17	0.39
DSST	0.80	−0.24	−0.20
IST	0.73	−0.23	−0.09
ZCTspeed	0.73	−0.16	−0.32
ZCTtot	0.34	−0.04	−0.14
WST	0.58	−0.10	0.06
MMSori	0.36	0.24	0.47
MMScal	0.57	−0.15	0.07
MMSrec	0.41	−0.08	0.61
Telephone	0.33	0.59	0.11
Transportation	0.43	0.33	−0.43
Medication	0.30	0.70	−0.01
Finances	0.49	0.58	−0.05

did not include either the MMS orientation and recall subscore, or any of the IADL items. The four IADL items had moderate loading on this factor, ranging from 0.33 to 0.49. The second factor explained 11.3% of variance and showed high loading of three IADL items (responsibility for own medication, telephone use, and handling finances) ranging from 0.70 to 0.58 and, to a lesser extent, of the item "mode of transportation" (0.33). The third factor had high loading of the MMSE recall, the orientation score, the "mode of transportation item," and the WPATr score. When the first three factors were all entered simultaneously as explanatory variables into the Cox model with delayed entry, a high score on the first factor was significantly associated with a decreased risk of incident dementia ($p < .001$), whereas the association with the second and third factors was not significant.

Discussion

In this study, each IADL item had specific associations with neuropsychological tests. Conceptual abilities contribute to autonomy in using the telephone and handling finances, orientation contributes to autonomy in using the telephone and handling finances, and memory contributes to the responsibility for medication and handling finances. It is, however, worth noting that speed of processing was the only cognitive component strongly associated with autonomy for each of the four IADL. If slower speed of processing is a consequence of decline in attention and inhibition, which are two of the main components of executive control, then this strongly suggests that decline in executive control is one of the main determinants of decline in functional activities. This is confirmed by the PCA results, which show that the first factor represents the cognitive component of the four IADL and is the only one associated with prediction of dementia. The predictive value of the IADL is, therefore, explained by their cognitive components. Given the previous interpretation of the neuropsychological test loading on Factor 1, this suggests that a slight deterioration of IADL corresponds to the deterioration of the executive control processes at the predemented phase of dementia. This is consistent with the fact that instrumental tasks such as using the telephone or handling finances require a high degree of planning and executive abilities.

Other studies have shown the impact of MCI on functioning. In the Kungsholmen Project mild, nondementing, cognitive impairment was associated with poorer health, especially with a higher rate of disability (Frisoni, Fratiglioni, Fastbom, Guo, Viitanen, & Winblad, 2000). In the Italian Longitudinal Study on Aging, the presence of cognitive impairment without dementia or age-related cognitive decline was linked to a significantly high impact on activity restriction (Di Carlo et al., 2000). However, should disability be considered as a direct consequence of MCI or as an overall marker of frailty in MCI patients? In another population sample of elderly French people without dementia, all participants with an attentional, memory, or visuospatial deficit demonstrated significantly lower functional capacity than those without cognitive impairment, independently of physical handicaps (Artero, Touchon, & Ritchie, 2001). Royall, Palmer, Chiodo, and Polk (2004) showed that declining executive control functions predicted changes in IADL. Tuokko, Morris, and Ebert (2005) showed, in the Canadian Study of Health and Aging, that neuropsychological measures of memory and psychomotor speed were significantly related to impairments in eight areas of functioning. In addition, memory measure was strongly associated with future impairment in money management. This confirms the correlation we found between handling finances and memory. Executive control, however, seems to work together with memory to mediate functional association with cognitive decline, as shown by our results. This is confirmed by Royall, Palmer, Chiodo, and Polk (2005), who also demonstrate that changes in executive control functions mediate memory association with functional decline. These authors suggest that amnesic MCI cases may have little risk of conversion to dementia unless they develop executive impairment.

Changes in complex, cognitively loaded, everyday life activities should then, as Nygard (2003) underlined, be included rather than excluded in the diagnosis of MCI. In the Cardiovascular Health Study, Lopez et al. (2003) did not exclude individuals with mild defects on IADL from a diagnosis of MCI. The International Working Group on MCI (Winblad et al., 2004), which met in Stockholm in 2003, proposed to include the following within the diagnosis criteria "Preserved basic ADL with some minimal impairment in complex instrumental functions."

There is, however, a need to define high-level function measures, including advanced functions not captured in IADL such as taking part in professional, recreational, or household activities that may suffer from slow reaction times, planning difficulties, or poor judgment. Any degree of cognitive decline, as assessed by neuropsychological tests, could have a measurable impact on functioning in daily life, provided we have sensitive enough instruments and reliable informants to document activity restriction. Changes in complex everyday life activities should, therefore, definitely be taken into account when diagnosing MCI.

General conclusion

In our population-based longitudinal study, MCI was certainly associated with a risk of both dementia and AD. Although this construct was more specific of AD than OCIND, it also demonstrated both instability (about 40% of those with MCI reverted to normal) as well as a lack of sensitivity (few people having incident AD within the next 5 years were characterized as MCI at entry).

Results of the PAQUID study also confirmed that various neuropsychological performances were affected in the transition to dementia and AD, which agrees with other longitudinal results. Our results strongly suggest that the most controlled and executive aspects are affected on the way to AD, whatever the primary function of the task: language, attention, and memory. Our results and those of others in the literature imply that executive deficits should be incorporated in any definition of MCI. If we assume that executive processes are at the heart of compensatory abilities, then demonstration of executive deficits alongside those of memory may signal the failure of compensatory abilities.

This may, in turn, explain why a slight decline in IADL should be considered as an essential constituent of MCI. In our study, the four IADL were consistently associated with the speed of information treatment, generally considered to be a good indicator of the ability to recruit executive resources. Moreover, the predictive value of IADL for conversion to dementia was explained by their executive control component, which agrees with the results of Royall et al. (2005), suggesting that amnesic MCI can convert to dementia only through comorbid changes in executive control function.

There is still ample room for improving MCI definition, if we are to obtain better predictive value for conversion to AD and other types of dementia. Different types of MCI, each corresponding to a prodromal phase of the differential types of dementia, have to be defined. On the basis of results presented in the PAQUID study and other studies, it seems essential to include executive decline as well as subtle IADL decline in defining MCI, whatever its type.

Further work is necessary to improve our knowledge of the preclinical phase leading to AD and other dementia. A variety of different approaches need to be used. In addition to clinical and epidemiological studies aimed at finding out the clinical characterization best associated with the risk of conversion to AD or to any other type of dementia, it is crucial to improve our knowledge of which cognitive components are affected, and why. Cognitive deficits are at the heart of MCI definition. Two major questions, at least, need to be addressed. The first question concerns what types of memory process are affected first. Our results would seem to suggest that memory tasks requiring a great deal of cognitive control during both encoding and retrieval are the first to be affected. The second question concerns the repeated demonstration of an early decline of executive control. From a neuropsychological point of view, these phenomena remain hard to understand if we can only appeal to what we currently know about the progression of AD lesions. A full understanding of the real nature of and reasons for the full pattern of cognitive decline in the predemented phase will require both longitudinal studies using precise, theoretically grounded cognitive tools and the use of cutting-edge imaging studies. These imaging studies, in particular, are needed if we are to acquire better knowledge of the temporospatial course of the different types of AD specific lesions at the predemented stage, and if we are to learn more about brain compensatory responses.

Acknowledgments

The PAQUID project was funded by Association pour la Recherche Médicale en Aquitaine (ARMA); Caisse Nationale d'Assurance Maladie des Travailleurs Salariés (CNAMTS); Conseil Général de la Dordogne; Conseil Général de la Gironde; Conseil Régional d'Aquitaine; France Alzheimer; Institut National de la Santé et de la Recherche Médicale (INSERM); Mutuelle Générale de l'Education Nationale (MGEN); Mutualité Sociale Agricole (MSA); NOVARTIS Pharma; SCOR Insurance Co.

References

Amieva, H., Rouch-Leroyer, I., Fabrigoule, C., & Dartigues, J. F. (2000). Deterioration of controlled processes in the preclinical phase of dementia: A confirmatory analysis. *Dementia and Geriatric Cognitive Disorders, 11*(1), 46–52.

Amieva, H., Rouch-Leroyer, I., Letenneur, L., Dartigues, J. F., & Fabrigoule, C. (2004). Cognitive slowing and learning of target detection skills in pre-demented subjects. *Brain and Cognition, 54,* 212–214.

American Psychiatric Association. (1987). *Diagnostic and Statistical Manual of mental disorders (DSM-III-R)* (Edition III Rev. ed.). Washington, DC: American Psychiatric Association.

Artero, S., Touchon, J., & Ritchie, K. (2001). Disability and mild cognitive impairment: A longitudinal population-based study. *International Journal of Geriatric Psychiatry, 16,* 1092–1097.

Bäckman, L., Jones, S., Berger, A. K., Laukka, E. J., & Small, B. J. (2004). Multiple cognitive deficits during the transition to Alzheimer's disease. *Journal of Internal Medecine, 256*, 195–204.
Baddeley, A. D. (1987). *Working memory.* Oxford: Oxford University Press.
Barberger-Gateau, P., Commenges, D., Gagnon, M., Letenneur, L., & Sauvel, C. (1992). Instrumental activities of daily living as a screening tool for cogntive impairment and dementia in elderly community dwellers. *Journal of American Geriatrics Society, 40*, 1129–1134.
Barberger-Gateau, P., Dartigues, J. F., & Letenneur, L. (1993). Four instrumental activities of daily living score as predictor of one year incident dementia. *Age and Ageing, 22*, 457–463.
Barberger-Gateau, P., Fabrigoule, C., Helmer, C., Rouch, I., & Dartigues, J. F. (1999a). Functional impairment in instrumental activities of daily living: An early clinical sign of dementia? *Journal of American Geriatrics Society, 47*, 456–462.
Barberger-Gateau, P., Fabrigoule, C., Rouch, I., Letenneur, L., & Dartigues, J. F. (1999b). Neuropsychological correlates of self-reported performance in instrumental activities of daily living and prediction of dementia. *Journal of Gerontology, B: Psychological Sciences, Social Sciences, 54B*, 293–303.
Benton, A. (1965). *Manuel pour l'application du test de rétention visuelle. Applications cliniques et expérimentales.* Paris: Centre de psychologie appliquée.
Bruscoli, M., & Lovestone, S. (2004). Is MCI really just early dementia? A systematic review of conversion studies. *International Psychogeriatrics, 16*(2), 129–140.
Dartigues, J. F., Commenges, D., Letenneur, L., Barberger-Gateau, P., Gilleron, V., Fabrigoule, C., et al. (1997). Cognitive predictors of dementia in elderly community residents. *Neuroepidemiology, 16*, 29–39.
Dartigues, J. F., Gagnon, M., Barberger-Gateau, P., Letenneur, L., Commenges, D., Sauvel, C., et al. (1992). The PAQUID epidemiological program on brain ageing. *Neuroepidemiology, 11*(Suppl. 1), 14–18.
Di Carlo, A., Baldereschi, M., Amaducci, L., Maggi, S., Grigoletto, F., Scarlato, G., et al. (2000). Cognitive impairment without dementia in older people: Prevalence, vascular risk factors, impact on disability. The Italian Longitudinal Study on Aging. *Journal of American Geriatrics Society, 48*, 775–782.
Duncan, J., & Owen, A. M. (2000). Common regions of the human frontal lobe recruited by diverse cognitive demands. *Trends in Neurosciences, 23*(10), 475–483.
Fabrigoule, C., Lafont, S., Letenneur, & Dartigues, J. F. (1996). WAIS similarities subtest performances as predictor of dementia in elderly community residents. *Brain and Cognition, 30*(3), 323–326.
Fabrigoule, C., Rouch, I., Taberly, A., Letenneur, L., Commenges, D., Mazaux, J. M., et al. (1998). Cognitive process in preclinical phase of dementia. *Brain, 121*, 135–141.
Flicker, C., Ferris, S. H., & Reisberg, B. (1991). Mild cognitive impairment in the elderly: Predictors of dementia. *Neurology, 41*, 1006–1009.
Folstein, M. F., Folstein, S. E., & McHugh, P. R. (1975). Mini-mental state. A practical method for grading the cognitive state of patients for the clinicians. *Journal of Psychiatric Research, 12*, 189–198.
Frisoni, G. B., Fratiglioni, L., Fastbom, J., Guo, Z., Viitanen, M., & Winblad, B. (2000). Mild cognitive impairment in the population and physical health: Data on 1,435 individuals aged 75 to 95. *Journal of Gerontology, A: Biological Sciences, Medical Sciences, 55A*, M322–M328.

Gauthier, S., Gelinas, I., & Gauthier, L. (1997). Functional disability in Alzheimer's disease. *International Psychogeriatry, 9*, 163–165.

Geerlings, M. I., Schmand, B., Jonker, C., Lindeboom, J., & Bouter, L. M. (1999). Education and incident Alzheimer's disease: A biased association due to selective attrition and use of a two-step diagnostic procedure? *International Journal of Epidemiology, 28*, 492–497.

Grady, C. L. (2000). Functional brain imaging and age-related changes in cognition. *Biological Psychology, 54*, 259–281.

Grady, C. L., McIntosh, A. R., Beig, S., Keightley, M. L., Burian, H., & Black, S. E. (2003). Evidence from functional neuroimaging of a compensatory prefrontal network in Alzheimer's disease. *Journal of Neuroscience, 23*(3), 986–993.

Hachinski, V. C., Iliff, L. D., Zilhka, F., Du Boulay, G. H., McAllister, V. L., Marshall, et al. (1975). Cerebral blood flow in dementia. *Archives of Neurology, 32*, 632–637.

Hasher, L., & Zacks, R. T. (1979). Automatic and effortful processes in memory. *Journal of Experimental Psychology, General, 108*, 356–388.

Isaacs, B., & Akhtar, A. (1972). The set test: A rapid test of mental function in old people. *Age and Aging, 1*, 222–226.

Jacobs, D. M., Sano, M., Dooneief, G., Marder, K., Bell, K. L., & Stern, Y. (1995). Neuropsychological detection and characterization of preclinical Alzheimer's disease. *Neurology, 45*, 957–962.

Jacoby, L. L. (1991). A process dissociation framework: Separating automatic from intentional uses of memory. *Journal of Memory and Language, 30*, 513–541.

Jorm, A. F. (1986). Controlled and automatic information processing in senile dementia: A review. *Psychological Medicine, 16*, 77–88.

Katz, S., Downs, T. D., Cash, H. R., & Grotz, R. C. (1970). Progress in development of the index of ADL. *Gerontologist, 10*, 20–30.

Larrieu, S., Letenneur, L., Orgogozo, J. M., Fabrigoule, C., Amieva, H., Le Carret, N., et al. (2002). Incidence and outcome of mild cognitive impairment in a population-based prospective cohort. *Neurology, 59*, 1594–1599.

Lawton, M. P., & Brody, E. M. (1969). Assessment of older people: Self-maintaining and instrumental activities of daily living. *Gerontologist, 9*, 179–186.

Letenneur, L., Commenges, D., Dartigues, J. F., & Barberger-Gateau, P. (1994). Incidence of dementia and Alzheimer's disease in elderly community residents of south-western France. *International Journal of Epidemiology, 23*, 1256–1261.

Letenneur, L., Gilleron, V., Commenges, D., Helmer, C., Orgogozo, J. M., & Dartigues, J. F. (1999). Are sex and educational level independent predictors of dementia and Alzheimer's disease? Incidence data from the PAQUID project. *Journal of Neurology, Neurosurgery and Psychiatry, 66*, 177–183.

Linn, R. T., Wolf, P. A., Bachman, D. L., Knoefel, J. E., Cobb, J. L., Belanger, A. J., et al. (1995). The 'preclinical phase' of probable Alzheimer's disease. *Archives of Neurology, 52*(5), 485–490.

Lopez, O. L., Jagust, W. J., DeKosky, S. T., Becker, J. T., Fitzpatrick, A., Dulberg, C., et al. (2003). Prevalence and classification of mild cognitive impairment in the Cardiovascular Health Study Cognition Study: Part 1. *Archives of Neurology, 60*, 1385–1389.

Masur, D., Sliwinski, M., Lipton, R. B., Blau, A., & Crystal, H. (1994). Neuropsychological prediction of dementia and the absence of dementia in healthy elderly persons. *Neurology, 44*, 1427–1432.

McKhann, G., Drachman, D., Folstein, M., Katzman, R., Price, D., & Stadlan, E. M. (1984). Clinical diagnosis of Alzheimer's disease: Report of the NINCDS-ADRDA Work Group under the auspices of Department of Health and Human Services Task Force on Alzheimer's Disease. *Neurology, 34*, 939–944.

Moscovitch, M. (1992). A neuropsychological model of memory and consciousness. In L. R. Squire & N. Butters (Eds.), *Neuropsychology of memory* (2nd ed.). New York: The Guildford Press.

Nygard, L. (2003). Instrumental activities of daily living: A stepping-stone towards Alzheimer's disease diagnosis in participants with mild cognitive impairment? *Acta Neurologica Scandinavian, Suppl., 179*, 42–46.

Petersen, R. C., Smith, G. E., Waring, S. C., Ivnik, R. J., Kokmen, E., & Tangalos, E. G. (1997). Aging, memory, and mild cognitive impairment. *International Psychogeriatry, 9*, 65–69.

Petersen, R. C., Smith, G. E., Waring, S. C., Ivnik, R. J., Tangalos, E. G., & Kokmen, E. (1999). Mild cognitive impairment—Clinical characterization and outcome. *Archives of Neurology, 56*, 303–308.

Ritchie, K., Artero, S., & Touchon, J. (2001). Classification criteria for mild cognitive impairment: A population-based validation study. *Neurology, 9*, 37–42.

Royall, D. R., Palmer, R., Chiodo, L. K., & Polk, M. J. (2004). Declining executive control in normal aging predicts change in functional status: The freedom house study. *Journal of American Geriatrics Society, 52*, 346–352.

Royall, D. R., Palmer, R., Chiodo, L. K., & Polk, M. J. (2005). Executive control mediates memory's association with change in instrumental activities of daily living: The Freedom house study. *Journal of the American Geriatrics Society, 53*, 11–17.

Schneider, W., & Shiffrin, R. M. (1977). Controlled and automatic information processing: I. Detection, search and attention. *Psychological Review, 84*(1), 1–66.

Tuokko, H., Morris, C., & Hebert, P. (2005). Mild cognitive impairment and everyday functioning in older adults. *Neurocase, 11*, 40–47.

Wechsler, D. (1945). A standardized memory scale for clinical use. *Journal of Psychology, 19*, 87–95.

Wechsler, D. (1981). *Wechsler Adult Intelligence Scale manual*. New York: The Psychological Corporation.

Winblad, B., Palmer, K., Kivipelto, M., Jelic, V., Fratiglioni, L., Wahlund, L. O., et al. (2004). Mild cognitive impairment—beyond controversies, towards a consensus: Report of the International Working Group on Mild Cognitive Impairment. *Journal of International Medicine, 256*(3), 240–246.

Zazzo, R. (1974). *Test des deux barrages*. Actualités pédagogiques et psychologiques. Neuchatel.

3 Cognitive impairment in elderly persons without dementia: Findings from the Kungsholmen Project

Katie Palmer, Lars Bäckman, Brent J. Small, and Laura Fratiglioni

The Kungsholmen Project (KP) is a longitudinal, population-based study on aging and dementia based in Stockholm, Sweden. Beginning in 1987, the health and cognitive status of persons aged 75 and older were evaluated over four follow-ups of data collection. Within the framework of the KP, a number of studies have been conducted to investigate different facets of aging, including cognitive and physical functioning, well-being, care and public health, drug use, and health economics, as well as mortality and comorbidity. One of the main emphases of the project has been on dementia disorders such as Alzheimer's disease (AD) and vascular dementia (VaD), from natural history to primary prevention. For example, studies from the KP have shown that low education (Qiu, Bäckman, Winblad, Aguero-Torres, & Fratiglioni, 2001), high systolic blood pressure (Qiu, von Strauss, Fastbom, Winblad, & Fratiglioni, 2003), low diastolic blood pressure, high pulse pressure (Qiu, Winblad, Viitanen, & Fratiglioni, 2003), and poor social network (Fratiglioni, Wang, Ericsson, Maytan, & Winblad, 2000) are associated with an increased risk of AD and dementia, whereas antihypertensive medication (Qiu, Winblad, Fastbom, & Fratiglioni, 2003) and intellectual and social stimulation (Wang, Karp, Winblad, & Fratiglioni, 2002) protect against the development of these diseases. Discovering risk factors for dementia disorders has important implications for primary prevention, but the issue of early identification of disease has also become increasingly relevant in recent years, due to the prospect of secondary prevention. This topic has been addressed using the 13-year long database of the KP. Two distinct approaches have been implemented: (1) retrospective assessment of the preclinical symptoms and signs of subjects who developed AD or dementia 3–6 years later, and (2) a prospective examination of the progression to dementia among subjects with cognitive deficits, including mild cognitive impairment (MCI).

This chapter is organized in three main sections. First, we provide an overview of the KP study design and participants, and describe relevant aspects of the data collection including details of the cognitive test battery and procedure for dementia diagnosis. Second, we describe the methods used to operationalize different definitions of cognitive impairment and MCI, and summarize major findings from the KP with regard to cognitive functioning in preclinical dementia, the prevalence and evolution of syndromes of cognitive impairment in nondemented elderly persons, and risk factors for cognitive impairment. Finally, we discuss the significance and implications of the major findings from our longitudinal population-based study.

The Kungsholmen Project

The KP was initiated on 1 October 1987, and included all inhabitants aged 75 and above living in the Kungsholmen area of Stockholm, Sweden at that time ($n = 1810$). One baseline and four follow-up examinations were conducted on average every 3 years (Figure 3.1), to identify prevalent and incident cases of dementia and assess cognitive and health status. At baseline, a two-phase procedure was used to detect prevalent dementia cases (Fratiglioni et al., 1991; Fratiglioni, Grut, Forsell, Viitanen, & Winblad, 1992). First, all 1810 participants underwent a structured interview with nurses, and global cognitive functioning was assessed with Folstein's Mini-Mental State Examination (MMSE) (Folstein, Folstein, & McHugh, 1975) with a subsequent clinical phase conducted on a sample of 668 persons. The baseline examination was the only measurement occasion when a two-phase study design was adopted, with an extensive clinical examination performed after a screening phase. At every other occasion, all participants underwent the full clinical examination including an interview by nurses, a thorough examination by physicians, extensive neuropsychological testing with a large cognitive battery administered by psychologists, and a next-of-kin interview concerning the subjects' cognitive and functional status. Details of the project have been extensively reported elsewhere (Fratiglioni et al., 1991, 1992), but a brief outline of the data collection and details specifically related to the topics discussed in this chapter is described below.

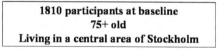

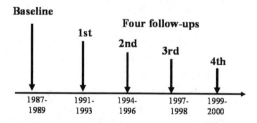

Figure 3.1 The Kungsholmen Project: 13-year population-based longitudinal study in Kungsholmen, Sweden.

Nurse examination

The nurse interview involved measurements of blood pressure, height, and weight, collection of blood samples, and assessment of cognitive status with the MMSE as well as assessment of physical functioning. Nurses also collected information regarding drug use within the preceding 3 months, including prescription drugs and over-the-counter medications. Genomic DNA was extracted from peripheral blood samples and apolipoprotein E genotyping was done using a standard polymerase chain reaction. Blood samples were also used to assess, for example, hemoglobin, vitamin levels such as folate and B12, white blood cell count, etc.

Clinical examination

The clinical examination involved a comprehensive assessment, including personal and family medical history, and physical, neurological, and psychiatric examinations. The examining physicians made diagnoses of current diseases according to standardized criteria, which were then reviewed by two senior clinicians. Furthermore, data on medical history were derived from the computerized Stockholm Inpatient Registry System, which encompasses all discharge diagnoses from hospital admissions in the Stockholm area since 1969.

Next-of-kin interview

A family interview with a next-of-kin or a close person was carried out. The interview concerned past and current health status and cognitive functioning of the subject, as well as selective risk factors of the most common chronic neurodegenerative diseases. Information was gathered on specific topics, such as detailed occupational-life history, caregiver burden, and use of home help and home services.

Cognitive assessment

At baseline, global cognitive functioning was assessed in all participants using the MMSE, and a sample of individuals underwent neuropsychological assessment (668 persons who underwent baseline clinical assessment as described above). The battery was administered by trained psychologists and included an extensive range of tasks covering an array of cognitive domains. Full details of the test battery are given elsewhere (Bäckman & Forsell, 1994) and only the tasks used to assess the three cognitive domains of particular interest to the current chapter are described here.

Four-word recall tasks were used to assess episodic memory: free recall of rapidly presented random words, free recall of slowly presented random words, free recall of organizable words, and cued recall of organizable words. In the two free recall of random words tasks, 12 concrete, semantically unrelated nouns were presented consecutively. The rapid list was presented at a rate of

2 s per word and the slow list was presented at a rate of 5 s per word. Subjects were asked to orally recall as many words as possible over a period of 2 min. For free and cued recall of organizable words, subjects were presented with a list containing 12 nouns belonging to four taxonomic categories. First, the subjects were asked to freely recall as many words from the list as possible and then the category names were presented and they were asked to recall the words again with the category names as cues. This cognitive domain was also assessed with face recognition tasks. Persons were shown 40 photographs of familiar and unfamiliar faces (20 per category). The photos were then shown in a recognition test mixed with 40 new faces, and persons were asked to state whether they had previously seen each of the 80 faces.

Verbal ability was assessed with letter and category fluency tasks. Subjects were asked to produce words belonging to the category of grocery items, and then to produce words beginning with the letters "S" or "L". Scores were based on the number of words produced within a 60-s period for each task.

Three tests were used to assess visuospatial functioning: block design, clock setting, and clock reading. For block design, which was taken from Wechsler's WAIS-R Block Design test, subjects were presented with seven designs, involving four blocks, and given 60 s to replicate each pattern using blocks. Scores were based on the number of correctly replicated designs. For clock setting, subjects were asked to indicate a specific time by drawing the hands on five numberless clocks. Scoring was based on the number of correctly drawn clocks. For clock reading, subjects were shown five predrawn clocks, where the hands depicted a specific time but no numbers were shown. Subjects were asked to tell the time of each clock. Scoring was based on the number of correctly drawn clocks.

Diagnosis of dementia and Alzheimer's disease

Dementia diagnoses at baseline and all follow-up examinations were made according to DSM-III-R criteria (American Psychiatric Association, 1987). The diagnosis of AD was similar to the NINDSC-ADRDA (McKhann, Drachman, Folstein, Katzman, Price, & Stadlan, 1984) criteria. A double diagnostic procedure was adopted where a preliminary diagnosis was made by the examining physician, and independently reviewed by a specialist. In the case of agreement, the diagnosis was accepted; otherwise, a second specialist examined the case to reach the final diagnosis. Dementia diagnoses for deceased subjects were made by consulting hospital medical records and death certificates using the same procedure.

Major findings from the Kungsholmen Project

Within the framework of the KP, we have investigated preclinical AD and MCI from two perspectives (Figure 3.2). In order to establish the patterns of cognitive functioning in the preclinical stages of the disease process, we first

3. Cognitive impairment in patients without dementia

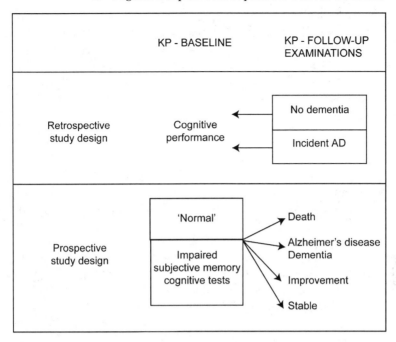

Figure 3.2 Retrospective and prospective study designs used in the Kungsholmen Project (KP) for identifying early symptoms and cognitive deficits in preclinical dementia.

retrospectively examined cognitive performance levels of subjects who developed dementia 3–6 years later, and compared their preclinical cognitive performance to that of persons who remained free of dementia during the same time period. Second, we were able to investigate identifiable conditions, such as MCI, that might progress to dementia with a prospective study design using various symptoms, signs, and different classifications for syndromes of cognitive impairment.

Cognitive functioning in preclinical AD and VaD

In the KP, our retrospective research on cognitive deficits during the preclinical phase of AD has focused on two principal issues: the pattern of cognitive deficits and the longitudinal time course of these impairments. With regard to the first point, we examined baseline performance on a variety of cognitive tests among persons who would or would not go on to be diagnosed with AD 3 years later. Baseline differences, in favor of the group who would remain free of dementia, were observed on tests of episodic memory, visuospatial skill, letter fluency, and category fluency (Small, Herlitz, Fratiglioni, Almkvist, & Bäckman, 1997). However, when the measures were examined simultaneously using logistic regression procedures, tests assessing episodic memory were found to be the strongest predictors of impending AD. A similar pattern of results was seen when the MMSE served as a measure of cognitive performance. In this case, preclinical cognitive deficits were seen for the total score 3 years prior to dementia diagnosis. However, when the individual item scores from the MMSE were examined, only those with a memory referent exhibited statistically significant differences between persons who would or would not go on to be diagnosed with AD. Specifically, preclinical differences were seen for the delayed recall item, as well as the orientation to time items. Taken together, these results suggest that memory deficits may be a cardinal feature of preclinical AD.

The second issue that our work has addressed deals with the longitudinal course of preclinical cognitive deficits in AD. In many cases, cognitive performance is measured only once before the diagnosis of AD is made and, as a result, only group differences can be compared. In our work, as well as that of other researchers (Chen, Ratcliff, Belle, Cauley, DeKosky, & Ganguli, 2001; Goldman & Morris, 2001), we have examined multiple measurement points prior to the diagnosis of AD in order to describe the trajectory of changes among persons who will or will not be diagnosed with AD. In two studies, we examined changes in episodic memory (Bäckman, Small, & Fratiglioni, 2001) and MMSE performance (Small, Fratiglioni, Viitanen, Winblad, & Bäckman, 2000) among persons who were measured at three time points across a 7-year interval. All individuals were free of a dementia diagnosis at the first two measurement points, whereas some would go on to be diagnosed with AD at the final follow-up point. The results of both studies were similar in that cognitive deficits were observed at the initial measurement point, 7 years before a dementia diagnosis would be rendered. Note that the deficits observed on the MMSE (Small et al., 2000) were most pronounced on the delayed recall (i.e., episodic memory) item. However, the magnitude of these deficits remained relatively stable at the second time of testing, 3 years later. Specifically, the incident AD cases did not exhibit selective decline from 6 to 3 years before diagnosis when compared to the nondemented subjects. However, during the last 3 years preceding the diagnosis, precipitous decline in performance was observed. The data from both of these studies suggest that the cognitive deficits in preclinical AD are characterized by an early onset followed by relative stability, at least until a few years before a diagnosis may be rendered (Bäckman et al., 2001; Small et al., 2000). To illustrate this pattern, the data for the delayed recall item in the MMSE (Small et al., 2000) are portrayed in Figure 3.3.

The demonstration of a preclinical phase with cognitive deficits has been extended to VaD in recent KP research. Indeed, the facts that (1) circulatory disturbances may cause gradual brain changes before the event of an actual stroke and (2) different forms of vascular alterations (e.g., high blood pressure, atherosclerotic disease, and cardiovascular signs) influence cognitive functioning in nondemented persons (Backman, Wahlin, Small, Herlitz, Winblad, & Fratiglioni, 2004) suggest that a preclinical phase is probable in VaD as well.

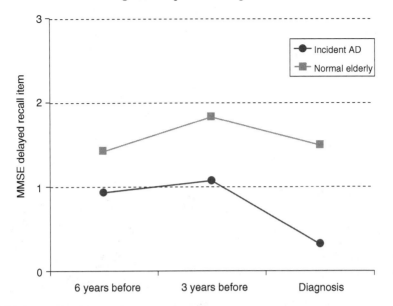

Figure 3.3 Decline in episodic memory performance 3 and 6 years before AD diagnosis, compared in persons who do not go on to develop dementia.

Initial evidence suggests striking similarities between VaD and AD with regard to the patterns of cognitive deficits for episodic memory and MMSE both 3 (Jones, Jonsson Laukka, Small, Fratiglioni, & Bäckman, 2004; Laukka, Jones, Small, Fratiglioni, & Bäckman, 2004) and 6 years (Laukka, Jones, Fratiglioni, & Bäckman, 2004) prior to dementia diagnosis. However, it is important to note that the VaD diagnosis in the KP focuses on multiinfarcts and strategic infarcts. Thus, it remains unknown whether the preclinical cognitive deficits observed in VaD and the apparent similarity to AD in this regard generalizes to other VaD etiologies (e.g., small-vessel disease).

Syndromes of cognitive impairment and the preclinical phase of AD

Considering that cognitive deficits are apparent in persons who go on to develop AD, we sought to prospectively identify a group of persons with a high risk of developing a dementia disorder. As numerous definitions and criteria for cognitive syndromes have been proposed in the literature, different signs of cognitive deficits and symptoms of cognitive decline have been investigated and compared in the KP, including cognitive impairment–no dementia (CIND), MCI, and individual subjective (i.e., memory complaints) and objective (i.e., cognitive test performance) indicators. We have investigated both the prevalence and evolution of these syndromes. In accordance with our findings that a precipitous decline in cognitive performance is seen primarily during the last 3 years before AD diagnosis (Backman et al., 2001;

Small et al., 2000), we have mainly focused on the 3-year evolution of these syndromes of cognitive impairment.

Definition of cognitive impairment–no dementia (CIND)

As we found that deficits in global cognitive functioning were evident in persons who went on to develop AD, we investigated the predictivity of a syndrome defined according to a widely used test of global cognitive functioning, the MMSE. Persons scoring 1 standard deviation (SD) below the mean MMSE performance compared to persons with the same age and educational level were considered as having CIND (Palmer, Wang, Bäckman, Winblad, & Fratiglioni, 2002). Although the terminology is similar, it is noteworthy that there are some disparities among research groups on definitions of the term "CIND". For example, in the Canadian Study of Health and Aging (Hogan & Ebly, 2000; Tuokko et al., 2003), a consensus diagnosis based on clinical evidence of cognitive impairment was implemented, as opposed to a specific cutoff on an objective test. In an Italian study, CIND was defined as having cognitive performance at a slightly higher cutoff of $2SD$ lower than the norm (De Ronchi et al., 2004). Despite these discrepancies, most definitions of CIND are conceptually common in that they refer to general deficits that are not limited to a specific cognitive domain.

Evolution of cognitive impairment–no dementia (CIND)

Among the 1435 nondemented elderly persons at the baseline phase of the KP, approximately 15% were classified with CIND, and the remaining 85% performed within normal ranges for their age and educational level. Individuals were followed for 3 and 6 years in relation to four outcomes: death, progression to dementia, cognitive improvement, and stability of CIND status.

Over 3 years of follow-up, the evolution of CIND was quite heterogeneous: one-third died, one-third developed dementia, and one-third either remained stable or improved in cognitive functioning (Figure 3.4). Persons with CIND were three times more likely to progress to dementia over 3 years than cognitively intact persons, with a relative risk (RR) of 3.6 (95% confidence interval [CI]: 2.6–4.8). After following subjects with CIND for a period of 6 years, we found that progression from CIND to dementia was time-dependent, occurring primarily within 3 years: 84% of those CIND subjects who progressed to dementia over 6 years already had the diagnosis at the 3-year follow-up examination.

In addition to an increased risk of dementia, subjects with CIND had an almost twofold mortality risk over 3 years compared to cognitively intact subjects (RR: 1.9, 95% CI: 1.4–2.5). However, one quarter (25%) of the CIND subjects actually improved in cognitive functioning over the 3-year follow-up, and returned to a level of cognitive performance considered normal

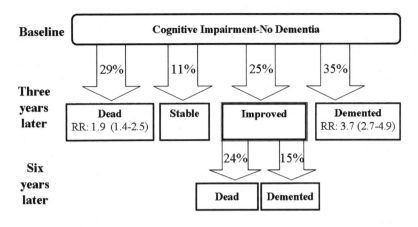

Figure 3.4 Evolution of cognitive impairment–no dementia over 3 and 6 years of follow-up.

for their age and educational level. Different cutoffs on the MMSE were administered to define CIND to ensure that this improvement was not due to the relatively mild definition of CIND implemented. However, improvement over 3 years occurred in one quarter of the cognitively impaired subjects, even if CIND was defined as performing 1.5 or even 2SD below age- and education-specific norms. These CIND subjects who improved were followed for a further 3 years to investigate whether they were still at higher risk of developing dementia. The results showed that these persons did not have a significantly increased risk of either dementia (RR: 1.4, 95% CI: 0.8–2.6) or death (RR: 1.4, 95% CI: 0.7–3.2) compared to persons who had never been classified as cognitively impaired.

Multistep procedure to identify persons at high risk for dementia

As we found that the evolution of CIND was heterogeneous, we sought to find a way to positively predict persons who would develop dementia by adding other potential predictors. In doing so, we evaluated the efficacy of a multistep procedure to identify persons who would progress to dementia 3 years later (Palmer, Bäckman, Winblad, & Fratiglioni, 2003). A combination of three factors was examined, including: (1) subjective memory complaints, (2) impairment on a test of global cognitive functioning (CIND), and (3) deficits on specific cognitive domains, including episodic memory and verbal fluency. These steps were chosen to reflect an analogy of clinical practice; an elderly individual with subjective memory problems first might report symptoms at the primary care level and undergo a brief test of global cognitive functioning by a general practitioner, and finally would be sent for a more thorough examination in a specialized clinical setting.

In order to test this three-step procedure, we used subjective and objective measurements from the baseline phase of the KP. Nurses asked subjects whether they felt that their memory had declined. Impairment in global cognitive functioning was defined as CIND, that is, performing 1*SD* below age- and education-specific norms on the MMSE. Domain-specific cognitive impairment was defined as scoring 1*SD* below age- and education-specific norms on a composite of tasks measuring episodic memory (word recall and recognition) and language (category fluency).

When all predictors were applied at the general population level without screening, the positive predictivity for dementia at the 3-year follow-up was low: less than 37% for each separate predictor. In fact, the positive predictive value for dementia was virtually identical for both CIND (35%) and episodic memory impairment (37%). Two screening procedures were implemented to increase the predictivity for dementia. The first screening was subjective memory complaints and the second was impairment on the test of global cognitive functioning (MMSE). When tests of episodic memory and verbal fluency were applied to persons with memory complaints and CIND, the positive predictive values for dementia ranged between 75 and 100%. Specifically, 95% of persons with subjective memory complaints, CIND, and verbal fluency impairment either progressed to dementia over 3 years or died during the follow-up period.

Despite the extremely high positive prediction of this three-step process, the procedure was limited by an extremely low sensitivity (Figure 3.5). Only 18% of future dementia cases had a combination of all three predictors (subjective memory complaint, CIND, and impairment on a domain-specific cognitive test) when they were assessed 3 years before their dementia diagnosis. The remaining 82% of those who developed dementia had only one or two symptoms or signs present, or were completely asymptomatic 3 years before dementia diagnosis. A major reason for this low sensitivity was the small number of subjectively reported memory complaints. Only 51% of the persons

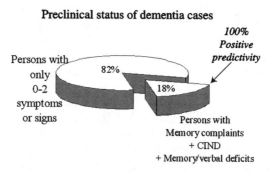

Figure 3.5 Proportion of clinically identifiable cognitive symptoms or signs 3 years before the diagnosis of dementia.

who developed dementia felt that they had problems with their memory when asked 3 years before diagnosis.

Definition of mild cognitive impairment (MCI) subtypes

The symptoms and signs examined in the study using the multistep procedure for identifying early dementia are similar to the criteria for the amnestic type of MCI, which requires both subjective and objective memory deficits. However, the MCI criteria (Petersen et al., 2001; Petersen, Smith, Waring, Ivnik, Tangalos, & Kokmen, 1999) specify that general cognitive functioning is relatively well preserved, so the additional contribution of CIND in our three-step prediction model warranted further investigation. In order to examine the influence of global cognitive deficits in conjunction with other items in the MCI criteria, we compared the prevalence and predictivity of MCI according to different definitions. Furthermore, following Petersen et al.'s proposed subclassifications of MCI into three subtypes (Petersen et al., 2001), we extended our investigation to both amnestic and nonamnestic types of MCI, to verify the prevalence of MCI subtypes at the general population level and compare predictivity for AD.

We retrospectively applied the criteria for MCI to subjects at the baseline phase of the KP, and followed them for 3 years (Palmer, 2004). Persons were classified as MCI-amnestic if they were free of dementia, largely normal in activities of daily living, reported subjective memory complaints, and had normal levels of general cognition, verbal fluency, and visuospatial functioning, but significant deficits in episodic memory. The classification of MCI-single-nonmemory was defined in the same way, with the exception that episodic memory functioning was normal but the subject exhibited deficits in one of either the visuospatial or language domain. To be classified as MCI-multidomains, the same definition was used, except that impairment had to be present in two or more of episodic memory, visuospatial, and language tasks.

As there is no established method for operationalizing the items in the MCI criteria, we decided to apply the criteria in the following ways:

No dementia: All subjects underwent a detailed clinical examination at baseline and were diagnosed as nondemented according to DSM-III-R criteria using a double diagnostic procedure.

Largely normal activities of daily living: All subjects underwent a complete neurological and medical examination by specialists who excluded the possibility that the presence of any functional impairment was due to memory or other cognitive deficits.

Subjective memory complaint: We considered the presence of memory complaints reported by the subject, a close informant, or both.

Objective cognitive impairment: We examined MCI with regard to deficits in three cognitive domains assessed with a range of tasks. Episodic memory included a composite score of four-word recall tasks: free recall of rapidly presented random words, free recall of slowly presented random words, free recall of organizable words, and cued recall of organizable words. For language, a test of verbal fluency was used where subjects were asked to produce as many grocery items as possible within a 60-s period. Visuospatial functioning was assessed using a composite score derived from tests of block design, clock setting, and clock reading. Impairment was defined as scoring 1*SD* below the age- and education-specific mean on the respective tasks.

Essentially normal general cognition: Our previous MMSE-based definition of CIND was used to indicate normal general cognition. One standard deviation below the age- and education-specific mean on the MMSE was taken as a cutoff to indicate impaired functioning (Palmer et al., 2002), and all persons scoring above that cutoff were considered to be normal.

The final item in the criteria, "essentially normal general cognition", was removed in some analyses in order to assess whether the inclusion of subjects with CIND within the MCI definition would affect the prevalence or predictivity of the three MCI subtypes.

Prevalence of MCI among nondemented persons

Among the 1435 nondemented persons in the KP, the prevalence of MCI per 100 dementia-free persons ranged from 1.8 to 7.2 depending on the specific cognitive deficits, as shown in Figure 3.6. More than a tenth (11.1%) of the nondemented elderly persons fulfilled the criteria for one of the MCI subtypes. The most common form was MCI-single-nonmemory, which was present in 7.2% of the subjects. MCI-amnestic and MCI-multidomains had a

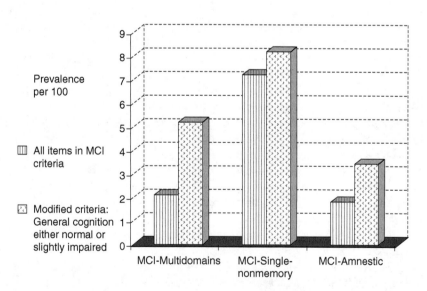

Figure 3.6 Prevalence of MCI subtypes per 100 nondemented persons according to two criteria.

similar prevalence rate of 2.1 and 1.8 per 100 persons, respectively. Further, a large number of persons were diagnosed as nondemented by the examining physician, but had significant deficits in specific cognitive tasks, yet did not fulfill all criteria for MCI due to the fact that their general cognition was not "normal". Removing this item from the criteria led to an increased prevalence of all MCI subtypes. Specifically, 3.4% were now classified with MCI-amnestic, 8.2% with MCI-single-nonmemory, and 5.2% with MCI-multidomains.

Evolution of MCI subtypes

After following the cohort for 3 years, we calculated the risk of progressing to a diagnosis of AD in persons with each type of MCI compared to persons who were cognitively intact. Persons with the form of MCI characterized by impairment in a single nonmemory domain such as language or visuospatial functioning did not have an increased risk for developing AD. By contrast, three quarters (75%) of persons with MCI-multidomains progressed to AD over 3 years (RR: 25.3, 95% CI: 7.2–88.2). Progression was also high for persons with MCI-amnestic; one-third (33.3%) developed AD, with a ninefold risk compared to cognitively intact subjects (RR: 9.5, 95% CI: 1.6–57.8). When we removed the requirement of "normal general cognition" from the definition, so that persons with deficits in domain-specific tasks as well as significant impairment on MMSE would be reclassified as MCI-amnestic, not only did the prevalence increase, but also the predictivity for AD was higher. More than half (53.3%) of the persons with specific deficits in episodic memory, with or without significant impairment on MMSE, developed AD over 3 years, with a 20-fold RR of AD (RR: 21.2, 95% CI: 5.2–85.4), similar to the figure found for MCI-multidomains.

Risk factors for cognitive impairment in nondemented subjects (CIND)

As there is increasing evidence that a substantial proportion of nondemented persons with cognitive impairment do not develop a dementia syndrome, we were interested in examining other etiological mechanisms that might be associated with cognitive deficits. In the KP, one third of persons with CIND either improved in cognitive functioning over 3 years, or remained stable, as described earlier (Figure 3.4). Thus, in another study, we sought to identify risk factors for incident CIND among elderly persons with initially normal levels of cognitive functioning. To achieve this objective, a nondemented and CIND-free cohort ($n = 718$) was examined over 3 years to detect incident CIND cases (Monastero, Palmer, Qiu, Winblad, & Fratiglioni, in press). We examined a range of baseline risk factors clustered according to possible pathophysiological mechanisms, including frailty, vascular, neurobehavioral, and social factors. At the 3-year follow-up, there were 82 incident cases of CIND, and 636 persons had normal cognition. We identified a number of significant risk factors for incident CIND, including frailty-related factors such as older age, history of hip fracture (OR 3.3, 95% CI: 1.3–8.6), and a high consumption of prescription drugs at baseline (OR 2.8, 95% CI: 1.1–7.1). Psychiatric factors such as history of psychoses (OR 5.3, 95% CI: 1.2–24.0) and depressive symptoms (OR 1.7, 95% CI: 1.0–3.0) were also associated with the development of CIND. These risk factors were significantly related to incident CIND, even after adjusting for future development of AD. Contrary to previous reports, no vascular factors were associated with the development of incident CIND at the 3-year follow-up.

Significance of findings

The findings from the KP contribute to the fields of MCI and early detection of dementia by providing insights into the topic at the general population level. Findings from clinical studies on MCI patients provide important information on the clinical characteristics of the syndrome, but these findings lack generalizability to the general population. In comparison to population-based samples, clinical samples are usually characterized by more severe cognitive deterioration, younger age, higher education, and familial aggregation of dementia. These characteristics lead to a higher progression rate to dementia. Our findings from a population perspective provide information on the relevance of the cognitive impairment in terms of occurrence of the syndrome and its different subtypes, and provide a description of the natural evolution, which can be applied to all levels of medical care, including primary care. Finally, the lack of selection of community-based samples facilitates an unbiased identification of possible markers of AD cases in the preclinical phase.

The major conclusions that can be drawn from our findings derived from the KP can be summarized in the following main points:

Cognitive impairment is a common condition among the nondemented elderly. The prevalence of all types of MCI is quite high, with more than a tenth of the dementia-free persons fulfilling the criteria for the three subtypes of MCI according to Petersen et al.'s criteria. The prevalence may even be higher if persons with global cognitive deficits are not excluded. We found that if persons with additional impairments on the global test of cognitive functioning were also included in the classification of MCI subtypes, the prevalence rose to 17% per 100 dementia-free elderly.

Persons with cognitive impairment have an elevated risk of dementia, but at least one third of CIND cases in the general population are reversible or easily treatable. Our findings showed that cognitive impairment defined according to deficits on an easy-to-use test of global cognitive functioning, the MMSE, is associated with an increased risk of progression to dementia over a 3-year period. These results correspond well with much of the literature on cognitive impairment defined according to general and global deficits, where progression to dementia varies between 26 and 47% over

1.5–5 years (Braekhus, Laake, & Engedal, 1995; Hogan & Ebly, 2000; Larrieu et al., 2002; Tuokko et al., 2003; Unverzagt et al., 2001). Although, as discussed later, other more specific cognitive tasks and syndromes of cognitive impairment have higher positive predictivity for identifying future cases of dementia, tools such as the MMSE have some advantages. They are quick, easy to administer, and widely available, and thus may serve as a good overall assessment for identifying persons at high risk for dementia on a wide scale.

Although there is an increased risk of developing dementia in persons with CIND, the evolution is heterogeneous. One third of CIND subjects either remain stable or improve in cognitive functioning over 3 years, with no increased risk for future dementia, suggesting that there are other causes of cognitive impairment, independent of AD and dementia. Our study investigating risk factors for incident CIND provides some clues to other etiological mechanisms that play a role in cognitive impairment such as multimorbidity, polypharmacy, and psychiatric illnesses. All these factors are common in old age (Bäckman & Forsell, 1994) and may also interact with each other, providing a much more complicated clinical and etiological picture. The identification of persons with other comorbidities who develop AD has been largely ignored in the past, due to the strict exclusion criteria often applied in order to eliminate the confounding effects of various somatic disorders on cognitive functioning. These questions will be the focus of future research within the KP.

The progression of MCI to AD varies depending on the MCI subtypes and on the use of original or modified criteria. When the criterion for normal general cognition was relaxed, about one half of MCI-amnestic progressed to AD, representing a 20-fold RR, similar to the risk seen for persons with MCI-multidomains. This result is in line with other studies (Bozoki, Giordani, Heidebrink, Berent, & Foster, 2001; Fisk, Merry, & Rockwood, 2003), which have shown that people with deficits in multiple cognitive domains are at a very high risk of progressing to AD. Conceivably, this reflects the fact that changes in multiple brain regions and alterations in numerous brain processes are commonly observed in the preclinical phase of AD (Fox, Warrington, & Rossor, 1999; Silverman et al., 2001; van der Flier et al., 2002; Wolf, Ecke, Bettin, Dietrich, & Gertz, 2000; Yamaguchi, Sugihara, Ogawa, Oshima, & Ihara, 2001). Consistent with this notion, findings from a recent meta-analysis from our group (Bäckman, Jones, Berger, Laukka, & Small, 2004, 2005) demonstrate that the cognitive deficits in preclinical AD are rather general in terms of the abilities that are affected. Specifically, based on the analysis of results from 47 studies, which comprised almost 10,000 control and over 1200 preclinical AD cases, we found that there were marked preclinical deficits in global cognitive ability (e.g., MMSE), episodic memory, perceptual speed, executive functioning, verbal ability, visuospatial skill, and attention. The only domain for which no preclinical deficits were observed was that of primary memory.

It is possible to identify with very high predictivity subjects who will develop dementia over 3 years by using clinical and psychological assessment, but only a fifth of all future cases are detected. The assessment consists of a three-step procedure which simulates clinical practice: reporting memory complaints at primary care level, assessment of global cognitive functioning by a general practitioner, and, finally, domain-specific cognitive testing in a specialized setting. Although up to 95% of persons with impairment at all three levels progressed to dementia over 3 years, the sensitivity was low as less than a fifth of the future dementia cases exhibited all three symptoms 3 years before diagnosis. This low sensitivity is mainly due to the low proportion of future dementia cases who report subjective memory problems 3 years before their dementia diagnosis. This finding has important clinical implications as any classification of MCI which includes an item requiring subjective reports of memory loss will include only that small proportion of preclinical AD cases. Some studies have suggested that removing subjective memory complaints or other items from the Petersen et al. MCI criteria increases the prevalence of MCI without diminishing predictivity for dementia (Busse, Bischkopf, Riedel-Heller, & Angermeyer, 2003; Fisk et al., 2003; Ganguli, Dodge, Shen, & DeKosky, 2004). However, currently no alternatives have been proposed for selecting elderly persons in need of cognitive assessment. Indeed, as our study showed, none of the three examined measures were sufficiently predictive for future dementia when applied to the whole cohort, suggesting that widespread screening of elderly populations for objective cognitive deficits may not be feasible at present.

Conclusions

Cognitive impairment in nondemented older adults is a common condition present in 10–15% of persons over 75 years. The progression to AD and other dementing disorders is high, but highly variable depending on the clinical definition of the cognitive impairment syndrome. At least one third of the cases are reversible, indicating that CIND is not only a transitional phase between normal aging and AD, but also a syndrome with multiple risk factors and outcomes. At the moment, the possibility to identify future AD cases at the population level by using clinical and psychological assessment is limited by the low sensitivity of the measurements, which provide only the possibility to identify with very high predictivity one fifth of the future AD cases 3 years before a diagnosis can be made.

Acknowledgment

Preparation of this chapter was supported by a grant from the Swedish Council for Working Life and Social Research (FAS) to Lars Bäckman and Laura Fratiglioni.

References

American Psychiatric Association. (1987). *Diagnostic and Statistical Manual of mental disorders: DSM-III-R* (3rd ed., Rev.). Washington, DC: American Psychiatric Association.

Bäckman, L., & Forsell, Y. (1994). Episodic memory functioning in a community-based sample of old adults with major depression: Utilization of cognitive support. *Journal of Abnormal Psycholology, 103*, 361–370.

Bäckman, L., Jones, S., Berger, A. K., Laukka, E. J., & Small, B. J. (2004). Multiple cognitive deficits during the transition to Alzheimer's disease. *Journal of Internal Medicine, 256*, 195–204.

Bäckman, L., Jones, S., Berger, A. K., Laukka, E. J., & Small, B. J. (2005). Cognitive impairment in preclinical Alzheimer's disease: A meta-analysis. *Neuropsychology, 19(4)*, 520–531

Bäckman, L., Small, B. J., & Fratiglioni, L. (2001). Stability of the preclinical episodic memory deficit in Alzheimer's disease. *Brain, 124*(Pt 1), 96–102.

Bäckman, L., Wahlin, A., Small, B. J., Herlitz, A., Winblad, B., & Fratiglioni, L. (2004). Cognitive functioning in aging and dementia: The Kungsholmen Project. *Aging, Neuropsychology, and Cognition, 11*, 212–244.

Bozoki, A., Giordani, B., Heidebrink, J. L., Berent, S., & Foster, N. L. (2001). Mild cognitive impairments predict dementia in nondemented elderly patients with memory loss. *Archives of Neurology, 58*, 411–416.

Braekhus, A., Laake, K., & Engedal, K. (1995). A low, 'normal' score on the Mini-Mental State Examination predicts development of dementia after three years. *Journal of the American Geriatric Society, 43*, 656–661.

Busse, A., Bischkopf, J., Riedel-Heller, S. G., & Angermeyer, M. C. (2003). Mild cognitive impairment: Prevalence and incidence according to different diagnostic criteria. Results of the Leipzig Longitudinal Study of the Aged (LEILA75+). *British Journal of Psychiatry, 182*, 449–454.

Chen, P., Ratcliff, G., Belle, S. H., Cauley, J. A., DeKosky, S. T., & Ganguli, M. (2001). Patterns of cognitive decline in presymptomatic Alzheimer disease: A prospective community study. *Archives of General Psychiatry, 58*, 853–858.

De Ronchi, D., Berardi, D., Menchetti, M., Ferrari, G., Serretti, A., Dalmonte, E., et al. (2004). Occurrence of cognitive impairment and dementia after the age of 60: A population-based study from northern Italy. *Dementia and Geriatric Cognitive Disorders, 19*, 97–105.

Fisk, J. D., Merry, H. R., & Rockwood, K. (2003). Variations in case definition affect prevalence but not outcomes of mild cognitive impairment. *Neurology, 61*, 1179–1184.

Folstein, M., Folstein, S., & McHugh, P. (1975). "Mini-mental state." A practical method for grading the cognitive state of patients for the clinician. *Journal of Psychiatric Research, 12*, 189–198.

Fox, N. C., Warrington, E. K., & Rossor, M. N. (1999). Serial magnetic resonance imaging of cerebral atrophy in preclinical Alzheimer's disease. *Lancet, 353(9170)*, 2125.

Fratiglioni, L., Grut, M., Forsell, Y., Viitanen, M., Grafstrom, M., Holmen, K., et al. (1991). Prevalence of Alzheimer's disease and other dementias in an elderly urban population: Relationship with age, sex, and education. *Neurology, 41*, 1886–1892.

Fratiglioni, L., Grut, M., Forsell, Y., Viitanen, M., & Winblad, B. (1992). Clinical diagnosis of Alzheimer's disease and other dementias in a population survey. Agreement and causes of disagreement in applying Diagnostic and Statistical Manual of mental disorders, Revised Third Edition, Criteria. *Archives of Neurology, 49*, 927–932.

Fratiglioni, L., Wang, H. X., Ericsson, K., Maytan, M., & Winblad, B. (2000). Influence of social network on occurrence of dementia: A community-based longitudinal study. *Lancet, 355(9212)*, 1315–1319.

Ganguli, M., Dodge, H. H., Shen, C., & DeKosky, S. T. (2004). Mild cognitive impairment, amnestic type: An epidemiologic study. *Neurology, 63*, 115–121.

Goldman, W. P., & Morris, J. C. (2001). Evidence that age-associated memory impairment is not a normal variant of aging. *Alzheimer Disease and Associated Disorders, 15*, 72–79.

Hogan, D. B., & Ebly, E. M. (2000). Predicting who will develop dementia in a cohort of Canadian seniors. *Canadian Journal of Neurological Sciences, 27*, 18–24.

Jones, S., Jonsson Laukka, E., Small, B. J., Fratiglioni, L., & Bäckman, L. (2004). A preclinical phase in vascular dementia: Cognitive impairment three years before diagnosis. *Dementia and Geriatric Cognitive Disorders, 18*, 233–239.

Larrieu, S., Letenneur, L., Orgogozo, J. M., Fabrigoule, C., Amieva, H., Le Carret, N., et al. (2002). Incidence and outcome of mild cognitive impairment in a population-based prospective cohort. *Neurology, 59*, 1594–1599.

Laukka, E. J., Jones, S., Fratiglioni, L., & Bäckman, L. (2004). Cognitive functioning in preclinical vascular dementia: A 6-year follow-up. *Stroke, 35*, 1805–1809.

Laukka, E. J., Jones, S., Small, B. J., Fratiglioni, L., & Bäckman, L. (2004). Similar patterns of cognitive deficits in the preclinical phases of vascular dementia and Alzheimer's disease. *Journal of the International Neuropsychological Society, 10*, 382–391.

McKhann, G., Drachman, D., Folstein, M., Katzman, R., Price, D., & Stadlan, E. M. (1984). Clinical diagnosis of Alzheimer's disease: Report of the NINCDS-ADRDA Work Group under the auspices of Department of Health and Human Services Task Force on Alzheimer's disease. *Neurology, 34*, 939–944.

Monastero, R., Palmer, K., Qiu, C., Winblad, B., & Fratiglioni, L. (in press). Heterogeneity in risk factors for cognitive impairment-no dementia in an elderly population: Longitudinal study from the Kungsholmen Project. *American Journal of Geriatric Psychiatry*.

Palmer, K. (2004). *Early detection of Alzheimer's disease and dementia in the general population: Findings from the Kungsholmen Project.* Karolinska Institutet Doctoral Thesis, Karolinska University Press, Stockholm, Sweden.

Palmer, K., Bäckman, L., Winblad, B., & Fratiglioni, L. (2003). Detection of Alzheimer's disease and dementia in the preclinical phase: Population based cohort study. *British Medical Journal, 326*, 245.

Palmer, K., Wang, H. X., Bäckman, L., Winblad, B., & Fratiglioni, L. (2002). Differential evolution of cognitive impairment in nondemented older persons: Results from the Kungsholmen Project. *American Journal of Psychiatry, 159*, 436–442.

Petersen, R. C., Doody, R., Kurz, A., Mohs, R. C., Morris, J. C., Rabins, P. V., et al. (2001). Current concepts in mild cognitive impairment. *Archives of Neurology, 58*, 1985–1992.

Petersen, R. C., Smith, G. E., Waring, S. C., Ivnik, R. J., Tangalos, E. G., & Kokmen, E. (1999). Mild cognitive impairment: Clinical characterization and outcome. *Archives of Neurology, 56*, 303–308.

Qiu, C., Bäckman, L., Winblad, B., Aguero-Torres, H., & Fratiglioni, L. (2001). The influence of education on clinically diagnosed dementia incidence and mortality data from the Kungsholmen Project. *Archives of Neurology, 58*, 2034–2039.
Qiu, C., Winblad, B., Fastbom, J., & Fratiglioni, L. (2003). Combined effects of APOE genotype, blood pressure, and antihypertensive drug use on incident AD. *Neurology, 61*, 655–660.
Qiu, C., Winblad, B., Viitanen, M., & Fratiglioni, L. (2003). Pulse pressure and risk of Alzheimer disease in persons aged 75 years and older: A community-based, longitudinal study. *Stroke, 34*, 594–599.
Qiu, C., von Strauss, E., Fastbom, J., Winblad, B., & Fratiglioni, L. (2003). Low blood pressure and risk of dementia in the Kungsholmen Project: A 6-year follow-up study. *Archives of Neurology, 60*, 223–228.
Silverman, D. H., Small, G. W., Chang, C. Y., Lu, C. S., Kung De Aburto, M. A., Chen, W., et al. (2001). Positron emission tomography in evaluation of dementia: Regional brain metabolism and long-term outcome. *Journal of the American Medical Association, 286*, 2120–2127.
Small, B. J., Fratiglioni, L., Viitanen, M., Winblad, B., & Bäckman, L. (2000). The course of cognitive impairment in preclinical Alzheimer disease: Three- and six-year follow-up of a population-based sample. *Archives of Neurology, 57*, 839–844.
Small, B. J., Herlitz, A., Fratiglioni, L., Almkvist, O., & Bäckman, L. (1997). Cognitive predictors of incident Alzheimer's disease: A prospective longitudinal study. *Neuropsychology, 11*, 413–420.
Tuokko, H., Frerichs, R., Graham, J., Rockwood, K., Kristjansson, B., Fisk, J., et al. (2003). Five-year follow-up of cognitive impairment with no dementia. *Archives of Neurology, 60*, 577–582.
Unverzagt, F. W., Gao, S., Baiyewu, O., Ogunniyi, A. O., Gureje, O., Perkins, A., Emsley, C. L., Dickens, J., Evans, R., Musick, B., Hall, K. S., Hui, S. L., & Hendrie, H. C. (2001). Prevalence of cognitive impairment: Data from the Indianapolis Study of Health and Aging. *Neurology, 57*, 1655–1662.
van der Flier, W. M., van den Heuvel, D. M., Weverling-Rijnsburger, A. W., Bollen, E. L., Westendorp, R. G., van Buchem, M. A., et al. (2002). Magnetization transfer imaging in normal aging, mild cognitive impairment, and Alzheimer's disease. *Annals of Neurology, 52*, 62–67.
Wang, H. X., Karp, A., Winblad, B., & Fratiglioni, L. (2002). Late-life engagement in social and leisure activities is associated with a decreased risk of dementia: A longitudinal study from the Kungsholmen Project. *American Journal of Epidemiology, 155*, 1081–1087.
Wolf, H., Ecke, G. M., Bettin, S., Dietrich, J., & Gertz, H. J. (2000). Do white matter changes contribute to the subsequent development of dementia in patients with mild cognitive impairment? A longitudinal study. *International Journal of Geriatric Psychiatry, 15*, 803–812.
Yamaguchi, H., Sugihara, S., Ogawa, A., Oshima, N., & Ihara, Y. (2001). Alzheimer beta amyloid deposition enhanced by apoE epsilon4 gene precedes neurofibrillary pathology in the frontal association cortex of nondemented senior subjects. *Journal of Neuropathology and Experimental Neurology, 60*, 731–739.

4 Population levels of mild cognitive impairment in England and Wales

Jane Fleming, Fiona E. Matthews, Mark Chatfield, and Carol Brayne

Introduction

Cognitive changes have been shown to be strongly age-related, but the boundary between normal ageing and cognitive decline is less clear. Several approaches to the examination of ageing and cognition have emerged over the last few decades, all of which have examples in the UK-based literature. This chapter draws on empirical data on cognitive performance and change with age from three population-based studies of the elderly in England and Wales: two based in Cambridgeshire—the rural East Cambridgeshire study and the Cambridge City over-75s Cohort (CC75C) study; and one national—the Medical Research Council Cognitive Function and Ageing Study (MRC CFAS).

This chapter is divided into a general introduction and a brief description of the three population-based studies and their methods in relation to definition of mild dementia and cognitive impairment. Population levels of normal and abnormal cognition from three perspectives are examined: cross-sectional prevalence, survival differences, and longitudinal change. Cross-sectional prevalences of measures of mild cognitive impairment are presented for all three studies, and population norms of three cognitive measures are shown in detail for nondemented individuals from CFAS. The differing proportions identified with different tests and cut-points are explored. Survival differences with mild and more severe levels of cognitive impairment are presented using both CC75C and CFAS findings. We illustrate how longitudinal changes have been explored in both of the Cambridge-based studies.

Context

Studies of dementia in the population and in clinical settings only began to incorporate comprehensive measurement in the last three decades. Studies on ageing routinely included detailed neuropsychological measurement and psychometrics, but it was only in the 1980s that population-based studies began to pull together the measurement methods from the different relevant disciplines including clinical medicine where diagnostic batteries were being developed using the diagnostic labels and criteria available at that time. These approaches had originally been developed for different types of sample to address different questions. Neuropsychology generated groups of tests, developed on individuals with specific brain lesions, that were felt to identify lesions in particular areas before the era of imaging. Psychometry examined the range of normality and changes in selected volunteers with age. The diagnostic batteries aimed to differentiate between normal ageing, depression, and dementia, and between the dementias. Thus these approaches generated different sets of questions and tests, both for the individual and informants, and were conducted by different groups of researchers. The studies described here were initiated in this environment, and at the time combining these approaches was unusual. Such combinations allowed examination of the data in both a diagnostic and a continuous manner. Now such multidisciplinary and diverse methodologies have become usual practice and are encouraged in research.

This blurring of methods is particularly useful in population studies as it allows specification of a diagnosis at any one point, as well as investigation of how likely a given individual with a particular profile is to develop dementia or severe cognitive impairment over the period of follow-up. It also allows characterization of the profile of those who subsequently refuse re-interview or die.

At the time the studies described here were designed—the 1980s—mild cognitive impairment was not an accepted categorical entity, and change across the spectrum of performance was the focus of examination, rather than categorization. However, there was already considerable discussion of the mild impairment end of the cognitive spectrum, a debate that has continued since with recent discussion of the need for consistent definition echoing similar calls two decades ago (Brayne & Calloway, 1988; Henderson & Huppert, 1984; Luis, Loewenstein, Acevedo, Barker, & Duara, 2003; Petersen, 2004; Winblad et al., 2004).

Description of the studies

The rural East Cambridgeshire study

The rural East Cambridgeshire study (Brayne, 1990; Brayne, Best, Muir, Richards, & Gill, 1997a; Brayne & Calloway, 1989; Muir & Brayne, 1992) was a defined and detailed study of a small geographical area for which complete population enumeration was available through a single primary care group practice. The study was conducted in the 12 months following October 1986. The sample comprised women aged 70–79 years, with 203 randomly selected from 270 in the 70–74 age range and all 207 from the older 75–79 age range. Of these 185 were interviewed in the younger and 180 in the older cohorts—an 89% response rate. The respondents were interviewed using the Cambridge Mental Disorders of the Elderly Examination—CAMDEX (Roth et al., 1986). This structured diagnostic interview for mental disorders in older populations included a medical examination including a comprehensive test designed to test the range of relevant cognitive domains (Cambridge Cognitive Exam—CAMCOG), selected blood tests, and informant interviews conducted by a trained physician. The interview included many of the established scales in embedded format. These included cognition (Mini-Mental State Examination—MMSE (Folstein, Folstein, & McHugh, 1975), CAMCOG (Huppert, Brayne, Gill, Paykel, & Beardsall, 1995), Abbreviated Mental Test—AMT (Hodkinson, 1972), Clifton Assessment Procedures for the Elderly—CAPE (Pettie & Gilleard, 1979)), function (Blessed Dementia Scale (Blessed, Tomlinson, & Roth, 1968)), and vascular (Hachinski Score (Hachinski et al., 1975)) scales as well as the battery of CAMDEX scales.

The population was contacted again five years later and re-interviewed using identical methods with a trained physician, blind to the original diagnosis. The purpose of this study was to examine dementia in a homogeneous rural area and to examine how measures of cognitive impairment recommended at that time were distributed in total populations, including institutionalized residents.

The Cambridge City over-75s Cohort (CC75C) study

The CC75C study methodology has been extensively reported elsewhere (Brayne et al., 1997b; Brayne, Huppert, Paykel, & Gill, 1992; Paykel, Huppert, & Brayne, 1998; http://www.mrc-bsu.cam.ac.uk/cc75c/). Briefly, all those aged 75 and over from patient lists of six general practices in Cambridge, and one in three from a seventh, were invited to join the first wave of the study, the Hughes Hall Project for Later Life, later re-named the Cambridge Project for Later Life. Consent to take part was given by 95% of those approached, or their relatives, equivalent to 40% of the city's population aged 75 and over. The study population was therefore highly representative of the sampling frame as a whole—the "old old" age group in Cambridge. Between 1985 and 1987, 2609 men and women were interviewed in their normal place of residence by trained lay interviewers using a structured questionnaire. The population is flagged for mortality and emigration with regular notification (Office of National Statistics, ONS).

CAMDEX was used for more detailed investigation of low MMSE scorers in the early stages of the study. All those with MMSE scores <23/30 in the baseline screen, and one in three of those scoring 24 or 25, were selected for these assessments in a structured interview designed to detect cognitive impairment, in particular mild dementia.

All those initially screened, except those from one practice, formed the basis of the on-going CC75C longitudinal study of ageing ($n = 2165$ from baseline), and the cohort have been re-interviewed regularly with five further full surveys at intervals of 2–4 years (years 2, 6, 10, 13, and 17).

The Medical Research Council Cognitive Function and Ageing Study (MRC CFAS)

The MRC CFAS is a population-based longitudinal study primarily of dementia, but also of other disorders and their potential risk factors. The initial phases of the study have been described in detail elsewhere (Chadwick, 1992; MRC CFAS, 1998; http://www-cfas.medschl.cam.ac.uk/). Briefly, five centres in England and Wales (East Cambridgeshire, Gwynedd, Newcastle-upon-Tyne, Nottingham, and Oxford) used identical methods to obtain approximately 2500 screening interviews in each centre. All centres except Gwynedd obtained the population information from the appropriate Family Health Service Authorities (FHSA); all individuals aged 64 and over on defined dates were enumerated. Population-based samples stratified to ages 65–74 years and 75 and above were taken to achieve the 2500 interviews at each centre. In Gwynedd the FHSA could not release names and addresses for sampling, hence enumeration was undertaken by searching records in GP surgeries and ascertainment was based on surgery size. Individuals have been flagged at the ONS for deaths and emigrations.

At wave one an initial screening interview was undertaken (initial response rate 80%) followed a few months later by a more detailed assessment interview on a 20% subsample of the respondents, biased towards the cognitively frail. The screening interview consisted of a battery of questions covering socio-demographic, disability, and self-reported health risk factors (see MRC CFAS, 1998 for details) as well as the cognitive battery that consisted of the MMSE, an Extended Mental State Examination—EMSE (Medical Research Council, 1987; Huppert, Cabelli, Matthews, & MRC Cognitive Function and Ageing Study, 2005), and the organicity component of the AGECAT algorithm (Copeland et al., 1976). The assessment interview consisted of the full Geriatric Mental State examinations for organicity and mood disorders (Copeland et al., 1976) together with the CAMCOG. Individuals were selected for this interview using stratified random sampling based on age, cognitive performance and date of interview, and analyses adjusted for this design to obtain population values. Data presented within the chapter are from CFAS data version 7.0.

Measures of cognition

All studies used similar measures of cognition. The MMSE and CAMCOG have been used as the main global measure of cognition in all three studies, with additional measurements varying between studies: further cognitive measurement in CFAS, the EMSE; full diagnostic CAMDEX with clinician diagnosis in CC75C and the rural East Cambridgeshire study as described in the East Cambridgeshire section. In CFAS the AGECAT (Copeland, Dewey, & Griffiths-Jones, 1986) diagnostic system was algorithmic and does not provide severity but gives levels of confidence in an organicity/dementia "diagnosis". In CC75C and the rural study, the diagnostic system applied was the

> *Box 4.1* Mild cognitive impairment as defined by CAMDEX criteria for minimal dementia*
>
> Limited and variable impairment in acquisition of new information and recalling recent events.
> An increased tendency to misplace and lose possessions.
> Minor and variable errors in orientation.
> Some blunting in the capacity to follow or pursue a reasoned argument and to solve problems.
> Occasional errors (but of a slowly advancing frequency) in occupational tasks and/or housework.
> Errors in tasks judgement on occasion in professional or highly skilled tasks or socially responsible roles requiring difficult decisions or choices.
> Self-care unimpaired.
> Emotional life and responses well preserved.
> Clinical examination usually yields negative results except for manifest anxiety when asked to carry out demanding tasks.

* In the pre-publication version of CAMDEX used at baseline in both the Rural East Cambridgeshire and CC75C studies this mild level of cognitive impairment was given the label "minimal/mild dementia", terminology that has been used in earlier publications from these studies. These criteria are clinical interpretations of specific items within the CAMDEX schedule and are affirmative when there are changes relative to the individual in the past, rather than absolute levels.

CAMDEX set of criteria. These map closely onto DSM-III-R and ICD-10 (American Psychiatric Association, 1987). The severity criteria were those specified in the prepublication version—the label "minimal/mild" was given for impairments insufficient to fulfil diagnostic criteria. This became minimal in the published version of CAMDEX, and detailed criteria are provided which resemble the criteria generated since that time to describe the mildest types of dementia (Box 4.1). Thus, the studies can generate estimates of mild cognitive impairment according to a wide range of definitions, including diagnostic information.

Methods of analysis

The three studies all used a whole population approach to investigate aspects of cognition and ageing. The analyses presented here summarize the population results from these studies that best reflect the current literature on mild cognitive impairment. Results from baseline and follow-up interview waves in CC75C, CFAS, and East Cambridgeshire have been used to present cross-sectional, longitudinal, and survival perspectives. Whilst emphasizing the difficulties of selecting cut-points in continuous distributions, prevalence of mild cognitive impairment has been estimated using a categorization of MMSE scores between 24 and 27 in all three studies. For CFAS alone, medians and percentiles by age of three different cognitive measures are compared to present the full population distribution in individuals who were not demented. Survival differences between individuals by baseline values of MMSE have been modelled using Cox-proportional hazards regression adjusted for other potential covariates. Longitudinal analyses in the CC75C and East Cambridgeshire studies have examined simple distributions of change and also used methods based on more complex modelling.

Findings

Prevalence of mild cognitive impairment—the cross-sectional view

There have been many studies that investigate the prevalence of mild cognitive impairment. None of the three population studies described in this chapter have produced specific prevalence estimates of the current definition of mild cognitive impairment as they pre-dated current definitions and investigated the total population spread of cognitive ability and change. Cut-points in a continuous spectrum are inevitably a matter of debate but for comparison purposes we report here the prevalence of cognition scoring in the MMSE range 24–27 at baseline in each of the three studies. The population levels of this intermediate cognitive group are comparable, with approximately 40% of the population aged above 75 showing this mild level of cognitive impairment. Age ranges were slightly different in each study sample but overlapped, so Table 4.1 presents the distributions of MMSE scores by age-bands in each study. The all female sample of East Cambridgeshire's rural population (Brayne, 1990; Brayne et al., 1989) tended to have lower scores on the MMSE than either of the other two studies' samples of men

Table 4.1 Distribution of MMSE in three population samples (%)

Study	Age (years)	MMSE (0–17)	MMSE (18–23)	MMSE (24–27)	MMSE (28–30)
CFAS	65–69	2	9	35	55
	70–74	3	12	39	46
	75–79	5	18	42	35
	80+	19	26	37	18
CC75C	75–79	5	16	44	36
	80+	15	27	36	22
East	70–74	1	33	49	16
Cambridgeshire[a]	75–79	11	27	49	14

[a]Women only.

and women. Missing data in the two larger studies may slightly affect the lowest score rate, especially in the older age groups where more MMSEs were incomplete but have been assumed to fall in the 0–17 category. It is interesting to note the apparent drop in prevalence of the mildly cognitively impaired scores 24–27 amongst over-80-year-olds due to the distributional shift towards lower MMSE scores with older age.

For the two studies that categorized their samples into diagnostic groupings using CAMDEX interviews by psychiatrists—the East Cambridgeshire study and CC75C—alternative estimated population levels of mild cognitive impairment might be made. The category "minimal/mild dementia", which the published CAMDEX criteria subsequently re-named "minimal dementia", could be said to correspond loosely to that of mild cognitive impairment in current terminology. In East Cambridgeshire 6.6% met the diagnostic criteria for this category (Brayne, 1990; Brayne et al., 1989), with the rate in the older age-band double that observed in the younger: 4.3% and 8.9% of the women aged 70–74 and 75–79, respectively. These rates are markedly lower than the proportion identified with the MMSE cut-points described above, suggesting that those identified by these different methods—MMSE scores and CAMDEX diagnostic assessment—are not comparable groups.

However, this cannot be examined in CC75C as it is impossible to give any rate for the equivalent diagnostic category. The study methodology was originally designed to identify moderate and severe dementia, so no-one scoring MMSE >25 underwent the full CAMDEX assessment. Reported prevalence rates of more severely graded cognitive impairment, as assessed by CAMDEX, used weighting to adjust for the sampling of only one in three respondents scoring MMSE 24–25 but cannot allow for the proportion of higher scorers who might have fitted the CAMDEX minimal criteria (O'Connor et al., 1989). Subsequent publications arising from follow-up of the sample reported attrition, MMSE scores, and severity changes for four graded categories of cognitive impairment including minimal dementia but no prevalence rates can be extrapolated from these figures for reasons described above (O'Connor, Pollitt, Hyde, Fellows, Miller, & Roth, 1990; O'Connor, Pollitt, Jones, Hyde, Fellows, & Miller, 1991).

The full extent of the population distribution of cognitive function amongst older people who do not have dementia is portrayed graphically in Figure 4.1 using three measures from CFAS. The figure shows cross-sectional norms for MMSE, EMSE, and CAMCOG scores at baseline. It can be seen that in all measures there are lower cognitive levels with increasing age, but that the CAMCOG appears most sensitive to this age difference. The striking fact from these data is that in each measure of cognition—MMSE, EMSE, and CAMCOG—a value of the score that represented the lowest 10% of the population at age 65–69 represents at least 60% of the population by age 90. This difference highlights the problems inherent in using cut-points at any level to define diagnostic entities, particularly from studies that do not represent the complete population spectrum of age or ability.

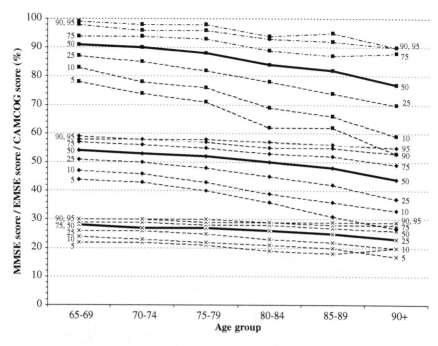

Figure 4.1 Percentiles of cognitive ability in nondemented individuals in MRC CFAS.

Association of mild cognitive impairment with mortality

It is now well established that severe, or even moderate, cognitive impairments predict reduced survival (Dewey & Saz, 2001). Most studies that have examined this association report between two and threefold increases in mortality. In CC75C, a 4-year survival analysis comparing a cognitively impaired group who scored ≤21 on baseline MMSE with both a physically frail and a healthy group with higher MMSE scores found a 26% lower survival rate in the cognitively impaired group compared with both of the other groups: RR 1.89, adjusted for age, sex, and physical health profile (Chi, Brayne, Todd, O'Connor, & Pollitt, 1995).

However, the literature regarding the effects of milder impairment of cognition on survival is scarcer and less clear-cut. Different populations sampled and methodologies, both in assessment and categorization of cognitive status, complicate the picture, making it difficult to make direct comparisons between the few studies to date. Estimates reported vary from no effect up to a 50% increase in risk. Nil effects were reported amongst people scoring only one error in the brief mental state test used in a study of cancer patients (Goodwin, Samet, & Hunt, 1996) and amongst those achieving a marginal score in the AMT (Hodkinson, 1972) in Gale et al.'s study of an elderly cohort (Gale, Martyn, & Cooper, 1996). By contrast, in a population-based sample Jagger and Clarke (1988) found a 30% increased risk of mortality, while Liu et al.'s estimate was 50% (Liu, LaCroix, White, Kittner, & Wolf, 1990).

4. Population levels of mild cognitive impairment in England and Wales

Reasons for attrition, including deaths, at reassessment 1 and 2 years after baseline have been reported on the subsample from the main CC75C cohort who underwent the full CAMDEX diagnostic assessment. There were no differences in mortality between those rated minimally or mildly demented but, as Figure 4.2 illustrates, death rates rose incrementally with increasing severity of cognitive impairment from 22 or 25% after 1 year and 32% after 2 years amongst those graded with these lower diagnostic grades, to 52% after 1 year and 66% after 2 years amongst those with severe dementia at baseline (O'Connor et al., 1991).

Mortality monitoring of the large MRC CFAS population sample, and the extensive data collected on a wealth of potential confounders, provided an ideal dataset for full exploration of the associations between survival and the full spectrum of cognition. Neale, Brayne, and Johnson (2001) categorized the baseline population for whom MMSE scores were available ($n = 12,552$ of 13,006 screened) into bands with MMSE scores 0–18, 19–23, 24–27, and 28–30 and found a consistent and strong reduction in survival probability for each decrement in MMSE from the highest scoring reference category. Deaths occurring before July 1, 1997 were censored (median follow-up time 4.7 years, range 3–6.5 years) in survival analyses using Cox-proportional hazards regression models. Age- and sex-adjusted hazard ratios, comparing the mild, moderate, and severely impaired groups to those with no cognitive dysfunction, were 1.24 (95% CI: 1.13–1.36), 1.77 (95% CI: 1.60–1.97), and 3.20 (95% CI: 2.82–3.63). These differences, whilst moderate, convey a separation of the survival curves.

Stratified analyses found little modification of these effects by education, smoking, marital status, housing, chronic disease, or self-perceived health except for a reduction of effect amongst the over-85-year-old age-band, particularly men, amongst whom life expectancy is markedly reduced for everyone. Besides the expected effects of age and sex, self-perceived health had the most effect, consistent with many other studies. Adjusting for these confounders still

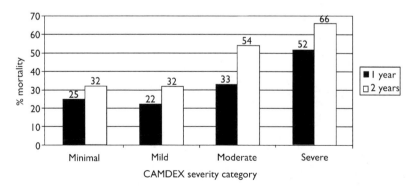

Figure 4.2 Mortality 1 and 2 years after CC75C baseline diagnostic assessment, by CAMDEX grades of dementia severity.

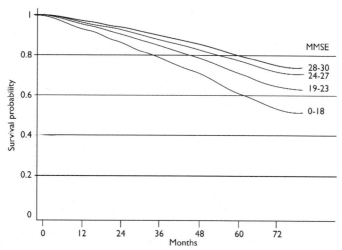

Adjusted for age, sex, education, self-perceived health, history of chronic disease, housing and smoking. Hazard ratios and 95% confidence intervals for each MMSE category relative to MMSE score 28-30 are
MMSE 24-27: HR 1.14 [95% CI 1.04 - 1.25]
MMSE 19-23: HR 1.49 [95% CI 1.33 - 1.66]
MMSE 0-17: HR 2.11 [95% CI 1.82 - 2.45]
Trajectories illustrated are for 75-year-olds.

Figure 4.3 Survival probability by baseline category of MMSE score in MRC CFAS.

left clearly significant effects of decreasing cognition on mortality, with severe impairment conferring an approximately twofold hazard, moderate impairment adding a 50% increase and even mild cognitive impairment increasing the hazard rate by approximately 10% (Figure 4.3).

The results confirm a picture of cognition as a continuum of impairment associated with a continuum of effect, such that even mild impairment in cognitive function is detrimental to survival.

Longitudinal analysis

Prospective studies of population samples allow for the exploration of temporal change in cognitive function with increasing age. Longitudinal analyses of the Cambridge-based cohorts have confirmed the picture of cognition as a continuum that was presented in the cross-sectional results. Change in cognition over time, as well as cognitive function at any given time, has been shown to be a continuous spectrum.

The rural female population in the East Cambridgeshire study were re-examined after a median of 5 years from baseline (Brayne et al., 1997a). The men and women in CC75C's representative urban sample have been followed up at intervals ranging from a few months to several years: incidence of dementia at the second main screening (Paykel et al., 1994) and trajectories of cognitive function over the first 4 years (Cullum et al., 2000) and 9 years (Brayne et al., 1999; Dufouil, Brayne, & Clayton, 2004; Dufouil et al., 2000) have been analysed to date. The differences between baseline and follow-up CAMCOG scores, including MMSE, were normally distributed around negative means in both CC75C and the East Cambridgeshire study, as were also the changes in East Cambridgeshire's additional measures, the Blessed Dementia Scale, and Choice Reaction Time. There was no evidence of more than one distribution underlying this, for example differential decline in scores between those with higher and lower baseline scores, despite the observation that those with lower baseline scores decline more.

In the East Cambridgeshire study slight cognitive decline was noted in the total population, increasing with age and marked in incident dementia (Brayne et al., 1997a). The baseline CAMDEX severity code "minimal" used at that time equates approximately to present concepts of mild cognitive impairment. Ten of the women with this minimal severity grading at baseline survived and were seen again after 5 years, and of them four had remained stable and six had progressed to frank dementia.

A clinically important result relevant to the question of mild cognitive impairment was the finding that those who subsequently developed dementia and their informants had been aware of decline 5 years earlier. Self-reported "difficulty in concentration now compared to the past" (CAMDEX) and informant report of decline in general mental faculties (Blessed Dementia Scale) were among the significant predictors of incident dementia.

CC75C's incidence study—the Cambridge Project for Later Life—reported incidence of minimal, mild, moderate, and severe dementia over a mean 2.4 years from baseline (Paykel et al., 1994). Annual incidence of the CAMDEX severity grading "minimal" was 5.4%, with a steep age-gradient from 2.8% at age 75–79 to 28.7% of those aged over 90.

A further longitudinal approach was used in CC75C to report population norms for MMSE scores, correcting for losses to follow-up due to death, dropout, and other reasons (Dufouil et al., 2000). Plotting selected quantiles of MMSE scores by gender and educational level showed gradual decline over time for the whole population and all subgroups. The normative data created placed the MMSE range 24–27 as spanning the 25th–50th centile of men and women in their early 80s, but by 87 years old this range falls in the 50th–75th centile. MMSE scores in this range, currently often classed as indicating mild cognitive impairment, represent only the 75th–90th centile of women aged 93–95 years old. The study has demonstrated the importance of adjusting for attrition in longitudinal analyses in order not to underestimate the extent of cognitive decline particularly in the oldest age-ranges (Brayne et al., 1999; Dufouil et al., 2004). Ten year follow-up data from CFAS will soon add to the literature on longitudinal cognitive change.

Analysis of different domains of cognitive function, measured by the various subscales in the CAMCOG, found that mean scores in each subscale declined over 4 years for men and women in CC75C (Cullum et al., 2000). Decline was steeper amongst those diagnosed as "cognitively impaired, no dementia" ($p = .01$, ANOVA adjusted for age), but still highly significant in the remainder of the sample and indeed the majority of participants showed evidence of decline in at least three domains. The findings suggest that the higher rates of decline from levels of mild cognitive impairment are on a continuum with the decline observed across populations with normal ageing.

Implications

Exceptionally good response rates have ensured that these studies are highly representative of the older population. The approach has been to apply standardized measurement scales to these populations, including those for informants, to examine the distributions of these measures of cognition at one time point and then to explore subsequent changes in cognitive function. This provides a different type of data to those from studies that use clinician judgement alone.

The studies described in this chapter all aimed to examine the full spectrum of normal to frail ageing over time, including the grey areas between ageing with no impairment and ageing with impairment. They used different measures, but all did include the MMSE. Mild cognitive impairment did not exist as a diagnostic category at the time these studies were set up and their results do not support the separation of a distinct entity of mild cognitive impairment any more than they support other categorizations. On the basis of group analysis there are clearly measures that are associated with subsequent decline, but these remain poor discriminators at the individual level. These findings concur with the findings from longitudinal clinical studies that show varying but substantial numbers of individuals remaining stable or even "recovering". It may be helpful to place such findings in the context of interventions for other continuously distributed variables such as blood pressure. The probability of adverse vascular events is relatively small for any individual receiving treatment but the weight of evidence regarding the benefits to the population is sufficient to warrant such intervention, even where there are side effects. Until the evidence regarding effective intervention to prevent progression to frank dementia is as strong as it is for control of hypertension in the prevention of stroke, it is unlikely that population-wide approaches will be advocated.

The concept of mild cognitive impairment remains valuable within both research and clinical settings. It defines a target group for possible interventions that may be tested in a screening context, at a later date when there is sufficient evidence of efficacy.

References

American Psychiatric Association. (1987). *Diagnostic and Statistical Manual* (III rev. ed.). Washington, DC: American Psychiatric Association.

Blessed, G., Tomlinson, B., & Roth, M. (1968). The association between quantitative measures of dementia and senile change in the cerebral grey matter of elderly subjects. *British Journal of Psychiatry, 114*, 797–811.

Brayne, C. (1990). *A study of dementia in a rural population*. MD Thesis, University of London.

Brayne, C., Best, N., Muir, M., Richards, S. J., & Gill, C. (1997a). Five-year incidence and prediction of dementia and cognitive decline in a population sample of women aged 70–79 at baseline. *International Journal of Geriatric Psychiatry, 12*, 1107–1118.

Brayne, C., & Calloway, P. (1988). Normal ageing, impaired cognitive function, and senile dementia of the Alzheimer's type: A continuum? *Lancet, 1*, 1265–1267.

Brayne, C., & Calloway, P. (1989). An epidemiological study of dementia in a rural population of elderly women. *British Journal of Psychiatry, 155*, 214–219.

Brayne, C., Huppert, F., Paykel, E., & Gill, C. (1992). The Cambridge Project for later life: Design and preliminary results. *Neuroepidemiology, 11*(Suppl. 1), 71–75.

Brayne, C., Huppert, F. A., Xuereb, J. H., Gertz, H.-J., Chi, L.-Y., McGee, M. A., et al. (1997b). An epidemiological study of the dementias in Cambridge: From clinical progression to neuropathology. In K. Iqbal, T. Winblad, M. Nishimura, M. Takeda, & H. M. Wisniewski (Eds.), *Alzheimer's disease: Biology, diagnosis and therapeutics* (pp. 11–20). Chichester, West Sussex, England: Wiley.

Brayne, C., Spiegelhalter, D. J., Dufouil, C., Chi, L. Y., Dening, T. R., Paykel, E. S., et al. (1999). Estimating the true extent of cognitive decline in the old old. *Journal of the American Geriatric Society, 47*, 1283–1288.

Chadwick, C. (1992). The MRC multicentre study of cognitive function and ageing: A EURODEM incidence study in progress. *Neuroepidemiology, 11*(Suppl. 1), 37–43.

Chi, L. Y., Brayne, C., Todd, C. J., O'Connor, D. W., & Pollitt, P. A. (1995). Predictors of hospital contact by very elderly people: A pilot study from a cohort of people aged 75 years and over. *Age Ageing, 24*, 382–388.

Copeland, J. R., Dewey, M. E., & Griffiths-Jones, H. M. (1986). A computerized psychiatric diagnostic system and case nomenclature for elderly subjects: GMS and AGECAT. *Psychological Medicine, 16*, 89–99.

Copeland, J. R., Kelleher, M. J., Kellett, J. M., Gourlay, A. J., Gurland, B. J., Fleiss, J. L., et al. (1976). A semi-structured clinical interview for the assessment of diagnosis and mental state in the elderly: The Geriatric Mental State Schedule. I. Development and reliability. *Psychological Medicine, 6*, 439–449.

Cullum, S., Huppert, F. A., McGee, M., Dening, T., Ahmed, A., Paykel, E. S., et al. (2000). Decline across different domains of cognitive function in normal ageing: Results of a longitudinal population-based study using CAMCOG [In Process Citation]. *International Journal of Geriatric Psychiatry, 15*, 853–862.

Dewey, M. E., & Saz, P. (2001). Dementia, cognitive impairment and mortality in persons aged 65 and over living in the community: A systematic review of the literature. *International Journal of Geriatric Psychiatry, 16*, 751–761.

Dufouil, C., Brayne, C., & Clayton, D. (2004). Analysis of longitudinal studies with death and drop-out: A case study. *Statistical Medicine, 23,* 2215–2226.

Dufouil, C., Clayton, D., Brayne, C., Chi, L. Y., Dening, T. R., Paykel, E. S., et al. (2000). Population norms for the MMSE in the very old: Estimates based on longitudinal data. Mini-Mental State Examination. *Neurology, 55,* 1609–1613.

Folstein, M. F., Folstein, S. E., & McHugh, P. R. (1975). "Mini-mental state". A practical method for grading the cognitive state of patients for the clinician. *Journal of Psychiatric Research, 12,* 189–198.

Gale, C. R., Martyn, C. N., & Cooper, C. (1996). Cognitive impairment and mortality in a cohort of elderly people. *British Medical Journal, 312,* 608–611.

Goodwin, J. S., Samet, J. M., & Hunt, W. C. (1996). Determinants of survival in older cancer patients. *Journal of the National Cancer Institute, 88,* 1031–1038.

Hachinski, V. C., Iliff, L. D., Zilhka, E., Du Boulay, G. H., McAllister, V. L., Marshall, J., et al. (1975). Cerebral blood flow in dementia. *Archives of Neurology, 32,* 632–637.

Henderson, A. S., & Huppert, F. A. (1984). The problem of mild dementia. *Psychological Medicine, 14,* 5–11.

Hodkinson, H. M. (1972). Evaluation of a mental test score for assessment of mental impairment in the elderly. *Age Ageing, 1,* 233–238.

Huppert, F. A., Brayne, C., Gill, C., Paykel, E. S., & Beardsall, L. (1995). CAMCOG—A concise neuropsychological test to assist dementia diagnosis: Sociodemographic determinants in an elderly population sample. *British Journal of Clinical Psychology, 34*(Pt 4), 529–541.

Huppert, F. A., Cabelli, S. T., Matthews, F., & MRC Cognitive Function and Ageing Study (MRC CFAS). (2005). Brief cognitive assessment in a UK populations sample—Distributional properties and the relationship between the MMSE and an extended mental state examination. *BMC Geriatrics, 5*(1), 7.

Jagger, C., & Clarke, M. (1988). Mortality risks in the elderly: Five-year follow-up of a total population. *International Journal of Epidemiology, 17,* 111–114.

Liu, I. Y., LaCroix, A. Z., White, L. R., Kittner, S. J., & Wolf, P. A. (1990). Cognitive impairment and mortality: A study of possible confounders. *American Journal of Epidemiology, 132,* 136–143.

Luis, C. A., Loewenstein, D. A., Acevedo, A., Barker, W. W., & Duara, R. (2003). Mild cognitive impairment: Directions for future research. *Neurology, 61,* 438–444.

Medical Research Council. (1987). *Report from the MRC Alzheimer's Disease Workshop.*

Medical Research Council Cognitive Function and Ageing Study (MRC CFAS). (1998). Cognitive function and dementia in six areas of England and Wales: The distribution of MMSE and prevalence of GMS organicity level in the MRC CFA Study. *Psychological Medicine, 28,* 319–335.

Muir, M. S., & Brayne, C. (1992). A longitudinal study in progress: A five-year follow-up of women aged 70–79 years living in a rural community. *Neuroepidemiology, 11*(Suppl. 1), 67–70.

Neale, R., Brayne, C., & Johnson, A. L. (2001). Cognition and survival: An exploration in a large multicentre study of the population aged 65 years and over. *International Journal of Epidemiology, 30,* 1383–1388.

O'Connor, D. W., Pollitt, P. A., Hyde, J. B., Fellows, J. L., Miller, N. D., Brook, C. P., et al. (1989). The prevalence of dementia as measured by the Cambridge Mental Disorders of the Elderly Examination. *Acta Psychiatrica Scandinavica, 79,* 190–198.

O'Connor, D. W., Pollitt, P. A., Hyde, J. B., Fellows, J. L., Miller, N. D., & Roth, M. (1990). A follow-up study of dementia diagnosed in the community using the Cambridge Mental Disorders of the Elderly Examination. *Acta Psychiatrica Scandinavica, 81*, 78–82.

O'Connor, D. W., Pollitt, P. A., Jones, B. J., Hyde, J. B., Fellows, J. L., & Miller, N. D. (1991). Continued clinical validation of dementia diagnosed in the community using the Cambridge Mental Disorders of the Elderly Examination. *Acta Psychiatrica Scandinavica, 83*, 41–45.

Paykel, E. S., Brayne, C., Huppert, F. A., Gill, C., Barkley, C., Gehlhaar, E., Beardsall, L., Girling, D. M., Pollitt, P., & O'Connor, D. (1994). Incidence of dementia in a population older than 75 years in the United Kingdom. *Archives of General Psychiatry, 51*, 325–332.

Paykel, E. S., Huppert, F. A., & Brayne, C. (1998). Incidence of dementia and cognitive decline in over-75s in Cambridge: Overview of cohort study. *Social Psychiatry and Psychiatric Epidemiology Index, 33*, 387–392.

Petersen, R. C. (2004). Mild cognitive impairment as a diagnostic entity. *Journal of International Medicine, 256*, 183–194.

Pettie, A. H., & Gilleard, C. J. (1979). *Manual of the Clifton Assessment Procedures for the Elderly (CAPE)*. Kent: Hodder and Stoughton.

Roth, M., Tym, E., Mountjoy, C. Q., Huppert, F. A., Hendrie, H., Verma, S., et al. (1986). CAMDEX. A standardized instrument for the diagnosis of mental disorder in the elderly with special reference to the early detection of dementia. *British Journal of Psychiatry, 149*, 698–709.

Winblad, B., Palmer, K., Kivipelto, M., Jelic, V., Fratiglioni, L., Wahlund, L. O., et al.(2004). Mild cognitive impairment—beyond controversies, towards a consensus: Report of the International Working Group on mild cognitive impairment. *Journal of International Medicine, 256*, 240–246.

5 The Melbourne Aging Study

Alexander Collie, Paul Maruff, David G. Darby, Colin Masters, and Jon Currie

Background

The Melbourne Aging Study arose from our observations of the dissociation between the progressive nature of the biochemical and clinical manifestations of Alzheimer's disease (AD), and the criteria for diagnosing AD in its earliest stages. Our review of the criteria for mild cognitive impairment (MCI) identified that while all criteria required objective evidence of a cognitive *deficit*, none required objective evidence of cognitive *decline* (Collie & Maruff, 2002a). This is inconsistent with neuropathological evidence for a long prodromal period in the AD process (Price & Morris, 1998), during which time aspects of cognition, particularly memory, demonstrate progressive deterioration (Collie & Maruff, 2000; Elias, Beiser, Wolf, Au, White, & D'Agostino, 2000). At the same time, we were aware that prospective studies of individuals classified as having MCI were reporting conversion to AD of only approximately 50% over 5–10 years (Bowen, Teri, Kukull, McCormick, McCurry, & Larson, 1997; Hanninen, Hallikainen, Koivisto Helkala, Reinikainen, & Soininen et al., 1995). Further, studies that challenged groups of MCI patients with other putative risk factors for AD were reporting conflicting results. For example, there was disagreement regarding the proportion of older individuals with MCI who carry the apolipoprotein E epsilon 4 (ApoE-4) allele, a genetic predictor of late onset sporadic AD (Reed et al., 1994; Smith et al., 1998). When considered together, these findings suggested that criteria for MCI based on a single assessment, aimed at identifying dysfunction or impairment, were inaccurate predictors of conversion to AD. Our hypothesis was that a more potent predictor of risk for developing AD was evidence of cognitive, particularly memory, decline demonstrated objectively. The Melbourne Aging Study was designed to address this hypothesis.

This chapter is divided into three sections. The first section describes the study cohort, the inclusion and exclusion criteria, the study design, and the types of measurements taken throughout the study. This includes a detailed description of the neuropsychological techniques used throughout the Melbourne Aging Study. The second section describes the major outcomes from this study to date, including a discussion of serial cognitive assessment for identifying MCI, the stability or reliability of current MCI criteria, and the development and validation of computerized cognitive screening tests for MCI. Finally, the third section briefly summarizes the major findings of the Melbourne Aging Study.

Study description

Participants and recruitment

Recruitment for this study began in 1996, after funding was obtained from the National Health and Medical Research Council (NH&MRC) of Australia. Advertisements were placed in local media calling for volunteers for a study of healthy aging. Study investigators also gave a number of interviews with local radio stations discussing the early stages of AD and the study. Over 600 people volunteered to participate. The study aimed to enrol a very healthy group of volunteers, and so screening proceeded in a number of stages. The first stage involved a telephonic screening interview with all potential volunteers, the aim of which was to identify and exclude those volunteers who obviously failed our exclusion criteria. Exclusion criteria at this stage included a history of respiratory, circulatory, or endocrine disease, although participants with minor episodes (e.g., bronchitis) and chronic conditions controlled with medications (e.g., high blood pressure) were not excluded. Personal or family history of psychiatric illness, head injury, and substance abuse were also exclusion criteria. Potential participants were also excluded if English was not their first language. The second stage was a general medical, psychiatric, and neurological assessment (Collie, Shafiq-Antonacci, Maruff, Tyler, & Currie, 1999). At this point in time all remaining volunteers were assessed by a neurologist, a neuropsychologist, and a psychiatric nurse. Exclusion criteria included meeting the National Institute of Neurological and Communicative Disorders and Stroke–Alzheimer's Disease and Related Disorders Association (NINCDS-ADRDA) criteria for dementia (McKhann, Drachman, Folstein, Katzman, Price, & Stadlan, 1984), a score below 28 on the Mini-Mental State Examination (MMSE) (Folstein, Folstein, & McHugh, 1975) or above the age-appropriate limit on the Short Blessed Test (SBT) (Katzman, Brown, Fuld, Peck, Schechter, & Schimmel, 1983), the presence of two or more abnormal neurological signs indicated by the CERAD neurological examination (Morris, Mohs, Rogers, Fillenbaum, & Heyman, 1988), past or current history of stroke, hypertension, major vascular disorder, heart disease, head injury, epilepsy, diabetes, thyroid disease, major depressive or anxiety disorder, or any other psychiatric illness. Factors such as education, race, intelligence, and socioeconomic status were not included in the criteria for selection. A total of 254 people over 50 years of age were recruited into the study.

Table 5.1 Demographic breakdown of the Melbourne Aging Study

Group	No.	%
Male	80	31.1
Female	174	68.9
50–69 years of age	188	74.0
70+ years of age	66	26.0
≥12 years of education	138	54.3
<12 years of education	116	45.7
Total	254	100.0

The vast majority of individuals were aged between 50 and 69 years of age, with a smaller group over 70 years. Most participants were well educated and there were a greater proportion of females to males (Table 5.1). Average age on enrolment to the study was 63.1±8.9 years, and the average MMSE score was 28.5±1.4.

Procedure

All participants enrolled in the study were assessed twice yearly for 5 years between 1996 and 2001. At the first assessment, a comprehensive medical history was taken to determine health status. All participants completed the General Health Questionnaire and the National Adult Reading Test (NART). At this assessment participants also gave blood for apolipoprotein (ApoE) genotyping. Each assessment included the following as a minimum:

(1) neuropsychological screening using the Consortium to Establish a Registry for Alzheimer's Disease (CERAD) test battery;
(2) a series of questionnaires examining recent levels of anxiety (State-Trait Anxiety Inventory [STAI]) and depression;
(3) an ocular-motor assessment including recording of prosaccades and antisaccades;
(4) collection of blood for biochemical analysis and genotyping; and
(5) staging of cognitive function according to the Clinical Dementia Rating (CDR) scale.

Approximately 1 month prior to the scheduled assessment of the participants, a study investigator made contact with them via telephone to confirm their appointment. The vast majority of examinations were undertaken at the Mental Health Research Institute of Victoria in Melbourne, Australia. On arrival at the institute, participants were asked to complete the anxiety and depression rating scales. Fasting blood was taken immediately and participants were then provided with breakfast. A self-report medical history covering the previous 6 months was taken by a clinical psychiatric nurse, followed by a neurological examination. The neuropsychological tests were then administered by a neuropsychologist or trained research assistant. Finally, participants completed the ocular-motor assessment. Occasionally it was necessary to conduct the assessment in the participant's home, due to illness or lack of transport. While this increased the time required for each assessment, it also led to high rates of compliance and retention.

Study timeline

The study was initiated in early 1996 and continues till today. The assessment schedule has changed somewhat during this time. For the first 5 years, assessments were undertaken semiannually. From 2001 onwards, assessments were undertaken on a yearly basis. From time to time additional assessment techniques were administered to study participants, in order to investigate specific hypotheses.

After 5 years of semiannual assessments (end of year 2000), two groups of individuals with different patterns of MCI were identified. These groups, along with a control group, became the focus of the study from 2001 onwards, where more detailed neuropsychological and neuroimaging investigations were undertaken. This timeline is described in Table 5.2, below.

Table 5.2 Timeline of the Melbourne Ageing Study

Year	Event
1995	Application for funding submitted
	Funding approved
	Ethics application submitted
1996	Ethics approval granted
	Study initiation
	Participant screening
	254 participants recruited
	Full medical history and ApoE genotyping
	First assessments undertaken
1996–2000	Semiannual assessments undertaken
	Approx. 180 participants continuing at end 2000
	MCI groups identified at end 2000
2001–2004	Annual assessment schedule adopted
	Detailed neuropsychological studies of MCI groups
	Neuroimaging studies of MCI groups
2005	Study continues, focusing on MCI

Materials and methods

Throughout the study a number of assessment procedures were utilized. These are described in more detail below.

Neuropsychological tests

CONSORTIUM TO ESTABLISH A REGISTRY FOR ALZHEIMER'S DISEASE (CERAD) NEUROPSYCHOLOGICAL TEST BATTERY

This battery consists of the Modified Boston Naming Test (Kaplan, Goodglass, & Weintraub, 1983), Categorical Verbal Fluency, Word List Learning, Word List Delayed Recall, Constructional Praxis "line drawing", Word List Recognition, and the MMSE. Four alternate forms of the CERAD battery are available, and these have been described in detail elsewhere (Morris et al., 1988; Welsh et al., 1994). All CERAD tests were administered and scored according to standard protocols. Briefly, in the word list learning and recall tests, subjects are read a list of 10 words and asked to immediately recall as many of those words as possible. This procedure is repeated three times with the same word list, with the order of word presentation changed on each occasion. After a 5 min delay in which subjects are distracted by other tasks, subjects are required to free recall as many words from the word list as possible. In all conditions, the number of words recalled is recorded. In the category verbal fluency test, subjects are required to name as many exemplars as possible from a predefined category (e.g., animals, clothing, first names) within 60 s. The number of exemplars named is recorded. In the confrontational naming test, subjects are shown a series of 15 line drawings and asked to name each one. The line drawings are graded on the basis of difficulty, and the number accurately named is recorded. On the Constructional Praxis line drawing test, subjects are asked to copy four abstract line drawings as accurately as possible. Both easy and difficult line drawings are shown, and each receives a score proportionate with the difficulty of the drawing. Scoring on this test reflects the extent to which the subject was able to accurately copy all aspects of the line drawings. The MMSE is a cognitive screening test that assesses five domains of cognition: (1) attention and calculation, (2) orientation in time and place, (3) recall, (4) language, and (5) registration. For a detailed description of the MMSE, see Folstein et al. (1975).

COMPUTERIZED COGNITIVE TESTS

A number of computerized neuropsychological assessment batteries were used throughout the study. These included the CogState system, the Automated Cognitive Test (ACT), and the Cambridge Neuropsychological Test Automated Battery (CANTAB).

The CANTAB requires subjects to respond via a touch sensitive screen to stimuli presented visually. Responses for the ACT system are collected via the computer keyboard in the form of a yes or no response. For both test systems, accuracy and response time data are recorded automatically by the computer for later analysis. Subjects were seated approximately 0.5 m from the computer's monitor and were instructed to respond to stimuli presented in each task by touching the screen (CANTAB) or by pressing the appropriate key on the keyboard (ACT). The testing session lasted between 90 and 120 min, and each task was administered according to standard protocols that have been described extensively elsewhere (Owen, Beksinska, James, Leigh, Summers, & Marsden, 1993; Stollery, 1996). The CANTAB subtests were administered in order to assess recognition memory (pattern and spatial recognition), associative learning (pattern-location associative learning [AL]), episodic memory (delayed matching to sample and spatial span), working memory (spatial working memory), executive function (set shifting), and planning and problem solving (Tower of London). The ACT subtests were administered to assess verbal reasoning (semantic and syntactic reasoning) and verbal memory (category search and repeated words).

CogState is a series of computerized card tasks that requires 15–18 min to complete. The test battery includes seven distinct tasks, including tests of simple reaction time, choice reaction time, working memory, simple and divided attention, and AL. For each task, both reaction times (RTs, measured in ms) and accuracy scores (measured as percentage correct) were calculated. Written instructions are presented on the screen indicating the response requirements. Participants were given a brief practice version of each task, before formal testing commenced. Participants were required in all cases to respond with two keyboard keys: the "D" key, which indicated a "no" response and the "K" key which indicated a "yes" response. These keys were reversed if participants were left-handed. A detailed description of the five tasks can be found elsewhere (Collie, Maruff, Darby, & McStephen, 2003).

OTHER NEUROPSYCHOLOGICAL TESTS

On occasion other cognitive/neuropsychological tests were administered to the group. For example, the logical memory subtest from the Weschler Memory Scales was employed (Weschler, 1987). In addition to this, we also developed some computerized cognitive tasks to examine specific hypotheses. For example, face-name and pattern-word AL tasks were developed to examine a hypothesis about hippocampal formation function in older people with memory decline (Collie, Myers, Schnirman, Wood, & Maruff, 2002c).

Subjective rating scales

The STAI and Centre for Epidemiological Studies Depression rating scale (CES-D) were also administered on each visit to assess anxiety and depressive symptomatology. The STAI requires the subject to indicate the degree to which a series of statements describe their current (state anxiety scale) or general (trait anxiety scale) state of mind. All questions on the STAI are rated from 1 (not at all) to 4 (very much so). The CES-D requires the subject to estimate the number of times they have experienced each of 20 statements during the previous week, and each question is rated from 0 (rarely or none of the time) to 3 (most or all of the time).

The NART was administered to all subjects on the first occasion as an estimate of intellect. The NART requires subjects to pronounce a series of irregular words of increasing difficulty, and correct pronunciation is taken to indicate knowledge of the meaning of that word. The number of words pronounced correctly as well as the number of errors made are recorded.

A self-rating cognitive function questionnaire, the Cognitive Failures Questionnaire, was also administered on numerous assessments. The Cognitive Failures Questionnaire requires participants to rate how often they have experienced a range of cognitive failures during the last 6 months on a scale from 0 (never) to 4 (very often). Participants are questioned about 25 broad examples of cognitive failures covering the domains of memory (8 questions), motor function (10 questions), and perception (7 questions). The total score from each domain, as well as the overall score, is taken to indicate the severity of subjective cognitive failures.

Outcomes

As stated above, the primary aim of the Melbourne Aging Study was to examine the use of serial cognitive assessment as a predictor for the onset of AD. However, the study also allowed us to examine a number of other important hypotheses. These included investigation of the stability of diagnostic criteria for MCI, and the properties of screening tests for detecting very early memory impairment. The study also allowed us to establish normative data for neuropsychological outcomes in older people. The most important outcomes of the Melbourne Aging Study are described in turn below.

Serial assessment of cognition

As stated above, the primary aim of the study was to investigate the use of serial memory assessment for the early detection of MCI and AD. This objective arose from observations that criteria for MCI and AD were based on a single assessment of cognition, whereas the clinical hallmark of the disease is a progressive decline in memory and cognitive functions. During the year 2000, we had reviewed the available diagnostic guidelines for MCI and observed a surprising lack of consensus (Collie & Maruff, 2002a). At the time, we were able to identify nine distinct criteria that had been developed for the classification of MCI. In addition, a number of other terms have been used to describe cognitive dysfunction in older individuals. These are described in Table 5.3.

On close examination of these criteria, it became obvious that there were a number of inconsistencies between them. While an individual must display evidence of a memory deficit before a classification of cognitive impairment

Table 5.3 Terminology for mild cognitive impairment

Acronym	Title	Reference
AACD	Aging associated cognitive decline	Levy (1994)
AAMI	Age-associated memory impairment	Crook et al. (1986)
ACMD	Age-consistent memory decline	Crook (1993)
ACMI	Age-consistent memory impairment	Blackford and La Rue (1989)
ARCD	Age-related cognitive decline	DSM-IV[a]
ARMD	Age-related memory decline	Blesa, Adroer, Santacruz, Ascaso, Tolosa, and Oliva (1996)
BSF	Benign senescent forgetfulness	Kral (1962)
IMD	Isolated memory decline	Small, Perera, DeLaPaz, Mayeux, and Stern (1999)
IMI	Isolated memory impairment	Berent et al. (1999)
IML	Isolated memory loss	Bowen et al. (1997)
LCD	Limited cognitive disturbance	Gurland, Copeland, and Kuriansky (1982)
LLF	Late life forgetfulness	Blackford and La Rue (1989)
MCD	Mild cognitive disorder	Reisberg, Ferris, de Leon, and Crook (1982)
MCI	Mild cognitive impairment	Petersen et al. (1999)
MD	Minimal dementia	Roth et al. (1986)
MND	Mild neurocognitive disorder	DSM-IV[a]
QD	Questionable dementia	Morris, Edland, Clark, Galasko, Koss, & Mohs et al. (1993)

[a]DSM-IV = Diagnostic and Statistical Manual of mental disorders—Version 4, published by the American Psychiatric Association (1994).

can be made according to all of these systems, other inclusion and exclusion criteria were much less uniform. Most surprisingly, none of these criteria required objective evidence of cognitive decline.

We were also aware that retrospective studies of individuals with probable AD had shown that subtle impairments in episodic memory could be detected up to 20 years before diagnosis (Elias et al., 2000; Jacobs, Sano, Dooneief, Marder, Bell, & Stern, 1995; Masur, Sliwinski, Lipton, Blau, & Crystal, 1994). This suggested that the careful assessment of memory in older people would provide the earliest indication of AD.

We therefore sought to analyze the serial neuropsychological data collected during the study, with the aim of identifying two groups of older people: (1) those with objective evidence of memory decline; and (2) those without such decline. We also sought to determine the relationship between memory decline and other putative risk factors for AD, including ApoE genotype, self-rated cognitive function, and performance on neuropsychological measures. CDRs were also calculated in order to determine the proportion of older people with memory decline who met a standard clinical criteria for MCI. One hundred and one participants who had completed five consecutive assessments at intervals of 6 months were selected. Participants who had missed an assessment, or who had not yet completed five assessments, were excluded from the analysis.

For each participant, serial performance on the CERAD word list delayed recall test was plotted with performance on the y-axis and assessment on the x-axis. A linear regression or "line of best fit" was then plotted on this data, and the slope of this equation calculated. Participants were classified as having memory decline if the slope of their performance on the WLDR test was less than zero. In contrast, participants were classified as having no decline if the slope of their word list delayed recall test performance was 0 or positive.

Thirty-five participants (34.7%) were classified as having declining memory, while the remaining participants ($N = 66$; 65.3%) were assigned to the nondeclining memory group. For the declining memory group, the mean yearly decrease in performance was recorded at 7.75% per year, or 0.775 of 10 possible words (Figure 5.1).

Importantly, the MMSE scores of all participants remained above 25/30 on all assessments, and no participant met criteria for probable AD at the final assessment. Further, upon entry to the study (assessment 1), there were no differences between the declining memory and nondeclining memory

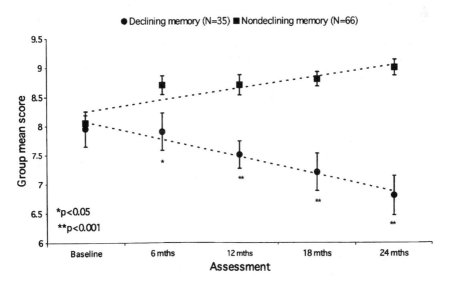

Figure 5.1 Serial word list delayed recall performance of older people with memory decline ($N = 35$) and controls ($N = 66$).

groups on word list delayed recall score, suggesting that initial level of memory test performance could not predict final group membership.

A substantial proportion of the memory decline group (34.3%) was rated as impaired using the CDR criteria at the final assessment, compared to only 6.3% of the control group. While this difference was statistically significant, it does suggest that the sensitivity of the CDR criteria for detecting memory decline in healthy older people is poor, as two thirds of older individuals with objective evidence of memory decline were misclassified as having normal cognitive function when this instrument was applied in the current study (i.e., false negative diagnoses).

All participants completed a more extensive neuropsychological assessment at the end of this analysis (i.e., at the 24-month assessment). This assessment included the STAI, the CES-D rating scale, and the Cognitive Failures Questionnaire. Interestingly, ratings of cognitive failures did not differ between older individuals with declining and nondeclining memory. One potential explanation for this finding is that memory impairment may only become apparent to the individual when performance drops below a certain level. The memory decline observed in this study was quite subtle and may not have been manifested as cognitive failures that occur in the individuals' daily environment. Further, there were no differences between groups on self-rated levels of anxiety and depression.

These findings suggested that episodic memory *decline* can be detected among healthy older people before an objective memory *deficit* is evident using standard clinical criteria (i.e., the CDR scale). We felt that this finding has important implications for the design and implementation of classification systems aimed at identifying individuals at increased risk for AD on the basis of cognitive performance, as it suggests that the inclusion criteria for such systems should require objective evidence of cognitive decline. This finding led to a further analysis of these classification systems, described below.

Reliability of MCI criteria

One of the striking observations from our literature reviews (Collie & Maruff, 2000, 2002a) was the rate of conversion to AD among older individuals classified as having MCI. In many studies, only approximately half of MCI patients developed AD or other neurodegenerative diseases within the period of investigation (up to 5 years: Berent et al., 1999; Bowen et al., 1997; Petersen, Smith, Waring, Ivnik, Tangalos, & Kokmen, 1999). This suggested that the specificity of MCI classification systems as predictors of AD is poor as they identify memory impairments in individuals who do not develop AD. A number of possible explanations for lack of progression to AD exist, including that length of follow-up was not sufficient, and that the remaining, nondementing MCI subjects may be normal older people with long-standing poor memory (Petersen et al., 1999). The memory impairment identified in these subjects may also be due to state factors associated with the behavioral assessment (e.g., test-related anxiety).

These findings raise the question of the specificity of diagnostic criteria for MCI. The aim of our second major analysis was to determine the stability of a commonly used MCI criteria (Petersen et al., 1999). We applied Petersen's criteria to data generated from three consecutive assessments of our aging cohort. We then sought to determine the proportion of the cohort with transient or inconsistent cognitive impairments and to differentiate this group from individuals with consistently impaired cognitive function (MCI).

Data from 174 individuals who had complete data sets available for three consecutive assessments were included in this analysis. The mean age of this group was 64.3 years, and 104 were female. At each assessment, classifications of MCI were made if the following criteria were met: (1) objective evidence of a memory impairment relative to age-matched norms. Memory impairment was defined as performance on the CERAD word list delayed recall task 1.5*SD*s below the norms described in Collie et al. (1999); (2) normal activities of daily living; (3) normal general cognitive function; (4) no dementia; and (5) no depression or anxiety. The proportion of the group meeting the MCI criteria at each assessment was then determined. At the first assessment, 46 (26.4%) of the group were classified as MCI. The corresponding figures for the second and third assessments were 39 (22.4%) and 45 (25.9%), respectively. Taken at face value, these figures appear relatively consistent and seem to suggest that the MCI criteria were very stable. However, a secondary analysis demonstrated that this was not the case.

This second analysis involved determining what proportion of the group had been classified as having MCI on 0, 1, 2, or all of the three consecutive assessments. It was observed that only 23 (13.3%) of the group met the criteria for MCI on all three assessments. A much larger proportion of the group displayed transient memory impairment, with 38 (21.8%) meeting the MCI criteria once, and 27 (15.5%) meeting the criteria twice. A group of 86 (49.4%) individuals were never classified as having MCI (Figure 5.2).

Estimates of the proportion of older individuals exhibiting mild cognitive deficits have ranged from 7 to 96%, depending on the classification system used to define impairment and the population in which that classification system was implemented (Smith, Ivnik, Petersen, Malec, Kokmen, & Tangalos, 1991). Higher estimates are often observed in studies that use less strict rules for classification. For example, estimates of the prevalence of AAMI among people aged over 50 years are most often reported as approximately 50–60% (Reinikainen, Koivisto, Mykkanen, Hanninen, Soininen, & Riekkinen, 1990). A recent proposal by Almkvist et al. (1998) supports this view. Almkvist states that both the severity of the initial cognitive impairment and the rigor of inclusion and exclusion criteria are highly correlated with outcomes. Therefore, subjects diagnosed according to criteria which require quite severe impairments are observed to progress to AD (Bowen et al., 1997; Petersen et al., 1999), while those diagnosed according to criteria which

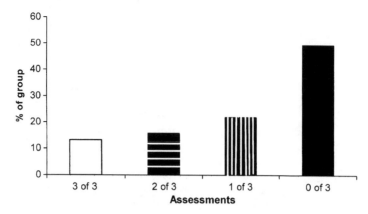

Figure 5.2 Proportion of group meeting MCI criteria on 0, 1, 2, or 3 of three assessments.

require only very mild impairments are less likely to develop AD (Hanninen et al., 1995; Snowdon & Lane, 1994).

As noted above, Petersen et al. (1999) proposed that groups of MCI subjects may be contaminated by older people with long-standing poor memory. Similarly, we have suggested that false positive diagnoses of MCI may also be made when the individual's cognition is affected by state factors associated with the behavioral assessment, and that these state factors will have greatest effect on the composition of MCI groups when a single behavioral assessment is used to rate cognitive function. Therefore, one appealing alternative explanation for the low prevalence of MCI observed in the current study (13.3%) is that it reflects a reduction in false positive classifications associated with the criteria employed. That is, only individuals who met the impairment criteria on three consecutive occasions were considered to have MCI.

Development of screening tests

Another focus of our study was the development of tests that had particular sensitivity to the impairments observed in MCI and early AD. We approached this issue in two ways. First, we sought to develop tests that measured those domains of cognition that are affected in the earliest stages of AD (Collie & Maruff, 2002b). Second, we sought to develop tests that were highly reliable and appropriate for repeated assessment of cognition, in order to identify the earliest signs of cognitive decline in older individuals (Darby, Maruff, & Collie, 2004; Darby, Maruff, Collie, & McStephen, 2002; Maruff, Collie, Darby, Weaver-Cargin, Masters, & Currie, 2004). These approaches will be discussed in turn, below.

One consistent observation in the MCI and aging literature is that the earliest stages of AD are characterized by an impairment in the ability to learn associations between stimuli (Collie & Maruff, 2000; Petersen et al., 1999).

The hippocampal formation is thought to play a key role in learning novel associations, with substantial evidence from studies of both humans and non-human primates supporting this proposal (AL; Henke, Weber, Kneifel, Wieser, & Buck, 1999; Squire & Zola-Morgan, 1991; Wallenstein, Eichenbaum, & Hasselmo, 1998). Specifically, these studies suggest that the hippocampal formation is necessary for learning arbitrary relationships between stimuli. One potential explanation for the AL deficits observed in MCI is therefore that they are a consequence of hippocampal dysfunction. This is consistent with neuroimaging findings of hippocampal formation atrophy in both MCI and early AD (Jack et al., 1999) and also with neuropsychological evidence that cognitive decline is restricted to the domain of episodic memory in individuals who later progress to develop AD (Collie & Maruff, 2000).

In our earlier analyses, we had proposed that progressive cognitive decline in older people (in the absence of other medical or psychiatric conditions) may be indicative of a neurodegenerative process that is limited to the hippocampus (Collie et al., 2001). Consistent with this proposal, the predominant impairments in this group appear to involve learning and remembering events and episodes (episodic or explicit memory; Collie & Maruff, 2000). In our "memory decline" group, we had observed that this episodic memory impairment was most reliable and robust on tasks that required AL (Collie et al., 2001). When considered in conjunction with findings suggesting that the hippocampal formation is involved in novelty detection (Knight, 1996) and spatial navigation (Maguire, Burgess, & O'Keefe, 1999), we proposed that older people with cognitive decline would display AL impairments most prominently on tasks containing novel stimuli, or stimuli presented in a spatial context, and that this impairment represented a behavioral manifestation of hippocampal formation dysfunction.

In order to investigate this hypothesis, we designed an experiment to challenge our "cognitive decline" group (from Collie et al., 2001) with a series of AL tasks. Three distinct tasks were designed, requiring the participants to associate (1) a pattern with a spatial location; (2) a pattern with a word; or (3) a face with a name. We hypothesized that the pattern-spatial location association would differentiate MCI from control participants, because of the novel nature of the association and the requirement to make a spatial association. In contrast, the face-name and pattern-word associations were presented in a nonspatial context and were relatively familiar (i.e., not novel) to most people.

Sixteen MCI participants and a group of sixteen matched control participants completed the study. Their results are shown in Figure 5.3, below. The outcome was consistent with our hypotheses: the MCI group displayed a large and significant impairment in the pattern-location AL task (Cohen's d effect size = 1.02), while there was no between-group differences on the other AL tasks.

Our interpretation of these results is that the stimuli for the face-name task are encountered daily and may invoke cognitive processing other than that required to simply make an association. This task may therefore be less difficult

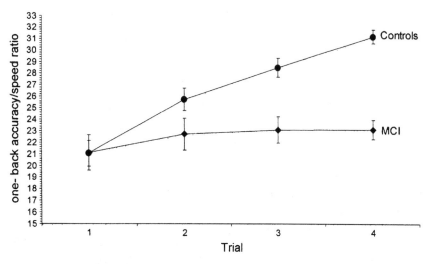

Figure 5.3 Performance of MCI and control groups on four assessments conducted within a single day.

than the pattern-location AL task, where the stimuli are abstract and unfamiliar. In addition, we felt that the combination of spatial localization and abstract pattern recognition in the pattern-location task may have contributed to these results, given the role of the hippocampal formation in spatial navigation (Maguire et al., 1999) and novelty detection (Knight, 1996), and the finding of hippocampal formation atrophy in MCI (Jack et al., 1999). Tasks that require the individual to make such associations may therefore be most suitable for the identification of early memory changes in MCI and AD.

In addition to developing tests of highly specific aspects of cognition, we also sought to develop tests with excellent metric properties for serial assessment. This approach arose from our observations that most conventional cognitive tests are designed for the identification of brain dysfunction, rather than the assessment of change in brain functions over time (Collie, Maruff, Falleti, Silbert, & Darby, 2002b). Although such tests are suitable for the investigation of brain–behavior relationships in cognitively impaired individuals, they possess two psychometric properties that restrict their applicability for serial assessment. First, many cognitive tests have limited or nonequivalent alternate forms that may result in performance changes due to practice effects (Benedict & Zgaljardic, 1998; McCaffrey, Ortega, Orsillo, & Welles, 1992), and low test–retest reliability resulting in increased measurement error and regression to the mean (McCaffrey, Duff, & Westervelt, 2000). Second, many of these tests have floor or ceiling effects when they are administered to normal people, and often have only a limited range of possible scores (e.g., 0–10 on a word learning test). These factors ensure that large changes in cognitive status are required for small changes in test score to be observed, and may mean that mild but "true" changes in cognition are not reflected as a change in test score. We therefore sought to develop tests that had appropriate metric properties for serial assessment and the detection of mild changes in cognition early in the AD process.

Our own research on the detection of change in memory function in nondemented older people suggests that the sensitivity to change of neuropsychological tests can be improved by increasing the number of times they are given to the same individual (Collie et al., 2001). To achieve this, however, it is necessary to have a brief test that possesses multiple parallel forms, has a standardized administration, requires simple responses, and yields performance data with sufficient range for true variation to occur (i.e., tests that yield a wide range of possible scores). As noted above, we observed that the false positive classification rate for memory impairment in healthy older people was 50% when based on a measure of word list delayed recall (Collie, Maruff, & Currie, 2002a). Some memory tests also facilitate considerable improvement with practice that can mask detection of true serial change (McCaffrey et al., 1992). Therefore, it is important to develop tests that possess only minimal and known practice effects so that the ability to detect change over time is not obscured by practice.

In one study, we selected a computerized cognitive test battery designed and validated for rapid and repeated use (Collie et al., 2003). We sought to determine whether the participants classified as having "memory decline" could be identified by multiple assessments conducted in a single 3-h testing session. Twenty MCI participants, and 40 healthy controls, participated in this study. All participants completed a battery of cognitive tests (CogState) on four occasions within a 3-h period. Tests within this battery were chosen to sample from a range of cognitive domains, including psychomotor speed, attention, working memory, and episodic learning and memory. The test has been described above.

All subjects were tested in a quiet computer laboratory. They were given instructions on how to perform the tasks but were not given any practice before they commenced the first assessment. Two test sessions (T1, T2) were completed 5 min apart prior to a lunch break (1 h), and the final two test sessions (T3, T4) were then completed separated by 5 min. Hence, total testing time was about 2.5–3 h with sufficient breaks to ensure maintenance of motivation and minimize fatigue. Results indicated that the MCI participants failed to demonstrate the normal learning or practice effect. While there was no difference between groups at the first test session, significant differences were observed by the third and fourth test sessions (Darby et al., 2002; Figure 5.4, below). A discriminant function analysis correctly classified 38 (95%) of the control participants and 16 (80%) of the MCI participants.

Whereas the normal older people demonstrated practice effects over the course of the four tests, the MCI patients tested here displayed only minor effects of practice with a performance plateau. As far as we are aware, this study is the first report of the use of a multiple assessment approach on a single day to successfully differentiate MCI patients from normal subjects.

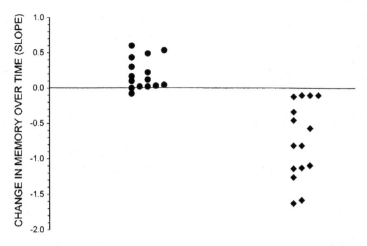

Figure 5.4 Performance of MCI and control participants on three different associate learning tasks.

The results support the hypothesis that multiple assessments using appropriate tools can leverage a lack of normal practice effects in impaired populations (Horton, 1992; Rapport, Brines, Axelrod, & Theisen, 1997). The cognitive instrument used in the current study was specifically designed for frequent serial assessment, but it remains possible that standard tests could also be used in this manner. For example, alternative forms of a verbal memory test repeated within minutes may cause disproportionately greater interference effects for patients with MCI, which may provide similar diagnostic specificity.

A further longitudinal study by our group compared this computerized cognitive test to a battery of conventional paper-and-pencil tests. This study was conducted in 15 MCI patients and 35 healthy matched control participants. All participants were assessed on eight occasions over a 12-month period. The data analytic procedure reported in Collie et al. (2001) was replicated with the computerized tests in this study. That is, linear regression equations were plotted against each individual participant's serial performance on the AL task, and the slope and intercept of those regression equations calculated. A between-group analysis was conducted to compare the mean slopes of the MCI and control groups (Figure 5.5).

Data demonstrated that the memory task performance of the MCI group deteriorated over a 12-month period, compared to that of the control group whose performance remained stable or improved slightly. These results indicate that subtle decline in memory function does occur in individuals classified as having early MCI, and that this can be detected using a brief computerized memory task. This accords well with previous data that identified a significant decline in word list delayed recall test performance in a group of neurologically normal individuals from the same aging study before

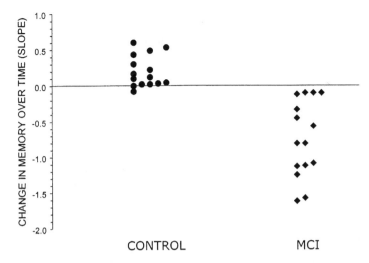

Figure 5.5 Scatterplot of slopes (change in memory accuracy per month) from the linear relationships fitted to the score on the computerized associate learning task and time for the MCI group and controls. Note a negative slope = memory decline.

they met any clinical criteria for MCI. We believe that both sets of results underscore the importance of considering objective decline in cognitive performance as a marker for the preclinical or prodromal phases of neurodegenerative diseases such as AD.

Summary

The Melbourne Aging Study was designed to address specific hypotheses regarding the validity of serial assessment of cognition for the early detection of cognitive decline in older people. Unlike other cohort studies where very large groups of individuals are assessed at intervals of 1–5 years, we undertook more regular, intensive assessments of a smaller cohort. This unique study design has provided some unique insights about the potential and limits of serial assessment models. Our studies have suggested that many criteria for MCI are inappropriate for the detection of memory/cognitive decline associated with neurodegenerative disease. Further, we have demonstrated that criteria for MCI are unreliable when applied to the same cohort on more than one occasion. Our early studies with conventional paper-and-pencil neuropsychological tests led us to the conclusion that many such tests were inappropriate for serial administration, due to the presence of practice effects, limited alternate forms, and other confounding factors. This led us to develop a series of "cognitive screening" tests with very different psychometric properties. Early results from these further studies are encouraging, suggesting that older people with

MCI may be identified with very rapid serial assessment. Work continues with the Melbourne Aging Study, and our research team is now embarking on other studies into age-related cognitive and neurological illnesses.

References

Almkvist, O., Basun, H., Backman, L., Herlitz, A., Lannfelt, L., Small, B., et al. (1998). Mild cognitive impairment: An early stage of Alzheimer's disease? *Journal of Neural Transmission, Suppl., 54*, 21–29.

American Psychiatric Association. (1994). *Diagnostic and Statistical Manual of mental disorders—Fourth Edition (DSM-IV)*. Washington, DC: American Psychiatric Association.

Benedict, R., & Zgaljardic, D. J. (1998). Practice effects during repeated administrations of memory test with and without alternate forms. *Journal of Clinical and Experimental Neuropsychology, 20*, 339–352.

Berent, S., Giordani, B., Foster, N., Minoshima, S., Lajiness-O'Neill, R., Koeppe, R., et al. (1999). Neuropsychological function and cerebral glucose utilization in isolated memory impairment and Alzheimer's disease. *Journal of Psychiatric Research, 33*, 7–16.

Blackford, R., & La Rue, A. (1989). Criteria for diagnosing age-associated memory impairment: Proposed improvements from the field. *Developmental Neuropsychology, 5*, 295–306.

Blesa, R., Adroer, R., Santacruz, P., Ascaso, C., Tolosa, E., & Oliva, R. (1996). High apolipoprotein e epsilon 4 allele frequency in age-related memory decline. *Annals of Neurology, 39*, 548–551.

Bowen, J., Teri, L., Kukull, W., McCormick, W., McCurry, S. M., & Larson, E. B. (1997). Progression to dementia in patients with isolated memory loss. *The Lancet, 349*, 763–765.

Collie, A., & Maruff, P. (2000). The neuropsychology of preclinical Alzheimer's disease and mild cognitive impairment. *Neuroscience and Biobehavioural Reviews, 24*(3), 365–374.

Collie, A., & Maruff, P. (2002a). An analysis of systems of classifying mild cognitive impairment in older people. *Australian and New Zealand Journal of Psychiatry, 36*(1), 133–140.

Collie, A., & Maruff, P. (2002b). Memory decline in healthy elderly people. In Vellas B, Grundman, M., Feldman, H., Fitten, L.J., Wingblad, B., & Giacobini, E. (Eds). *Research and practice in Alzheimer's disease and cognitive decline*. (Vol. 6, pp. 22–26). New York: Springer Publishing Company.

Collie, A., Maruff, P., & Currie, J. (2002a). Behavioural characterization of mild cognitive impairment. *Journal of Clinical and Experimental Neuropsychology, 24*(6), 720–733.

Collie, A., Maruff, P., Darby, D. G., & McStephen, M. (2003). The effects of practice on the cognitive test performance of neurologically normal individuals assessed at brief test-retest intervals. *Journal of the International Neuropsychological Society, 9*(3), 419–428.

Collie, A., Maruff, P., Falleti, M., Silbert, B., & Darby, D. G. (2002b). Determining the extent of cognitive change following coronary artery bypass grafting: A review of statistical procedures. *Annals of Thoracic Surgery, 73*, 2005–2011.

Collie, A., Maruff, P., Shafiq-Antonacci, R., Smith, M., Hallup, M., Schofield, P., et al. (2001). Memory decline in healthy older people: Implications for identifying mild cognitive impairment. *Neurology, 54*, 1353–1358.

Collie, A., Myers, C. E., Schnirman, G., Wood, S., & Maruff, P. (2002c). Selectively impaired associative learning in older people with cognitive decline. *Journal of Cognitive Neuroscience, 14*(3), 484–492.

Collie, A., Shafiq-Antonacci, R., Maruff, P., Tyler, P., & Currie, J. (1999). Norms and the effects of demographic variables on a neuropsychological test battery for use in healthy aging Australian populations. *Australian and New Zealand Journal of Psychiatry, 33*, 568–575.

Crook, T. H. (1993). Diagnosis and treatment of memory loss in older patients who are not demented. In R. Levy, R. Howard, & A. Burns (Eds.), *Treatment and care in old age psychiatry* (pp. 95–111). London: Wrightson Biomedical.

Crook, T., Bartus, R. T., Ferris, S. H., Whitehouse, P., Cohen, G. D., & Gershon, S. (1986). Age-associated memory impairment: Proposed diagnostic criteria and measures of clinical change – Report of a National Institute of Mental Health Work Group. *Developmental Neuropsychology, 2*, 261–276.

Darby, D., Maruff, P., & Collie, A. (2004). Mild cognitive impairments can be identified by multiple assessments in a single day. In B. Vellas, M. Grundman, H. Feldman, L. J. Fitten, B. Wingblad, & E. Giacobini (Eds.), *Research and practice in Alzheimer's disease* (Vol. 8). New York: Springer Publishing Company.

Darby, D. G., Maruff, P., Collie, A., & McStephen, M. (2002). Detection of mild cognitive impairment by multiple assessments in a single day. *Neurology, 59*, 1042–1046.

Elias, M. F., Beiser, A., Wolf, P., Au, R., White, R. F., & D'Agostino, R. B. (2000). The preclinical phase of Alzheimer's disease: A 22-year prospective study of the Framingham cohort. *Archives of Neurology, 57*, 808–813.

Folstein, M. F., Folstein, S. E., & McHugh, P. R. (1975). Mini-mental state: A practical method for grading the cognitive status of patients for the clinician. *Journal of Psychiatric Research, 12*, 189–198.

Gurland, B. J., Copeland, J. R., & Kuriansky, J. (1982). *The mind and mood of ageing. Mental health problems of community elderly in New York and London.* Beckenham: Croom Helm.

Hanninen, T., Hallikainen, M., Koivisto, K., Helkala, E. L., Reinikainen, K. J., Soininen, H., et al. (1995). A follow-up study of age-associated memory impairment: Neuropsychological predictors of dementia. *Journal of the American Geriatrics Society, 43*, 1007–1015.

Henke, K., Weber, B., Kneifel, S., Wieser, H. G., & Buck, A. (1999). Human hippocampus associates information in memory. *Proceedings of the National Academy of Science of the United States of America, 96*, 5884–5889.

Horton, A. M. Jr. (1992). Neuropsychological practice effects X age: A brief note. *Perceptual and Motor Skills, 75*, 257–258.

Jack, C. R., Petersen, R. C., Xu, Y. C., O'Brien, P. C., Smith, G. E., Ivnik, R. J., et al. (1999). Prediction of AD with MRI-based hippocampal volume in mild cognitive impairment. *Neurology, 52*, 1397–1403.

Jacobs, D. M., Sano, M., Dooneief, G., Marder, K., Bell, K. L., & Stern, Y. (1995). Neuropsychological detection and characterization of preclinical Alzheimer's disease. *Neurology, 45*, 957–962.

Kaplan, E., Goodglass, H., & Weintraub, S. (1983). *Boston naming test* (2nd ed.). Philadelphia, PA: Lea & Febiger.

Katzman, R., Brown, T., Fuld, P., Peck, A., Schechter, R., & Schimmel, H. (1983). Validation of a short orientation-memory-concentration test of cognitive impairment. *American Journal of Psychiatry, 140,* 734–739.

Knight, R. T. (1996). Contribution of human hippocampal region to novelty detection. *Nature, 383,* 256–259.

Kral, V. A. (1962). Senescent forgetfulness, benign and malignant. *Journal of the Canadian Medical Association, 86,* 257–260.

Levy, R. (1994). Ageing-associated cognitive decline. *International Psychogeriatrics, 6,* 63–68.

Maguire, E. A., Burgess, N., & O'Keefe, J. (1999). Human spatial navigation; cognitive maps, sexual dimorphism and neural substrates. *Current Opinion in Neurobiology, 9,* 171–177.

Maruff, P., Collie, A., Darby, D., Weaver-Cargin, J., Masters, C., & Currie, J. (2004). Subtle memory decline over 12 months in mild cognitive impairment. *Dementia & Geriatric Cognitive Disorders, 18*(3), 342–348.

Masur, D. M., Sliwinski, M., Lipton, R. B., Blau, A. D., & Crystal, H. A. (1994). Neuropsychological prediction of dementia and the absence of dementia in healthy older persons. *Neurology, 44,* 1427–1432.

McCaffrey, R. J., Duff, K., & Westervelt, H. J. (2000). *Practitioner's guide to evaluating change with neuropsychological assessment instruments.* New York: Kluwer Academic/Plenum Publishers.

McCaffrey, R. J., Ortega, A., Orsillo, S. M., & Welles, A. (1992). Practice effects in repeated neuropsychological assessments. *Clinical Neuropsychologist, 6,* 32–42.

McKhann, G., Drachman, D., Folstein, M., Katzman, R., Price, D., & Stadlan, E. M. (1984). Clinical diagnosis of Alzheimer's disease: Report of the NINCDS-ADRDA work group under the auspices of Department of Human Services Task Force on Alzheimer's disease. *Neurology, 34,* 939–944.

Morris, J. C., Edland, S. D., Clark, C., Galasko, D., Koss, E., Mohs, R., et al. (1993). The consortium to establish a registry for Alzheimer's disease (CERAD). Part IV. Rates of cognitive change in the longitudinal assessment of probable Alzheimer's disease. *Neurology, 43,* 2457–2465.

Morris, J. C., Mohs, R. C., Rogers, H., Fillenbaum, G., & Heyman, A. (1988). Consortium to establish a registry for Alzheimer's disease (CERAD): Clinical and neuropsychological assessment of Alzheimer's disease. *Psychopharmacology Bulletin, 24,* 641–652.

Owen, A. M., Beksinska, M., James, M., Leigh, P. N., Summers, B. A., & Marsden, C. D. (1993). Visuospatial memory deficits at different stages of Parkinson's disease. *Neuropsychologia, 31,* 627–644.

Petersen, R. C., Smith, G. E., Waring, S. C., Ivnik, R. J., Tangalos, E. G., & Kokmen, E. (1999). Mild cognitive impairment: Clinical characterization and outcome. *Archives of Neurology, 56,* 303–308.

Price, J. L., & Morris, J. C. (1998). Tangles and plaques in nondemented aging and 'preclinical' Alzheimer's disease. *Annals of Neurology, 45,* 358–368.

Rapport, L. J., Brines, D. B., Axelrod, B. N., & Theisen, M. E. (1997). Full scale IQ as mediator of practice effects: The rich get richer. *The Clinical Neuropsychologist, 11,* 375–380.

Reed, T., Carmelli, D., Swan, G. E., Breitner, J. C., Welsh, K. A., Jarvik, G. P., et al. (1994). Lower cognitive performance in normal older adult male twins carrying the Apolipoprotein E e4 allele. *Archives of Neurology, 51,* 1189–1192.

Reinikainen, K. J., Koivisto, K., Mykkanen, L., Hanninen, T., Soininen, H., & Riekkinen, P. (1990). Age-associated memory impairment in aged population: An epidemiological study. *Neurology, 40*(Suppl. 1), 177.

Reisberg, B., Ferris, S. H., de Leon, M. J., & Crook, T. (1982). The global deterioration scale for assessment of primary degenerative dementia. *American Journal of Psychiatry, 139*, 1136–1139.

Roth, M., Tym, E., Mountjoy, C. Q., Huppert, F. A., Hendrie, H., Verma, S., & Goddard, R. (1986). CAMDEX: A standardized instrument for the diagnosis of mental disorders in the elderly with special reference to the early detection of dementia. *British Journal of Pyschiatry, 149*, 698–709.

Small, S. A., Perera, G. M., DeLaPaz, R., Mayeux, R., & Stern, Y. (1999). Differential regional dysfunction of the hippocampal formation among elderly with memory decline and Alzheimer's disease. *Annals of Neurology, 45*, 466–472.

Smith, G. E., Bohac, D. L., Waring, S. C., Kokmen, E., Tangalos, E. G., Ivnik, R. J., et al. (1998). Apolipoprotein E genotype influences cognitive 'phenotype' in patients with Alzheimer's disease but not in healthy control subjects. *Neurology, 50*, 355–362.

Smith, G. E., Ivnik, R. J., Petersen, R. C., Malec, J. F., Kokmen, E., & Tangalos, E. G. (1991). Age-associated memory impairment diagnosis: Problems of reliability and concerns for terminology. *Psychology and Aging, 6*, 551–558.

Snowdon, J., & Lane, F. (1994). A longitudinal study of age-associated memory impairment. *International Journal of Geriatric Psychiatry, 9*, 779–787.

Squire, L., & Zola-Morgan, S. M. (1991). The medial temporal lobe memory system. *Science, 253*, 1380–1386.

Stollery, B. T. (1996). The Automated Cognitive Test (ACT) system. *Neurotoxicology and Teratology, 18*, 493–497.

Wallenstein, G. V., Eichenbaum, H., & Hasselmo, M. E. (1998). The hippocampus as an associator of discontiguous events. *Trends in Neurosciences, 21*, 317–323.

Welsh, K., Butters, N., Mohs, R., Beekly, D., Edland, S., Fillenbaum, G., et al. (1994). The consortium to establish a registry for Alzheimer's disease (CERAD). Part V: A normative study of the neuropsychological battery. *Neurology, 44*, 609–614.

Weschler, D. (1987). *Weschler Memory Scale—Revised*. Sidcup, UK: The Psychological Corporation.

Part III

Specific Samples

6 Mild cognitive impairment in the Religious Orders Study

Robert S. Wilson, Neelum T. Aggarwal, and David A. Bennett

With the dramatic increase in longevity during the past century, the proportion of older persons in most industrialized populations has substantially increased. As a result of this demographic shift, chronic medical conditions of old age have become an increasing public health burden. Prominent among these conditions are Alzheimer's disease, stroke, and Parkinson's disease, which are common contributors to impaired cognitive and motor function in old age. Current research suggests that loss of cognitive and motor abilities in old age reflects the interaction of genetic and experiential risk factors with the accumulation of age-related neuropathology occurring within nervous systems whose structure and functional capabilities differ from person to person. Prevention of cognitive and motor decline in old age, therefore, is likely to require detailed information about risk factors, cognitive and motor abilities proximate to death, and postmortem data on neuropathologic lesions and neurobiologic structure and function. The Rush Religious Orders Study was designed to confront these issues. Participants are older persons who have agreed to detailed annual clinical evaluations and brain autopsy upon death. It has three broad aims: to identify risk factors for Alzheimer's disease and for decline in cognitive and motor function; to clarify the neurobiologic bases of cognitive and motor impairment; and to examine the neurobiologic mechanisms linking risk factors to clinical outcomes.

This chapter is divided into two sections. In the first section, we provide an overview of the design and operational components of the Religious Orders Study, an ongoing clinicopathologic investigation of risk factors for common chronic conditions of old age. In the second section, we describe the clinical classification of mild cognitive impairment in the Religious Orders Study, its clinical consequences, and its neurobiological basis.

Rush Religious Orders Study

Religious Orders Study participants are older Catholic nuns, priests, and brothers. Eligibility requires that the participant agrees to annual clinical evaluations and signs an Anatomical Gift Act donating his/her brain to Rush

Investigators at death. The study was approved by the Institutional Review Board of Rush University Medical Center.

The decision to study Catholic clergy members was based on several factors. First, given the church's history of charitable works, it was felt that clergy members might be more willing than lay persons to volunteer for a study from which they would be unlikely to derive personal benefit. Second, religious orders often form tight-knit communities, some of which include communal living, making it easier to maintain participation in follow-up and, because evaluations are conducted at the religious orders' facilities, reducing the operational costs of the project. Third, socioeconomic status and related lifestyle variables are relatively homogeneous during adulthood and old age in Catholic religious orders relative to the general population of older persons in the United States. An advantage of this homogeneity is that it reduces the potentially confounding effects of socioeconomic status in some analyses. On the other hand, the relatively restricted range of socioeconomic-related factors makes it difficult to study the effects of such variables in the Religious Orders Study.

Data collection for the Religious Orders Study began in January 1994 and is continuing. As of February 2005, 1009 persons had completed the baseline evaluation. They had a mean age of 75.6 (SD = 7.4), a mean of 18.1 years of education (SD = 3.3), a mean score of 28.1 (SD = 2.4) on the Mini-Mental State Examination (Folstein, Folstein, & McHugh, 1975), with 67.7% women and 89.1% White and non-Hispanic.

At baseline, each participant undergoes a uniform structured clinical evaluation that includes a medical history and assessment of selected risk factors, a complete neurological examination, as described in detail elsewhere (Wilson, Bienias, Evans, & Bennett, 2004), and cognitive function testing.

Cognition is assessed with a battery of 21 tests in an approximately 1-h session. The tests are used to inform the diagnoses of dementia and mild cognitive impairment, as outlined below. Because the tests are repeated annually, they are also used to assess change in cognitive function. One test, the Mini-Mental State Examination, assesses global cognition. There are seven measures of episodic memory: immediate and delayed recall of the East Boston Story (Albert, Smith, Scherr, Taylor, Evans, & Funkenstein, 1991; Wilson et al., 2002b) and Story A from the Wechsler Memory Scale-Revised (Wechsler, 1987) and Word List Memory, Word List Recall, and Word List Recognition (Morris et al., 1989). Semantic memory is assessed with a 20-item version of the Boston Naming Test (Kaplan, Goodglass, & Weintraub, 1983), category fluency (Morris et al., 1989; Wilson et al., 2002b), a 15-item version of the Extended Range Vocabulary Test (Ekstrom, French, Harman, & Kermen, 1976), a 20-item version of the National Adult Reading Test and subsequent modifications (Blair & Spreen, 1989; Grober & Sliwinski, 1991; Nelson, 1982), and Complex Ideational Material from the Boston Diagnostic Aphasia Examination (Goodglass & Kaplan, 1983). Four tests of working memory are administered: Digit Span Forward and Digit Span Backward from the Wechsler Memory Scale-Revised (Wechsler, 1987), a modified version

(Wilson et al., 2002b) of the Digit Ordering Test (Cooper & Sager, 1993), and Alpha Span (Craik, 1986). Perceptual speed is assessed with the oral version of the Symbol Digit Modalities Test (Smith, 1982) and Number Comparison (Ekstrom et al., 1976), and visuospatial ability is assessed with a 15-item version of Judgment of Line Orientation (Benton, Sivan, Hamsher, Varney, & Spreen, 1994) and a 17-item version of Standard Progressive Matrices (Raven, Court, & Raven, 1992).

The Mini-Mental State Examination is primarily used for descriptive purposes and scores on Complex Ideational Material are highly skewed. As a result, most analyses have been based on the remaining 19 tests. To reduce floor and ceiling artifacts and other forms of measurement error, composites of two or more individual tests have been used in analyses. To take advantage of all cognitive data, a composite measure of global cognition was constructed from all 19 tests. Based in part on a factor analysis of the 19 tests at baseline, composite measures of episodic memory (seven tests), semantic memory (four tests), working memory (four tests), perceptual speed (two tests), and visuospatial ability (two tests) were also formed. To compute the composite measures, scores on each component test are converted to z scores, using the baseline mean and SD for the entire Religious Orders Study cohort, and the z scores are averaged to yield the composite, with the composite treated as missing if less than half of the component tests have valid scores, as previously described (Wilson et al., 2002b).

The essential details of the baseline evaluation are repeated at annual intervals thereafter. These follow-up evaluations serve two purposes. First, they provide detailed clinical information proximate to death for clinicopathologic analyses. Second, they permit assessment of change in cognitive and motor function and of the incidence of Alzheimer's disease and other common conditions of old age. An important feature of the Religious Orders Study is that all persons collecting clinical data or making clinical decisions are blinded to previously collected clinical data. As a result, change in cognitive function is independent of incident Alzheimer's disease, and showing that a risk factor is associated with both outcomes suggests that its association with incident disease is unlikely to be due to diagnostic bias or imprecision (Wilson et al., 2002a, 2002c; Wilson, Evans, Bienias, Mendes de Leon, Schneider, & Bennett, 2003a; Wilson, Schneider, Bienias, Evans, & Bennett, 2003c).

Follow-up participation in the Religious Orders Study has been expressed as the proportion of those who survived the first follow-up evaluation completing at least one follow-up evaluation, and among those with follow-up data, as the proportion of evaluations completed in survivors. Both rates have exceeded 95% in all studies published to date.

The Religious Orders Study is designed to achieve a high autopsy rate and to minimize the postmortem interval. An eligibility criterion is that persons sign a Uniform Anatomical Gift Act form at the time of enrollment donating their brain to Rush investigators for studies of aging and Alzheimer's disease. Pathology groups in 11 cities outside of Chicago have been trained in the protocol for brain removal. The study coordinator is available 24 h a day with a beeper with a toll-free number and, on notification of a death, directs the activity of persons at the facility of the religious group, the funeral home, and the pathology group. Through September of 2002, brain autopsies had been performed on 202 participants out of 217 deaths (92.3%), with a mean of less than 8 months between death and the last clinical evaluation and a mean postmortem interval of less than 8 h.

After the brain is removed and weighed, it is cut into 1-cm-thick coronal slabs. Slabs from one hemisphere are initially fixed in 4% paraformaldehyde before being placed in 2% dimethylsulfoxide/10% glycerol in phosphate buffered saline for long-term storage except for tissue from six regions that are cut into 0.5-mm-thick blocks and embedded in paraffin. Slabs from the other hemisphere are stored in a −80 °C freezer. A structured neuropathological examination is performed on each case by a person blinded to all clinical data, focusing on lesions with the potential to impair cognition (e.g., neurofibrillary tangles, cerebral infarction).

Mild cognitive impairment in the Religious Orders Study

Clinical classification of mild cognitive impairment

Clinical classification of mild cognitive impairment and dementia in the Religious Orders Study is accomplished in three steps (Bennett et al., 2002). First, the battery of cognitive performance tests is administered. Second, a board-certified neuropsychologist, blinded to all clinical information other than the participant's education, occupation, sensory or motor deficits, and level of effort on the tests, reviews the test results and renders a clinical judgment regarding the presence of impairment in five cognitive functions (i.e., orientation, attention, memory, language, and visuospatial ability). To date, these judgments have been rendered by a single neuropsychologist (RSW). To inform these judgments and maximize their consistency, the neuropsychologist is provided with educationally adjusted cutoff scores for determining impairment on 11 of the tests (Bennett et al., 2002). These cutoff scores were developed from a review of published research and extensive pilot testing in the Religious Orders Study and in a geographically defined population of older people in a biracial community in Chicago (Bienias, Beckett, Bennett, Wilson, & Evans, 2004). They are intended to guide clinical thinking, but the final decision about cognitive impairment is a clinical judgment. Third, based on an examination of the participant and review of all available data, including the neuropsychologist's judgments, an experienced clinician classifies each person with respect to dementia. Classification of dementia is based on the criteria of the joint working group of the National Institute of Neurological and Communicative Disorders and Stroke and the Alzheimer's Disease and Related Disorders Association (McKhann, Drachman, Folstein, Katzman, Price, & Stadlan, 1984). These criteria require a history of cognitive decline and evidence of impairment in at least two cognitive domains, one of which must be memory if the dementia is to meet criteria for Alzheimer's disease, as previously described (Bennett et al., 2002; Wilson et al., 2003c, 2004).

There is no secure agreement on how best to diagnose mild cognitive impairment. In the Religious Orders Study, classification of mild cognitive impairment is based on two criteria: presence of cognitive impairment as determined by the neuropsychologist's judgment and absence of dementia as determined by the clinician's judgment, as previously reported (Aggarwal, Wilson, & Beck, 2005a; Aggarwal, Wilson, Beck, Bienias, Berry-Kravis, & Bennett, 2005b; Bennett et al., 2002; Wilson et al., 2004). These criteria, which most closely resemble the syndrome of cognitive impairment–no dementia (Elby, Hogan, & Parhad, 1995; Tuokko & Frerichs, 2000), have three important features. First, they require evidence of cognitive impairment on performance testing so that people with reported cognitive impairment or with impairment in activities of daily living but not in cognition are not included. Second, the criteria permit all older persons to be classified as having one and only one of three conditions: dementia, mild cognitive impairment, or no cognitive impairment. Third, the criteria do not assume that some subtypes of cognitive impairment are more important than others. This definition of mild cognitive impairment does allow description of subtypes such as those with versus without memory impairment.

Consequences of mild cognitive impairment

Of 872 persons who had enrolled in the Religious Orders Study through November of 2000, 211 (24.2%) met criteria for mild cognitive impairment, 74 (8.5%) met criteria for dementia, and 587 (67.3%) had no cognitive impairment (Bennett et al., 2002). Compared to those without cognitive impairment, persons with mild cognitive impairment were older and had slightly lower scores on the Mini-Mental State Examination (27.4 [$SD = 2.0$] vs. 28.8 [$SD = 1.4$]).

During a mean of 4.5 years of follow-up, about 30% (63/211) of those with mild cognitive impairment died compared to about 13% (75/587) of those without cognitive impairment (Bennett et al., 2002). In a Cox proportional hazards model that controlled for age, sex, and education, risk of death was about 75% higher in persons with mild cognitive impairment compared to those without cognitive impairment, consistent with other research on mild cognitive impairment (Frisoni, Fratiglioni, Fastbom, Viitanene, & Winblad, 1999; Gussekloo, Westendorp, Remarque, Lagaay, Heeren, & Knook, 1997).

Of the 798 people without dementia at baseline, 22 died before the first follow-up and 54 had yet to reach the date of the first follow-up evaluation. Of the remaining 722 people, follow-up data were available on 708 (98.1%), 188 with mild cognitive impairment and 520 without it. During 4.5 years of follow-up, about 34% (64/188) of those with mild cognitive impairment developed

Alzheimer's disease compared to about 10% (51/520) of persons with no cognitive impairment. In a proportional hazards model adjusted for age, sex, and education, risk of incidence Alzheimer's disease was increased more than threefold in those with mild cognitive impairment relative to those without it (Bennett et al., 2002).

The increased risk of dementia associated with mild cognitive impairment might be due entirely to having an initially lower level of cognition than those without cognitive impairment. Alternatively, those with mild cognitive impairment might also be experiencing more rapid cognitive decline than those without cognitive impairment. To examine this issue, we constructed a mixed-effects model with a term for time (in years since baseline), an indicator for no (reference group) versus mild cognitive impairment at baseline, and the interaction of time with the indicator. The model also included terms to control for the potentially confounding effects of age, sex, and education. In this analysis, those without baseline cognitive impairment declined a mean of 0.03 unit per year on the measure of global cognition. The global cognitive score was 0.46 unit lower at baseline in those with mild cognitive impairment compared to those without cognitive impairment. In addition, those with mild cognitive impairment declined an additional 0.04 unit per year in global cognition compared to those without cognitive impairment, an increase of approximately 133% (Bennett et al., 2002). The results suggest that persons with mild cognitive impairment not only have a lower level of cognition than persons without cognitive impairment, but they also experience more rapid cognitive decline.

Cognition is not a unitary construct but rather is composed of multiple systems, and in mild cognitive impairment, some systems appear to be affected more than others (Bennett et al., 2002). Thus, rates of episodic memory and semantic memory decline in mild cognitive impairment were more than double the rates in those without cognitive impairment; decline in perceptual speed was increased by about 40%, whereas rates of decline in working memory and visuospatial ability were not associated with mild cognitive impairment. Further research is needed to establish the generalizability and possible bases of these selective effects.

Although risk of dementia is increased in those with mild cognitive impairment relative to those without cognitive impairment, a substantial proportion of those with mild cognitive impairment do not subsequently develop dementia. Two recent sets of analyses of Religious Orders Study data examined factors contributing to individual differences in risk. One study examined apolipoprotein E genotype (Aggarwal et al., 2005b). The apolipoprotein E is a plasma protein involved in cholesterol transport. It is coded by a gene on chromosome 19 that has three alleles: $\varepsilon 2$, $\varepsilon 3$, and $\varepsilon 4$. Possession of one or more copies of the $\varepsilon 4$ allele has been shown to increase risk of Alzheimer's disease (Corder et al., 1993; Saunders et al., 1993). Studies of the relation of the $\varepsilon 4$ allele to risk of dementia or Alzheimer's disease among persons with mild cognitive impairment have been mixed, however, with some studies (Coria, Rubio,

6. Mild cognitive impairment in the Religious Orders Study 123

Bayon, Santaengracia, & Rodriquez-Artalejo, 1995; Petersen et al., 1995; Tierney et al., 1996) but not others (Jack et al., 1999; Johnson et al., 1998; Visser, Verhey, Ponds, Cruts, Van Broekhoven, & Joles, 2000) suggesting an association. In analyses of 181 Religious Orders Study participants, with mild cognitive impairment, 56 (30.9%) had at least one copy of the ε4 allele. Those with an ε4 allele were 93% more likely to develop Alzheimer's disease than those without an ε4 allele in a proportional hazards model that controlled for age, sex, and education (Aggarwal et al., 2005b).

Persons with mild cognitive impairment differ in the nature and severity of their impairment in cognition, but the association of these factors with subsequent risk of disease has been difficult to establish. A particular problem in this research is that in Cox proportional hazards models, a common choice for such analyses, the nonproportionality of hazard functions cannot be safely assumed. That is, it is likely that the ability of a cognitive test score to predict development of dementia changes with the passage of time. Therefore, we used accelerated failure-time models (Allison, 1995; Carroll, 2003) that permit estimation of relative risk ratios even when the proportional hazards assumption is not tenable.

In 218 Religious Orders Study participants with mild cognitive impairment, 82 (37.6%) developed Alzheimer's disease during a mean of 5.1 years of follow-up. Three persons who developed other forms of dementia were excluded from further analyses. In a series of accelerated failure-time models that controlled for age, sex, and education, risk of developing dementia was inversely related to baseline levels of episodic memory, semantic memory, working memory, and perceptual speed but not visuospatial ability. When those with mild cognitive impairment were divided into subgroups with ($n = 126$) versus without ($n = 116$) impaired episodic memory, there was an approximately 2.5-fold increase in risk of dementia-associated impairment in episodic memory compared to impairment in other cognitive domains (Aggarwal et al., 2005a). In addition, those with episodic memory impairment experienced more rapid decline in semantic memory and visuospatial ability but not in other cognitive domains compared to persons with impairment in domains other than episodic memory.

To examine how the relation of cognitive impairment to risk of Alzheimer's disease changed with time, we divided the 82 incident cases into five subgroups: 26 who were diagnosed at the first year follow-up evaluation, 15 at year 2, 16 at year 3, 13 at years 4 and 5 combined, and 12 diagnosed at year 6 or later. We then constructed separate series of logistic regression models to assess how baseline level of function in each domain predicted disease incidence at each follow-up point (Aggarwal et al., 2005a). In these analyses, low episodic memory was associated with increased risk of AD at the first and second year follow-up points and after 6 or more years of follow-up, with similar trends at the two intermediate follow-up points. Lower semantic memory, working memory, and perceptual speed were each associated with increased risk at the first year follow-up evaluation but rarely thereafter, and visuospatial ability was not related to risk at any follow-up point. Together, these analyses suggest that episodic memory impairment is associated with a substantial and persistent increase in risk of developing Alzheimer's disease compared to impairment in other cognitive systems.

Neuropathological basis of mild cognitive impairment

Over 90% of Religious Orders Study participants who died had undergone a brain autopsy, as described elsewhere (Bennett et al., 2002; Bennett, Schneider, Bienias, Evans, & Wilson, 2005; Wilson et al., 2003a; Wilson, Schneider, Bienias, Arnold, Evans, & Bennett, 2003b). The high autopsy rate and the availability of comparable and clinically well-characterized persons with and without mild cognitive impairment make the Religious Orders Study an excellent setting within which to investigate the neurobiological basis of mild cognitive impairment.

One study focused on 180 participants who died and underwent brain autopsy, of whom 37 had mild cognitive impairment proximate to death, 60 did not have cognitive impairment, and 83 had dementia (Bennett et al., 2005). Those with mild cognitive impairment had an intermediate level of AD pathology, expressed either as composite measures of cortical plaques and tangles or as the proportion meeting various pathologic dementia criteria (i.e., Braak stage (Braak & Braak, 1991), CERAD (Mirra, Heyman, McKeel, Sumi, Crain, Brownlee et al., 1991), or NIA-Reagan (Consensus recommendations for the postmortem Diagnosis of Alzheimer's disease, 1997)), in comparison to those with dementia and those without cognitive impairment. In addition, the correlation between AD pathology and cognition was similar in the subgroups with dementia, mild cognitive impairment, and no cognitive impairment.

Persons with mild cognitive impairment also had an intermediate level of cerebral infarctions relative to those with dementia and those with no cognitive impairment (Bennett et al., 2005). Intermediate levels of myelin basic protein in the subfrontal white matter have also been reported in mild cognitive impairment, consistent with subcortical white matter changes (Wang, Bennett, Mufson, Cochran, & Dickson, 2004a).

About 15% met criteria for Lewy body disease that was slightly more common among those with dementia in comparison to the other two subgroups, but the infrequency of the condition precluded analyses. Similar results were found in a small study that examined soluble alpha synuclein in the frontal cortex (Wang, Bennett, Mufson, Cochran, & Dickson, 2004b).

Another study (Mufson, Chen, & Cochran, 1999) found the level of beta-amyloid in the entorhinal cortex of persons with mild cognitive impairment to be intermediate to levels in persons with clinical Alzheimer's disease and those without cognitive impairment. In addition, neuronal loss in the entorhinal cortex in mild cognitive impairment resembled that seen in dementia and exceeded that seen in those without cognitive impairment (Kordower et al., 2001). Tau changes in the medial temporal lobe have also been examined using antibodies to paired helical filaments or other tau epitopes (Ghoshal, García-Sierra, Wuu, Leurgans, Bennett, Berry et al., 2002; Mitchell et al., 2002). In these studies, the density of tau-positive neurofibrillary tangles in mild cognitive impairment was intermediate to the other two subgroups or resembled findings in those with clinical Alzheimer's disease, whereas tau-positive neuropil threads did not differentiate the subgroups. Overall, these data suggest that mild cognitive impairment represents an early manifestation of the leading causes of dementia, Alzheimer's disease pathology, and cerebral infarction.

The cholinergic system is known to be compromised in Alzheimer's disease and has long been a target of pharmacological attempts to treat the disease. The viability of cholinergic neurons in the basal forebrain depends in part on nerve growth factor that is regulated by high-affinity (TrkA) and low-affinity (P75NTR) receptors. Mild cognitive impairment is characterized by loss of TrkA and P75NTR immunoreactive neurons (Mufson et al., 2000, 2002) and downregulation of TrkA mRNA (Chu, Cochran, Bennett, Mufson, & Kordower, 2001) in the nucleus basalis. By contrast, choline acetyltransferase activity appears to be unaffected in mild cognitive impairment (DeKosky et al., 2002; Ikonomovic, Mufson, Wuu, Cochran, Bennett, & DeKosky, 2003), suggesting that the synthesis of this enzyme may be upregulated as the number of cholinergic neurons in the basal forebrain decreases. Thus, changes in the cholinergic system in mild cognitive impairment are complex and in need of further study.

Oxidative stress is another characteristic finding in the brain of persons with Alzheimer's disease. To examine the role of oxidative stress in mild cognitive impairment, the percentage of astrocytes expressing heme oxygenase-1 was quantified in the hippocampus and temporal neocortex (Schipper, Bennett, Lieberman, Bienias, Schneider, Kelly et al., 2006). Astroglial heme oxygenase-1 expression was markedly elevated in mild cognitive impairment and similar to the Alzheimer's disease group, both of which differed from those without cognitive impairment. Astroglial heme oxygenase-1 immunoreactivity in the temporal cortex, but not hippocampus, correlated with the burden of neurofibrillary pathology. These data suggest that oxidative stress may be a very early event in the pathogenesis of Alzheimer's disease.

Conclusions

A wide spectrum of cognitive function is seen in older persons in the Religious Orders Study ranging from no cognitive impairment to frank dementia. Persons in the Religious Orders Study who show some cognitive impairment on neuropsychological examination but do not meet criteria for dementia are designated as having mild cognitive impairment. Although the syndrome of mild cognitive impairment is heterogeneous, it includes a substantial proportion of individuals undergoing a transition from normal cognition to manifest dementia. Thus, as a group, persons with mild cognitive impairment are intermediate between those without cognitive impairment and those with dementia, not only in risk of death and rate of cognitive decline but also in level of Alzheimer's disease pathology and cerebral infarction. The relation of markers of the cholinergic system and oxidative stress to mild cognitive impairment appears to be complex. Further, the transition from mild cognitive impairment is associated with possession of an apolipoprotein E ε4 allele, a well-established risk factor for Alzheimer's disease, and with episodic memory impairment, a defining characteristic of Alzheimer's disease. Together, these observations suggest that the syndrome of mild cognitive impairment, despite its heterogeneity, can be thought of as a prodromal stage that usually precedes late life dementia. As such, it represents a suitable target for therapies designed to prevent or delay loss of cognition in old age.

Acknowledgments

The authors thank the hundreds of nuns, priests, and brothers from the following groups participating in the Religious Orders Study: Archdiocesan priests, Chicago, IL, Dubuque, IA, and Milwaukee, WI; Benedictine monks, Lisle, IL, and Collegeville, MN; Benedictine Sisters, Erie, PA; Benedictine Sisters of the Sacred Heart, Lisle, IL; Capuchins, Appleton, WI; Christian Brothers, Chicago, IL, and Memphis, TN; Diocesan priests, Gary, IN; Dominicans, River Forest, IL; Felician Sisters, Chicago, IL; Franciscan Handmaids of Mary, New York, NY; Franciscans, Chicago, IL; Holy Spirit Missionary Sisters, Techny, IL; Maryknolls, Los Altos, CA, and Maryknolls, NY; Norbertines, De Pere, WI; Oblate Sisters of Providence, Baltimore, MD; Passionists, Chicago, IL; Presentation Sisters, BVM, Dubuque, IA; Servites, Chicago, IL; Sinisinawa Dominican Sisters, Chicago, IL, and Sinsinawa, WI; Sisters of Charity, BVM, Chicago, IL, and Dubuque, IA; Sisters of the Holy Family, New Orleans, LA; Sisters of the Holy Family of Nazareth, Des Plaines, IL; Sisters of Mercy of the Americans, Chicago, IL, Aurora, IL, and Erie, PA; Sisters of St. Benedict, St. Cloud, MN and St. Joseph, MN; Sisters of St. Casimir, Chicago, IL; Sisters of St. Francis of Mary Immaculate, Joliet, IL; Sisters of St. Joseph of LaGrange, LaGrange Park, IL; Society of Divine Word, Techny, IL; Trappists, Gethsemane, KY, and Peosta, IA; and Wheaten Franciscan Sisters, Wheaton, IL. They also thank Julie Bach, MSW, Tracy Colvin, MPH, and George Hoganson for coordinating the Religious Orders Study; George Dombrowski, MS and Greg Klein for data management; Todd Beck, MS for analytic programming; and Sherry Carroll for preparing the manuscript. This work was supported by National Institute on Aging grants RO1 AG15819 and P30 AG10161.

References

Aggarwal, N. T., Wilson, R. S., & Beck, T. L. (2005a). Mild cognitive impairment in different functional domains and incident Alzheimer's disease. *Journal of Neurology, Neurosurgery and Psychiatry, 76*, 1479–1484.

Aggarwal, N. T., Wilson, R. S., Beck, T. L., Bienias, J. L., Berry-Kravis, E., & Bennett, D. A. (2005b). The apolipoprotein E ε4 allele and incident Alzheimer's disease in persons with mild cognitive impairment. *Neurocase, 11,* 3–7.

Albert, M., Smith, L., Scherr, P., Taylor, J., Evans, D., & Funkenstein, H. (1991). Use of brief cognitive tests to identify individuals in the community with clinically diagnosed Alzheimer's disease. *International Journal of Neuroscience, 57,* 167–178.

Allison, P. D. (1995). *Survival analysis using the SAS® system: A practical guide.* Cary, NC: SAS Institute Inc.

Bennett, D. A., Schneider, J. A., Bienias, J. L., Evans, D. A., & Wilson, R. S. (2005). Mild cognitive impairment is related to Alzheimer disease pathology and cerebral infarctions. *Neurology, 64,* 834–842.

Bennett, D. A., Wilson, R. S., Schneider, J. A., Evans, D. A., Beckett, L. A., Aggarwal, N. T. et al. (2002). Natural history of mild cognitive impairment in older persons. *Neurology, 59,* 198–205.

Benton, A. L., Sivan, A. B., Hamsher, K. DeS., Varney, N. R., & Spreen, O. (1994). *Contributions to neuropsychological assessment* (2nd ed.). New York: Oxford University Press.

Bienias, J. L., Beckett, L. A., Bennett, D. A., Wilson, R. S., & Evans, D. A. (2004). Design of the Chicago Health and Aging Project. *Journal of Alzheimer's Disease, 5,* 349–355.

Blair, J. R., & Spreen, O. (1989). Predicting premorbid IQ: A revision of the National Religious Orders Study Adult Reading Test. *The Clinical Neuropsychologist, 3,* 129–136.

Braak, H., & Braak, E. (1991). Neuropathological staging of Alzheimer-related changes. *Acta Neuropathologica (Berlin), 82,* 239–259.

Carroll, K. J. (2003). On the use and utility of the Weibull model in the analysis of survival data. *Controlled Clinical Trials, 24,* 682–701.

Chu, Y., Cochran, E. J., Bennett, D. A., Mufson, E. J., & Kordower, J. H. (2001). Down-regulation of trkA mRNA within nucleus basalis neurons in individuals with mild cognitive impairment and Alzheimer's disease. *Journal of Comparative Neurology, 437,* 296–307.

Consensus recommendations for the postmortem diagnosis of Alzheimer's disease. (1997). The National Institute on Aging and Reagan Institute Working Group on Diagnostic Criteria for the Neuropathological Assessment of Alzheimer's Disease. *Neurobiology of Aging, 18*(Suppl. 4), 51–52.

Cooper, J. A., & Sager, H. J. (1993). Incidental and intentional recall in Parkinson's disease: An account based on diminished attentional resources. *Journal of Clinical and Experimental Neuropsychology, 15,* 713–731.

Corder, E. H., Saunders, A. M., Strittmatter, W. J., Schmechel, D. E., Gaskell, P. C., Small, G. W., et al. (1993). Gene dose of apolipoprotein E type 4 allele and the risk of Alzheimer's disease in late onset families. *Science, 261,* 921–923.

Coria, F., Rubio, I., Bayon, C., Santaengracia, N., & Rodriquez-Artalejo, F. (1995). Apolipoprotein E allele variants predict dementia in elderly people with memory impairment. *European Journal of Neurology, 2,* 191–193.

Craik, F. I. M. (1986). A functional account of age differences in memory. In E. Klix & H. Hagendorf (Eds.), *Human memory and cognitive capabilities: Mechanisms and performances* (pp. 409–422). Amsterdam: Elsevier Science.

DeKosky, S. T., Ikonomovic, M. D., Styren, S. D., Beckett, L. A., Wisniewski, S., Bennett, D. A., et al. (2002). Upregulation of choline acetyltransferase activity in

hippocampus and frontal cortex of elderly subjects with mild cognitive impairment. *Annals of Neurology, 51,* 145–155.
Ekstrom, R. B., French, J. W., Harman, H. H., & Kermen, D. (1976). *Manual for kit of factor-referenced cognitive tests.* Princeton, NJ: Educational Testing Service.
Elby, E. M., Hogan, D. B., & Parhad, I. M. (1995). Cognitive impairment in the nondemented elderly: Results from the Canadian Study of Health and Aging. *Archives of Neurology, 52,* 612–619.
Folstein, M., Folstein, S., & McHugh, P. (1975). Mental-mental state: A practical method for grading the mental state of patients for the clinician. *Journal of Psychiatric Research, 12,* 189–198.
Frisoni, G. B., Fratiglioni, L., Fastbom, J., Viitanene, M., & Winblad, B. (1999). Mortality in nondemented subjects with cognitive impairment: The influence of health-related factors. *American Journal of Epidemiology, 150,* 1031–1044.
Ghoshal, N., García-Sierra, F., Wuu, F. G. J., Leurgans, S., Bennett, D.A., Berry, R. W., et al. (2002). Tau conformational changes correspond to impairments of episodic memory in mild cognitive impairment and Goodglass Kaplan 1983 Alzheimer's disease. *Experimental Neurology, 177,* 475–493.
Goodglass, H., & Kaplan, E. (1983). *Boston Diagnostic Examination for Aphasia.* Philadelphia: Lea & Febiger.
Grober, E., & Sliwinski, M. (1991). Development and validation of a model for estimating premorbid verbal intelligence in the elderly. *Journal of Clinical and Experimental Neuropsychology, 13,* 933–949.
Gussekloo, J., Westendorp, R. G. J., Remarque, E. J., Lagaay, A. M., Heeren, T. J., & Knook, D. L. (1997). Impact of mild cognitive impairment on survival in very elderly people: Cohort study. *British Medical Journal, 315,* 1053–1054.
Ikonomovic, M. D., Mufson, E. J., Wuu, J., Cochran, E. J., Bennett, D. A., & DeKosky, S. T. (2003). Cholinergic plasticity in hippocampus of individuals with mild cognitive impairment: Correlation with Alzheimer's neuropathology. *Journal of Alzheimer's Disease, 5,* 39–48.
Jack, C. R., Petersen, R. C., Xu, Y. C., O'Brien, P. C., Smith, G. E., Ivnik, R. J., et al. (1999). Prediction of AD with MRI based hippocampal volume in mild cognitive impairment. *Neurology, 53,* 1397–1403.
Johnson, K. A., Jones, K., Holman, B. L., Becker, J. A., Spiers, P. A., Satlin, A., et al. (1998). Preclinical prediction of Alzheimer's disease using SPECT. *Neurology, 50,* 1563–1571.
Kaplan, E. F., Goodglass, H., & Weintraub, S. (1983). *The Boston Naming Test.* Philadelphia: Lea & Febiger.
Kordower, J. H., Chu, Y., Stebbins, G. T., DeKosky, S. T., Cochran, E. J., Bennett, D. A., et al. (2001). Loss and atrophy of layer II entorhinal cortex neurons in elderly people with mild cognitive impairment. *Annals of Neurology, 49,* 202–213.
McKhann, G., Drachman, D., Folstein, M., Katzman, R., Price, D., & Stadlan, E. (1984). Clinical diagnosis of Alzheimer's disease: Report of the NINCDS/ADRDA Work Group under the auspices of Department of Health and Human Services Task Force on Alzheimer's Disease. *Neurology, 34,* 939–944.
Mirra, S. S., Heyman, A., McKeel, D., Sumi, S. M., Crain, B. J., Brownlee, L. M., et al. (1991). The consortium to establish a registry for Alzheimer's disease (CERAD). Part II. Standardization of the neuropathologic assessment of Alzheimer's disease. *Neurology, 41,* 479–486.

Mitchell, T. W., Mufson, E. J., Schneider, J. A., Cochran, E. J., Nissanov, J., Han, L. Y., et al. (2002). Parahippocampal tau pathology in healthy aging, mild cognitive impairment, and early Alzheimer's disease. *Annals of Neurology, 51*, 182–189.

Morris, J., Heyman, A., Mohs, R., Hughes, J., van Belle, G., Fillenbaum, G., et al. (1989). The consortium to establish a registry for Alzheimer's disease (CERAD). Part I. Clinical and neuropsychological assessment of Alzheimer's disease. *Neurology, 39*, 1159–1165.

Mufson, E. J., Chen, E. Y., & Cochran, E. J. (1999). Entorhinal cortex β-amyloid load in individuals with mild cognitive impairment. *Experimental Neurology, 158*, 469–490.

Mufson, E. J., Ma, S. Y., Cochran, E. J., Bennett, D. A., Beckett, L. A., Jaffar, S., et al. (2000). Loss of nucleus basalis neurons containing trkA innumoreactivity in individuals with mild cognitive impairment and early Alzheimer's disease. *Journal of Comparative Neurology, 427*, 19–30.

Mufson, E. J., Ma, S. Y., Dills, J., Cochran, E. J., Leurgans, S., Wuu, J., et al. (2002). Loss of forebrain P75 (NTR) immunoreactivity in subjects with mild cognitive impairment and Alzheimer's disease. *Journal of Comparative Neurology, 443*, 136–153.

Nelson, H. E. (1982). *National Adult Reading Test (NARI): Test manual.* Windsor, England: NFER Nelson.

Petersen, R. C., Smith, G. E., Ivnik, R. J., Tangalos, E. G., Schaid, D. J., Thibodeau, S. N., et al. (1995). Apolipoprotein E status as a predictor of the development of Alzheimer's disease in memory impaired individuals. *Journal of American Medical Association, 273*, 1274–1278.

Raven, J. C., Court, J. H., & Raven, J. (1992). *Manual for Raven's progressive matrices and vocabulary: Standard Progressive Matrices.* Oxford: Oxford Psychologists Press.

Saunders, A. M., Strittmatter, W. J., Schmechel, D. E., George-Hyslop, P. H., Pericak-Vance, M. A., Joo, S. H., et al. (1993). Association of apolipoprotein E allele ε4 with late-onset familial and sporadic Alzheimer's disease. *Neurology, 43*, 1467–1472.

Schipper, H. M., Bennett, D. A., Lieberman, A., Bienias, J. L., Schneider, J. A., Kelly, J. F., et al. (2006). Glial heme oxygenase-1 expression in Alzheimer's disease and mild cognitive impairment. *Neurobiology of Aging, 27*, 252–261.

Smith, A. (1982). *Symbol Digit Modalities Test manual-revised.* Los Angeles: Western Psychological Services.

Tierney, M. C., Szalai, J. P., Snow, W. G., Fisher, R. H., Tsuda, T., Chi, H., et al. (1996). A prospective study of the clinical utility of ApoE genotype in the prediction of outcome in patients with memory impairment. *Neurology, 46*, 149–154.

Tuokko, H., & Frerichs, R. J. (2000). Cognitive impairment with no dementia (CIND): Longitudinal studies, the findings, and the issues. *The Clinical Neuropsychologist, 14*, 505–525.

Visser, P. J., Verhey, F. R., Ponds, R. W., Cruts, M., Van Broekhoven, C. L., & Joles, J. (2000). Course of objective memory impairment in non-demented subjects attending a memory clinic and predictors of outcome. *International Journal of Geriatric Psychiatry, 15*, 363–372.

Wang, D. S., Bennett, D. A., Mufson, E. J., Cochran, E. J., & Dickson, D. W. (2004a). Contribution of changes in ubiquitin and myelin basic protein to age-related cognitive decline. *Neuroscience Research, 48*, 93–100.

Wang, D. S., Bennett, D. A., Mufson, E. J., Cochran, E. J., & Dickson, D. W. (2004b). Soluble α-synuclein in frontal cortex correlates with cognitive decline in the elderly. *Neuroscience Letters, 359*, 104–108.

Wechsler, D. (1987). *Wechsler Memory Scale-Revised manual*. San Antonio, TX: Psychological Corporation.

Wilson, R. S., Barnes, L. L., Mendes de Leon, C. F., Aggarwal, N. T., Schneider, J. S., Bach, J., et al. (2002a). Depressive symptoms, cognitive decline, and risk of AD in older persons. *Neurology, 59*, 364–370.

Wilson, R. S., Beckett, L. A., Barnes, L. L., Schneider, J. A., Bach, J., Evans, D. A., et al. (2002b). Individual difference in rates of change in cognitive abilities of older persons. *Psychology and Aging, 17*, 179–193.

Wilson, R. S., Bienias, J. L., Evans, D. A., & Bennett, D. A. (2004). Religious Orders Study: Overview and change in cognitive and motor speed. *Aging Neuropsychology and Cognition, 11*, 280–303.

Wilson, R. S., Evans, D. A., Bienias, J. L., Mendes de Leon, C. F., Schneider, J. A., & Bennett, D. A. (2003a). Proneness to psychological distress is associated with risk of Alzheimer's disease. *Neurology, 61*, 1479–1485.

Wilson, R. S., Mendes de Leon, C. F., Barnes, L. L., Schneider, J. A., Bienias, J. L., Evans, D. A., et al. (2002c). Participation in cognitively stimulating activities and risk of incident Alzheimer's disease. *Journal of the American Medical Association, 287*, 742–748.

Wilson, R. S., Schneider, J. A., Bienias, J. L., Arnold, S. E., Evans, D. A., & Bennett, D. A. (2003b). Depressive symptoms, clinical AD, and cortical plaques and tangles in older persons. *Neurology, 61*, 1102–1107.

Wilson, R. S., Schneider, J. A., Bienias, J. L., Evans, D. A., & Bennett, D. A. (2003c). Parkinsonianlike signs and risk of incident Alzheimer's disease. *Archives of Neurology, 60*, 539–544.

7 A perspective from the Mayo Clinic

Glenn Smith, Mary Machulda, and Kejal Kantarci

Overview

Studies of the transition from normal aging to early dementia have been a primary focus of dementia research at the Mayo Clinic for over two decades. Our studies of mild cognitive impairment (MCI) have occurred in concert with our Mayo Older Americans Normative studies (MOANS). The bulk of the MOANS and MCI studies have been based on the Mayo Alzheimer's Disease Patient Registry (ADPR). In this chapter, we briefly review the history of the Mayo ADPR, including its methods. We will next review our criteria for MCI and the evolution of our conceptualization of this issue. We will then describe a series of studies of the correlates and outcomes of MCI as defined in this manner. Finally, we will discuss several considerations and concerns that have arisen from this body of work.

History of the Mayo Alzheimer's Disease Patient Registry

The Mayo ADPR was one of six ADPRs established in 1986 in response to a Research Fund Announcement (RFA) from the National Institute on Aging. The RFA requested development of registries to address epidemiologic issues of incidence, prevalence, and risk factors for dementias, especially Alzheimer's disease (AD) and to develop cohorts of prospectively studied subjects to refine diagnostic criteria for dementia and AD. Mayo's ADPR has been continuously funded since 1986. The Mayo ADPR initially responded to the RFA by (1) developing a set of population-based, retrospective studies using the Mayo Clinic medical records linkage system to address the epidemiologic questions and (2) developing prospective, longitudinally studied cohorts of cognitively impaired and normal subjects to refine diagnostic techniques and criteria for dementia and AD. The population studies based on medical records were a resource for incidence, prevalence, and risk factor studies, while the prospective cohort was subjected to intensive clinical study which gave rise to questions concerning patterns of normal aging versus the earliest signs of cognitive impairment. As such, the registry allowed the information gleaned from the retrospective studies to be applied to the study of aging, dementia, and AD in the prospective work. Mayo's studies of MCI have been conducted primarily with the participants of the prospective arm of the ADPR.

From the perspective of epidemiology, we believe our community-based studies reside somewhere between population-based and referral-based patient populations. These various data sources may complement each other (Kokmen, Ozsarfati, Beard, O'Brien, & Rocca, 1996). Community-based studies of aging and dementia provide important information on base rates of disease, risk factors, etiology, mechanisms, and clinical outcome, which supplement other research databases in an important fashion. And, in fact, having simultaneous population-based (ADPR records linkage), community-based (ADPR prospective), and referral-based (the Mayo Alzheimer's Disease Research Center P50 AG-16574) cohorts has enabled us to conduct methodological studies. For example, we used findings from the ADPR to compare sociodemographic and clinical characteristics in three groups of AD patients. The first group included ADPR incidence cases occurring among residents of Rochester, MN ($n = 241$). The second group was a sample of patients referred to the Mayo Clinic from the remainder of Minnesota and the four surrounding states ($n = 58$). The third was a sample referred from the remainder of the US ($n = 94$). Patients from Rochester were more frequently women, less highly educated, less commonly white collar workers, more frequently institutionalized, less frequently married, and more often lived alone than those in the two referral groups. Patients from Rochester also had a more advanced age of onset of dementia. For occupation, education, and living arrangement, the differences across groups increased with increasing distance of referral. We were thus able to assess the extent of selection bias from clinical and epidemiological studies based on patients referred from primary to secondary or tertiary care settings (Kokmen et al., 1996; Rocca & Kokmen, 1997).

Prospective cohorts

The history of the Mayo ADPR prospective cohort is divided into three epochs: (1) From 1986 to 1999 recruitment involved a case-control format. Each cognitively impaired subject was age- and gender-matched to a control subject. Approximately 50–60 pairs of subjects were recruited each year. (2) Beginning in 1999, a cohort of 500 unimpaired subjects aged 70–89 was recruited in an "unyoked" fashion vis-a-vis cases. This expansion allowed us to more extensively examine the boundary between normal aging and very early dementia. (3) In 2004, a new population-based prospective study was initiated to address the incidence of various forms of MCI. Data from this phase of the Mayo ADPR will not be available until sometime after 2008.

1986–1999: Case–control recruitment

CASE RECRUITMENT

Since 1986, the Mayo ADPR has collaborated with the Division of Community Internal Medicine of the Mayo Clinic, which is responsible for providing much of the primary care for the residents of Rochester, MN. This group of 30+ physicians knows its patient population very well and has been supportive of our research efforts. We enrolled our case and control subjects from persons obtaining their general medical care through the Division of Community Internal Medicine. Our staff reviewed the medical records of every person over the age of 65 years who obtained a general medical evaluation. If the record noted: (1) any type of cognitive impairment by the patient, (2) a question of cognitive change by a family or friend, or (3) a change in the patient's cognitive status noted by the examining physician, the patient became eligible for recruitment. At that point, the primary care physician was contacted for permission to contact the patient, and then our staff contacted the patient and family for permission to participate. Note that this mechanism permitted us to recruit participants who had just received a general medical evaluation by an internist.

CONTROL RECRUITMENT

For each cognitively impaired index case, we identified an age- and gender-matched control subject from the same population of older persons obtaining their primary care through the Mayo Division of Community Internal Medicine. Control status was operationalized as the next consenting age- and gender-appropriate individual who came for a periodic general medical evaluation, and did not trigger one of the criteria for referral as discussed below. These control subjects underwent virtually the same evaluation as the cases without some of the laboratory or imaging studies. Because we were using these participants to conduct our normative studies, we required the behavioral neurologist to certify that the subjects met normal criteria (as listed below) without the benefit of neuropsychological data. This avoided criteria contamination in the development of our norms. If the behavioral neurologist felt the person recruited actually had some cognitive compromise, this person was diverted to the case sample and a new control was recruited for the index case.

1999–2004: Enhancement of normal cohort

A major thrust of the ADPR in the 1994–2004 grant cycle was to recruit 500 new cognitively normal subjects aged 70–89 years. These 500 participants were recruited from the same community internal medicine sampling frame described for the controls above. This goal was accomplished by 2002. These participants were not "yoked" to cases but were recruited in an age-stratified way to observe the process of converting from normal to MCI. The majority of this cohort is being re-evaluated currently for any change in cognitive status. We are now analyzing data from this cohort in combination with control subjects from our previous grant cycles, whom we have continued to follow (Ferman, Ivnik, & Lucas, 1998; Ivnik, Malec, Smith, Tangalos, & Petersen, 1996). At present, we have over 1000 subjects in the database who were enrolled as normal and the majority have been seen for at least one follow-up. These subjects have been followed for a median of 4.5 years (range 1–15 years). Over 15+ year time frame, 75 had converted to either MCI or AD and 122 subjects had developed dementia.

2004 and beyond: Population-based sampling

In our latest grant cycle, we are recruiting a population-based, stratified, random sample of 2300 persons aged 70–90 years residing in Olmsted County, MN. We will study prevalence and incidence of MCI in this project. Data from this cohort will not be available until sometime after 2007.

Methods

Neurological exam

For all participants, across all grant cycles, a behavioral neurologist or geriatrician took a history and performed a neurologic exam, along with the Short Test of Mental Status (Kokmen, Smith, Petersen, Tangalos, & Ivnik, 1991), Hachinski Ischemic Scale (Hachinski et al., 1975), and the Unified Parkinson's Disease Rating Scale (Fahn, Elton, & Members of the UPDRS Development Committee, 1987). A study nurse completed a family history form (Lautenschlager et al., 1996; Rao et al., 1995), Record of Independent Living (Weintraub, 1986), and the Mini-Mental State Exam (Folstein, Folstein, & McHugh, 1975). Routine laboratory studies were performed, including a hematology group, chemistry group, chest x-ray, and electrocardiogram, which are done as part of the general medical examination. Additional studies included a vitamin B_{12} level, folic acid level, sensitive TSH determination, and a syphilis serology for research purposes. A head imaging study (CT/MRI) was done as part of the evaluation of the cognitive disorder. Additional MRIs were done for select subjects as part of other research protocols but that information was not used in the diagnostic decision-making process. Psychiatric consultations or other studies (e.g., cerebral spinal fluid analysis, electroencephalogram, single photon emission computer tomography scan, or other laboratory studies) were done on occasion as dictated by the clinical situation.

Neuropsychological testing

Extensive neuropsychological testing has been done for all participants. In the 1986–1998 period, we used some measures for diagnostic purposes and others for research purposes. The first set includes the Wechsler Adult Intelligence Scale-Revised (WAIS-R) (Wechsler, 1981), Wechsler Memory Scale-Revised (WMS-R) (Wechsler, 1987), Auditory Verbal Learning Test (AVLT) (Rey, 1964), and the reading subtest of the Wide-Range Achievement

Test-Revised (Jastak & Wilkinson, 1984). The second set for research purposes consists of the Dementia Rating Scale (Mattis, 1988), Free and Cued Selective Reminding Test (Buschke, 1984a, 1984b), Controlled Oral Word Association Test (COWAT) (Benton, Hamsher, Varney, & Spreen, 1983), Category Fluency (Monsch et al., 1994), and The Boston Naming Test (Kaplan, Goodglass, & Weintraub, 1983). In the 1999–2004 grant cycle, the WAIS-R and WMS-R were replaced with the WAIS-III and the WMS-III and the Rey Complex Figure was added. In this era, separate neurological and neuropsychological diagnoses were generated before a consensus diagnosis, including all information, was made. The neuropsychological diagnosis was based on all tests in the battery.

Consensus diagnosis

Following these evaluations a consensus committee including two neurologists, a geriatrician, two neuropsychologists, nurses, and psychometricians assembled to render the research diagnosis. In addition to a primary diagnosis, secondary and tertiary diagnoses and qualifying features of each diagnosis were assigned as appropriate. Qualifying features included family history, early onset, unusual behavioral features, mood features, etc. Following the diagnosis, level of severity was graded on the Clinical Dementia Rating Scale (Morris, 1993) and the Global Deterioration Scale (Reisberg, Ferris, deLeon, & Crook, 1982).

Longitudinal evaluation

Clinical re-evaluations were performed approximately annually. In the 1986–1998 era, there was a complete readministration of the neuropsychological battery as well as the Record of Independent Living (Weintraub, 1986), the Mini-Mental State Exam, and an update of the family history form (Lautenschlager et al., 1996; Rao et al., 1995). These evaluations were discussed at the consensus conference and changes in the diagnostic classifications and/or severity ratings were made by the committee. After 1998 those not cognitively impaired began receiving only an abbreviated neuropsychological follow-up (DRS and AVLT). If significant change was noted on these instruments, they were brought in for a full evaluation (identical to the initial evaluation).

Diagnostic criteria

Normal

Because we were engaged in normative neuropsychological studies early on, we felt it important to have formal criteria for normal status. These criteria were: (1) they have no cognitive complaints, (2) they have no active neurological or psychiatric disorder, and (3) they are not taking psychoactive medications considered to impair cognition. These individuals may have comorbid illnesses such as hypertension, diabetes mellitus, and coronary artery disease, but in the opinions of their treating physicians, these disorders or their therapies are not considered to be influencing the subject's cognitive function. As such, these individuals were "typical" normal subjects rather than optimally or supernormal subjects (Petersen, 1995).

Dementia

Diagnostic classifications were made according to the following criteria: dementia—Diagnostic and Statistical Manual of Mental Disorders III-R (American Psychiatric Association, 1987); AD—NINCDS/ADRDA criteria (McKhann, Drachman, Folstein, Katzman, Price, & Stadlan, 1984); vascular dementia—NINDS/AIREN criteria (Roman et al., 1993); mixed (degenerative and vascular)—NINCDS/ADRDA and NINDS/AIREN criteria; Lewy body dementia (McKeith et al., 1996); frontotemporal dementia—Lund Manchester criteria (The Lund and Manchester Groups, 1994).

Mild cognitive impairment

Our group has published our MCI criteria in several places. Three sets of published criteria are listed in Table 7.1. All were meant to describe the same population (see the section "Conceptual issues involving MCI"). Regrettably, subtle variations in our statements may have produced some confusion. The primary sources of confusion have involved how we defined cognitive complaint, whether we used a strict psychometric cutoff, and whether there was a biconditional relationship between CDR scores of 0.5 and MCI diagnoses.

To be clear, in all three publications we intended that "cognitive complaint" reflected a spontaneous concern about cognitive function on the part of either the patient, his or her informants, or his or her primary medical provider. Further, we intended -1.5 standard deviations (SD) on objective cognitive tests to reflect the typical performance for MCI patients, not a rigorous cutoff. We have always believed that cognitive impairment on objective measures was a determination requiring clinical judgment. So, for example, a high-functioning individual could meet our MCI criteria even if their score of memory testing fell within $1SD$ of the mean. In addition, a person with memory scores below $-1.5SD$ could be labeled as normal if judged to have always functioned at that level. And finally, it is our perspective that although all MCI patients, by definition, receive CDR scores of 0.5, not all persons who receive CDR scores of 0.5 necessarily meet MCI criteria. Use of clinical judgment raises concern about the reliability of diagnosis. In our setting this problem is mitigated a bit by use of a consensus conference. Moreover, use of clinical judgment is common in dementia studies where reliability concerns have been surmounted.

Table 7.1 Variation and evolution of "Mayo" criteria for mild cognitive impairment

	Petersen et al. (1992)	Smith et al. (1996)	Petersen et al. (1999)
Cognitive concern	Cognitive complaint usually involving memory	Memory complaint by patient, family, or physician	Memory complaint
Global cognition	Results of cognitive screening tests such as the MMSE in the normal range for age	Normal global cognitive function	Normal general cognitive function
Focal cognitive impairment	Memory tests... *tended* to fall more than 1.5*SD* below age-appropriate norms	Objective memory impairment or impairment in one other cognitive domain as evidenced by scores >1.5*SD* below age appropriate means	Abnormal memory for age
Activities of daily living (ADLs)	ADLs assessed by history and functional scales were generally preserved	Normal ADLs	Normal ADLs
Dementia	Such participants do not meet DSM-III-R criteria for dementia since only one cognitive domain is involved and ADLs are not impaired	Not demented	Not demented
Clinical Rating Scale	CDR = 0.5	CDR = 0.5	—

Conceptual issues involving MCI

Other terms

We recognize that there is substantial overlap between our MCI concept and other terms including CIND, AACD, AAMI, which are described elsewhere in this book. Importantly, we conceptualize a dichotomy in these terms with some reflecting normal age-related processes and others meant to mark increased risk for neurodegenerative disease. Figure 7.1 reflects this dichotomy. For example, age-associated memory impairment is a concept meant to capture typical age-related changes in an individual's cognitive function. As originally described, it was not expected to associate with a

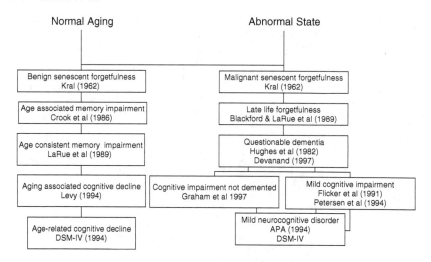

Figure 7.1 Proposed terms for benign and malignant cognitive aging.

specific neuropathology. Questionable dementia on the other hand was expected to commonly associate with Alzheimer's neuropathology. Our notion of MCI is that it is not a typical condition of aging and that in *many* cases it marks a neuropathological process.

Our initial concept of MCI

We adopted the term MCI for studies of a boundary condition. This term had already been introduced into the literature by Flicker, Ferris, and Reisberg (1991). They used the term to describe people obtaining a score of 3 on the Global Deterioration Scale. Our conceptualization did not tie MCI to any scale. As applied cross-sectionally to groups of people, we viewed MCI as that level of cognitive function wherein it is difficult to distinguish low-functioning normals and high-functioning dementia patients. Figure 7.2 depicts this overlap. We conceived of all persons labeled as MCI as belonging in either a normal population, not destined to develop dementia, or in a population that is developing dementia. However, at a given evaluation, some of our ADPR participants met neither our normal criteria nor our dementia criteria. We recognized that some "normals" may have life-long weakness in a single cognitive domain and simply reflect the "tail" of the normal distribution. Conversely, some people who did not meet criteria for normal or dementia may have declined from a higher level of function. But without prior testing this deteriorating course could not be documented. Since, in the absence of valid biomarkers, the ultimate neuropathological status in both types of cases was initially unknowable, we applied the label "MCI." As might be expected, it turns out that this intermediate MCI state ultimately reflects increased risk for the person to subsequently attain a dementia diagnosis.

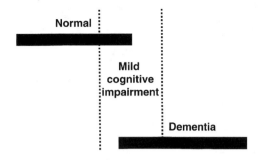

Figure 7.2 Conceptual model of mild cognitive impairment as the overlap of the distributions of cognitive functioning of "low normal" and early dementia.

Thus our use of MCI originated in a cross-sectional, nomothetic context. However, this concept has subsequently been applied to individuals followed to the development of dementia. In the context of declining individuals, MCI has come to be seen as reflecting an epoch in the longitudinal course of dementia. In this longitudinal model, MCI reflects a time when cognition is no longer normal relative to age expectations, but also wherein daily function is not sufficiently disrupted to warrant the diagnosis of dementia. Thus, it is considered a transitional stage in individuals (Figure 7.3). But this concept only applies to individuals known to be declining. It is important to recognize that until the longitudinal trajectory of a given individual with MCI has been established, we are operating with the cross-sectional model, that is, a state of uncertainty about his or her course. Though outcome studies suggest a high likelihood that a person fitting MCI criteria will progress to dementia, we do not expect that all such persons will do so.

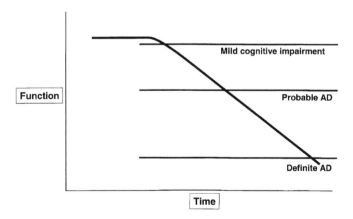

Figure 7.3 Theoretical cognitive and functional trajectory of degenerative dementia in an individual.

Evolution of the MCI concept

Of course not all dementia is AD, so the idea that MCI could only include memory problems was quickly recognized as a limitation of the concept (Petersen et al., 2001). For example, we know that early in subcortical dementias such as Parkinson's dementia, memory is spared but basic attention and processing speed are compromised. This led to the recognition of the need to broaden the concept of MCI to include presentations that are not amnestic or not exclusively amnestic in nature. Petersen et al. (2001) have proposed a new conceptual model that combines clinical profile with presumed etiology (Table 7.2). The clinical profile is established by clinical and neuropsychological evaluation. Presumed etiology is assessed by clinical history, clinical evaluation, and appropriate studies. The cells in Table 7.2 reflect the likely outcome for MCI patients with given combinations of clinical profile and presumed etiology.

Although this conceptualization of MCI is relatively new, preliminary studies argue that multidomain MCI or single nonmemory domain MCI may be more common than single-domain amnestic MCI (aMCI) (Lopez et al., 2002). Single- and multidomain MCI with an amnestic component (aMCI) progress at roughly equal rates to AD (Petersen et al., 2004). Nonamnestic MCI (nMCI) is also a risk factor for AD, but may give rise to non-AD dementias, like Lewy body dementia or frontotemporal dementia, more commonly than aMCI (Boeve et al., 2004; Ferman et al., in press; Petersen et al., 2001).

Those knowledgeable of DSM-IV (American Psychiatric Association, 1994) diagnostic criteria will ask "why does multidomain MCI not meet criteria for dementia?" Two fundamentals of neuropsychology are relevant in this regard. First, a low score is not necessarily the same thing as impairment. A certain percentage of the normal population will score below clinical cutoffs on any measure. If a cutoff is set, for example, at $-1.5SD$, 7% of the general population will fall below the cutoff. In persons with appropriate histories e.g., low academic attainment, low IQ) it is entirely possible for a score below this cutoff to be deemed clinically normal for that person. So persons may have worrisome scores

Table 7.2 A possible model of MCI and associated etiologies

MCI type	Number of affected domains	Etiology Degenerative	Vascular	Psychiatric
Amnestic	Single	AD	VaD	Depression
	Multiple	AD		Depression
Nonamnestic	Single	FTD		
	Multiple	DLB	VaD	

Note: AD, Alzheimer's disease; DLB, Lewy body dementia; FTD, Frontotemporal dementia; VaD, Vascular dementia.

in more than one domain but do not meet the criteria requiring a decline from a higher level of cognitive function. The second fundamental issue is that low scores on tests do not necessarily imply "significant impairment in social or occupational functioning" (American Psychiatric Association, 1994). There are plenty of people who live normal day-to-day lives that would "fail" specific cognitive measures.

Caution: Not all MCI is early dementia

If all MCI patients progress to dementia, it would not be necessary to have a concept called MCI, we could just say "early dementia." Morris et al. (1991) and others have argued that aMCI is simply early AD. These investigators base this opinion in part on their neuropathological study of patients who died with questionable dementia. In nearly all of their cases there was sufficient neuropathological burden to justify the CERAD (Gearing, Mirra, Hedreen, Sumi, Hansen, & Heyman, 1995; Mirra, Heyman, McKeil, Sumi, & Crain, 1991) diagnosis of AD. This neuropathological diagnostic system suffers in its failure to distinguish between neuritic and non-neuritic plaques and in not incorporating tangle burden in any fashion. Mufson et al. (2003), for example, found that nearly half of their aMCI cases coming to autopsy had "low" NIA-Reagan neuropathological findings. Our preliminary analyses also suggest that not all MCI patients have or are developing AD (Petersen et al., 2000). These findings would argue that it is not appropriate to simply conclude that all MCI is necessarily early AD. Yet, these neuropathological findings also affirm that the clinical syndrome of MCI in many cases reflects a transitional neuropathological state.

Correlates of MCI

Although the diagnosis of MCI is based predominantly on a pattern of impaired and preserved cognitive functions, we have found that MCI, particularly aMCI, reliably associates with a variety of neuroimaging and genetic markers and with patterns of clinical outcome. We will describe each of these in turn, and their interactions, and finally discuss the evolution and future of the MCI concept as we see it.

Neuroimaging studies

Structural MRI

Volumetric MRI studies have aided in understanding brain changes that characterize aMCI. One of the earliest studies examined hippocampal volume (Jack et al., 1999). This longitudinal study found that degree of hippocampal atrophy at baseline was associated with the development of AD (Figure 7.4). A follow-up cross-sectional study addressed whether

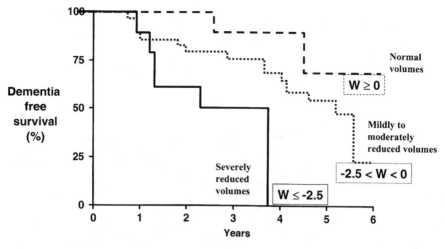

Figure 7.4 Survival time from mild cognitive impairment to dementia diagnosis by hippocampal volume at initial evaluation. W = age-normalized volume.

MRI-based measurements of the transentorhinal/entorhinal cortex are more sensitive than hippocampal volume in discriminating normal controls, aMCIs, and ADs, given that the earliest pathology of AD has been identified in this brain region (Xu et al., 2000). Contrary to expectations, measurements of the hippocampus and entorhinal cortex were approximately equivalent at discriminating between the two patient groups.

Subsequent studies have focused on the utility of serial MRI scans to serve as a biomarker of disease progression along the continuum from normal aging to aMCI to AD. The first of these studies focused on rate of hippocampal atrophy (Jack et al., 2000). The annualized rate of hippocampal volume loss was greatest in the ADs followed by the aMCIs and then the normal controls. Amongst the controls and aMCIs, those who experienced a greater loss of hippocampal volume over time also showed more decline in their cognitive status. Jack et al. (2004) also examined whole brain and ventricular volume in addition to medial temporal lobe structures (i.e., hippocampus, entorhinal cortex) in normal elderly and individuals with aMCI and AD and found that atrophy rates in all four brain regions were greater in subjects who evidenced clinical decline than in those who remained stable. A more recent serial MRI study examined atrophy rates in these same brain regions in normal elderly and subjects with aMCI over a relatively short period of time (i.e., 1–2 year interval) (Jack et al., 2004). Interestingly, whole brain and ventricular volume atrophy rates were helpful in predicting progression in the MCI subjects while the hippocampal and entorhinal cortex measures were not. There was, however, overlap in the atrophy rates in the medial temporal lobe structures between the subjects who converted versus those who did not.

¹H Magnetic resonance spectroscopy

Proton MR spectroscopy (¹H MRS) is a diagnostic imaging technique that is sensitive to the changes in the brain at the cellular level. With ¹H MRS, major proton-containing metabolites in the brain are measured during a common data acquisition period. The metabolite changes in aMCI are generally intermediate between normal elderly and patients with AD. The metabolite N-acetyl aspartate (NAA) is a marker for neuronal integrity, and NAA decreases in a variety of neurological disorders including AD (Kantarci et al., 2000; Klunk, Panchalingam, Moossy, McClure, & Pettegrew, 1992; Tsai & Coyle, 1995). Another metabolite that is elevated in people with aMCI and AD is myo-inositol (mI) (Catani et al., 2001; Kantarci et al., 2000). MI levels also correlate with performance on the AVLT and Dementia Rating Scale in patients with aMCI (Kantarci, Smith et al., 2002). The mI peak consists of glial metabolites that are responsible for osmoregulation (Brand, Richter-Landsberg, & Leibfritz, 1993; Urenjak, Williams, Gadian, & Noble, 1993). Elevated mI levels correlate with glial proliferation in inflammatory CNS demyelination (Bitsch et al., 1999). We speculate that the elevation of the mI peak is related to glial proliferation and astrocytic activation during the evolution of AD pathology. One other metabolite peak of interest in aMCI and AD is choline (Cho). The largest amount of choline in the brain is bound in membrane phospholipids that are precursors of choline and acetylcholine synthesis. It has been postulated that the elevation of the Cho peak is the consequence of membrane phosphotidylcholine catabolism in order to provide free choline for the chronically deficient acetylcholine production in AD (Wurtman & Marie, 1985) (Figure 7.5).

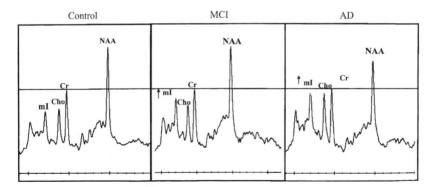

Figure 7.5 ¹H Magnetic resonance spectroscopy metabolite ratios for cognitively normal, mild cognitive impairment (MCI), and early Alzheimer's disease (AD) samples. MCI patients have elevated myo-inositol (mI) to creatine (Cr) levels. AD patients have elevated mI/Cr ratios and reduced *N*-acetyl aspartate to Cr ratios.

Diffusion weighted MR imaging (DWI)

DWI is sensitive to the random motion of water molecules in brain tissue. Measures of apparent diffusion coefficient (ADC) from DWI can quantify the alterations in water diffusivity resulting from microscopic structural changes. The ADC measurements of DWI indicate that the diffusivity of water is higher in the hippocampus of patients with aMCI and AD than cognitively normal elderly (Fellgiebel et al., 2004; Kantarci et al., 2001). We attribute the elevation of the ADCs in the hippocampi of people with aMCI and AD to the expansion of the extracellular space owing to the loss of neuron cell bodies and dendrites. In a comparative study of different MR techniques in aMCI, we found that hippocampal diffusivity was not superior to hippocampal volumetry in distinguishing patients with MCI from normal (Kantarci, Xu et al., 2002). However, when we followed these patients with MCI, elevated hippocampal diffusivity predicted progression to AD as well or better than hippocampal volumetry (Kantarci et al., 2005) (Figure 7.6).

Functional magnetic resonance imaging (fMRI)

fMRI is a noninvasive technology that offers the ability to examine changes in blood oxygenation (i.e., an indirect measure of neuronal activation) as subjects engage in cognitive tasks. We studied fMRI activation during a complex scene-encoding task in a group of normal elderly, individuals with aMCI, and individuals with early AD. Using ROC curve analysis, we found that activation in the medial temporal lobe was greater in normal subjects than in patients with MCI and AD, while the aMCI patients were not significantly different from AD patients (Machulda et al., 2003). Decreased hippocampal activation has also been reported in a subgroup of subjects with "isolated

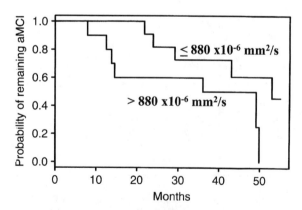

Figure 7.6 Survival time free of dementia in MCI patients grouped by hippocampal apparent diffusion coefficients obtained in diffusion-weighted magnetic resonance imaging.

memory decline" during a face-encoding task (Small, Perera, DeLaPaz, Mayeux, & Stern, 1999). Another study found that the medial temporal lobe response during repeated presentations of faces is compromised in individuals with MCI (Johnson, Baxter, Susskind-Wilder, Connor, Sabbagh, & Caselli, 2004). In contrast, Dickerson et al. (2004) showed that a subgroup of MCI subjects who demonstrated greater clinical impairment over time activated a greater extent of the right parahippocampal gyrus during a scene-encoding task compared to subjects who remained clinically stable. However, they did not require that their MCI subjects demonstrate objective memory impairment, which is one of the criteria for aMCI required by most research groups.

Investigators have also used fMRI to examine the effects of cholinesterase inhibitors on brain function in aMCI. Increased frontal activity was observed during a working memory task in individuals with aMCI who were on stable doses of donepezil relative to unmedicated controls (Saykin et al., 2004). A group of aMCI patients were also studied after prolonged exposure to galantamine (i.e., 6 days). Relative to their activation patterns at baseline, these aMCI subjects showed increased activation in the left prefrontal areas, anterior cingulate, left occipital areas, and left posterior hippocampus during a face-encoding task, and increased activation in the right precuneus and right middle frontal gyrus during a working memory task (Goekoop et al., 2004).

Flurodeoxyglucose positron emission tomography (FDG PET)

As with other imaging modalities, FDG PET findings in aMCI suggest that MCI is an intermediate stage between normality and AD. The spatial distribution of the decrease in glucose metabolism in patients with MCI is similar to but less pronounced than patients with AD (Kantarci et al., 2004). In keeping with the distribution of the early neurofibrillary pathology of AD, the decrease in glucose metabolism involves the limbic and paralimbic cortex, as well as the temporal, and parietal association cortices in aMCI. Longitudinal studies indicate that FDG PET may predict progression to AD in people with aMCI (Chetelat, Desgranges, de la Sayette, Viader, Eustache, & Baron, 2003; Drzezga et al., 2003).

Genetics studies

The E-4 polymorphism of the apolipoprotein E (ApoE) gene has been widely established to increase risk for AD especially in those cases with onset before age 80. E-4 allelic frequency in AD samples is consistently in the range of 40%. In contrast, the frequency of the E-4 gene in the normal population is approximately 13%. If cross-sectional MCI cohorts (especially aMCI) are a mix of a large proportion of pre-AD cases and a smaller proportion of low-functioning normals or non-AD cases (such as hippocampal sclerosis or Lewy body disease), then we can expect intermediate ApoE allelic frequencies. For example, if MCI cohorts comprise approximately 75% pre-AD and 25% normals, then we would expect ApoE allelic frequencies in aMCI to be (.75)(.40) + (.25)(.13) = .33. Table 7.3 reflects ApoE genotype data from our ADPR for persons aged 80 and younger. Note that aMCI patients have ApoE allelic frequencies more similar to AD patients (Petersen et al., 1995).

Cognition

As noted above, history, neurological examination, and neuropsychological test performance all contribute to our diagnoses. In our hands MCI is a neuropsychological as well as a neurological diagnosis. It thus goes without saying that an MCI diagnosis is associated with neuropsychological test performance and that these performances help subclassify MCI patients into amnestic versus nonamnestic as well as single versus multidomain MCI. Figure 7.7 reflects patterns of mean performance for controls, AD patients, and MCI patients at their initial neuropsychological evaluations on a select subset of our neuropsychological battery.

Several features of our neuropsychological approach that are embedded in this diagram are worthy of comment:

(1) It is well established that delayed recall is more sensitive in pre-AD than immediate recall (see the section "Nature of memory assessment"). However, we believe these memory problems are most clearly seen in measures of savings or retention (e.g., percent retention). We demonstrated (Smith, Ivnik, Malec, Petersen, Tangalos, & Kurland, 1992; Smith, Ivnik, Malec, & Tangalos, 1993) that the calculation of percent retention scores permits the emergence of a retention construct in factor analyses of a neuropsychological battery. This factor may not appear in analyses of simple delayed scores, since delayed scores are highly correlated with immediate recall scores. Percent retention scores

Table 7.3 Apolipoprotein E genotypes for Mayo normals, aMCIs, and AD patients

Genotype	Normal (%) (n = 563)	aMCI (%) (n = 143)	AD (%) (n = 114)
2/2	0.5	0	0
2/3	12.4	8.3	3.5
2/4	2.3	4.2	5.3
3/3	61.2	39.8	36.0
3/4	22.0	39.2	41.2
4/4	1.4	8.4	14.3
E-4 allelic frequency	13	30	37

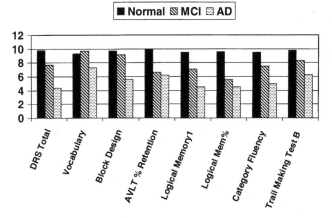

Figure 7.7 Mean cognitive performance on select neuropsychological measures for normal, mild cognitive impairment, and early Alzheimer's disease patients. DRS = Dementia Rating Scale (Mattis, 1988). Vocabulary and Block Design from Wechsler Adult Intelligence Scale-Revised (Wechsler, 1981). AVLT = Rey Auditory Verbal Learning Test (Rey, 1964). Logical Memory from the Wechsler Memory Scale-Revised (Wechsler, 1987). Category Fluency = One-minute trials of animals, fruits, and vegetables. All scores presented as MOANS standard scores (Ivnik et al., 1992a, 1992b, 1996).

isolate the variance associated with forgetting, and it is this variance that is crucial in distinguishing normal aging from preclinical AD (aka, aMCI).

(2) Even in single-domain aMCI, there are mean differences between normals and MCI groups on nonmemory measures. Note, however, that on average these nonmemory measures do not fall in the impaired range. MCI diagnoses are made on an individual basis. The common profile of a single-domain aMCI patient will include impaired memory function, but may also include semantic fluency or executive function performances that are "impoverished" but nevertheless within normal limits for age.

(3) We approach MCI as a clinical diagnosis (see the section "Mild cognitive impairment" in "Diagnostic criteria"). This includes the clinical judgment of the neuropsychologist. We have diagnosed people with average memory performance as aMCI if, in our clinical judgment, they were memory impaired relative to their baseline. In fact, in one interim analysis of nine neuropsychological measures, 23% of our MCI population had no cognitive performances that fell >1.5SD below the mean. In the same analysis of nine measures, 21% of our "normals" had at least one measure more than 1.5SD below age-appropriate means. Thus, we clearly do not assign the diagnosis of MCI simply because a person has a poor memory performance. Our

neuropsychologists and neurologists have exercised clinical judgment including consideration of life-long patterns of function and expectations established from general cognitive function in rendering an MCI diagnosis.

Interaction of neuroimaging, genetic, and cognitive factors

Logically, different associates of MCI should associate with each other. Thus, it is not surprising that in aMCI patients annual change in hippocampal and whole brain volume correlates with annual change in Dementia Rating Scale score (Jack et al., 2004), or that MI metabolite levels in HMRS also correlate with performance on the AVLT and Dementia Rating Scale in patients with MCI (Kantarci, Smith et al., 2002), or that patients with ApoE-4 genotype show more advanced memory dysfunction at comparable durations of illness (Smith, Petersen, Ivnik, Malec, & Tangalos, 1996) than E-4 negative patients. It is perhaps more useful to note that these types of variables contribute unique added value in predictions of rate of progression to dementia. We have noted that ApoE genotype and cognitive measures independently predict progression from aMCI to dementia (Petersen et al., 2004).

Outcomes

Clinical diagnosis

In following their group of MCI patients, Flicker, Ferris, and Reisberg (1991) found a conversion rate to the full syndrome of dementia of approximately 72% over 2 years of follow-up (i.e., approximately 36% per year). Our conversion rate is about 12% per year over the initial 7 years of follow-up (Figure 7.8). An age- and gender-matched group of normal controls had only a cumulative 5% rate of developing cognitive impairment in the comparable 7-year interval (Petersen et al., 1995). Other researchers have found progression to dementia rates ranging from 6 to 24% for variously defined boundary conditions (Bowen, Teri, Kukull, McCormick, McCurry, & Larson, 1997; Bozoki, Giordani, Heidebrink, Berent, & Foster, 2001; Daly, Zaitchik, Copeland, Schmahmann, Gunther, & Albert, 2000; Kluger, Ferris, Golomb, Mittelman, & Reisberg, 1999; Morris et al., 2001; Tierney et al., 1996).

Residential outcomes

We examined residential outcome in MCI. Patterns of and time to relocation from home were compared in persons entering the ADPR as MCI, normal, or persons already having dementia. Relocation was defined as move from initial independent living to assisted living or nursing home care. Study groups consisted of 846 normal controls, 171 MCI patients, and 292

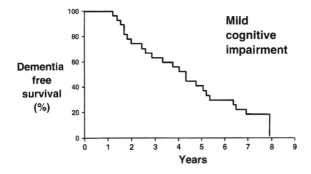

Figure 7.8 Survival free from dementia in Mayo mild cognitive impairment patients.

dementia patients. In these groups, respectively, a total of 21, 58, and 201 relocations occurred during our surveillance. At each of the three annual follow-up times, patients entering the study as MCI were significantly more likely than controls but less likely than dementia patients to be in assisted living or nursing homes. Median time to relocation in the MCI cohort was 8.5 years compared to 4.8 years in a dementia cohort. However, age at placement did not differ between groups. This suggests that persons with MCI at enrollment were in fact identified "early" and were not merely persons with a slower rate of decline. Figure 7.9 presents Kaplan–Meier data of time from enrollment to relocation. A set of risk factors for relocation, as established in prior publications (Severson et al., 1994; Smith, Kokmen, & O'Brien, 2000;

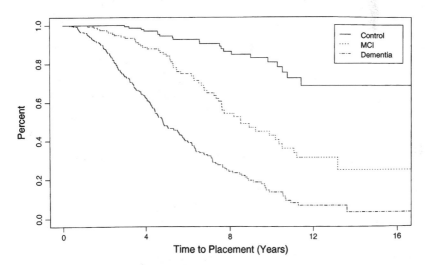

Figure 7.9 Time to relocation for persons who were normal (solid line), had mild cognitive impairment (dotted line), or early Alzheimer's disease (dashed line) at initial evaluation.

Smith, O'Brien, Ivnik, Kokmen, & Tangalos, 2001; Smith, Tangalos, Ivnik, Kokmen, & Petersen, 1995), were examined for their association with time to relocation in the MCI cohort. In univariate analysis, 7 of 11 candidate variables were predictors of time to relocation. These included age at onset, number of cohabitants, global cognitive status, functional status, neuropsychiatric status, marital status, and medical comorbidity. In multivariate modeling, only neuropsychiatric symptoms, marital status (married vs. unmarried), and functional status (Record of Independent Living) score remained significant predictors in the proportional hazards model.

Considerations

Reconciling MCI prevalence, progression rates, and dementia incidence

The annual incidence (number of new cases in a year) of dementia in the over 65 population is well established at 1–2% (Edland, Rocca, Petersen, Cha, & Kokmen, 2002). If we make the reasonable assumption that all dementia patients will pass through the MCI state before displaying dementia, then basically dementia incidence = MCI point prevalence × Annual progression rate × Cumulative progression rate. We can thus use epidemiological concepts and data to assure concordance between these percentages, or to estimate MCI prevalence. First we will define some terms. Point prevalence is the number of MCI cases in the population at any one time. This value is not well studied. Annual progression rate refers to the percentage of MCI cases progressing to dementia in a year. As seen above, rates of annual progression from MCI to dementia have been widely studied and are widely variable but tend to fall around the 12% we have reported. Cumulative progression refers to the total number of MCI patients who will progress to dementia. Some have reported that "100% of their MCI equivalent group had neuropathologic dementing illness at autopsy, 88% with AD" (Morris et al., 2001). In our autopsy sample, however, one of 15 MCI patients was pathology free, and two others had only hippocampal sclerosis. This suggests that 20% of our MCI group did not have pathology that would have led to dementia, that is, cumulative progress could be estimated to be 80%. Perhaps an intermediate estimate of 90% cumulative progression is reasonable.

So, if 90–93% of MCI patients will ultimately have a progressive neuropathology at autopsy and about 12% of MCI patients will progress to dementia per year (Figure 7.8), we can back-calculate estimated prevalence of MCI. Dementia incidence (1–2%) is divided by annual progression (12%) and divided again by cumulative progression (90%), which results in an estimated prevalence of 9–18%.

Epidemiologically determined MCI point prevalence rates are only beginning to be reported in the literature (Bennett et al., 2002; Larrieu et al., 2002; Lopez et al., 2002). The prevalence varies from 3 to 54% mainly because of the different methods and criteria used. The Cardiovascular Health Study

(CHS) evaluated several definitions of MCI in their nondemented cohort aged 65 years or older and provided useful prevalence figures (Lopez et al., 2002). The CHS included aMCI and multidomain MCI defined in a very similar fashion to the Petersen et al. (2001) criteria. They concluded that the prevalence of MCI among nondemented individuals was 19%, and it increased with increasing age. These results are similar to the estimate of MCI prevalence calculated above. Lopez et al. (2002) found a rate ratio of 2.5:1 for the prevalence of multiple domain type MCI (which included memory impairment) compared to single-domain aMCI (Lopez et al., 2002). The CHS findings thus provide preliminary support for the assumptions that almost all dementia patients will pass through the MCI state, and that MCI cohorts include a proportion of people who will not develop dementia. Ultimately a research group's prevalence of MCI, and annual and cumulative rates of progression to dementia, should reconcile with known dementia incidence rates.

Differences across studies

Throughout this chapter we have noted that definitions and "rates" of MCI or related concepts vary across studies. We believe there are at least four important dimensions along which these studies must be compared in order to understand their discrepant findings: (1) the population sampled, (2) the nature of memory complaint, (3) the types of memory assessment used, and (4) the number and type of other cognitive domains assessed.

Population sampled

As has been emphasized by the editors via this book's structure, it is important to note the population sampled for studies of boundary conditions. Our studies and those of several others (e.g., Bowen et al., 1997; Tierney et al., 1996) use a clinical sample, that is, there was a clinical concern regarding the index cases. This is not necessarily the same as a clinic sample, such as samples recruited from memory disorder clinics at tertiary medical centers. Heretofore, our sample has been somewhat unique in that we recruited patients for whom a clinical concern existed, even if the person or that family was not yet pursuing a dementia evaluation. That a clinical concern existed for these patients increased the likelihood that they were drawn for the predementia group. A variety of other studies have identified their cohorts by recruiting normal, older adults (e.g., Albert, Moss, Tanzi, & Jones, 2001; Ritchie & Touchon, 2000). These may be controls in clinical trials or longitudinal aging studies, or may be a general population of normal elderly samples selected to be representative of the entire population. MCI "patients" are often culled from these normal samples by using a psychometric cutoff based on their memory performance. Thus, by definition, these normal patients scored at the lowest end of the memory score distributions. Selection in this fashion necessarily increases the likelihood that these MCI patients arise from the normal population, rather than cognitively impaired population.

Nature of memory complaint

The Mayo criteria for MCI (Petersen, Smith, Waring, Ivnik, Tangalos, & Kokmen, 1999) called for a memory complaint to be present. Differences in the nature of memory complaints across studies are a corollary of the recruitment method. In clinical samples any memory complaint is generally "spontaneous." It arises as a concern from some members of the health care process (e.g., patient, family, provider). Such memory concerns, especially from family or physicians, may have a better correspondence with objectively established cognitive dysfunction (Carr, Gray, Baty, & Morris, 2000). In studies that recruit general or normal samples, memory complaint is typically established by administration of standardized subjective ratings of memory function. Numerous studies have demonstrated that scores on such instruments are more likely to associate with mood or self-efficacy than with actual cognitive dysfunction (Smith et al., 1996; Taylor, Miller, & Tinklenberg, 1992).

Nature of memory assessment

Another key difference across studies of boundary conditions is their approach to memory assessment. The term "memory impairment" has been used to describe a wide variety of cognitive impairments, which may have different neural substrates. Most studies have focused on episodic memory. However, even within the realm of episodic memory, differences may exist in the extent to which impairments are associated with risk for subsequent decline to dementia. It is possible and important to distinguish between encoding and retrieval phases of memory tasks (cf. Delis, Jacobson, Bondi, amilton, & Salmon, 2003; Smith et al., 1992). Encoding is typically assessed by aspects of immediate recall while retrieval is assessed by delayed recall. The encoding phase of memory is sensitive to aging effects, and may thus be nonspecific for detecting incipient dementia (Petersen, Smith, Ivnik, Kokmen, & Tangalos, 1994; Petersen, Smith, Kokmen, Ivnik, & Tangalos, 1992). For example, a recent study of nine people who died and were observed to have healthy brains, compared to five people who were nondemented at death but observed to have AD changes in the brain, showed no cognitive differences between the groups. However, all memory test scores in this very small study focused on the immediate recall (Goldman et al., 2001). Numerous studies suggest that delayed recall measures, especially those expressed as saving or retention, are most sensitive and specific for early discrimination of dementia (Bondi, Monsch, Galasko, Butters, Salmon, & Delis, 1994; Ivnik, Smith, Petersen, Boeve, Kokmen, & Tangalos, 2000; Tierney et al., 1996). Studies that focus on immediate recall (encoding) versus delayed recall (retrieval) in establishing the memory impairment criteria for MCI may engender very different samples.

Number and type of cognitive domains assessed

The number and type of nonmemory cognitive domains assessed in studies of MCI are important. As the number of cognitive domains assessed in a given individual increases, there is an increasing probability that cognitive measure will fall in the impaired range by chance alone. Moreover, all cognitive domains tend to be correlated at least to a moderate degree. For example, retention and perceptual organization function correlate at .38 in our sample of participants with normal cognitive functioning (Ivnik, Smith, Malec, Petersen, & Tangalos, 1995). Thus, excluding nondemented persons with multiple impairments from MCI samples because of a low score in another domain increases the probability that the memory score for that patient is spuriously low. A study by Ritchie, Artero, and Touchon (2001) provides an example of this problem. In this study, seven nonmemory domains were assessed. Seventy five percent of persons with a loosely defined memory impairment (scores < $-1SD$ below age norms) also had at least one nonmemory score fall below this cutoff. Of the remaining 25% of their "MCI" patients, only 7% continued to have memory scores below their cutoff at follow-up. By excluding persons with modestly low nonmemory scores from their sample, these investigators appeared to exclude persons with true memory impairments from their MCI sample. This common finding that aMCI patients have poor performance on sensitive measures in other cognitive domains as well as the relatively common presentation of persons with isolated cognitive concerns in nonmemory domains has motivated the evolution of the concept of MCI described above.

Use of strict psychometric cutoffs

A corollary of the above issue is that rates of MCI are predictable when psychometric cutoffs alone are used to establish the presence of MCI. Most cognitive functions tend to be normally distributed in the population. So we know that 16% of the population will fall below $-1SD$ and 7% will fall below $-1.5SD$ on a given neuropsychological measure. We can predetermine a base rate above 7% by choosing a liberal ($-1SD$) cutoff and/or by adding measures to our neuropsychological battery until we reach the desired base rate (aka prevalence). If our measures were completely independent, the number of measures "n" we need could be estimated by desired prevalence = $1 - .93^n$. Since our measures are correlated it may take a few more measures than n to reach the desired prevalence. In any event, if we employ no restrictions in MCI diagnosis save for psychometric cutoffs then we can derive the MCI base rate we want in normal samples via choices we make with the neuropsychological battery.

In fact, we have studied the utility of psychometric cutoffs in comparison to clinical judgment in defining MCI (Smith, Cerhan, & Ivnik, 2002). We applied 1.5SD cutoffs to determine "impairment" with 200 clinically defined MCI patients and 943 normals. The base rate of clinical MCI in this analysis was 21%, not far off from the CHS estimates. The battery included memory (percent retention on AVLT, WMS-R Logical Memory, and Visual Reproduction) and nonmemory (Perceptual Organization, Boston Naming, COWAT, Category Fluency, and Trails B) measures. Of the clinically defined MCI patients, 23% had no impairments by the psychometric definition, 47% had impaired performance only in memory, 8.5% had only impaired nonmemory performance, and 21% had memory plus nonmemory impairments. Among the normals, 79% had no impairments, 10% memory only, 8% nonmemory impairment, and 3% memory plus nonmemory impairment. Clearly the strict cutoffs would identify somewhat different MCI and normal groups than were defined clinically. As expected from the normal distribution, a significant percentage (21%) of individuals determined by a behavioral neurologist to be clinically normal, nevertheless fell below −1.5SD on at least one measure. Longitudinal data revealed that persons with clinically defined MCI were more likely to convert to dementia than psychometrically defined MCI. The likelihood ratios for progression were 5.2 for clinical MCI versus 2.1 for psychometric MCI (Smith, Cerhan, & Ivnik, 2002). These data suggest that any strictly psychometric approach to MCI will produce a cohort with a substantial proportion of low-scoring normals and will generate a progression rate much lower than that observed in studies of clinical MCI.

Conclusion

Boundary concepts remain important to dementia research and clinical practice. One such concept, MCI, appears associated with biomarkers of AD even before patients meet AD criteria. MCI patients are at elevated risk for progressing to dementia. While MCI cross-sectional samples predominantly comprise persons with incipient dementia, these samples also include some persons with non-AD neuropathology, persons with transient poor performance, *and* normal older persons with poor cognitive function (Figure 7.10). The relative proportion of each group in an MCI sample will be influenced by the sampling frame (clinical vs. general or normal), the nature of the memory complaint (spontaneous vs. elicited), the type of memory assessment used in selecting patients (e.g., immediate vs. delayed recall), and the number, type, and interpretation of measures of nonmemory domains. These factors need to be considered when comparing outcomes from studies of boundary conditions.

The use of a concept such as MCI avoids the problem of knowing for sure whether a person at the boundary between normal and dementia has a disease entity or not. This diagnosis acknowledges the overlapping distributions of normal function, temporary deviations for normal function, and early degenerative disease, yet identifies risk status. Identifying persons in this way

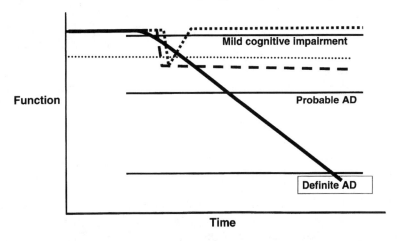

Figure 7.10 Possible cognitive and functional trajectory for individuals recruited in a cross-sectional mild cognitive impairment cohort; degenerative dementia (solid line), life-long low-functioning normal (dotted line), transient poor performance, e.g., depression (short dashed line), static cognitive dysfunction, e.g., head injury, stroke, hippocampal sclerosis (long dashed line).

permits their involvement in intervention research. In fact being able to identify such persons has clearly given impetus to early intervention research. In DSM-IV (American Psychiatric Association, 1994) mild neurocognitive disorder (MND) is listed as a diagnosis for future consideration. This concept is congruent with the idea of a boundary area or preclinical status. The criteria for MND are similar but not identical to MCI. Whether CIND, MCI, or MND labels and criteria ultimately gain widest acceptance, there will likely be substantial research and clinical benefits to including a boundary condition as a "legitimate" diagnosis in the next DSM.

Acknowledgments

MCI research endeavors at the Mayo Clinic have been supported by a variety of funding mechanisms including Grants P50 AG16574, UO1 AG06786, RO1 AG15866, and the Robert H. and Clarice Smith and Abigail Van Buren Alzheimer's Disease Research Program of the Mayo Foundation. This research is a team effort. We acknowledge all physicians, psychologists, epidemiologists, statisticians, nurses, psychometrists, technicians, data analysts, and other support staff that make up this team. They have all contributed to the Mayo studies cited herein. We would particularly like to thank Ron Petersen and Cliff Jack for their review and commentary on this chapter. However, the views and opinions expressed in this chapter are strictly those of the authors. Finally, we would like to express our thanks to the people of Rochester, MN for their willingness to participate in this research, some for over a decade.

References

Albert, M., Moss, M., Tanzi, R., & Jones, K. (2001). Preclinical prediction of AD using neuropsychological tests. *Journal of the International Neuropsychological Society*, 7, 631–639.

American Psychiatric Association. (1987). *Diagnostic and Statistical Manual of mental disorders* (3rd Rev. ed.). Washington, DC: American Psychiatric Association.

American Psychiatric Association. (1994). *Diagnostic and Statistical Manual of mental disorders* (4th ed.). Washington, DC: American Psychiatric Association.

Bennett, D., Wilson, R., Schneider, J., Evans, D., Beckett, L., Aggarwal, N., et al. (2002). Natural history of mild cognitive impairment in older persons. *Neurology*, 59, 198–205.

Benton, A., Hamsher, K., Varney, N., & Spreen, O. (1983). *Contributions to neuropsychological assessment. A clinical manual.* New York: Oxford University Press.

Bitsch, A., Bruhn, H., Vougioukas, V., Stringaris, A., Lassmann, H., Frahm, J., et al. (1999). Inflammatory CNS demyelination: Histopathologic correlation with in vivo quantitative proton MR spectroscopy. *American Journal of Neuroradiology*, 20(9), 1619–1627.

Blackford, R. C., & LaRue, A. (1989). Criteria for diagnosing age associated memory impairment. *Developmental Neuropsychology*, 5, 295–306.

Boeve, B., Ferman, T., Smith, G., Knopman, D., Jicha, G., Geda, Y., et al. (2004). Mild cognitive impairment preceding dementia with Lewy bodies. *Neurology*, 62(Suppl. 5), A86.

Bondi, M., Monsch, A., Galasko, D., Butters, N., Salmon, D., & Delis, D. (1994). Preclinical cognitive markers of dementia of the Alzheimer type. *Neuropsychology*, 8, 374–384.

Bowen, J., Teri, L., Kukull, W., McCormick, W., McCurry, S., & Larson, E. (1997). Progression to dementia in patients with isolated memory loss. *Lancet*, 349(9054), 763–765.

Bozoki, A., Giordani, B., Heidebrink, J., Berent, S., & Foster, N. (2001). Mild cognitive impairments predict dementia in nondemented elderly patients with memory loss. *Archives of Neurology*, 58, 411–416.

Brand, A., Richter-Landsberg, C., & Leibfritz, D. (1993). Multinuclear NMR studies on the energy metabolism of glial and neuronal cells. *Developmental Neuroscience*, 15(3–5), 289–298.

Buschke, H. (1984a). Control of cognitive processing. In L. Squire & N. Butters (Eds.), *Neuropsychology of memory* (pp. 37–40). New York: Guilford.

Buschke, H. (1984b). Cued recall in amnesia. *Journal of Clinical Neuropsychology*, 6, 433–440.

Carr, D., Gray, S., Baty, J., & Morris, J. (2000). The value of informant versus individual's complaints of memory impairment in early dementia. *Neurology*, 55(11), 1724–1726.

Catani, M., Cherubini, A., Howard, R., Tarducci, R., Pelliccioli, G., Piccirilli, M., et al. (2001). (1)H-MR spectroscopy differentiates mild cognitive impairment from normal brain aging. *Neuroreport*, 12(11), 2315–2317.

Chetelat, G., Desgranges, B., de la Sayette, V., Viader, F., Eustache, F., & Baron, J. (2003). Mild cognitive impairment: Can FDG-PET predict who is to rapidly convert to Alzheimer's disease? *Neurology*, 60(8), 1374–1377.

Crook, T., Bartus, R. T., Ferris, S. H., Whitehouse, P., Cohen, G. D., & Gershon, S. (1986). Age-associated memory impairment: Proposed diagnostic criteria and measures of clinical change—Report of a National Institute of Mental Health Work Group. *Developmental Neuropsychology, 2*, 261–276.

Daly, E., Zaitchik, D., Copeland, M., Schmahmann, J., Gunther, J., & Albert, M. (2000). Predicting conversion to Alzheimer disease using standardized clinical information. *Archives of Neurology, 57*(5), 675–680.

Delis, D., Jacobson, M., Bondi, M., Hamilton, J., & Salmon, D. (2003). The myth of testing construct validity using factor analysis or correlations with normal or mixed clinical populations: Lessons from memory assessment. *Journal of the International Neuropsychological Society, 9*(6), 936–946.

Devanand, D. P., Folz, M., Gorlyn, M., Moeller, J. R., & Stern, Y. (1997). Questionable dementia: Clinical course and predictors of outcome. *Journal of the American Geriatrics Society, 45*, 321–328.

Dickerson, B., Salat, D., Bates, J., Atiya, M., Killiany, R., Greve, D., et al. (2004). Medial temporal lobe function and structure in mild cognitive impairment. *Annals of Neurology, 56*(1), 27–35.

Drzezga, A., Lautenschlager, N., Siebner, H., Riemenschneider, M., Willoch, F., Minoshima, S., et al. (2003). Cerebral metabolic changes accompanying conversion of mild cognitive impairment into Alzheimer's disease: A PET follow-up study. *European Journal of Nuclear Medicine & Molecular Imaging, 30*(8), 1104–1113.

Edland, S., Rocca, W., Petersen, R., Cha, R., & Kokmen, E. (2002). Dementia and Alzheimer's disease incidence rates do not vary by sex in Rochester, Minn. *Archives of Neurology, 59*(10), 1589–1593.

Fahn, S., Elton, R., & Members of the UPDRS Development Committee. (1987). Unified Parkinson's Disease Rating Scale. In S. Fahn, C. Marsden, D. Calne, & M. Golstein (Eds.), *Recent developments in Parkinson's disease* (Vol. II). New York: MacMillan.

Fellgiebel, A., Wille, P., Muller, M., Winterer, G., Scheurich, A., Vucurevic, G., et al. (2004). Ultrastructural hippocampal and white matter alterations in mild cognitive impairment: A diffusion tensor imaging study. *Dementia & Geriatric Cognitive Disorders, 18*(1), 101–108.

Ferman, T., Ivnik, R., & Lucas, J. (1998). Boston naming test discontinuation rule: "Rigorous" vs. "lenient" interpretations. *Assessment, 5*, 13–18.

Ferman, T., Smith, G., Boeve, B., Graff-Radford, N., Lucas, J., Knopman, D., et al. (in press). Neuropsychological differentiation of dementia with Lewy body from normal aging and Alzheimer's disease. *The Clinical Neuropsychologist*.

Flicker, C., Ferris, S., & Reisberg, B. (1991). Mild cognitive impairment in the elderly: Predictors of dementia. *Neurology, 41*, 1006–1009.

Folstein, M., Folstein, S., & McHugh, P. (1975). "Mini-Mental State": A practical method for grading the cognitive state of patients for the clinician. *Journal of Psychiatric Research, 12*, 189–198.

Gearing, M., Mirra, S., Hedreen, J., Sumi, S., Hansen, L., & Heyman, A. (1995). The consortium to establish a registry for Alzheimer's disease (CERAD). Part X. Neuropathology confirmation of the clinical diagnosis of Alzheimer's disease. *Neurology, 45*, 461–466.

Goekoop, R., Rombouts, S., Jonker, C., Hibbel, A., Knol, D. L., Truyen, L., et al. (2004). Challenging the cholinergic system in mild cognitive impairment: A pharmacological fMRI study. *NeuroImage, 23*, 1450–1459.

Goldman, W., Price, J., Storandt, M., Grant, E., McKeel, D., Jr., Rubin, E., et al. (2001). Absence of cognitive impairment or decline in preclinical Alzheimer's disease. *Neurology, 56*(3), 361–367.

Graham, J. E., Rockwood, K., Beattie, B. L., Eastwood, R., Gauthier, S., Tuokko, H., et al. (1997). Prevalence and severity of cognitive impairment with and without dementia in an elderly population. *Lancet, 349*, 1793–1796.

Hachinski, V., Iliff, L., Zilhka, E., Du Boulay, G., McAllister, V., Marshall, J., et al. (1975). Cerebral blood flow in dementia. *Archives of Neurology, 32*, 632–637.

Hughes, C. P., Berg, L., Danziger, W. L., Cohen, L. A., & Martin, R. L. (1982). A new clinical scale for the staging of dementia. *British Journal of Psychiatry, 140*, 566–572.

Ivnik, R., Malec, J., Smith, G., Tangalos, E., & Petersen, R. (1996). Neuropsychological Tests' norms above age 55: COWAT, BNT, MAE Token, WRAT-R Reading, AMNART, STROOP, TMT and JLO. *The Clinical Neuropsychologist, 10*(3), 262–278.

Ivnik, R. J., Malec, J. F., Smith, G. E., Tangalos, E. G., Petersen, R. C., Kokmen, E., et al. (1992a). Mayo's Older Americans Normative Studies: WMS-R norms for ages 56 to 94. *The Clinical Neuropsychologist, 6*(Suppl.), 49–82.

Ivnik, R. J., Malec, J. F., Smith, G. E., Tangalos, E. G., Petersen, R. C., Kokmen, E., et al. (1992b). Mayo's Older Americans Normative Studies: WAIS-R norms for ages 56 to 97. *The Clinical Neuropsychologist, 6*(Suppl.), 1–30.

Ivnik, R., Smith, G., Malec, J., Petersen, R., & Tangalos, E. (1995). Long-term stability and inter-correlations of cognitive abilities in older persons. *Psychological Assessment: A Journal of Consulting and Clinical Psychology, 7*, 155–161.

Ivnik, R., Smith, G., Petersen, R., Boeve, B., Kokmen, E., & Tangalos, E. (2000). Diagnostic accuracy of four approaches to interpreting neuropsychological test data. *Neuropsychology, 14*, 163–177.

Jack, C., Jr., Petersen, R., Xu, Y., O'Brien, P., Smith, G., Ivnik, R., et al. (2000). Rates of hippocampal atrophy correlate with change in clinical status in aging and AD. *Neurology, 55*, 484–489.

Jack, C., Jr., Petersen, R., Xu, Y., O'Brien, P., Smith, G., Ivnik, R., et al. (1999). Prediction of AD with MRI-based hippocampal volume in mild cognitive impairment. *Neurology, 52*, 1397–1403.

Jack, C., Jr., Shiung, M., Gunter, J., O'Brien, P., Weigand, S., Knopman, D., et al. (2004). Comparison of different MRI brain atrophy rate measures with clinical disease progression in AD. *Neurology, 62*(4), 591–600.

Jastak, S., & Wilkinson, G. (1984). *The Wide Range Achievement Test-Revised. Administration manual*. Wilmington: Jastak Associates, Inc.

Johnson, S., Baxter, L., Susskind-Wilder, L., Connor, D., Sabbagh, M., & Caselli, R. (2004). Hippocampal adaptation to face repetition in healthy elderly and mild cognitive impairment. *Neuropsychologia, 42*(7), 980–989.

Kantarci, K., Boeve, B., Knopman, D., Weigand, S., O'Brien, P., Shiung, M., et al. (2005). DWI predicts future progression to Alzheimer's disease in amnestic mild cognitive impairment. *Neurology, 64*, 902–904.

Kantarci, K., Jack, C., Jr., Xu, Y., Campeau, N., O'Brien, P., Smith, G., et al. (2000). Regional metabolic patterns in mild cognitive impairment and Alzheimer's disease: A 1H MRS study. *Neurology, 55*(2), 210–217.

Kantarci, K., Jack, C. J., Xu, Y., Campeau, N., O'Brien, P., Smith, G., et al. (2001). Mild cognitive impairment and Alzheimer's disease: Regional diffusivity of water. *Radiology, 219*(1), 101–107.

Kantarci, K., Lowe, V., Petersen, R., Boeve, B., Knopman, D., Edland, S., et al. (2004). Glucose metabolic patterns in amnestic mild cognitive impairment and Alzheimer's disease: An 18F-FDG-PET study. *Neurobiology of Aging*, 25(S2), S280.

Kantarci, K., Smith, G., Ivnik, R., Petersen, R., Boeve, B., Knopman, D., et al. (2002). 1H MRS, cognitive function, and apolipoprotein E genotype in normal aging, mild cognitive impairment and Alzheimer's disease. *Journal of the International Neuropsychology Society*, 8(7), 934–942.

Kantarci, K., Xu, Y., Shiung, M., O'Brien, P., Cha, R., Smith, G., et al. (2002). Comparative diagnostic utility of different MR modalities in mild cognitive impairment and Alzheimer's disease. *Dementia & Geriatric Cognitive Disorders*, 14(4), 198–207.

Kaplan, E., Goodglass, H., & Weintraub, S. (1983). *The Boston Naming Test* (2nd ed.). Philadelphia: Lea & Febiger.

Kluger, A., Ferris, S., Golomb, J., Mittelman, M., & Reisberg, B. (1999). Neuropsychological prediction of decline to dementia in nondemented elderly. *Journal of Geriatric Psychiatry & Neurology*, 12, 168–179.

Klunk, W., Panchalingam, K., Moossy, J., McClure, R., & Pettegrew, J. (1992). N-acetyl-L-aspartate and other amino acid metabolites in Alzheimer's disease brain: A preliminary proton nuclear magnetic resonance study. *Neurology*, 42(8), 1578–1585.

Kokmen, E., Ozsarfati, Y., Beard, C., O'Brien, P., & Rocca, W. (1996). Impact of referral bias in clinical and epidemiological studies of Alzheimer's disease. *Journal of Clinical Epidemiology*, 49, 79–83.

Kokmen, E., Smith, G., Petersen, R., Tangalos, E., & Ivnik, R. (1991). The short test of mental status: Correlations with standardized psychometric testing. *Archives of Neurology*, 48, 725–728.

Kral, V. A. (1962). Senescent forgetfulness: Benign and malignant. *Canadian Medical Association Journal*, 86, 257–260.

Larrieu, S., Letenneur, L., Orgogozo, J., Fabrigoule, C., Amieva, H., Le Carret, N., et al. (2002). Incidence and outcome of mild cognitive impairment in a population-based prospective cohort. *Neurology*, 59, 1594–1599.

Lautenschlager, N., Cupples, L., Rao, V., Auerbach, S., Becker, R., Burke, J., et al. (1996). Risk of dementia among relatives of Alzheimer disease patients in the MIRAGE study: What is in store for the "oldest old"? *Neurology*, 46, 641–650.

Levy, R. (1994). Aging-associated cognitive decline. *International Psychogeriatrics*, 6, 63–68.

Lopez, O., Kuller, L., DeKosky, S., Becker, J., Jagust, W., Dulberg, C., et al. (2002). Prevalence and classification of mild cognitive impairment in a population study. *Neurobiology of Aging*, 23, S138.

Machulda, M., Ward, H., Borowski, B., Gunter, J., Cha, R., O'Brien, P., et al. (2003). Comparison of memory fMRI response among normal, MCI, and Alzheimer's patients. *Neurology*, 61(4), 500–506.

Mattis, S. (1988). *Dementia Rating Scale. Professional manual.* Odessa, FL: Psychological Assessment Resources, Inc.

McKeith, I., Galasko, D., Kosaka, K., Perry, E., Dickson, D., Hansen, L., et al. (1996). Consensus guidelines for the clinical and pathologic diagnosis of dementia with Lewy bodies (DLB): Report of the consortium on DLB international workshop. *Neurology*, 47, 1113–1124.

McKhann, G., Drachman, D., Folstein, M., Katzman, R., Price, D., & Stadlan, E. (1984). Clinical diagnosis of Alzheimer's disease: Report of the NINCDS-ADRDA work group under the auspices of Department of Health and Human Services Task Force on Alzheimer's Disease. *Neurology, 34*, 939–944.

Mirra, S., Heyman, M., McKeil, D., Sumi, S., & Crain, B. (1991). The Consortium to Establish a Registry for Alzheimer's Disease (CERAD). Part II. Standardization of the neuropathologic assessment of Alzheimer's disease. *Neurology, 41*(4), 479–486.

Monsch, A., Bondi, M., Butters, N., Paulsen, J., Salmon, D., Brugger, P., et al. (1994). A comparison of category and letter fluency in Alzheimer's disease and Huntington's disease. *Neuropsychology, 8*, 25–30.

Morris, J. (1993). The Clinical Dementia Rating (CDR): Current version and scoring rules. *Neurology, 43*(11), 2412–2414.

Morris, J., McKeel, D., Storandt, M., Rubin, E., Price, J., Grant, E., et al. (1991). Very mild Alzheimer's disease: Informant based clinical, psychometric, and pathologic distinction from normal aging. *Neurology, 41*, 469–478.

Morris, J., Storandt, M., Miller, J., McKeel, D., Price, J., Rubin, E., et al. (2001). Mild cognitive impairment represents early-stage Alzheimer's disease. *Archives of Neurology, 58*, 397–405.

Mufson, E., Ikonomovic, M., Styren, S., Counts, S., Wuu, J., Leurgans, S., et al. (2003). Preservation of brain nerve growth factor in mild cognitive impairment and Alzheimer disease. *Archives of Neurology, 60*(8), 1143–1148.

Petersen, R. (1995). Normal aging, mild cognitive impairment, and early Alzheimer's disease. *The Neurologist, 1*, 326–344.

Petersen, R., Dickson, D., Parisi, J., Braak, H., Johnson, K., Ivnik, R., et al. (2000). Neuropathological substrate of mild cognitive impairment. *Neurobiology of Aging, 21*(1S), S198.

Petersen, R., Doody, R., Kurz, A., Mohs, R., Morris, J., Rabins, P., et al. (2001). Current concepts in mild cognitive impairment. *Archives of Neurology, 58*, 1985–1992.

Petersen, R., Ivnik, R., Smith, G., Knopman, D., Boeve, B., Tangalos, E., et al. (2004). Predictors of progression in amnestic MCI and multiple-domain MCI with memory impairment. *Neurobiology of Aging, 25*(S2), S107 (P101–046).

Petersen, R., Smith, G., Ivnik, R., Kokmen, E., & Tangalos, E. (1994). Memory function in very early Alzheimer's disease. *Neurology, 44*, 867–872.

Petersen, R., Smith, G., Ivnik, R., Tangalos, E., Schaid, D., Thibodeau, S., et al. (1995). Apolipoprotein E status as a predictor of the development of Alzheimer's disease in memory-impaired individuals. *Journal of the American Medical Association, 273*, 1274–1278.

Petersen, R., Smith, G., Kokmen, E., Ivnik, R., & Tangalos, E. (1992). Memory function in normal aging. *Neurology, 42*, 396–401.

Petersen, R., Smith, G., Waring, S., Ivnik, R., Tangalos, E., & Kokmen, E. (1999). Mild cognitive impairment: Clinical characterization and outcome. *Archives of Neurology, 56*, 303–308.

Rao, V., Cupples, L., Auerbach, S., Becker, R., Burke, J., Chui, H., et al. (1995). Age at onset of Alzheimer disease is influenced by multiple genetic and non-genetic factors: The Mirage Study. *Alzheimer's Research, 1*, 159–168.

Reisberg, B., Ferris, S., deLeon, M., & Crook, T. (1982). The Global Deterioration Scale for assessment of primary degenerative dementia. *American Journal of Psychiatry, 130*, 1136–1139.

Rey, A. (1964). *L'examen clinique en psychologie*. Paris: Presses Universitaires de France.
Ritchie, K., Artero, S., & Touchon, J. (2001). Classification criteria for mild cognitive impairment: A population-based validation study. *Neurology, 56*(1), 37–42.
Ritchie, K., & Touchon, J. (2000). Mild cognitive impairment: Conceptual basis and current nosological status. *Lancet, 355*(9199), 225–228.
Rocca, W., & Kokmen, E. (1997). Referral bias in Alzheimer's disease (Response). *Journal of Clinical Epidemiology, 50*, 365–366.
Roman, G., Tatemichi, T., Erkinjuntti, T., Cummings, J., Masdeu, J., Garcia, J., et al. (1993). Vascular dementia: Diagnostic criteria for research studies. Report of the NINDS-AIREN International Workshop. *Neurology, 43*(2), 250–260.
Saykin, A., Wishart, H., Rabin, L., Flashman, L., McHugh, T., Mamourian, A., et al. (2004). Cholinergic enhancement of frontal lobe activity in mild cognitive impairment. *Brain, 127*(Pt 7), 1574–1583.
Severson, M., Smith, G., Tangalos, E., Petersen, R., Kokmen, E., Ivnik, R., et al. (1994). Patterns and predictors of institutionalization in community-based dementia patients. *Journal of the American Geriatrics Society, 42*, 181–185.
Small, S., Perera, G., DeLaPaz, R., Mayeux, R., & Stern, Y. (1999). Differential regional dysfunction of the hippocampal formation among elderly with memory decline and Alzheimer's disease. *Annals of Neurology, 45*(4), 466–472.
Smith, G., Cerhan, J., & Ivnik, R. (2002). Diagnostic utility of select WAIS-III/WMS-III indices for Alzheimer's disease. *Journal of the International Neuropsychological Society, 8*, 195.
Smith, G., Ivnik, R., Malec, J., Petersen, R., Tangalos, E., & Kurland, L. (1992). Mayo's Older Americans Normative Studies (MOANS): Factor structure of a core battery. *Psychological Assessment: A Journal of Consulting and Clinical Psychology, 4*, 382–390.
Smith, G., Ivnik, R., Malec, J., & Tangalos, E. (1993). Factor structure of the MOANS core battery: Replication in a clinical sample. *Psychological Assessment: A Journal of Consulting and Clinical Psychology, 5*, 121–124.
Smith, G., Kokmen, E., & O'Brien, P. (2000). Risk factors for nursing home placement in a population-based dementia cohort. *Journal of the American Geriatrics Society, 48*, 519–525.
Smith, G., O'Brien, P., Ivnik, R., Kokmen, E., & Tangalos, E. (2001). Prospective analysis of risk factors for nursing home placement of dementia patients. *Neurology, 57*, 1467–1473.
Smith, G., Petersen, R., Ivnik, R., Malec, J., & Tangalos, E. (1996). Subjective memory complaints, psychological distress, and longitudinal change in objective memory performance. *Psychology and Aging, 11*(2), 272–279.
Smith, G., Tangalos, E., Ivnik, R., Kokmen, E., & Petersen, R. (1995). Tolerance weighted frequency indices for non-cognitive symptoms of dementia. *American Journal of Alzheimer's Disease, 10*, 2–10.
Taylor, J., Miller, T., & Tinklenberg, J. (1992). Correlates of memory decline: A 4-year longitudinal study of older adults with memory complaints. *Psychology and Aging, 7*, 185–193.
The Lund and Manchester Groups. (1994). Clinical and neuropathological criteria for frontotemporal dementia. *Journal of Neurology, Neurosurgery and Psychiatry, 57*, 416–418.
Tierney, M., Szalai, J., Snow, W., Fisher, R., Nores, A., Nadon, G., et al. (1996). Prediction of probable Alzheimer's disease in memory-impaired patients: A prospective longitudinal study. *Neurology, 46*, 661–665.

Tsai, G., & Coyle, J. (1995). *N*-acetyl aspartate in neuropsychiatric disorders. *Progress in Neurobiology, 46*(5), 531–540.

Urenjak, J., Williams, S., Gadian, D., & Noble, M. (1993). Proton nuclear magnetic resonance spectroscopy unambiguously identifies different neural cell types. *Journal of Neuroscience, 13*(3), 981–989.

Wechsler, D. (1981). *Wechsler Adult Intelligence Scale-Revised.* New York: Psychological Corporation.

Wechsler, D. (1987). *Wechsler Memory Scale-Revised.* New York: Psychological Corporation.

Weintraub, S. (1986). The Record of Independent Living: An informant-completed measure of activities of daily living and behavior in elderly patients with cognitive impairment. *American Journal of Alzheimer's Care and Related Disorders, 7*, 35–39.

Wurtman, R., & Marie, J. (1985). Autocannibalism of choline-containing membrane phospholipids in the pathogenesis of Alzheimer's disease. *Neurochemistry International, 7*, 369–372.

Xu, Y., Jack, C., Jr., Petersen, R., O'Brien, P., Smith, G., Ivnik, R., et al. (2000). Usefulness of MRI measures of entorhinal cortex vs. hippocampus in AD. *Neurology, 54*, 1760–1767.

8 Prediction of probable Alzheimer's disease: The Sunnybrook Memory Study

Mary C. Tierney

Prediction of probable Alzheimer's disease: The Sunnybrook Memory Study

The Sunnybrook Memory Study is an ongoing prospective study that commenced in 1991. It was designed to examine the usefulness of neuropsychological, behavioral, and genetic measures in the prediction of Alzheimer's disease (AD) in nondemented patients. We attempted to optimize the selection of participants most likely to progress to AD by including patients identified by their family physicians as having memory problems but no other neurological disorders. Because family physicians are the first point of contact with the health care system by older individuals and their families, we wanted to ensure that our findings would be generalizable to patients of family physicians. Thus, our first selection criterion to define participants for this study was judgment by the family physician that cognitive impairment was present, regardless of whether this was confirmed by subsequent neuropsychological testing. Our second criterion was that participants not meet the criteria for dementia, which we verified by a thorough diagnostic work-up, including specialist medical and neuropsychological assessments. In an attempt to reduce the number of participants with dementia required to undergo the diagnostic work-up, we also requested that family physicians not refer their patients with dementia. In addition, all referred patients underwent an initial screening examination and those who scored below established cut-points on the Dementia Rating Scale (DRS) and the Mini-Mental State Examination (MMSE) were excluded. Those remaining participants who scored above the cut-points underwent a rigorous diagnostic examination to exclude dementia. Finally, because we were specifically interested in the prediction of progression to probable AD, we excluded referred patients who showed evidence of any conditions affecting the brain (e.g., stroke, Parkinson's disease, etc.).

We designed the Sunnybrook Memory Study to maintain independence between predictors and outcome measures by using different sets of tests to predict and diagnose AD and by ensuring that the diagnosticians did not have access to the predictor tests. This criterion of independence was subsequently noted in a series of articles (Users' Guide to the Medical Literature) as an important evidence-based criterion to demonstrate the validity of a diagnostic (or prognostic) test (Jaeschke, Guyatt, & Sackett, 1994a, 1994b).

The goal of this prospective study was to determine whether we could identify neuropsychological, behavioral, and genetic measures that would accurately predict progression to AD. In addition, we were also interested in the identification of easily administered predictive test batteries, sensitive and specific in a primary care patient population, that could be used by family physicians to recognize early symptoms of AD. Our specific objectives to achieve these goals were to examine the following:

(1) the accuracy of neuropsychological tests in the prediction of probable AD over 2 years;
(2) the relative contribution of ApoE ε4 genotype and neuropsychological tests to the prediction of probable AD;
(3) the accuracy of the MMSE in the prediction of probable AD and the contribution of informant and patient ratings to this prediction by the MMSE;
(4) the construct of mild cognitive impairment (MCI) and its accuracy in the prediction of AD.

The rationale for each of these objectives is provided in detail below after a description of the participants and procedure of the Sunnybrook Memory Study. Following this, a report of the findings related to each of the objectives is provided along with the implication of our findings for clinical practice and research. The implications of the findings from this study are also discussed in relation to the construct of MCI as it has been defined in previous research investigations.

Method

Participants

Family physicians in Toronto, Ontario, Canada were asked to refer patients whom they suspected of memory impairment to a research investigation being conducted at Sunnybrook & Women's College Health Sciences Centre (formerly Sunnybrook Medical Centre), a University of Toronto teaching hospital. Letters were sent to all physicians describing the purpose of the study and the inclusion and exclusion criteria. Specifically, physicians were asked to refer patients who had not been diagnosed with a dementing illness but for whom (1) there were complaints of a memory deficit from either patients themselves or from someone who knew them well, but no objective deficits were found in the clinical interview, or in employment or social situations; or (2) coworkers noticed poor performance; they showed word- and name-finding deficits or a concentration deficit; or the patient felt lost in a familiar location. Physicians were asked to exclude patients who had a history of heavy alcohol abuse, stroke, hypoxia, brain tumors, brain trauma, or known neurological disorder, e.g., Parkinson's disease. Because of the nature of the cognitive testing involved in the study, physicians were also asked to refer only those who were fluent in English and were not deaf or blind. A history of medical and neurological problems was obtained from the family physician. The Research Ethics Board of Sunnybrook & Women's College Health Sciences Centre approved this study.

After informed consent was obtained from patient and family, a psychometrist administered the MMSE (Folstein, Folstein, & McHugh, 1975) and the DRS (Mattis, 1988). Referred patients were included only if they obtained a score of ≥23 on the MMSE or a score of ≥123 on the DRS. See Figure 8.1 for a flow diagram describing the number of participants referred to the study and those meeting inclusion and exclusion criteria for the 2-year duration.

Procedure

Participants were seen by one of four experienced geriatricians for a formal baseline diagnostic assessment. During the geriatrician examination, the MMSE was administered and standard questions were posed to patients and their informants (a relative or close friend) about their functioning in their normal environment. A work-up consisting of a thorough physical examination, CT scan, SPECT scan, and laboratory tests including hematological, renal, hepatic, and metabolic function tests was conducted to rule out alternative causes of memory impairment. This followed the guidelines of the Workgroup of the National Institute of Neurological and Communicative Disorders and Stroke and the Alzheimer's Disease and Related Disorders Association (NINCDS-ADRDA) (McKhann, Drachman, Folstein, Katzman, Price, & Stadlan, 1984), which is the reference standard for a diagnosis of AD. These criteria exclude chronic alcohol or drug abuse, chronic infections, stroke, hypoxia, metabolic disorders, nutritional disorders, intracranial mass lesions, psychoses, brain trauma, or other neurological diseases including Parkinson's disease and Huntington's.

Next, patients were administered a diagnostic neuropsychological test battery by a psychometrist who was unaware of the physician's diagnosis. This assessment consisted of the Wechsler Memory Scale (WMS) Information and Orientation subtests (Wechsler & Stone, 1974); Wechsler Memory Scale-Revised Visual Reproduction (Wechsler, 1987)—immediate and delayed recall; California Verbal Learning Test (Delis, Massman, Butters, & Salmon, 1991); odd or even items of the Boston Naming Test (Kaplan, Goodglass, & Weintraub, 1983); Controlled Oral Word Association Test (letters P, R, W) (Spreen & Benton, 1969); Category Fluency (animal names); Wechsler Adult Intelligence Scale—Revised Digit

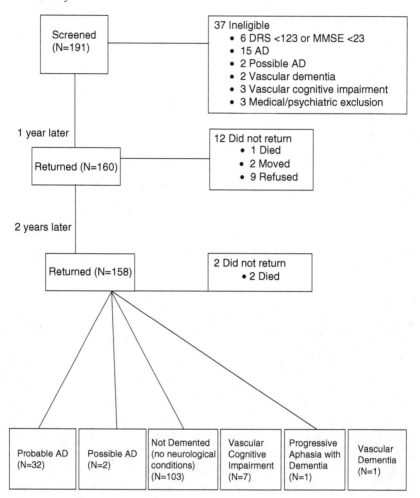

Figure 8.1 Flow chart of participants through the 2 years of the study with diagnoses after 2 years.

Span, Similarities, and Digit Symbol subtests (Wechsler, 1981); Read Perceptual Closure Test (Read, 1988); Finger Tapping Test (Reitan, 1977); and Token Test (Benton & Hamsher, 1983).

At this session, participants were also administered a research battery of tests, the results of which were not provided to the diagnosticians. See below for a complete description of the tests used to predict probable AD.

After formulating their own diagnostic judgments independently, the experienced board-certified neuropsychologist met with the geriatrician to decide whether the patient met the criteria for dementia of the *Diagnostic and Statistical Manual, Revised Third Edition* (DSM-III-R) (American Psychiatric Association, 1987).

Eligible patients received two subsequent medical and neuropsychological diagnostic assessments at 12-month intervals, which were similar to the baseline assessment. Neither the geriatrician nor the neuropsychologist had access to participants' previous diagnostic assessments at baseline. If the patient was diagnosed as demented or found to have new clinical evidence of a neurological condition other than AD by either diagnostician, a radiological and laboratory work-up was conducted as previously described. As can be seen in the figure, after 2 years 32 participants progressed to probable AD, 2 to possible AD, 103 remained nondemented with no new neurological conditions, 7 met criteria for vascular cognitive impairment, 1 for progressive aphasia with dementia, and 1 for vascular dementia.

Measures used to predict probable AD

Neuropsychological tests

Several additional tests were administered that were not part of the diagnostic work-up and the results of these tests were not given to the diagnosticians. The following 10 test scores were derived from the research battery: raw scores on the Wechsler Memory Scale (1) Mental Control, (2) Paired-Associate (PA) Easy, and (3) PA Hard and (4) Logical Memory subtests (Wechsler & Stone, 1974); Rey Auditory Verbal Learning Test (RAVLT) (Rey, 1964; Tuokko, Kristjansson, & Miller, 1995), (5) mean number of words recalled over five learning trials (immediate recall), (6) number of words recalled after an interference list (delayed recall), and (7) percentage of true positives and true negatives from a recognition list; Controlled Oral Word Association Test (Spreen & Benton, 1969): (8) number of words beginning with F, A, and S generated in 1 min for each letter; and Trail Making Test (Reitan, 1977) (intermediate form): time taken to complete (9) Trails A and (10) Trails B.

Patient and informant ratings of cognitive functioning

Participants also received the 19-item rating scale from Section H of the Cambridge Mental Disorders Examination (CAMDEX) (Neri, Roth, Rubichi, DeVreese, Bolzani, & Cipolli, 2001; Roth et al., 1986). All patients were asked to provide the name of a study informant, i.e., the person with whom they were most familiar and who knew them well. A trained research assistant then administered the same set of 19 items from Section H of the CAMDEX to this informant at a time when the patient was not present. These 19 items addressed either the patient's or informant's perceptions of the patient's difficulties in several areas of cognitive functioning. The scale has a maximum score of 19, a higher score indicating that more difficulties were acknowledged.

Genotyping at ApoE

Genotypes at ApoE were deduced using the methods previously described by this group (Tierney et al., 1996b). Three different observers read each autoradiograph independently.

Results

Participants

The mean baseline age and education as well as performance on the DRS and MMSE screening instruments of the participants who returned for their year 2 assessments and received either a diagnosis of AD or did not develop dementia nor any other neurological condition are provided in Table 8.1. As can be seen, the participants who did not develop dementia were significantly younger and scored significantly higher on the MMSE and DRS. The remainder of this section will describe the findings of the various individual studies designed to examine the predictive utility of neuropsychological, behavioral, and genetic measures for the early identification of incident AD.

Accuracy of neuropsychological tests in the prediction of probable AD over 2 years

The baseline scores on the neuropsychological research battery of 29 participants who progressed to probable AD and of 98 who did not convert to

Table 8.1 Baseline mean (±standard deviations) on demographic measures and test scores of the participants who returned for their diagnostic assessments at year 2 and were diagnosed with AD or did not develop dementia nor any other neurological condition

	Developed probable or possible AD	*Did not develop dementia nor any other neurological conditions*	*t-test difference between groups*
n	34.0	103.0	
Age (years)	74.26 (5.67)	70.86 (7.59)	$t = 2.4\ (135) = 0.02$
Education (years)	12.82 (2.76)	13.9 (3.35)	$t = 1.70\ (135) = 0.09$
MMSE	26.00 (2.17)	28.09 (1.72)	$t = 5.74\ (135) < .0001$
DRS	124.56 (6.56)	137.52 (4.27)	$t = 10.80\ (42.6) < .0001$

Note: MMSE = Mini-Mental State Examination; DRS = Dementia Rating Scale.

dementia nor had any other neurological conditions were examined in order to determine the accuracy of this battery to predict progression to AD over 2 years. This sample was smaller than the original sample because it only included participants who completed all aspects of the baseline research neuropsychological battery. First, we examined the intercorrelation matrix derived from 10 scores on the tests in our neuropsychological research battery and eliminated variables if there were correlations of $\geq.80$ to reduce multicollinearity. The correlation between the mean number of words recalled immediately after presentation over five trials on the RAVLT and delayed recall on the same measure met this criterion. Because previous research has shown that delayed recall is important to diagnostic outcome, we conducted logistic regression (Swets & Pickett, 1982) without the immediate recall score, leaving nine test scores in the model. Age and education were included as covariates in all analyses.

The model that included the nine research neuropsychological test scores was highly significant, $\chi^2(11) = 109.36$, $p < .0001$. The sensitivity was 76%, and specificity was 94%. Sensitivity represents the number of AD cases with predicted probabilities $\geq.50$. Specificity is the number of cognitively impaired cases with predicted probability of AD < .50. Two tests contributed significantly to this model: RAVLT delayed recall, $\chi^2(1) = 9.79$, $p = .0018$, and WMS Mental Control, $\chi^2(1) = 4.55$, $p = .033$. We ran another logistic regression that included only the two measures that significantly contributed to the full model. This reduced model was also significant, $\chi^2(4) = 78.022, p < .0001$. The sensitivity and specificity of the reduced model were identical to the full model, i.e., 76 and 94%.

Likelihood ratios (LRs) determine the extent to which a test result will improve a diagnostic judgment that has been based simply on prevalence of the disease (or pretest probability). The LR of a positive test (LR+) for AD tells us how much the pretest odds of having the disease increase following a positive test. LR+ is the quotient of two measures: (1) the likelihood of obtaining a given test result among people with the target disorder (sensitivity); and (2) the likelihood of obtaining the same test result among people without the target disorder (1−specificity). The pretest probability refers to the diagnostician's judgment about the presence of the disease in a patient before seeing the results of the test. The post-test probability is the diagnostician's judgment about the presence of the disease after knowing the test results. If the test does not appreciably raise or lower the pretest probability, it is not useful diagnostically (Sackett, Haynes, Guyatt, & Tugwell, 1991). The LR+ was 12.67 and the LR− was 0.26. Following the guidelines provided by Jaeschke et al. (1994b), the LR+ would generate a large change in pretest to post-test probability of developing AD within 2 years and the LR− would generate a small but potentially important change in pretest to post-test probability. If we assume that the pretest probability of progression to AD is 50% (1:1 odds), the LR+ value of 12.67 indicates that a positive test result would increase the post-test probability of progression to AD to 93%

(12.67/13.43), whereas the LR– value of 0.26 indicates that a negative test result would decrease the post-test probability to 21% (0.26/1.26).

Thus this battery of two tests with the covariates of age and education, heretofore referred to as the Alzheimer Predictive Index (API), is a useful predictive tool for early identification of probable AD. The reproducibility of these findings with computer-intensive methods using bootstrapping and split-sample procedures has been demonstrated elsewhere (Tierney & Szalai, 1998).

Table 8.2 provides the regression coefficients for the two tests, two covariates, and the intercept in the reduced predictive model, which were published elsewhere (Tierney et al., 1996a). One can calculate the probability of a new patient's progression to AD using these regression coefficients. An example of the application of these findings to a new patient is as follows. The patient is a 70-year-old woman with 10 years of education, whose husband reports she has memory problems. The results of a medical work-up indicate that she does not meet criteria for dementia nor does she have any other identifiable cause for her memory problem. The API (RAVLT delayed recall and WMS Mental Control) is administered and the regression coefficients are applied to her scores on the two tests and her age and education. The patient receives a RAVLT delayed recall score of 2 and a WMS Mental Control of 5. First calculate the linear combination (X) of the products of the regression coefficients using the values for age, education, RAVLT short delay, and Mental Control in our example as follows: X = 2.3110 + .0339 (70) + .1163 (10) + (–.8511) (2) + (–.4665) (5) = 1.866. The predicted probability of AD for this specific case is then calculated using the following equation: $e^x/(1 + e^x)$ = .8596. The probability of AD can range from 0 to 1: the larger the value the higher the probability of having AD. Thus, this woman would have an 86% probability of developing AD in 2 years and should be considered for a more detailed diagnostic work-up.

Replication of the accuracy of neuropsychological prediction of AD is required in new samples. One such replication study that used different participants, tests, and language of administration was conducted in Montpellier, France (Artero, Tierney, Touchon, & Ritchie, 2002). In this investigation, a sample of 128 subjects was randomly selected from a larger cohort of 397 cognitively impaired participants who did not meet diagnostic criteria for dementia. The tests used to predict incident AD were part of a computerized battery of tests that have been described in detail elsewhere (Ritchie, Huppert, Nargeot, Pinek, & Ledesert, 1993). In brief, these tests assessed working memory, visual and verbal span, verbal and visuospatial secondary memory, implicit memory, language skills, visuospatial performance, object matching, visual reasoning, and focused and divided attention. This battery was administered at baseline and was independent of the diagnostic process. Using logistic regression analyses, the results indicated that three of these tests, which measured delayed narrative recall, construction of an abstract figure, and category fluency, showed a sensitivity of 73% and specificity of

Table 8.2 Results of logistic linear regression analyses of the relationship between diagnostic classification at year 2 and variables in the reduced model

Variables	Regression coefficient	p value
Intercept	2.3110	.5414
Age	0.0339	.4495
Education	0.1274	.3614
Delayed recall	−0.8511	.0001
Mental control	−0.4665	.0129

99% in the prediction of AD 2 years later. The regression coefficients and instructions for their application to new patients are provided in this paper (Artero et al., 2002).

We also examined the accuracy of neuropsychological prediction of progression to AD over a longer period in participants of the Canadian Study of Health and Aging (CSHA). The CSHA is a 10-year longitudinal study designed to examine the prevalence and incident of dementia in Canada. Specifically we examined whether neuropsychological tests accurately predicted incident AD 5 and 10 years prior to diagnosis in participants who were initially nondemented and free of any condition likely to affect the brain (Tierney, Yao, Kiss, & McDowell, 2005). The CSHA was conducted in three waves: CSHA-1 (1991–92), CSHA-2 (1996–97), and CSHA-3 (2001–02). The 10-year prediction study included those who completed neuropsychological testing at CSHA-1 and received a diagnostic assessment at CSHA-3 ($n = 263$). The 5-year prediction study included those who completed neuropsychological testing at CSHA-2 and received a diagnostic assessment at CSHA-3 ($n = 551$). The diagnostic work-up for dementia at CSHA-3 was formulated without knowledge of neuropsychological test performance at CSHA-1 or CSHA-2. We excluded cases with a baseline diagnosis of dementia or a prior history of any condition likely to affect the brain. Age and education were included in all analyses as covariates. In the 10-year follow-up study, only one test (RAVLT delayed verbal recall) emerged from the forward regression analyses. The model with this test and two covariates was significant, $X^2(3) = 31.61, p < .0001$ (sensitivity = 73%, specificity = 70%). In the 5-year follow-up study, three tests (RAVLT delayed verbal recall, animal fluency, and WMS Information subtest) emerged from the forward logistic regression analyses. The model was significant, $X^2(5) = 91.34, p < .0001$ (sensitivity = 74%, specificity = 83%). Both models were supported with bootstrapping estimates. These results provide evidence that neuropsychological tests can accurately predict progression to AD 5 and 10 years prior to diagnosis in a large epidemiological sample of nondemented participants. The regression coefficients and illustration of their application to new patients are provided in this paper.

The relative contribution of ApoE ε4 genotype and neuropsychological tests to the prediction of probable AD

We examined the predictive utility of ApoE genotype in a subsample of the memory-impaired participants of the Sunnybrook Memory Study who agreed to provide blood samples to perform the genotyping. (The characteristics of the participants and methods used in the Sunnybrook Memory Study have been fully described earlier in this chapter.) The subsample of patients who gave blood in these two groups included 27 patients who progressed to AD and 78 who did not progress to AD. We found that the predictive model that included ApoE genotype, together with age and education, significantly predicted progression to AD (Tierney et al., 1996b). We also wanted to examine whether ApoE genotype improved the prediction of progression to AD by the API. To do this, we added genotype to the model consisting of the RAVLT delayed recall, WMS Mental Control, age, and education. The model with both genotype and the API measures was not a significantly better predictor of progression to AD than the model with only the API measures (Tierney et al., 1996a). Based on these findings, we cannot conclude that ApoE genotype improves the prediction obtained with the API alone.

We also examined the role of ApoE ε4 genotype in the 10- and 5-year neuropsychological predictive models generated from the CSHA longitudinal study (Tierney et al., 2005). We found that the genotype contributed significantly to the 10-year predictive model but not to the 5-year model. Prior studies have shown that ApoE genotype is predictive of progression to AD but the results of the Sunnybrook Memory Study and the CSHA study suggest that when one is five or fewer years away from a diagnosis of AD, cognitive test performance accounts for more of the variation in diagnostic outcome than genotype and hence is relatively more predictive of AD. However, when progression to AD is 10 years away, neuropsychological test performance accounts for less of the variation in diagnostic outcome because there is less cognitive impairment, and as a result, genotyping adds to the predictive model. Further investigation is needed to examine whether the inclusion of additional biomarkers and other cognitive or neuroradiological measures may improve the 5- and 10-year prediction of progression to AD.

Role of MMSE in prediction of probable AD

The two API tests (the RAVLT delayed recall and WMS Mental Control subtest of the WMS) require approximately 20 min testing time as well as expertise in their administration and thus are unlikely to be used by the primary care physician. Therefore, we wanted to determine if briefer simpler-to-administer tests were sufficiently accurate that they could be used by the primary care physician and other clinicians in the prediction of progression to AD. First, we examined the utility of the MMSE in predicting who would develop AD (Tierney, Szalai, Dunn, Geslani, & McDowell, 2000) in nondemented patients, who were referred by their family physicians to the Sunnybrook Memory Study (described earlier), and who were followed for 2 years. We found that a cut-off score of 24 or less produced a sensitivity of only 31% but a specificity of 96% in the prediction of progression to AD. The optimal combination, which maximized both sensitivity and specificity, was a cut-off score of 27. This produced a sensitivity of 69% and a specificity of 70%, indicating that knowledge of performance on the MMSE, relative to this cut-off score, would produce a small but potentially important change in pretest to post-test probability of developing AD.

Next, we wanted to determine whether we could improve the predictive accuracy of the MMSE in the 2-year prediction of probable AD with the addition of an informant and participant rating scale. We examined the combined predictive accuracy of the MMSE and the 19-item Informant Rating Scale from section H of the Cambridge Diagnostic Examination (CAMDEX) (Tierney, Herrmann, Geslani, & Szalai, 2003). The participant and an informant who knew the participant well completed the latter 19-item scale. Informants included 61 spouses, 31 adult children, 8 siblings, and 24 friends or nonrelatives who were familiar with the participants. The relationship between type of informant and diagnostic outcome 2 years later was not significant, $X^2(3) = 4.79$, $p = .188$. With the covariates of age and education included, we found that the MMSE and Informant Rating Scale showed a significant improvement over MMSE alone $p < .0001$, with a sensitivity of 83%, specificity of 79%, LR+ of 3.93, and LR– of 0.22. The magnitude of these LRs indicates that the use of these two measures would produce a small to moderate change from the clinician's pretest judgment of probability of progressing to AD to his or her post-test judgment of this probability (Jaeschke et al., 1994b) and thus would meet evidence-based criteria for their use as diagnostic or prognostic tests. We also examined the predictive accuracy of the Participant Rating Scale but it, however, did not add significantly to the predictive utility of the MMSE.

The regression coefficients for the MMSE and Informant Rating Scale, which are provided in the paper (Tierney et al., 2003), can be applied to new patients' scores on these tests to determine their predicted probability of progression to AD by using the same method as described for the API. Alternatively, the health-care professional can go to our website to print the test forms and enter the test data so that the predicted probability of progression to AD for a new patient can be automatically calculated. This website is located at http://alzheimerprediction.ca.

Although the combination of the MMSE and Informant Rating Scale produce an acceptable change from pretest to post-test probability of progression to AD, this combination was less accurate than the API (RAVLT delayed recall and WMS Mental Control). A comparison of the area under the curve of the API (AUC = 0.95) with the combined MMSE and Informant Rating Scale (AUC = 0.87) indicates that the API is significantly more accurate, $p < .01$. Thus if one has training in the administration of the API and the time to administer it, it would be the preferred approach to identification of patients at risk, but in situations where this is not the case, the combined MMSE and Informant Rating Scale is an acceptable alternative.

The construct of mild cognitive impairment (MCI) and its accuracy in the prediction of AD

Petersen and colleagues (Petersen, Smith, Waring, Ivnik, Tangalos, & Kokmen, 1999) defined MCI as the transitional state between normal aging and early AD. The criteria for MCI proposed by Petersen's group at the Mayo Clinic are subjective memory complaint, normal performance of activities of daily living, normal general cognitive function, abnormal memory for age on a memory test, and no evidence of dementia. Petersen defines abnormal memory as "generally" >$1.5SD$ below the mean on a memory test. If MCI is considered a transitional state between normal aging and AD, its validity can only be determined by the extent to which it predicts progression to AD. Progression rates for MCI rates reported by Petersen's group are approximately 12% per year (Petersen et al., 1999). Ritchie and colleagues (Ritchie, Artero, & Touchon, 2001) attempted to replicate the conversion rates reported by the Mayo Clinic group in a subgroup of their epidemiological population sample of elderly (over 60 years of age) people in France. Their subgroup consisted of nondemented people who had subjective memory complaints plus proxy rating of some degree of deterioration over the last year. They used a computerized battery of neuropsychological tests to apply the criteria of MCI to their sample. However, the abnormal memory criterion they used was a cut-off score of $-1SD$ below the mean on a memory test. They found the prevalence rate of MCI in their sample to be only 9%. Furthermore, only 11% of the participants classified as MCI converted to senile dementia by year 3.

A similar epidemiological study (Ganguli, Dodge, Shen, & DeKosky, 2004) attempted to estimate the prevalence and progression rate to AD, also using Petersen's criteria. This study reported a 3–4% prevalence of MCI in their community-based sample, and a conversion rate to AD after 2 years between 10 and 17%. Because of these large discrepancies between these findings, we undertook a study in which we operationalized MCI according to the criteria originally proposed by Petersen's group at the Mayo Clinic. In our investigation (Geslani, Tierney, Herrmann, & Szalai, 2005), participants were the 160 nondemented patients referred to the Memory Study by their family physicians who returned the next year for follow-up assessments. Our criterion for abnormal memory was $-1.5SD$ below the mean on age- and sex-corrected norms of the California Verbal Learning Test. The application of these criteria to our sample of patients resulted in a baseline MCI prevalence of 35%, considerably higher than the

3 or 9% reported in epidemiological studies (Ganguli et al., 2004; Ritchie et al., 2001). Each participant in our study was followed for 2 years and reassessed annually to determine rate of conversion to AD. After 1 year, our conversion rate was 41% and after 2 years it was 60%. There were several differences between our study and those conducted by Petersen, Ganguli, and Ritchie, the most notable of which were differences in the participants included in the studies. Ritchie's sample included participants from a representative sample of general practices in the south of France who had subjective memory complaints and deterioration in at least one area of cognitive function over the past year as judged by a proxy. Ganguli included a random sample drawn from Pennsylvania voter registration lists. Petersen included a mixture of participants, some referred by their physicians and some referred on the basis of their own complaints. We, on the other hand, asked family physicians to refer their own patients to the study if there was a concern about their memory. Therefore one explanation for the higher conversion rate found in our study is that family physicians were referring those patients from their practice who had experienced a decline over time and thus, although not meeting criteria for dementia, were already on the trajectory towards AD. These different conversion rates cannot be attributed to greater baseline cognitive impairment in the MCI sample of the Sunnybrook Memory Study because performance by this group was similar to, if not slightly better than, that of the participants in the study by Petersen (Petersen et al., 1999) on those neuropsychological tests that were used in common in the two studies, including the MMSE, Controlled Oral Word Association Test, and the Boston Naming Test.

Another explanation for the differences is the use of different normative cut-off scores for abnormal memory. We used the more stringent criteria of $-1.5SD$ below the mean for age and sex matched individuals on a memory test, compared to $-1SD$ (Ganguli et al., 2004; Ritchie et al., 2001), and Petersen's was somewhere in the middle ("generally" -1.5). Our inclusion of participants with a greater degree of memory impairment at baseline no doubt contributed to the higher rate of conversion 1 and 2 years later. However, when we changed our inclusion criterion for MCI to $1.0SD$ below the mean, this reduced our progression rate to 30% in the first year and 48% in the second year. While these progression rates represent a decrease in the progression rates found at $-1.5SD$ below the mean, they are not as low as those reported by Ritchie or Ganguli and were still more than twice as high as those of Petersen et al. This suggests that while the cut-off for abnormal memory has implications for progression rates to AD, physician referral and history of memory decline may be more important contributors to this outcome. Finally, the three studies used different measures to determine whether an individual met criteria for abnormal memory, normal activities of daily living, and normal cognitive function, which may have had an additional effect on conversion rates. Taken together, these findings suggest that before MCI is used clinically to identify incipient AD it requires further refinement and evidence regarding its reliability and predictive utility.

Conclusions

The findings from the Sunnybrook Memory Study as well as the replication of the approach with a 2-year cohort study from the south of France and with the 5- and 10-year cohorts from the CSHA inform us that neuropsychological tests accurately predict progression to AD 2–10 years prior to diagnosis. In particular, these studies have consistently demonstrated the importance of delayed verbal recall in this prediction. These studies also have generated regression coefficients that can be applied to new patients' scores on the tests to determine new patients' individual risks of progression to AD. Of course as with any research finding, these findings can only be applied to new patients who are similar to the research sample from which the regression coefficients were generated. It is anticipated that the application of these findings to new people will assist with decisions about patient care in the clinical setting. For example, a family physician who learns that his or her patient has an 85% probability of developing AD within 2 years may decide to monitor the patient more carefully, mobilize community support for the individual to maintain independence, or refer for specialist opinion. This approach could also be used to make decisions regarding participant selection for clinical trials thereby permitting investigation of therapeutic interventions at a stage of the disease when the individual is still functioning in society. Details of this approach have been provided elsewhere (Szalai & Tierney, 1998).

Studies that have examined the accuracy of the construct of MCI for the prediction of AD suggest that the construct may be unstable and that there are considerable variations in its prevalence rates and progression rates to AD. These inconsistencies have been largely due to several reasons, including the use of criteria for this construct, use of different samples, and different tests to measure the criteria. The application of cut-off scores to members of cohorts from population studies is likely to generate a lower prevalence rate and rate of progression to AD than the application of the same cut-off scores to individuals who have been selected by clinicians knowledgeable of their past history. Thus, while MCI may prove to be a useful construct to identify those at risk for AD, this construct needs to be validated in terms of its accuracy to predict AD with diverse samples.

Given the shortcomings with the current construct of MCI, one recommendation is to define MCI based on its probability of progression to AD such that an individual would have to meet a predetermined probability of progressing to AD over a specific period of time. For example, if the probability of progression to AD was defined as at least 70% in 5 years, the individual would be administered the specific neuropsychological tests for which regression coefficients have been provided and then the probability of progression could be calculated. If the individual's probability of AD was >70%, then he or she would be included in the group. Similar to the original criteria intended to describe a group at risk for AD (Petersen et al., 1999), a clinical diagnosis of dementia would have to be ruled out first. Another criterion would be that the individual would have no other neurological conditions that might account for any cognitive impairment, as the regression coefficients could only be applied to individuals with this characteristic. This approach would allow for more specificity in group definition such that an individual could be considered to be MCI 2-year AD subtype, or MCI 5-year AD subtype, etc., and as a result, this approach would be more precise for patient care or clinical trial selection. As with the application of any research findings, these new criteria could only be applied to individuals who have been selected according to the criteria used in the studies that have generated the regression coefficients.

Future directions

Future research should address the question of whether other neuropsychological tests would improve prediction of progression to AD. Another important consideration is the role of noncognitive measures and whether they would improve the predictive accuracy of AD, whether alone or when added to the cognitive and behavioral measures that have been found to accurately predict incident AD. Other noncognitive markers that are promising early predictors are neuroradiological measures (Convit, de Asis, de Leon, Tarshish, De Santi, & Rusinek, 2000) and cerebral spinal fluid markers (Blennow & Hampel, 2003), for example. ApoE genotype is a significant predictor of progression to AD and based on the findings presented in this chapter it is more likely to be a useful prognostic indicator the further an individual is from showing signs of cognitive deterioration and meeting clinical criteria for the disease. However, as the clinical symptoms progress and there is greater clinical expression of the disease, performance on neuropsychological measures then becomes more useful in the identification of those at risk. Examination of other biomarkers in a similar manner will be of importance. In future research, regression coefficients can be generated for prediction of other forms of dementia. It may well be that the neuropsychological tests that have been found to be predictive of incident AD will not also be predictive of other forms of dementia, such as vascular dementia or Lewy body dementia. These questions await further research.

Acknowledgments

This is to acknowledge the contribution to diagnostic assessments in the Sunnybrook Memory Study by Dr. Rory Fisher, Dr. W. Gary Snow, and Dr. Grant Nadon and to biostatistical guidance from the late Dr. John Paul Szalai. The Sunnybrook Memory Study was funded by the Ontario Ministry of Health and Long-term Care, Toronto, Ontario, Canada.

References

American Psychiatric Association. (1987). *Diagnostic and Statistical Manual of mental disorders* (3rd Rev. ed.). Washington, DC: American Psychiatric Association.

Artero, S., Tierney, M. C., Touchon, J., & Ritchie, K. (2002). Prediction of transition from cognitive impairment to senile dementia: A prospective, longitudinal study. *Acta Psychiatrica Scandinavica, 107*, 390–393.

Benton, A., & Hamsher, K. (1983). *Multilingual Aphasia Examination*. Iowa City: AJA Associates, Inc.

Blennow, K., & Hampel, H. (2003). CSF markers for incipient Alzheimer's disease. *Lancet Neurology, 2*, 605–613.

Convit, A., de Asis, J., de Leon, M., Tarshish, C., De Santi, S., & Rusinek, H. (2000). Atrophy of the medial occipitotemporal, inferior, and middle temporal gyri in nondemented elderly predict decline to Alzheimer's disease. *Neurobiology of Aging, 21*, 19–26.

Delis, D., Massman, P., Butters, N., & Salmon, D. (1991). Profiles of demented and amnesic patients on the California Verbal Learning Test: Implications for the assessment of memory disorders. *Psychological Assessment, 3*, 19–26.

Folstein, M., Folstein, S., & McHugh, S. (1975). Mini-Mental State: A practical method for grading the cognitive status of patients for the clinician. *Journal of Psychiatric Research, 12*, 189–198.

Ganguli, M., Dodge, H., Shen, C., & DeKosky, S. (2004). Mild cognitive impairment, amnestic type: An epidemiologic study. *Neurology, 63*, 115–121.

Geslani, D., Tierney, M. C., Herrmann, N., & Szalai, J. (2005). Mild cognitive impairment: An operational definition and its conversion rate to Alzheimer's disease. *Dementia and Geriatric Cognitive Disorders, 19*, 383–389.

Jaeschke, R., Guyatt, G., & Sackett, D. L. (1994a). Users' guides to the medical literature. III. How to use an article about a diagnostic test. A. Are the results of the study valid? *Journal of the American Medical Association, 271*, 389–391.

Jaeschke, R., Guyatt, G., & Sackett, D. L. (1994b). Users' guides to the medical literature. III. How to use an article about a diagnostic test. B. What are the results and will they help me in caring for my patients? *Journal of the American Medical Association, 271*, 703–707.

Kaplan, E., Goodglass, H., & Weintraub, S. (1983). *Boston Naming Test*. Philadelphia: Lea & Febiger.

Mattis, S. (1988). *Dementia Rating Scale: Professional Manual*. Florida: Psychological Assessment Resources, Inc.

McKhann, G., Drachman, D., Folstein, M., Katzman, R., Price, D., & Stadlan, E. (1984). Clinical diagnosis of Alzheimer's disease: Report of the NINCDS-ADRDA Work Group under the auspices of Department of Health and Human Services Task Force on Alzheimer's disease. *Neurology, 34*, 939–944.

Neri, M., Roth, M., Rubichi, S., DeVreese, L., Bolzani, R., & Cipolli, C. (2001). The validity of informant report for grading the severity of Alzheimer's disease. *Aging (Milano), 13*, 22–29.

Petersen, R., Smith, G., Waring, S., Ivnik, R., Tangalos, E., & Kokmen, E. (1999). Mild cognitive impairment: Clinical characterization and outcome. *Archives of Neurology, 56*, 303–308.

Read, D. E. (1988). Age-related changes in performance on a visual-closure test. *Journal of Clinical and Experimental Neuropsychology, 10*, 451–466.

Reitan, R. M. (1977). *Manual of administration of neuropsychological test batteries for adults and children.* Tucson, AZ: Neuropsychology Laboratories.

Rey, A. (1964). *L'examen clinique en psychologie.* Paris: Presses universitaires de France.

Ritchie, K., Artero, S., & Touchon, J. (2001). Classification criteria for mild cognitive impairment. *Neurology, 56,* 37–42.

Ritchie, K., Huppert, F. A., Nargeot, C., Pinek, B., & Ledesert, B. (1993). Computerized cognitive examination of the elderly (ECO): The development of a neuropsychological examination for clinic and population use. *International Journal of Geriatric Psychiatry, 8,* 899–914.

Roth, M., Tym, E., Mountjoy, C. Q., Huppert, F. A., Hendrie, H., Verma, S., et al. (1986). CAMDEX. A standardized instrument for the diagnosis of mental disorder in the elderly with special reference to the early detection of dementia. *British Journal of Psychiatry, 149,* 698–709.

Sackett, D. L., Haynes, R. B., Guyatt, G. H., & Tugwell, P. (1991). *Clinical epidemiology: A basic science for clinical medicine* (2nd ed.). Toronto: Little, Brown and Company.

Spreen, O., & Benton, A. (1969). *Neurosensory center comprehensive examination for aphasia.* Victoria: Neuropsychology Laboratory.

Swets, J., & Pickett, R. (1982). *Evaluation of diagnostic systems: Methods from signal detection theory.* New York: Academic Press.

Szalai, J. P. & Tierney, M. C. (1998). Preventing the emergence of Alzheimer's disease in high-risk patients: Part 2: The optimal design for clinical trials. *International Journal of Pharmaceutical Medicine, 8,* 75–78.

Tierney, M. C., Herrmann, F., Geslani, D., & Szalai, J. (2003). Contribution of informant and patient ratings to the accuracy of the Mini-Mental State Examination in predicting probable Alzheimer's disease. *Journal of the American Geriatrics Society, 51,* 813–818.

Tierney, M. C., & Szalai, J. P. (1998). Preventing the emergence of Alzheimer's disease in high-risk patients: Part 1: The optimal method for risk assessment. *International Journal of Pharmaceutical Medicine, 12,* 71–74.

Tierney, M. C., Szalai, J., Dunn, E., Geslani, D., & McDowell, I. (2000). Prediction of probable Alzheimer's disease in patients with symptoms suggestive of memory impairment: Value of the Mini-Mental State Examination. *Archives of Family Medicine, 9,* 527–532.

Tierney, M. C., Szalai, J. P., Snow, W. G., Fisher, R. H., Nores, A., Nadon, G., et al. (1996a). Prediction of probable Alzheimer's disease in memory-impaired patients: A prospective longitudinal study. *Neurology, 46,* 661–665.

Tierney, M. C., Szalai, J. P., Snow, W. G., Fisher, R. H., Tsuda, T., Chi, H., et al. (1996b). A prospective study of the clinical utility of ApoE genotype in the prediction of outcome in patients with memory impairment. *Neurology, 46,* 149–154.

Tierney, M. C., Yao, C., Kiss, A., & McDowell, I. (2005). Neuropsychological tests accurately predict incident Alzheimer's disease after five and ten years. *Neurology, 64,* 1853–1859.

Tuokko, H., Kristjansson, E., & Miller, J. (1995). Neuropsychological detection of dementia: An overview of the neuropsychological component of the Canadian Study of Health and Aging. *Journal of Clinical and Experimental Neuropsychology, 17,* 352–373.

Wechsler, D. (1981). *Wechsler Adult Intelligence Scale-Revised.* New York: Psychological Corporation.

Wechsler, D. (1987). *Wechsler Memory Scale-Revised.* San Antonio: Psychological Corporation.

Wechsler, D., & Stone, C. P. (1974). *Wechsler Memory Scale.* New York: Psychological Corporation.

9 Studies in the Leipzig Memory Clinic: Contribution to the concept of mild cognitive impairment

Henrike Wolf and Hermann-Josef Gertz

Introduction

The Leipzig Memory Clinic

The Leipzig Memory Clinic (MC) is placed in the Department of Psychiatry, at the University of Leipzig, Germany. It was founded in 1991 as an approach to bridge the gap between basic researchers and practitioners (Volker Bigl, Thomas Arendt, Dirk Zedlick).

Today, the Leipzig MC is a specialized diagnostic centre for putative dementia disorders, serving the larger Leipzig area. Referrals are received from specialists in the fields of neurology, psychiatry, and internal medicine as well as from general practitioners. There is no systematic or binding referral system—the current health system in Germany does allow such a setting. The main clinical–practical purpose of our MC is the diagnostic work-up in cases with suspected dementia disorders. The diagnostic procedures are based on consensus recommendations in the field (Lasek & Müller-Oerlinghausen, 1997; Muller, Wolf, Kiefer, & Gertz, 2003). Patients are examined clinically (psychiatric and neurological examination, Clinical Dementia Rating (CDR)) and neuropsychologically with different screening tests, the Structured Interview for Diagnosis of Alzheimer type, Multi-infarct dementia, and dementia of other aetiology according to ICD-10 and DSM-III-R (SIDAM; Zaudig, Mittelhammer, & Hiller, 1991), and neurocognitive battery tests, including the Consortium to Establish a Registry for Alzheimer's Disease (CERAD) battery, the Wechsler Logical Memory test, and trail-making tests A and B. To exclude secondary causes of dementia, a computerized tomography (CT) or magnetic resonance imaging (MRI) scan and standard laboratory tests are performed, including blood count, electrolytes, thyroid function, vitamin B_{12} and folate, cholesterol, HbA1C, homocysteine and if indicated treponema pallidum and borrelia serology, and cerebral spinal fluid (CSF) analyses. In addition, a variable set of research tools is being applied including volumetric MRI, quantitative electroencephalograms (qEEG), peripheral blood markers, and CSF markers. After the completion of the diagnostic process (sometimes in an in-patient setting), a treatment recommendation is given or treatment is initiated. At present, a significant proportion (approximately 50%) of the referrals remain in long-term treatment in our clinic with one to three annual follow-up visits. Information, education, and guided caregiver groups usually accompany the diagnostic and therapeutic process. Depending on the available resources, there were great variations in the number of patient visits over time (averaging 200–400 visits per year). Currently, we are 1 out of 14 centres in the German Competence Network of Dementia. Due to extra resources from this initiative, there are currently about 1200 visits per year, 300 of which are new referrals.

There are four common clinical diagnostic groups:

1. (Young-) elderly people without objective cognitive decline, seeking information or potential treatment because of subjective concern or a family history of dementia.
2. Referrals from practitioners because of cognitive decline/suspected dementia. This constitutes the largest subgroup of our referrals (approximately 70%). Most common diagnoses in this group are dementia in Alzheimer's disease (AD), often complicated by additional cerebrovascular pathology or vascular risk factors, and subcortical vascular dementia. A growing proportion of the latter group have cognitive impairment short of dementia. We generally refer to this diagnostically unclear group of patients as having mild cognitive impairment (MCI).
3. Referrals from specialists for differential diagnosis of atypical dementia disorders.
4. A relatively small group of patients with cognitive decline in somatic illnesses, for example after coronary surgery, or in neurological diseases, such as multiple sclerosis or Parkinson's disease.

In accordance with the original intention and following the tradition of research MCs, our clinic has become an important part of the local research infrastructure in clinical dementia research. Collaborations exist with several neighbouring institutions, including the Paul Flechsig Institute of Brain Research, the Max Planck Institute of Human Cognitive and Brain Sciences, and the Department of Nuclear Medicine.

In addition to the need to identify and select well-characterized patients for clinical studies, there was—from the earliest days of our MC—a special focus on the improvement of the recognition of dementia disorders, in particular in early stages. In this chapter, we will describe the conceptual influences affecting the development of our research and our approach to the study of MCI. We will also describe a series of our MCI studies focussing on MCI definitions and biological correlates of MCI. Finally, we will discuss our interpretation of the findings from these studies and some of our ideas about future research in this field.

Conceptual influences

It was in 1995/1996 when the first prospective longitudinal research project on MCI was established in our department. We used the German label "leichte kognitive Störungen" (mild cognitive disorders), which was understood as a broad generic term, to describe the border zone between dementia and physiological decline of cognitive function in old age. Naturally, it was meant to incorporate a variety of cognitive phenotypes and causes of cognitive decline short of dementia that can be found in old age. The main aim of this project was "to identify biological predictors of different progression types of MCI"; that is, as the approach to defining MCI, the main outcome measures were also restricted to the level of clinical phenomenology.

When planning this study under the label "MCI", we were not aware of Petersen's MCI concept and we could not foresee the enormous "boom" that the field of MCI research should undergo in the coming years. The invitation to write this chapter made us think about and review in retrospect the sources that influenced our ideas about MCI research at that time. Our awareness and perception of MCI was certainly influenced by opinions and concepts of the European and European-influenced psychiatric tradition that has addressed this border zone repeatedly, and from different perspectives.

Already at the beginning of the last century, the phenomenology of senile age-related mental disorders had been extensively studied and well described in the German psychiatric literature. Following Wernicke, *Spielmeyer* (1912) discussed a subtype of senile psychosis, so-called "presbyphrenia" and stressed that disturbances of memory are particularly pronounced in these cases, while order of thought (die Ordnung der Gedankengänge), global mental activity (die geistige Regsamkeit), and judgement (das Urteil) were often unexpectedly well preserved (Spielmeyer, 1912). As concerns the prognosis of these conditions, Spielmeyer stated: There is a regular transition of presbyphrenia to common senile dementia (in der Regel geht die Presbyphrenie in einen einfachen Altersblödsinn über), however in some cases the symptoms were reversible.

The German-Canadian *Viktor Kral* described a "mild type of memory dysfunction", a presumably benign form of senescent forgetfulness that progresses slowly and is characterized by the inability to recall on certain occasions relatively unimportant experiences of the (remote) past. This form was distinguished from "malignant forgetfulness", which was usually progressive. However, even some cases (5%) with "benign senescent forgetfulness" in Kral's studies were found to have progressed to dementia after 4 years (Kral, Cahn, & Mueller, 1964).

The existence of incomplete organic syndromes and the question of the reversibility of such syndromes were addressed by the concepts of Durchgangssyndrome ("transitory states"; Wieck, 1960) and pseudoneurasthenic syndromes (Huber, 1972). Both were categories of organic psychological disturbances. These concepts did not primarily focus on cognitive disturbances, but alterations of concentration and memory were among the broad symptomatology of organic mental disturbances described under these labels. With his concept of "Durchgangssyndrome", he summarized transient organic syndromes without disturbances of consciousness characterized by a broad psychiatric phenomenology, including amnestic symptoms, impairment of judgment, affective change, and lack of drive, thereby addressing the possible reversibility of mild cognitive disorders (Wieck, 1960). *Gerd Huber* described "pseudoneurasthenic syndromes" as a particularly mild or nonspecific form of chronic (irreversible) organic mental disturbance that could be distinguished from dementia (predominant and severe cognitive symptoms) and organic personality changes (predominant and severe personality changes). Pseudoneurasthenic syndromes ("Hirnleistungsschwäche", weakness of brain function) were typically characterized by changes in affect and drive ("reizbare Schwäche", irritable weakness) and mild cognitive changes (asthenia). They were presumed to be caused by manifold traumatic, encephalitic, dystrophic, and vascular injuries to the brain (Huber, 1972).

Beringer and Mallison (1949) proposed the concept of "vorzeitige Versagenszustände" (states of premature failure; Beringer & Mallison, 1949). It was assumed that a certain type of early (occurring in mid life) somatopsychic failure was accompanied by atrophic processes in the brain that were quantitatively and qualitatively different from those seen in classic presenile dementia disorders. Friedrich Wilhelm Bronisch raised the idea that the atrophic processes underlying mild cognitive, personality, and affective changes in these cases were not necessarily steadily progressive, but may have "got stuck" (steckengeblieben sein) in initial stages (Bronisch, 1951). Subsequent longitudinal studies in such patients confirmed the prognostic and aetiological heterogeneity of these conditions (Degenhardt & Greger, 1971).

In summary, there was a wealth of ideas about incomplete dementia syndromes. Not only cognitive symptoms but also affective, motivational, and personality changes were discussed, and a broad spectrum of possible aetiologies was taken into consideration. This apparent complexity on the one side was accompanied and on the other side partially opposed by the clinical knowledge about relatively typical and common cognitive phenotypes in old age that showed a tendency of progression to complete dementia syndromes. Based on retrospective clinical observations, staging procedures had been developed (Hughes, Berg, Danziger, Coben, & Martin, 1982; Reisberg, Ferris, de Leon, & Crook, 1982). Yet, predicting the further course in patients with mild cognitive disorders remained one of the most puzzling clinical questions.

By the time we were planning our study, the knowledge in this research field was further enriched with accumulating evidence about the preponderance of AD among the causes of dementia (Katzman, 1986; Schoenberg, Kokmen, & Okazaki, 1987), and correlative associations between Alzheimer-type lesions and cognition, even in nondemented elderly (Gertz et al., 1996; Petersen, Parisi, Johnson, Waring, & Smith, 1997). In addition, promising findings had been revealed by neuroimaging studies, suggesting that radiological measures, in particular atrophy of the hippocampal formation, could be feasible in vivo markers of the disease process in AD (de Leon et al., 1993; Jobst, Barnetson, & Shepstone, 1998). Pharmaceutical research in AD had just entered the era of new antidementia drugs, making the question of our research one of clinical–practical significance.

MCI studies in the Leipzig Memory Clinic

MCI studies in our MC were conducted in the frame of two larger studies: (1) an interdisciplinary clinical study on aging that served as a *pilot study* in our MCI research and informed the development of (2) the Leipzig Longitudinal Study of the Aged (LEILA).

Assumptions and hypotheses

We had a number of general assumptions that influenced the design of our studies:

1. Broad MCI definition/assumption of a cognitive continuum: We were aware of the potential of MCI research to improve the early recognition of dementia disorders. Some MCI concepts and definitions were based on aetiological assumptions. For example, the CDR scale (Hughes et al., 1982) was presumed to measure decline in cases with AD, other concepts stressed the benign age-related character of certain cognitive deficits and excluded subjects with somatic diseases that could possibly account for the cognitive decline. However, we decided neither to preselect subjects to fit such categories nor to use cutoffs on psychometric tests as a selection criterion. Instead, it seemed most ideal to recruit elderly subjects from the general population to represent the cognitive continuum in old age. Exclusion criteria were rather "soft" and comprised cases in which severe organic or (nonorganic) psychiatric illnesses or sensory deficits would have interfered with the ability to undergo neuropsychological or laboratory examinations. According to findings in the general population, we excluded less than 13% by this approach: major neuropsychiatric disorders were present in 0.8%, and sensory and motor deficits in 12% of the population aged 75 and over (Busse, Aurich, Zaudig, Riedel-Heller, Matschinger, & Angermeyer, 2002).
2. Assumption of aetiological heterogeneity within a spectrum of dementia diseases: Although being aware of the great impact of Alzheimer type pathology on cognitive decline in old age, our view on MCI and dementia was not "alzheimerized". We were also interested in other pathological processes and their interaction with degenerative changes to cause cognitive decline. Cerebrovascular pathology was presumed to be a common co-occurring pathological lesion in elderly subjects with Alzheimer type pathology. Following these ideas, we did not draw a

strict (but nevertheless arbitrary) line between vascular cognitive impairment/dementia and dementia in AD.
3. Consideration of biological factors in addition to neuropsychological and clinical methods: We assumed that the prognostic value of neuropsychological and clinical methods in MCI could be improved by taking biological factors into consideration. Candidates were chosen based on the knowledge from studies on AD and vascular dementia; that is, we considered that factors of significance in MCI were the same as those associated with cognitive decline in AD and VaD.

A systematic method for definition and measurement of MCI

Our approach to MCI ideally required a structured, operationalized instrument for the definition of MCI that involved both categorial aspects (i.e., the definition of an incomplete dementia syndrome) as well as a dimensional approach (i.e., a quantification of the severity of cognitive symptoms). With the Cambridge Mental Disorders of Elderly Examination (CAMDEX; Roth et al., 1986), a comprehensive instrument had become available.

Taking up the basic idea of CAMDEX, the structured interview for the diagnosis of dementia of the Alzheimer type, multi-infarct dementia, and dementias of other aetiology according to ICD-10 and DSM-III-R (SIDAM) was developed (Zaudig et al., 1991) in an attempt "to avoid disadvantage inherent in complex interview procedures and on the other hand, to assess cognitive deficits in a complex and comprehensive manner based on current classification systems". The SIDAM consists of a neuropsychological test battery including the Mini-Mental State Examination (MMSE), a section for clinical judgment (including the Hachinski–Rosen scale) and third party information on psychosocial impairment. The neuropsychological test battery covers six areas of neurocognitive functioning:

(1) orientation: assessment of orientation for time and place;
(2) memory (divided into the subscores "immediate recall", "short-term", and "long-term" memory): Short-term memory measures delayed verbal recall of a word list and fictitious name and address, and delayed visual reproduction;
(3) intellectual abilities: assessed by items of abstract thinking (differences explaining the meaning of idiomatic expressions) and judgment (describing pictures representing actions and plausibility judgment);
(4) verbal abilities and calculation: assessed by calculating serial sevens, spelling backwards, and digit span backwards;
(5) constructional abilities (visuospatial): assessed by copying figures;
(6) aphasia and apraxia: assessed by naming objects, reading and obeying a sentence, writing a sentence and performing a three-stage command.

The subscores in these six areas can be summed up to yield the SIDAM score (SISCO) that ranges from 55 (optimal cognitive performance) to 0 (most severe cognitive deficits).

Based on the current dementia definitions of the DSM-III-R and ICD-10 classification criteria, the SIDAM was accompanied with an algorithm for the diagnosis of "MCI". MCI was solely defined as an incomplete dementia syndrome, and three major types were distinguished according to ICD-10 dementia criteria (Type I—isolated memory impairment, Type II—impairment in memory and other cognitive functions, Type III—impairment in cognition plus emotional control, social behaviour, or motivation). In addition to this categorial approach, cutoffs on the global SIDAM test performance were proposed, based on a normative sample of 150 randomly selected subjects (Zaudig, 1992).

The pilot study

While we were planning the LEILA project and during the baseline recruitment phase, we examined existing data in our MC. In the years 1993–1994, an interdisciplinary study on aging had been carried out, including 117 subjects who had been examined at least once in our MC. The sample comprised referrals to

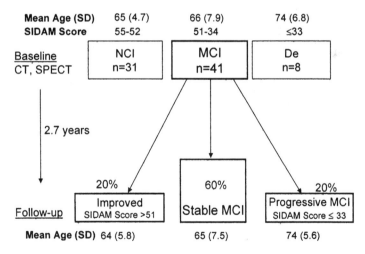

Figure 9.1 Study design of the pilot study. Note: Regardless of the source (referrals or convenience control population), baseline groups were formed according to cutoff values on the SIDAM score. These cutoff values for "mild cognitive impairment" had been derived from a normative sample of 150 elderly subjects, based on a syndromatic definition of MCI as an incomplete dementia syndrome according to ICD-10 dementia criteria (Zaudig, 1992) At the follow-up examination, the same cutoffs were used to define progression types (progressive MCI = MCI→dementia, stable MCI = MCI→MCI, improvement = MCI→NCI).

the MC and active healthy elderly subjects who had been recruited as a convenience sample from a society of elderly athletes. Two to three years after inclusion into the study, 80 were available for a follow-up examination, and completed the SIDAM, clinical examinations, and a second CT examination. This material was the basis for two pilot studies that focussed on the prognostic significance of radiological findings (medial temporal lobe [MTL] atrophy and white matter lesions [WMLs]) in MCI (Figure 9.1).

Main results from the pilot studies

Studies 1 and 2 were longitudinal studies in the frame of the pilot study, aiming to assess the prognosis of MCI and to identify possible biological predictors of the course. The main analyses focussed only on the subjects fulfilling the MCI criteria according to Zaudig; that is, the "dimension" MCI was defined by cutoffs on the global SIDAM performance (Zaudig, 1992).

In a short-term perspective (2–3 years), MCI had a variable outcome, the majority (60%) of subjects remained stable within the category of MCI, 20% of the subjects with MCI declined to dementia, and 20% improved back to normal test scores.

Higher age, thinner MTL, a measure of hippocampal formation atrophy, and a number of cognitive subdomains of the SIDAM were associated with decline to dementia.

The impact of WMLs as detected on CT was examined in an elderly subgroup. Both WML severity and MTL thickness were associated with the global SIDAM score at baseline in subjects with MCI, even when controlling for age and coexisting brain pathology. In univariate analyses, the extent of WMLs and MTL thickness were the only two parameters that separated the two outcome groups (stable vs. progressive MCI). Although not reported in the original publication, in multivariate analyses WML and MTL thickness were independent predictors and yielded a high prognostic/diagnostic accuracy when combined (area under the curve: 0.92). In subjects with progressive MCI, the severity of MTL atrophy was inversely correlated to the severity of white matter changes. Subjects with high WML scores who had progressed to dementia tended to have started off with higher SIDAM scores. This was interpreted as an indication that WML could accelerate cognitive decline in the presence of subtle AD pathology. However, the study sample was small, and the findings were based on only eight progressive cases.

MCI studies in the frame of the LEILA project

The LEILA 75+ was planned in 1995/1996 as a prospective, longitudinal population-based study of dementia and MCI. It comprised (1) an epidemiological part that focussed on the prevalence and incidence of dementia and MCI in the general population aged 75 and over, and (2) a clinical study, for which a subgroup of LEILA participants were invited to our MC for extensive clinical and paraclinical examinations.

Epidemiological study

Between January 1997 and June 1998, the baseline wave of the epidemiological study was performed (Riedel-Heller, Busse, Aurich, Matschinger, & Angermeyer, 2001; Riedel-Heller, Schork, Matschinger, & Angermeyer, 2000). The main instrument employed was the SIDAM (Zaudig et al., 1991). It was conducted during a home visit in 1265 (74.8%) of the originally selected random sample. Follow-up examinations took place after 1.5, 3, 4.5, and 6 years (ongoing). Due to several strategies to facilitate participation, comparably high response rates were reached throughout the whole investigation period (Riedel-Heller et al., 2000).

The LEILA/MC project

In the frame of the clinical study, a subsample of 101 largely nondemented LEILA participants in the age range from 75 to 85 were invited to participate in further investigations that took place in our MC. Clinical psychiatric, neurological, and laboratory examinations were performed. These included:

(1) repetition of neurocognitive tests (SIDAM) under clinic-based conditions;
(2) routine clinical procedures used in the general dementia work-up (clinical neurological and psychiatric examination, CDR, neuropsychological tests, CT or MRI, EEG, routine blood sample analyses);
(3) research tools (volumetric MRI, quantitative EEG, peripheral blood cell markers, apolipoprotein E genotype, 24-h blood pressure monitoring, serum lipid analyses).

Originally, we also planned postmortem pathological examinations, but this did not turn out to be practical in an epidemiological study.

The main candidate biological markers in our studies are listed in Table 9.1, where the rationale for their choice is briefly stated.

Focus on MRI

The main methodological focus of the clinical study was on MRI. As today, the role of structural neuroimaging in the diagnosis of Alzheimer's disease and other degenerative dementias is rather limited to the exclusion of secondary causes of dementia. Yet, modern volumetric MRI imaging techniques appear to be an appropriate tool for the detection and accurate quantification of atrophic processes (the macroscopic hallmark of degeneration) and cerebrovascular lesions (the underlying pathology in vascular dementia) (for review of the current literature see Wolf, Jelic, Gertz, Nordberg, Julin, & Wahlund, 2003a). Since the study was planned as a longitudinal project that should involve serial MRI examinations, it was important to adhere strictly to the original MRI protocols throughout the study and to use the same MRI scanner for all examinations. It was originally planned to study approximately

Table 9.1 A list of the main candidate biological markers in our studies

Candidate markers	Rationale
Hippocampal volume or atrophy Measurements: maximum width of the medial temporal lobe (MTL) on axial CT (pilot studies); hippocampal volume (HcV) on T1w MR, coronal plane; medial temporal lobe atrophy rating (MTA)	HcV consistently reduced in patients with AD High correlations between regional neurofibrillary tangles (NFT) and HcV in AD Early affection of Hc in the course of AD surrogate marker for AD pathology
Corpus callosum (CC) morphometry Measurements: mid-sagittal CC area	CC area consistently reduced in patients with dementia Topographical organization of cortical fibre connections within the CC in vivo indicator of cortical neuron loss staging parameter in AD
Other measures of brain atrophy Automated measurements: global brain, ventricular volume, grey matter, and white matter volume	Reflect the severity of atrophic processes
White matter lesions Measurements: white matter lucencies and lacunar infarcts on CT (pilot study); periventricular and deep white matter changes on T2w/T1w MR images; lacunar infarcts	Common pathology in elderly people, generally related to vascular cognitive impairment or dementia Possible interaction between vascular lesions and degenerative processes Semiquantitative rating scales to cause clinical symptoms
EEG theta activity Measurement: quantitative EEG under rest conditions and haptic	Consistent finding of an increase in theta power in AD Decrease in theta power during complex perceptive-cognitive tasks added prognostic value in MCI tasks
Apolipoprotein E genotype Measurement: blood leukocytes, PCR	ApoE-4 allele—main genetic susceptibility factor in AD Possible confounder for cognitive measures, brain volumetric measures, and serum lipids
Serum lipids Measurements: total cholesterol (TC), high-density lipoprotein cholesterol (HDL-C), low-density lipoprotein cholesterol (LDL-C)	Known vascular risk factor Brain cholesterol homeostasis failure as a possible mechanism in the pathological cascade in AD peripheral marker of brain lipid status
Mitogenic stimulation of peripheral blood lymphocytes Measurements: CD69 expression after stimulation	Cell-cycle dysregulation might be critically involved in the process of neurodegeneration in AD Peripheral blood lymphocytes express cell surface receptors comparable to neurons systemic marker of cellular proliferation control

250 subjects from the general population, but due to limitations in the availability of the MR scanner the eventual normative sample was smaller.

Normative study sample

Sixty-eight nondemented subjects from LEILA 75+ received MRI scans. They represent approximately 10% of the nondemented LEILA sample in the same age range. Even though representativity cannot be claimed in such a small subsample, the close connection to the epidemiological study allowed us to characterize our subsample in comparison to the general population. In addition, age- and education-adjusted normative values for the SIDAM score and its subscores could be derived from the epidemiological field study, as well as normative change scores over time. Comparison of our subsample with the remaining nondemented LEILA population showed no differences with regard to the prevalence of common medical diseases, such as myocardial infarction (9.5 vs. 10.5%, $p = .8$), diabetes mellitus (20 vs. 22%, $p = .4$), and stroke (9 vs. 6.4%, $p = .3$). There were slight, but significant differences in educational level (persons with low education are under-represented in the MC sample), and—as could be expected—indices of physical disability (patients in the MC study are slightly less physically impaired). Age- and education-specific norms for the SISCO subscores that were derived from the full LEILA sample (Busse et al., 2002) allowed us to estimate the prevalence of various types of MCI with operationalized criteria, such as "amnestic MCI" (Petersen et al., 2001) or "aging-associated cognitive decline" (AACD; Levy, 1994) in our subjects.

Due to our sampling procedure along a cognitive continuum, subjects with MCI were over-represented. Based on AACD criteria, the prevalence of MCI in our sample is 52% as compared to 17.7% among LEILA participants in the same age groups. The prevalence of amnestic MCI is 6% in our sample as compared to 3% in LEILA. Approximately one third of the participants with AACD in LEILA and one fifth with "amnestic MCI" were included in our study. This normative study sample has been "enriched" with consecutive referrals to our MC, the majority of which represents cases with mild to moderate dementia in AD. Among the referrals to our MC, the proportion of very mildly affected patients not (yet) fulfilling formal dementia criteria has steadily increased over the past years. Figure 9.2 summarizes the study design of our MC study in connection with LEILA 75+.

Main results from the LEILA/MC project

In the frame of the LEILA/MC project, the first studies were cross-sectional analyses of structural neuroimaging data, aiming to replicate earlier findings derived from clinic-based samples in the general elderly population. MCI was defined in broad clinical terms and involved a high proportion of rather minimally affected subjects. Furthermore, because of our sampling procedures,

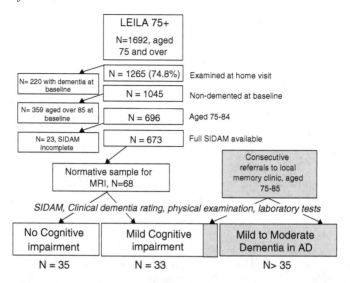

Figure 9.2 Design of the LEILA/MC project/baseline sample. *Note*: The study sample was derived from two major sources: the LEILA 75+ population and referrals to our MC. At inclusion, particular focus was on the age range 75–85. The baseline population was sampled along a presumed cognitive continuum using MMSE strata, rather than selected to fit into predefined categories. CDR seemed to be most appropriate to label subjects grossly along the continuum. Clinical follow-up examinations were performed after approximately 1.5 and 3 years, including a second MR scan.

"normal subjects" did not represent an extremely healthy group. The hippocampal volume (HcV) turned out to be significantly reduced in subjects with MCI (approximating 15% volume reduction) relative to cognitively unimpaired (Wolf et al., 2001, 2004b). There were no statistically significant reductions in global brain, grey and white matter volume, or corpus callosum area in MCI relative to dementia (Hensel, Wolf, Busse, Arendt, & Gertz, 2005; Wolf et al., 2004b). A priori defined subtypes of MCI, such as amnestic MCI or AACD, could not be distinguished on the basis of hippocampal volumetry.

The HcV was also highly correlated with continuous measures of cognition across sample, as well as in the nondemented subsample. HcV correlated significantly with SIDAM memory subscores as well as global cognitive measures, even after correction for the degree of global brain atrophy.

Multivariate logistic regression analyses suggested that from the limited angle of a cross-sectional study, HcV was the main determinant of the transition from "normal cognition" to MCI, whereas the global brain volume seemed to determine the transition from MCI to dementia. The multivariate models achieved from the whole sample also produced high predictive accuracies in presumed subtypes, such as "amnestic MCI", "AACD", and "dementia with CVD" (Wolf et al., 2004b).

In fact, our first longitudinal results confirmed the hypothesis that although hippocampal atrophy is typically present in MCI, other factors, in particular global brain volume or atrophy, may contribute more strongly to the progression of cognitive deficits, at least in a short-term perspective (Hensel et al., 2005). When baseline clinical and cognitive measures were taken into account, the global brain volume remained a significant, independent predictor of the rate of cognitive decline in a 2–3 year perspective. However, the added information to the clinical baseline assessments, in particular the CDR Sum-of-the-Boxes (SOB) score, appeared to be small (Hensel et al., 2005).

In our analyses, we considered improvement as a possible outcome measure in the nondemented participants at baseline. The majority of improvers, as well as decliners, came from the baseline group with MCI. Except for the HcV, all brain volumetric measurements including global brain volume, white matter volume, grey matter, corpus callosum area, and intracranial volume (ICV) tended to be larger in improvers (yielding positive z values) as compared to decliners (yielding negative z values), with stable MCI being intermediate (Hensel et al., 2005). In addition to the implication that MCI may be quite heterogeneous in outcome, this could be interpreted as an indication that hippocampal atrophy is associated with higher intraindividual performance variability.

In contrast to our previous CT study, semiquantitatively assessed WMLs were equally frequent across the cognitive stages and did not seem to contribute to cognitive decline over time (Hensel et al., 2005; Wolf et al., 2004b). More precisely, in our studies, virtually every person aged over 75 had at least some white matter abnormalities on MRI. Neither the severity of the lesions nor the proportion of subjects with extended WMLs (approximately 50% in all cognitive groups) distinguished the groups with MCI and dementia from cognitively unimpaired elderly subjects.

A rather unexpected finding in our sample was that our elderly subjects with MCI and dementia had significantly smaller intracranial and head volumes as compared to cognitively healthy subjects from the same birth cohort (Wolf, Kruggel, Hensel, Wahlund, Arendt, & Gertz, 2003b). The effect was more pronounced in women, but statistical analyses yielded no proof of a gender difference. After scrutinizing and cross-validating our methodological approach to the measurement of ICV, we became more interested in understanding the possible mechanisms behind this finding. Since the growth of the brain determines the size of the skull, measures of intracranial and head size are considered to be good estimates of the premorbid brain volume. A larger premorbid brain could provide an elderly person with a larger "structural" reserve against atrophic processes or vascular brain lesions. It could also reflect better early-life circumstances, such as nutrition and social factors that may contribute to the cognitive reserve capacity in later life. Subsequent analyses showed that the effect of ICV on late-life cognitive function was independent of education. Neither education nor ICV was related to the

Table 9.2 Brief summary of studies on MCI conducted in the Leipzig Memory Clinic

Study	Study sample	Setting	Design	Question	Concept of MCI	Main results
Wolf et al. (1998)	Total $n = 80$ with 2.7-year follow-up, $n = 31$ NCI, $n = 41$ MCI, $n = 8$ De/AD	MC/Research	Long	Prognosis of MCI, predictors of progressive MCI	Zaudig/SIDAM cutoffs for baseline cognitive state and decline	20% progressive/20% improved back to normal range, age, baseline memory function and medial temporal lobe atrophy distinguished progression types, SPECT measures at baseline did not
Wolf, Ecke, Bettin, Dietrich, and Gertz (2000)	$n = 27$, all with baseline MCI with 2.7-year follow-up	MC/Research	Long	Role of white matter lesions (WML) and medial temporal lobe thickness (MTT) in progression of MCI	Zaudig/SIDAM cutoffs for baseline cognitive state and decline	Both WML and MTT were associated with pMCI
Wolf et al. (2001)	Total $n = 39$, $n = 17$ NCI, $n = 12$ MCI, $n = 10$ De/AD	Pop	Cross	Hippocampal atrophy in elderly community-dwelling subjects with MCI	Cognitive continuum, CDR 0.5 excluding dementia	Significant hippocampal volume reduction in CDR 0.5 as compared to CDR 0
Grunwald et al. (2002)	Total $n = 51$, $n = 20$ NCI, $n = 16$ MCI, $n = 15$ De/AD	Pop/MC	Cross	qEEG in MCI under rest conditions and haptic tasks	CDR 0.5	EEG theta power differentiated CDR 0.5 from CDR 0 under haptic tasks, but not under rest conditions
Hensel et al. (2002)	Total $n = 83$, $n = 33$ NCI, $n = 27$ MCI, $n = 23$ De/AD	Pop/MC	Cross	Corpus callosum atrophy in MCI	Cognitive continuum, CDR 0.5	No significant reduction

Wolf et al. (2003b)	Total n = 99, n = 34 NCI, n = 34 MCI, n = 31 De/AD	Pop/MC	Cross	Head-size-cognition associations	Cognitive continuum, CDR 0.5 excluding dementia	Smaller intracranial and head volume in MCI and De/AD; impact of premorbid brain volume/early-life factors
Wolf et al. (2004c)	Total n = 181, n = 85 NCI, n = 39 MCI, n = 36 AD, n = 21 VaD	MC/Research	Cross	ICV-cognition-associations (replication study)	No dementia, at least 1.5 SD below average for their age in at least one neuropsychological test	Small ICV increased the risk of late-life cognitive impairment. ICV was related to severity of cognitive impairment in dementia
Wolf et al. (2004b)	Total n = 105, n = 35 NCI, n = 38 MCI, n = 32 De/AD	Pop/MC	Cross	MR structural correlates of MCI	Cognitive continuum, MCI = CDR 0.5 or modified AACD, excluding dementia	Significant hippocampal volume reduction in MCI, subtypes (amnestic MCI, AACD) were not structurally distinguishable
Hensel et al. (2005)	Total n = 74, n = 68 with follow-up information, n = 37 NCI, n = 31 MCI	Pop/MC	Long	MR predictors of cognitive decline in nondemented elderly	Cognitive continuum, CDR 0.5, excluding dementia; rate of decline + categorical definition of decline and improvement	Global brain volume, but not HcV, WML, or corpus callosum volume, was associated with the rate of cognitive decline (when correcting for baseline cognition). The added value to clinical and neuropsychological baseline assessments was small
Wolf et al. (2004a)	Total n = 86, n = 26 NCI, n = 35 MCI, n = 25 De/AD	Pop/MC	Cross	Role of serum cholesterol in AD pathogenesis?	Cognitive continuum (MCI defined as in study 7)	High serum HDL cholesterol may protect against hippocampal atrophy

(Contd)

Table 9.2 (Contd)

Study	Study sample	Setting	Design	Question	Concept of MCI	Main results
Wolf, Kivipelto, Hensel, Winblad, Riedel-Heller, and Gertz (2005)	Total $n = 70$, $n = 57$ non-demented, 23 AD	Pop/MC	Long	Role of serum cholesterol in AD pathogenesis?	"early AD" = PMCI /mild AD	Confirmation of association between serum HDL cholesterol and HcV in cases with early AD
Stieler et al. (2001)	27 AD, 45 age-matched controls	Pop/MC	Cross	Mitogenic activation of peripheral blood lymphocytes (Lc) in AD	n/a	Impairment in mitogenic activation of Lc in AD, strong correlations between stimulation index and MMSE in AD

Note: Cross, cross-sectional analyses; De/AD, dementia in Alzheimer's disease; ICV, intracranial volume; Long, longitudinal analyses; MCI, mild cognitive impairment; MC/research, typical research setting with convenience controls and referrals; NCI, no cognitive impairment; Pop/MC, population-based normative sample from LEILA 75+ enriched with referrals to MC.

severity of brain pathology, such as hippocampal atrophy, brain atrophy, or cerebrovascular lesions. In support for the assumption of reserve, persons with a large ICV (defined as ICV in the fourth quartile) had higher global cognitive scores at given levels of brain atrophy (quartiles of hippocampal atrophy; Wolf, Wahlund, Muller, Hensel, & Gertz, 2004d). Our replication study that was based on a considerably younger sample of consecutive referrals to the MC, Huddinge, Sweden, largely confirmed these findings (Wolf, Julin, Gertz, Winblad, & Wahlund, 2004c).

Because some studies suggested a link between serum cholesterol and AD-like pathology or risk of dementia, we were interested in the association between HcV—as a presumed index of AD pathology—and serum cholesterol. Serum HDL cholesterol, but not LDL or total cholesterol, was positively associated with HcV across the cognitive spectrum in our study. The same pattern was observed when only nondemented subjects were analysed. As in some previous studies, low HDL was also associated with an increased risk of dementia (Wolf, Hensel, Arendt, Kivipelto, Winblad, & Gertz, 2004a). This is compatible with protective effects of HDL cholesterol on hippocampal atrophy and possibly AD. We speculated that this finding might reflect the role of cholesterol and lipoproteins in facilitating synaptic plasticity in the aging human brain.

Discussion

Definitions of MCI

In our studies, we defined MCI broadly as objective cognitive impairment short of dementia and as part of a presumed cognitive continuum from physiological cognitive function in aging to dementia. Facing the obvious difficulties in labelling a part of a continuum, theoretical borders had to be defined to delineate this state from physiological cognitive function and dementia. Relatively clear qualitative and quantitative criteria exist for defining dementia, although part of the definition relies on the personal awareness (in patient or caregiver) and rather subjective judgement of impaired psychosocial functions. The delineation of physiological cognitive function from objective cognitive impairment appears even more complicated. Some aspects of cognition appear to decline as a function of age, regardless of the presence of degenerative brain changes (Nilsson, 2003). The concept of "normal aging" is fuzzy and depends largely on the definition of what is not normal. The assertion that MCI, dementia, or AD is not normal aging is more "a political statement than a scientific one" (Whitehouse, 2003).

Using previously "validated" cutoffs on a global performance measure, such as the SIDAM, offers an objective, easily reproducible, but nevertheless arbitrary solution to the problem. In our own experience, the cutoff scores by Zaudig for MCI appeared to be too sensitive, labelling some apparently healthy elderly as MCI (Busse et al., 2002). At the same time, cutoffs for dementia were too low in some of the cases that were already mildly demented if a clinical definition had been applied. The lack of age- and education-adjusted norms was another limitation of this original approach in our research.

With this experience in mind, we decided to use the global score of the CDR (Hughes et al., 1982) in our subsequent studies. Somewhat consistent with our clinical concept of MCI, it allowed us to label and quantify cognitive, behavioural, and psychosocial impairment even when it appeared of only questionable significance. Many subjects in our population-based sample showed no more than a questionable memory deficit on clinical examination. CDR may be criticized as a somewhat subjective approach, however it reflects well the levels and ways of clinical judgement. In the scientific discussion, it has been argued that some persons with CDR 0.5 are already demented. This holds true in our clinical experience. Therefore, our primary definition of dementia was independent of the CDR score (we defined dementia according to ICD-10 research criteria).

When age- and education-adjusted normative values became available (Busse et al., 2002) in the frame of LEILA, we entered into a third phase, and defined MCI as either CDR 0.5/no dementia or the fulfilment of modified AACD criteria (Busse, Bischkopf, Reidel-Heller, & Angermeyer, 2003b; Wolf et al., 2004b). Not surprisingly, the overlap between the clinical judgment of CDR 0.5 and the modified AACD criteria was substantial (79%), but not complete. This approach somewhat broadened our baseline "at-risk" stage. In contrast, the criteria for "amnestic MCI" as suggested by Petersen (Petersen et al., 2001) had a low prevalence in the general population (3% original vs. 5% modified, excluding memory complaint) (Busse et al., 2003b).

Longitudinal data from the LEILA epidemiological study confirmed that the use of the psychometric criteria of the AACD concept might be most appropriate if a broad definition of MCI is required. Psychometrically, AACD was defined as cognitive performance of more than $1SD$ below the age- and education-adjusted mean in any cognitive subdomain. These criteria had a prevalence of 19.7% in subjects aged 75 and older, and they also achieved the highest predictive value for dementia at follow-up (AUC 0.746 as compared to AUC 0.530 in amnestic MCI, modified).

In none of our studies did we consider the presence of subjective complaints of cognitive impairment or decline as a criterion for MCI. This was based on our perception of the literature (Riedel-Heller et al., 2000) and part of our broad approach to MCI. Criteria for MCI that require subjective complaints about cognitive impairment would exclude subjects who are either not aware of their deficits or deny them. Again, results from the LEILA field study support this approach: The diagnostic criterion of subjective memory complaints as used in the original definition of AACD and amnestic MCI had no additional power to predict dementia (Busse, Bischkopf, Riedel-Heller, & Angermeyer, 2003a).

Definitions of MCI progression

The progression of cognitive deficits is an important outcome measure in MCI studies. If clinical symptoms were progressive, and a specific dementia diagnosis could be made at follow-up, it is usually inferred that a preclinical dementia disorder was present at baseline. Strictly speaking, progression to dementia makes a degenerative dementia disorder more likely, but it could also be due to other factors, such as a stroke or other concomitant diseases. Likewise, the absence of progression does not exclude a preclinical dementia disorder. Nevertheless, predicting the further course in MCI is a crucial clinical question of high relevance for the patient and his/her relatives.

There are three principal approaches to define cognitive change:

(1) Subjective report of cognitive decline by individual or caregiver.
(2) Transition or "conversion" of the MCI syndrome to a complete dementia syndrome.
(3) Objective measurements of cognitive change.

(1) The subjective report of cognitive impairment, in particular of memory, is an essential aspect in clinic-derived MCI criteria (Petersen, 2004; Petersen et al., 2001; Petersen, Smith, Waring, Ivnik, Tangalos, & Kokmen, 1999). These criteria seem to be well suited to characterize typical referrals to MCs. In virtually every such case, the criterion "memory complaint by patient, caregiver, or physician" should be fulfilled. As already discussed, we disregarded subjective memory complaints as a criterion to define MCI in our population-based samples, and our field study provided no evidence that the predictive accuracy of MCI criteria could be improved by using this criterion. Nevertheless, the report of memory or cognitive decline by the individual or the caregiver could be a first indication for a progressive worsening of cognitive functions. Standardized informant-based assessments of cognitive decline, such as that provided by the CAMDEX section H, could add useful information if aspects of change are the particular focus (Tuokko et al., 2003).

(2) Because the syndromes of MCI and dementia lie on a continuum, the transition from MCI to dementia does not occur at a specific time point. Yet, the so-called "conversion" studies rely on determining the time point for this transition. This is obviously problematic, particularly in studies with short follow-up intervals. Using the transition through predefined cutoffs on cognitive tests as in our pilot study may take away some of the subjectivity of this approach, but is nevertheless quite arbitrary. It should be noted, however, that all patients who progressed to the SIDAM dimension "dementia" actually also fulfilled the ICD-10 criteria for dementia.

(3) Alternatively, cognitive change measures derived from multiple testing could be used for the identification of progressive MCI. In fact, this approach has support by the NINCDS research criteria for "possible AD" which propose

that in cases with a history suggestive of AD, possible AD should be diagnosed if a decline in cognitive scores can be demonstrated over time (Mckhann, Drachman, Folstein, Katzman, Price, & Stadlan, 1984). This approach is by no means trivial, and no generally accepted criteria exist to define clinically significant cognitive decline. Change could be defined on global cognitive measures or on one or several cognitive subscales, or using both global and specific cognitive measures.

To define significant change, measurement errors and practice effects should be taken into consideration. In our initial analyses, we used a cutoff of $1SD$ from the mean on the annualized change scores of global SIDAM performance to define cognitive change (categorized as improvement, stable MCI, and progressive MCI). At the time of our initial analyses, our normative data on cognitive change relied on the small LEILA/MC subsample, and only two measurement points were taken into account. Meanwhile, normative change values over 4.5–6 years with up to five measurement points have become available from the LEILA field study, providing an independent normative sample for our definitions of decline. This calls for rather sophisticated statistical modelling that should account for intraindividual performance variation over time and dependence on baseline cognitive levels.

Biological factors in MCI

Hippocampal atrophy in MCI

The finding of a significant HcV reduction in MCI relative to control groups of healthy elderly subjects is one of the most consistent findings in MCI research. The volume reduction in MCI groups averages 15% in a handful of cross-sectional studies (Wolf et al., 2003a). In light of pathological studies in AD that repeatedly showed high correlations between regional load of neurofibrillary pathology and HcV (Bobinski et al., 1995; Gosche, Mortimer, Smith, Markesbery, & Snowdon, 2002; Jack et al., 2002; Nagy et al., 1999), it is tempting to interpret this finding as an indication of AD pathology in subjects with MCI. In theory, a volume reduction is never specific, and it can be caused by various diseases and other mechanisms (Tittgemeyer & von Cramon, 2004). In practice, AD pathology appears to be the principal lesion associated with hippocampal atrophy in elderly subjects, followed by ischemic damage leading to hippocampal sclerosis (Gosche et al., 2002; Jack et al., 2002; Mortimer, Gosche, Riley, Markesbery, & Snowdon, 2004; Nagy et al., 1999; Zarow et al., 2005). Because the hippocampus is essentially involved in memory and other cognitive processes, any structural hippocampal lesion, regardless of its aetiology, is likely to cause cognitive impairment. Hence, consistent HcV reductions, even in heterogeneously defined MCI samples, are plausible, and associations between HcV and cognitive performance can be expected.

Beyond statistical group differences, the remarkable interindividual variations in HcV in MCI could be seen as the second most "consistent" finding.

Considerable overlap with the groups of cognitively unimpaired and demented subjects was present in our and most other studies. This could be interpreted as evidence for aetiological heterogeneity in MCI. Accordingly, subjects with small HcV within MCI groups should be more likely to show severe and progressive cognitive deficits than subjects with large hippocampi. Some studies in the literature have confirmed this assumption (including our pilot study); others (including our LEILA/MC study) failed to do so. From a meta-analytical point of view, HcV reductions at baseline seem to be associated with a modestly increased risk of progression to dementia (Wolf et al., 2003a), but a single measurement of HcV does not appear to be suitable to predict dementia or AD in an individual patient (Figure 9.3).

Our and other studies showed that in addition to HcV, measures of global brain volume and/or atrophy in several brain regions might be responsible for symptom progression in MCI. These areas include other limbic structures, such as the amygdala (Fischl et al., 2002), the thalamus (Fischl et al., 2002), as well as the isocortical regions in the temporal lobe (Convit, de Asis, de Leon, Tarshish, De Santi, & Rusinek, 2000).

Against the background of the hierarchical topographical evolution of neurofibrillary pathology in AD (Braak & Braak, 1991), these MRI findings could indicate that more widespread AD pathology in subjects with MCI is associated with more rapid decline or development of dementia. Yet, in light of the consistently high correlative associations between HcV and AD pathology in a number of studies (Gosche et al., 2002; Jack et al., 2002), the weakness of HcV as a prognostic marker in MCI is rather unexpected. Hence, one could call into question the assumption that AD pathology itself is the main determinant of cognitive decline. Other factors than the degree of AD pathology could influence the course of MCI.

The baseline HcV tended to be decreased in subjects with MCI. However, HcV was not a useful predictor of future cognitive change in the MCI group. In nondemented subjects, HcV was the only morphometric variable that did

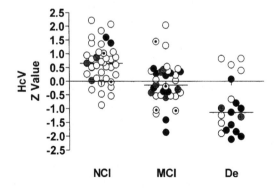

Figure 9.3 Hippocampal volume at baseline as a function of baseline cognitive state and cognitive change over a 2-year period (NCI, no cognitive impairment; De, dementia).

not distinguish improvers (grey dots) from decliners (black dots). All other measurements (brain volume, grey matter volume, white matter volume, and corpus callosum size) were larger in improvers as compared to decliners (Hensel et al., 2005). Circles with a dot are subjects who were lost to follow-up; white circles are subjects who remained stable.

What is the role of cerebrovascular factors in MCI?

Many other and our studies particularly focussed on the additional contribution of cerebrovascular lesions in MCI. Cerebrovascular disease (CVD) is thought to be the second most common cause of dementia. In elderly persons, CVD and AD commonly co-occur. Interactions between both pathologies may be complex. Clinicopathological studies suggest that CVD may enhance the capacity of AD lesions to cause dementia symptoms (Esiri, Nagy, Smith, Barnetson, & Smith, 1999; Snowdon, Greiner, Mortimer, Riley, Greiner, & Markesbery, 1997).

As regards the role of white matter changes and subcortical infarcts in MCI, our studies provided divergent findings. In our pilot study, which used semiquantitative CT assessments of WMLs, extended WMLs were associated with future dementia, and the results were suggestive of additive effects of both pathologies on symptom progression in MCI. The subsequent MRI study, also based on semiquantitative assessments, could not replicate our earlier findings in a somewhat more elderly sample that was followed up for 2.3 years. This apparent controversy within our studies is also reflected in the literature in this field.

While large-scale longitudinal studies focussing on cardiovascular risk factors (Breteler et al., 1994; Longstreth et al., 1996; Vermeer, Prins, den Heijer, Hofman, Koudstaal, & Breteler, 2003) and studies on old-age depression (Hickie, Scott, Wilhelm, Brodaty, 1997) support associations between WMLs and cognitive impairment or decline, clinical studies in smaller samples provided controversial evidence (Bronge & Wahlund, 2003; DeCarli et al., 1999, 2004; de Leeuw, Barkhof, & Scheltens, 2004). In the latter studies, bias toward under-reporting negative findings can be presumed.

There may be many reasons for this variability of findings. Certainly, one aspect is the quality of study designs and imaging procedures for the detection of pathological changes of clinical significance (Bronge, Bogdanovic, & Wahlund, 2002). Various neuroimaging techniques have become available. MRI seems to be superior to CT in detecting pathological changes in the white matter, and modern MRI techniques, such as fluid attenuated inversion recovery (FLAIR), further improve the conspicuousness of lesions (Bronge et al., 2002). However, MRI–CT comparison studies suggested that CT-detected lesions may be more specifically associated with clinical symptoms (Lopez et al., 1995). On the other hand, biological variability and complexity may be more substantial factors underlying small or absent effects in this field than methodological shortcomings.

To explore the latter idea, it may be worthwhile to take a closer look at clinicopathological correlation studies. As early as in 1937, D. Rothschild faced a similarly dissatisfying situation when trying to correlate pathological findings with the clinical symptoms in cases with "senile psychoses" (presumably presenting cases with "mixed AD and CVD" according to modern diagnostic criteria) (Rothschild, 1937). Realizing that there was "no simple quantitative relationship between pathologic and clinical changes", he concluded that "isolated consideration of the anatomic changes fails to solve some of the most important problems in senile psychoses". In light of the puzzling phenomenon that some persons with severe pathological lesions fail to show clinical abnormalities, he hypothesized that "such persons are able to compensate for the changes so well that a clinically recognizable disorder fails to develop". These observations and ideas coined the brain reserve hypothesis of dementia.

Subsequent studies, such as the seminal work by Tomlinson and colleagues (Tomlinson, Blessed, & Roth, 1968, 1970) disputed Rothschild's somewhat nihilistic interpretations by justifying the hypothesis that the degree of severity of brain changes relates to the severity of the clinical symptoms. This was also true for ischemic brain damage—tissue softening of more than 20 mL was more common in the demented group. Yet, the mean infarct volumes in the demented and in the control group were not significantly different (Tomlinson et al., 1970).

Figure 9.4 shows two examples for the typical associative pattern between measures of hippocampal atrophy and AD-type neurofibrillary pathology respectively with clinical-cognitive state. In fact, the pattern observed with a radiological routine *in vivo* marker seems to resemble nicely the situation based on histopathological findings. Even in studies that took several pathological factors into account or in samples carefully selected to represent the spectrum of "pure" AD-type neurodegenerative changes, the percentage of explained variance in cognitive function did not usually exceed 55% (Jack et al., 2002; Mortimer et al., 2004; Riley, Snowdon, & Markesbery, 2002; Zarow et al., 2005).

Brain reserve in MCI?

Several findings from our and many other previous studies suggest that beyond the capacity of hippocampal atrophy (a presumed index of AD pathology) and CVD to cause cognitive impairment, other factors must be present that mediate the relationship between degree of pathology and cognitive function. It has been repeatedly shown that there are subjects with severe hippocampal atrophy or advanced AD pathology (Braak stage IV or higher) with intact or only mildly impaired cognitive functions. Our data may give some answers as to why these persons could avoid the clinical manifestation of dementia despite severe pathological changes in their brains.

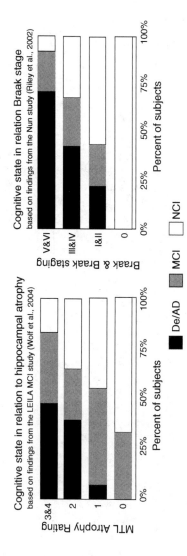

Figure 9.4 Medial temporal lobe atrophy rating in our study population as a function of cognitive state. *Note:* Left side—Visual rating of medial temporal lobe atrophy on a five-graded scale in relation to cognitive state in 105 subjects aged 75–85 from the LEILA/MC study (Wolf et al., 2004b). About 50% in both NCI and MCI groups in this age group had some degree of hippocampal atrophy, and the level of hippocampal atrophy varied from absent to very severe, even in nondemented elderly subjects. Although, hippocampal atrophy is significantly correlated to global cognitive state across the sample ($r = .44$, $p < .001$), there is a high interindividual variation in clinical symptom severity at given levels of hippocampal atrophy. Subjects with MCI can be found in all stages of hippocampal atrophy. The situation somewhat resembles the findings in pathological studies (right side). Right side—Braak & Braak stages (severity and topographical hierarchical evolution of neurofibrillary tangles) and cognitive state in 130 cases from the Nun Study. Modified/recalculated from Riley et al. (2002). MCI in this figure is defined as evidence of isolated memory impairment or memory impairment plus one or more other cognitive domains in the absence of dementia. The correlation between Braak stage and six cognitive states in this study was $r = .59$. Only subjects who were free from cerebral infarcts and from other neuropathological conditions, which could have caused cognitive decline, were included in this sample. De/AD, dementia in AD; MCI, mild cognitive impairment; MTL, medial temporal lobe; NCI, no cognitive impairment.

In 1988, Katzman et al. described 10 cases of cognitively unimpaired elders who showed the pathological features of AD but had fully intact cognitive functions. These subjects had larger brain weights and a higher number of neurons on average. It was speculated that they may have started with larger brains and thus avoided the development of dementia due to a greater reserve capacity (Katzman et al., 1988).

Three findings in our studies are compatible with brain reserve effects:

(1) Associations between ICV and late-life cognitive state.
(2) Larger baseline brain volumes were associated with improvement and stability of cognitive function.
(3) The absolute size of the hippocampus yielded significantly higher correlations with cognitive test scores than volumes that were normalized to ICV.

Associating a measurement of the skull with cognitive functions may appear rather awkward and could remind of the dubious practice of phrenologists in the 18th century (for review and excellent criticism: Gould, 1981). Nevertheless, because of its stability over time (Wolf et al., 2003b), ICV has some advantages over volumetric measures of brain tissue. Brain growth in childhood determines the size of the cranial vault. In midlife, the brain shrinks, but the shape of the cranium remains constant: hence, the total ICV and other measurements of head size can be used as estimates of the maximum attained brain size throughout life. This means that although this measurement may appear crude, because it is based on skull size, it is unaffected by degenerative changes during life. Interpreting findings that are based on actual brain volumes in relation to brain reserve is more difficult because it is unknown to what extent premorbid size and atrophy (e.g., due to degenerative or vascular changes) have contributed to the volume of a structure.

Epidemiological studies using head circumference measures as estimates of head size consistently supported various aspects of the brain reserve concept. They found associations between head size and cognitive performance in nondemented elderly subjects (Gale, Walton, & Martyn, 2003; Reynolds, Johnston, Dodge, DeKosky, & Ganguli, 1999; Tisserand, Bosma, Van Boxtel, & Jolles, 2001) and in subjects suffering from AD (Graves, Mortimer, Larson, Wenzlow, Bowen, & McCormick, 1996), as well as associations between head size and risk of prevalent (Mortimer, Snowdon, & Markesbery, 2003; Schofield, Logroscino, Andrews, Albert, & Stern, 1997) and incident AD (Borenstein et al., 2001) or future cognitive decline (Gale et al., 2003). Structural neuroimaging studies only occasionally addressed the relationship between late-life cognitive disorders and ICV (for review see Wolf et al., 2004c).

It must be said that the effect size of the observed relationship between ICV and cognition was relatively small in both of our studies. The question as to what extent the total brain volume represents factors such as nerve cell numbers, nerve cell size, synaptic density, dendritic branching, connectivity, and transmitter availability cannot be answered in detail. Estimations of how brain volume translates into neuron number are rare and may be subject to great error (Haug, 1987). Caveats aside, these findings suggest the intriguing possibility that early-life influences (the size of the skull is determined by adolescence) may be related to the risk of late-life cognitive impairment. ICV could be an indirect indicator of early-life factors, including environmental influences, such as general health in childhood, nutrition, social status, and education.

Added clinical value

The aim of our studies was to identify factors that may help to predict the further course in a patient with MCI. Several biological variables, including baseline HcV, MTL atrophy rating, corpus callosum size, and brain volume, were significantly associated with MCI and future cognitive decline in our studies when considered alone or in combination with each other. Taken alone, these measures had moderate predictive accuracies in nondemented subjects, as suggested by areas under the ROC curve between 0.6 and 0.8. This may be interpreted as indication of the validity of these measures to determine the course in MCI. However, any factor claiming to be a "biological marker" for cognitive decline or a dementia disorder should first be compared against the prognostic and diagnostic value of clinical tools and personal expertise of a clinician. We agree with Berg and Morris (Berg & Morris, 1994) who cited Elble with the statement that:

> "... none of the available laboratory tests contributes more to the diagnosis and management of dementia than a thorough and thoughtful clinical evaluation by a thoughtful physician."

We think that this statement should form the nil hypothesis for clinical research in the field of MCI. More specifically, the added clinical value of biological parameters should be proven in clinical settings.

In our study, the prognostic value of routine clinical assessments, including the CDR SOB score, MMSE, and SIDAM to predict cognitive decline in nondemented subjects, was very high (AUC 0.8–0.9). Having been classified as MCI at baseline, having a low MMSE (<26), and having a CDR SOB score greater than 0.5 or 1 considerably increased the risk of cognitive decline in the follow-up period. In multivariate models that combined clinical and paraclinical variables, some of the biological factors, primarily the global brain volume, remained significant predictors when controlling for baseline cognitive state. ROC statistics showed that the combination of these measurements could slightly improve the already high diagnostic accuracy of clinical variables (AUC 0.92), but there was no statistically significant difference to the model that was only based on the CDR SOB score. Yet, the combined model yielded higher sensitivity in the range of low false positive rates.

Thus, our findings support the notion that clinical assessments may already yield remarkably high predictive-diagnostic accuracies, leaving little room for a relevant contribution of other measurements. Yet, morphological parameters independently contributed to the prediction of future cognitive decline. Possibly, the proportional contribution of laboratory measurements may increase with the length of the predictive intervals.

Conclusion and outlook

MCI has been defined as an unclear boundary or transitional zone. The need for this category derives from a conceptual gap between dementia definitions and the concepts of normal aging. Despite its vagueness by definition, MCI is a valuable research category for the study of age- and disease-related mechanisms of cognitive decline. Many studies showed that MCI is associated with a higher risk of progression to dementia, and many pathological and radiological features in MCI are characteristic of AD. However, we think that global aetiological assumptions in MCI (such as "MCI is early AD") are not justified. This is in agreement with the most recent consensus statement on MCI (Winblad et al., 2004), and based on our theoretical understanding of current diagnostic systems and our perception of research findings.

In our experience, MCI is a dubious label for clinical use. According to current diagnostic standards, subjects with MCI do not have an identifiable disease, hence they should not be labelled with a "diagnosis" that means either that someone does not have AD, or has it or will or might get it. On the other hand, the identification of subjects with MCI may help to facilitate an early diagnosis of dementia disorders. In the current conceptual dilemma in AD, NINCDS-AIREN research criteria for "possible AD" may be best suited to enable a diagnosis at a very early time point of clinical symptoms. According to these criteria, clinical diagnosis of possible AD should be used when a single, gradually declining severe cognitive deficit is identified in the absence of other identifiable causes (McKhann et al., 1984). Hence, some patients with "amnestic MCI" as defined by Petersen would already meet criteria for possible AD.

New refined criteria for the diagnosis of early dementia disorders are needed to extract, at the earliest time point, persons with a diagnosable and potentially treatable disease from the unclear category of MCI. With potential causal treatment options for AD at hand, the disease process should be identified before isocortical structures are affected and most ideally also before limbic structures are involved. Modern imaging techniques, such as hippocampal volumetry, plaque and tangle imaging, and biological markers, could be the basis for new diagnostic systems. However, a substantial proportion of cases identified with these techniques will have no symptoms, and this will raise the question whether "clinically silent" AD should be diagnosed and treated. On the other hand, if the application of these techniques will be restricted to already symptomatic subjects with MCI, a large proportion will already have advanced AD pathology (Figure 9.4).

Therapeutic interventions should not only aim at features that characterize the disease process. These features presumably account for less than 50% of the variance in clinical symptoms. Cognitive and physical activity, somatic and cerebral comorbidity, and stabilization of brain metabolic homeostasis could be modifiable factors influencing brain reserve and thus the expression of clinical symptoms. The modulation of such factors may help to avoid or considerably delay the onset of cognitive symptoms in old age.

References

Berg, L., & Morris, J. C. (1994). Diagnosis. In R. D. Terry & K. L. Bick (Eds.), *Alzheimer Disease* (pp. 9–25). New York: Raven Press.

Beringer, K., & Mallison, R. (1949). Vorzeitige Versagenszustände. *Allgemeine Zeitschrift F?r Psychiarie, 124*, 100–130.

Bobinski, M., Wegiel, J., Wisniewski, H. M., Tarnawski, M., Reisberg, B., Mlodzik, B., et al. (1995). Atrophy of hippocampal formation subdivisions correlates with stage and duration of Alzheimer disease. *Dementia, 6*(4), 205–210.

Borenstein, G. A., Mortimer, J. A., Bowen, J. D., McCormick, W. C., Mccurry, S. M., Schellenberg, G. D., et al. (2001). Head circumference and incident Alzheimer's disease: Modification by Apolipoprotein E. *Neurology, 57*(8), 1453–1460.

Braak, H., & Braak, E. (1991). Neuropathological stageing of Alzheimer-related changes. *Acta Neuropathologica (Berl.), 82*(4), 239–259.

Breteler, M. M., Van Amerongen, N. M., Van Swieten, J. C., Claus, J. J., Grobbee, D. E., Van Gijn, J., et al. (1994). Cognitive correlates of ventricular enlargement and cerebral white matter lesions on magnetic resonance imaging. The Rotterdam Study. *Stroke, 25*(6), 1109–1115.

Bronge, L., Bogdanovic, N., & Wahlund, L. O. (2002). Postmortem MRI and histopathology of white matter changes in Alzheimer brains—A quantitative, comparative study. *Dementia and Geriatric Cognitive Disorders, 13*(4), 205–212.

Bronge, L., & Wahlund, L. O. (2003). Prognostic significance of white matter changes in a memory clinic population. *Psychiatry Research-Neuroimaging, 122*(3), 199–206.

Bronisch, F. W. (1951). *Hirnatrophische Prozesse Im Mittleren Lebensalter Und Ihre Psychischen Erscheinungsbilder*. Stuttgart: Georg Thieme Verlag.

Busse, A., Aurich, C., Zaudig, M., Riedel-Heller, S., Matschinger, H., & Angermeyer, M. C. (2002). Age- and education-specific reference values for the cognitive test of the Sidam (structured interview for the diagnosis of dementia of the Alzheimer type, multi-infarct dementia and dementias of other etiology according to ICD-10 and DSM-IV).*Zeitschrift Gerontologie Geriatrie, 35*(6), 565–574.

Busse, A., Bischkopf, J., Riedel-Heller, S. G., & Angermeyer, M. C. (2003a). Mild cognitive impairment: Prevalence and incidence according to different diagnostic criteria—Results of the Leipzig longitudinal study of the aged (LEILA 75+). *British Journal of Psychiatry, 182*, 449–454.

Busse, A., Bischkopf, J., Riedel-Heller, S. G., & Angermeyer, M. C. (2003b). Subclassifications for mild cognitive impairment: Prevalence and predictive validity. *Psychological Medicine, 33*(6), 1029–1038.

Convit, A., De Asis, J., De Leon, M. J., Tarshish, C. Y., De Santi, S., & Rusinek, H. (2000). Atrophy of the medial occipitotemporal, inferior, and middle temporal gyri in non-demented elderly predict decline to Alzheimer's disease. *Neurobiology of Aging, 21*(1), 19–26.

De Leeuw, F. E., Barkhof, F., & Scheltens, P. (2004). White matter lesions and hippocampal atrophy in Alzheimer's disease. *Neurology, 62*(2), 310–312.

De Leon, M. J., Golomb, J., George, A. E., Convit, A., Tarshish, C. Y., Mcrae, T., et al. (1993). The radiologic prediction of Alzheimer disease: The atrophic hippocampal formation. *American Journal of Neuroradiology, 14*(4), 897–906.

Decarli, C., Miller, B. L., Swan, G. E., Reed, T., Wolf, P. A., Garner, J., et al. (1999). Predictors of brain morphology for the men of the NHLBI twin study. *Stroke, 30*(3), 529–536.

Decarli, C., Mungas, D., Harvey, D., Reed, B., Weiner, M., Chui, H., et al. (2004). Memory impairment, but not cerebrovascular disease, predicts progression of MCI to dementia. *Neurology, 63*(2), 220–227.

Degenhardt, T., & Greger, J. (1971). Verlaufsuntersuchungen An Sogenannten Vorzeitigen Versagenzuständen. *Psychiatrie, Neurologie, Und Medizinische Psychologie, 23*, 615–649.

Esiri, M. M., Nagy, Z., Smith, M. Z., Barnetson, L., & Smith, A. D. (1999). Cerebrovascular disease and threshold for dementia in the early stages of Alzheimer's disease. *Lancet, 354*(9182), 919–920.

Fischl, B., Salat, D. H., Busa, E., Albert, M., Dieterich, M., Haselgrove, C., et al. (2002). Whole brain segmentation: Automated labeling of neuroanatomical structures in the human brain. *Neuron, 33*(3), 341–355.

Gale, C. R., Walton, S., & Martyn, C. N. (2003). Foetal and postnatal head growth and risk of cognitive decline in old age. *Brain, 126*, 1–6.

Gertz, H. J., Xuereb, J. H., Huppert, F. A., Brayne, C., Kruger, H., McGee, M. A., et al. (1996). The relationship between clinical dementia and neuropathological staging (Braak) in a very elderly community sample. *European Archives of Psychiatry and Clinical Neuroscience, 246*(3), 132–136.

Gosche, K. M., Mortimer, J. A., Smith, C. D., Markesbery, W. R., & Snowdon, D. A. (2002). Hippocampal volume as an index of Alzheimer neuropathology: Findings from the Nun Study. *Neurology, 58*(10), 1476–1482.

Gould, S. J. (1981). *The mismeasure of man.* New York: W.W. Norton & Company.

Graves, A. B., Mortimer, J. A., Larson, E. B., Wenzlow, A., Bowen, J. D., & McCormick, W. C. (1996). Head circumference as a measure of cognitive reserve. Association with severity of impairment in Alzheimer's disease. *British Journal of Psychiatry, 169*(1), 86–92.

Grunwald, M., Busse, F., Hensel, A., Riedel-Heller, S., Kruggel, F., Arendt, T., et al. (2002). Theta-power differences in patients with mild cognitive impairment under rest condition and during haptic tasks. *Alzheimer's Disease and Associated Disorders, 16*(1), 40–48.

Haug, H. (1987). Brain sizes, surfaces, and neuronal sizes of the cortex cerebri: A stereological investigation of man and his variability and a comparison with some mammals (primates, whales, marsupials, insectivores, and one elephant). *The American Journal of Anatomy, 180*(2), 126–142.

Hensel, A., Wolf, H., Busse, A., Arendt, T., & Gertz, H. J. (2005). Association between global brain volume and the rate of cognitive change in elderly humans without dementia—A 2-year follow-up study. *Dementia and Geriatric Cognitive Disorders, 19*(4), 213–221.

Hensel, A., Wolf, H., Kruggel, F., Riedel-Heller, S. G., Nikolaus, C., Arendt, T., et al. (2002). Morphometry of the corpus callosum in patients with questionable and mild dementia. *Journal of Neurology, Neurosurgery and Psychiatry, 73*(1), 59–61.

Hickie, I., Scott, E., Wilhelm, K., & Brodaty, H. (1997). Subcortical hyperintensities on magnetic resonance imaging in patients with severe depression—A longitudinal evaluation. *Biological Psychiatry, 42*, 367–374.

Huber, G. (1972). Klinik Und Psychopathologie Der Organischen Psychosen. In K. P. Kisker, J. E. Meyer, M. Müller, & E. Strömgren (Eds.), *Psychiatrie Der Gegenwart* (pp. 71–146). Berlin, Heidelberg, New York: Springer.

Hughes, C. P., Berg, L., Danziger, W. L., Coben, L. A., & Martin, R. L. (1982). A new clinical scale for the staging of dementia. *British Journal of Psychiatry, 140*, 566–572.

Jack, C. R., Dickson, D. W., Parisi, J. E., Xu, Y. C., Cha, R. H., O'Brien, P. C., et al. (2002). Antemortem MRI findings correlate with hippocampal neuropathology in typical aging and dementia. *Neurology, 58*(5), 750–757.

Jobst, K. A., Barnetson, L. P., & Shepstone, B. J. (1998). Accurate prediction of histologically confirmed Alzheimer's disease and the differential diagnosis of dementia: The use of NINCDS-ADRDA and DSM-III-R criteria, SPECT, X-ray CT, and Apo E4 in medial temporal lobe dementias. Oxford project to investigate memory and aging [in process citation]. *International Psychogeriatrics, 10*, 271–302.

Katzman, R. (1986). Alzheimer's disease. *New England Journal of Medicine, 314*(15), 964–973.

Katzman, R., Terry, R., Deteresa, R., Brown, T., Davies, P., Fuld, P., et al. (1988). Clinical, pathological, and neurochemical changes in dementia: A subgroup with preserved mental status and numerous neocortical plaques. *Annals of Neurology, 23*(2), 138–144.

Kral, V. A., Cahn, C., & Mueller, H. (1964). Senescent memory impairment and its relation to the general health of the aging individual. *Journal of the American Geriatrics Society, 12*(2), 101–113.

Lasek, R., & Müller-Oerlinghausen, B. (1997). Therapieempfehlungen Der Arzenimittelkommission Der Deutschen Ärzteschaft—Ein Instrument Zur Qualitätssicherung In Der Arzneimitteltherapie. *Zeitschrift F?r Ärztliche Fortbildung Und Qualitätssicherung, 91*, 375–383.

Levy, R. (1994). Aging-associated cognitive decline. *International Psychogeriatrics, 6*(1), 63–68.

Longstreth, W. T. J., Manolio, T. A., Arnold, A., Burke, G. L., Bryan, N., Jungreis, C. A., et al. (1996). Clinical correlates of white matter findings on cranial magnetic resonance imaging of 3301 elderly people. The cardiovascular health study [see comments]. *Stroke, 27*(8), 1274–1282.

Lopez, O. L., Becker, J. T., Jungreis, C. A., Rezek, D., Estol, C., Boller, F., et al. (1995). Computed tomography—but not magnetic resonance imaging—identified periventricular white-matter lesions predict symptomatic cerebrovascular disease in probable Alzheimer's disease. *Archives of Neurology, 52*, 659–664.

Mckhann, G., Drachman, D., Folstein, M., Katzman, R., Price, D., & Stadlan, E. M. (1984). Clinical diagnosis of Alzheimer's disease: Report of the NINCDS-ADRDA work group under the auspices of Department of Health and Human Services Task Force on Alzheimer's disease. *Neurology, 34*, 939–944.

Mortimer, J. A., Gosche, K. M., Riley, K. P., Markesbery, W. R., & Snowdon, D. A. (2004). Delayed recall, hippocampal volume and Alzheimer neuropathology: Findings from the Nun Study. *Neurology, 62*(3), 428–432.

Mortimer, J. A., Snowdon, D. A., & Markesbery, W. R. (2003). Head circumference, education and risk of dementia: Findings from the Nun Study. *Journal of Clinical and Experimental Neuropsychology, 25*(5), 671–679.

Muller, U., Wolf, H., Kiefer, M., & Gertz, H. J. (2003). A systematic comparison of national and international dementia guidelines. *Fortschritte Der Neurologie Psychiatrie, 71*(6), 285–295.

Nagy, Z., Hindley, N. J., Braak, H., Braak, E., Yilmazer-Hanke, D. M., Schultz, C., et al. (1999). Relationship between clinical and radiological diagnostic criteria for Alzheimer's disease and the extent of neuropathology as reflected by 'Stages': A prospective study. *Dementia and Geriatric Cognitive Disorders, 10*(2), 109–114.

Nilsson, L. G. (2003). Memory function in normal aging. *Acta Neurologica Scandinavica, 107*, 7–13.

Petersen, R. C. (2004). Mild cognitive impairment as a diagnostic entity. *Journal of Internal Medicine, 256*(3), 183–194.

Petersen, R. C., Doody, R., Kurz, A., Mohs, R. C., Morris, J. C., Rabins, P. V., et al. (2001). Current concepts in mild cognitive impairment. *Archives of Neurology, 58*(12), 1985–1992.

Petersen, R. C., Parisi, J. E., Johnson, K. A., Waring, S. C., & Smith, G. E. (1997). Neuropathological findings in patients with mild cognitive impairment. *Neurology, 48*(3), 2034.

Petersen, R. C., Smith, G. E., Waring, S. C., Ivnik, R. J., Tangalos, E. G., & Kokmen, E. (1999). Mild cognitive impairment—Clinical characterization and outcome. *Archives of Neurology, 56*(3), 303–308.

Reisberg, B., Ferris, S. H., De Leon, M. J., & Crook, T. (1982). The global deterioration scale for assessment of primary degenerative dementia. *American Journal of Psychiatry, 139*, 1136–1139.

Reynolds, M. D., Johnston, J. M., Dodge, H. H., Dekosky, S. T., & Ganguli, M. (1999). Small head size is related to low mini-mental state examination scores in a community sample of nondemented older adults. *Neurology, 53*(1), 228–229.

Riedel-Heller, S. G., Busse, A., Aurich, C., Matschinger, H., & Angermeyer, M. C. (2001). Prevalence of dementia according to DSM-III-R and ICD-10—Results of the Leipzig longitudinal study of the aged (LEILA 75+) Part 1. *British Journal of Psychiatry, 179*, 250–254.

Riedel-Heller, S. G., Schork, A., Matschinger, H., & Angermeyer, M. C. (2000). Recruitment procedures and their impact on the prevalence of dementia. Results from the Leipzig longitudinal study of the aged (LEILA 75+). *Neuroepidemiology, 19*(3), 130–134.

Riley, K. P., Snowdon, D. A., & Markesbery, W. R. (2002). Alzheimer's neurofibrillary pathology and the spectrum of cognitive function: Findings from the Nun Study. *Annals of Neurology, 51*(5), 559–566.

Roth, M., Tym, E., Mountjoy, C. Q., Huppert, F. A., Hendrie, H., Verma, S., et al. (1986). Camdex. A standardized instrument for the diagnosis of mental disorder in the elderly with special reference to the early detection of dementia. *British Journal of Psychiatry, 149*, 698–709.

Rothschild, D. (1937). Pathological changes in senile psychosis and their psychobiological signficance. *American Journal of Psychiatry, 93*, 757–788.

Schoenberg, B. S., Kokmen, E., & Okazaki, H. (1987). Alzheimer's disease and other dementing illnesses in a defined United States population: Incidence rates and clinical features. *Annals of Neurology, 22*(6), 724–729.

Schofield, P. W., Logroscino, G., Andrews, H. F., Albert, S., & Stern, Y. (1997). An association between head circumference and Alzheimer's disease in a population-based study of aging and dementia. *Neurology, 49*(1), 30–37.

Snowdon, D. A., Greiner, L. H., Mortimer, J. A., Riley, K. P., Greiner, P. A., & Markes-bery, W. R. (1997). Brain infarction and the clinical expression of Alzheimer disease. The Nun Study. *Journal of the American Medical Association, 277*, 813–817.

Spielmeyer, W. (1912). Die Psychosen Des Rückbildungs—Und Greisenalters. In Aschaffenburg, G. (Ed.), *Handbuch Der Psychiatrie* (pp. 85–164). Leipzig: Deuticke.

Stieler, J. T., Lederer, C., Bruckner, M. K., Wolf, H., Holzer, M., Gertz, H. J., et al. (2001). Impairment of mitogenic activation of peripheral blood lymphocytes in Alzheimer's disease. *NeuroReport, 12*(18), 3969–3972.

Tisserand, D. J., Bosma, H., Van Boxtel, M. P., & Jolles, J. (2001). Head size and cognitive ability in nondemented older adults are related. *Neurology, 56*(7), 969–971.

Tittgemeyer, M., & Von Cramon, D. Y. (2004). Morphometry using magnetic resonance imaging. Present results. *Nervenarzt, 75*(12), 1172–1178.

Tomlinson, B. E., Blessed, G., & Roth, M. (1968). Observations on the brains of nondemented old people. *Journal of the Neurological Sciences, 7*(2), 331–356.

Tomlinson, B. E., Blessed, G., & Roth, M. (1970). Observations on brains of demented old people. *Journal of the Neurological Sciences, 11*(3), 205–242.

Tuokko, H., Frerichs, R., Graham, J., Rockwood, K., Kristjansson, B., Fisk, J., et al. (2003). Five-year follow-up of cognitive impairment with no dementia. *Archives of Neurology, 60*(4), 577–582.

Vermeer, S. E., Prins, N. D., den Heijer, T., Hofman, A., Koudstaal, P. J., & Breteler, M. M. (2003). Silent brain infarcts and the risk of dementia and cognitive decline. *New England Journal of Medicine, 348* (13), 1215–1222.

Whitehouse, P. J. (2003). Classification of the dementias. *Lancet, 361(9364)*, 1227.

Wieck, H. H. (1960). Zur Klinischen Stellung Der Durchgangs-Syndroms. *Archiv für Neurologie und Psychiatrie, 88*, 409–419.

Winblad, B., Palmer, K., Kivipelto, M., Jelic, V., Fratiglioni, L., Wahlund, L. O., et al. (2004). Mild cognitive impairment—Beyond controversies, towards a consensus: Report of the International Working Group on mild cognitive impairment. *Journal of Internal Medicine, 256*(3), 240–246.

Wolf, H., Ecke, G. M., Bettin, S., Dietrich, J., & Gertz, H. J. (2000). Do white matter changes contribute to the subsequent development of dementia in patients with mild cognitive impairment? A longitudinal study. *International Journal of Geriatric Psychiatry, 15*(9), 803–812.

Wolf, H., Grunwald, M., Ecke, G. M., Zedlick, D., Bettin, S., Dannenberg, C., et al. (1998). The prognosis of mild cognitive impairment in the elderly. *Journal of Neural Transmission, 54*, 31–50.

Wolf, H., Grunwald, M., Kruggel, F., Riedel-Heller, S. G., Angerhofer, S., Hojjatoleslami, A., et al. (2001). Hippocampal volume discriminates between normal cognition, questionable and mild dementia in the elderly. *Neurobiology of Aging, 22*(2), 177–186.

Wolf, H., Hensel, A., Arendt, T., Kivipelto, M., Winblad, B., & Gertz, H. J. (2004a). Serum lipids and hippocampal volume: The link to Alzheimer's disease? *Annals of Neurology, 56*(5), 745–748.

Wolf, H., Hensel, A., Kruggel, F., Riedel-Heller, S. G., Arendt, T., Wahlund, L. O., et al. (2004b). Structural correlates of mild cognitive impairment. *Neurobiology of Aging, 25*(7), 913–924.

Wolf, H., Jelic, V., Gertz, H. J., Nordberg, A., Julin, P., & Wahlund, L. O. (2003a). A critical discussion of the role of neuroimaging in mild cognitive impairment. *Acta Neurologica Scandinavica, 107*, 52–76.

Wolf, H., Julin, P., Gertz, H. J., Winblad, B., & Wahlund, L. O. (2004c). Intracranial volume in mild cognitive impairment, Alzheimer's disease and vascular dementia: Evidence for brain reserve? *International Journal of Geriatric Psychiatry, 19*(10), 995–1007.

Wolf, H., Kivipelto, M., Hensel, A., Winblad, B., Riedel-Heller, S. G., & Gertz, H. J. (2005). Serum lipids and hippocampal volume: The link to Alzheimer's disease? Reply. *Annals of Neurology, 57*(5), 780.

Wolf, H., Kruggel, F., Hensel, A., Wahlund, L. O., Arendt, T., & Gertz, H. J. (2003b). The relationship between head size and intracranial volume in elderly subjects. *Brain Research, 973*(1), 74–80.

Wolf, H., Wahlund, L. O., Muller, U., Hensel, A., & Gertz, H. J. (2004d). Education and intracranial volume are independent predictors of late-life cognitive state. *Neurobiology of Aging, 25*, S313–S314.

Zarow, C., Vinters, H. V., Ellis, W. G., Weiner, M. W., Mungas, D., White, L., et al. (2005). Correlates of hippocampal neuron number in Alzheimer's disease and ischemic vascular dementia. *Annals of Neurology, 57*(6), 896–903.

Zaudig, M. (1992). A new systematic method of measurement and diagnosis of mild cognitive impairment and dementia according to ICD-10 and DSM-III-R criteria. *International Psychogeriatrics, 4*(Suppl. 2), 203–219.

Zaudig, M., Mittelhammer, J., & Hiller, W. (1991). Sidam—A structured interview for the diagnosis of dementia of the Alzheimer type, multi-infarct dementia and dementias of other aetiology according to ICD-10 and DSM-III-R. *Psychological Medicine, 21*, 223–225.

Part IV

Interventions

10 Emerging pharmacological therapies for mild cognitive impairment

Howard Chertkow

Introductory comments

If this chapter dealt with medications for MCI for which we have a set of robust, effective, and uncontroversial results arising from prospective, randomized, placebo-controlled clinical studies, it would be a very short chapter—there are none! Nevertheless, we will present an overview of potential and forthcoming treatments and treatment possibilities, painting with broad strokes the present putative treatments and future possible avenues which may prove productive. I will look at available evidence for pharmacological interventions. Later chapters will consider nonpharmacological as well as combination approaches. We will also address some basic issues regarding treatment trials in MCI.

Why treat individuals with MCI?

This is perhaps a good place to begin, because there are several different answers to this question, and we can formulate a number of initial key issues by stating the different responses to this critical question.

Answer (a) Because the symptom of memory loss is upsetting to some. In other words, treatment may be symptomatic because of the individual's concerns over memory loss in MCI. *Treatment of symptoms* must be differentiated from treatment to prevent progression to dementia. The latter represents *secondary prevention* treatments for AD, and overlaps with future *primary prevention* treatments to be administered to asymptomatic elderly individuals considered to be at high risk for AD (Figure 10.1).

The first thing to ask about treating memory loss in MCI is whether it is desired, requested, necessary, or important. In other words, if patients were not worried about getting worse and progressing to Alzheimer disease, would they be even seeking treatment? The answer varies in each case. In our experience at a tertiary care memory clinic, the majority of patients are not seeking current treatment, but rather prevention. When offered experimental research protocols, they often reply "well, I do not really feel sick, so I don't need medications." At the same time, other individuals who do not even meet

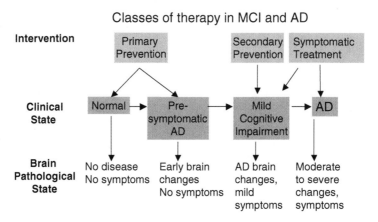

Figure 10.1 The classes of therapy in MCI and AD.

the objective criteria for MCI complain bitterly of their degree of memory impairment and seek over-the-counter and alternative medications for treatment. Furthermore, the economic results in the marketplace address a widespread desire for treatment of the memory loss associated with aging—sales of Ginkgo products in North America have apparently topped a billion dollars annually! Thus, a discussion of treatment approaches for MCI shades into the "slippery slope" of cognitive enhancement in the elderly (Rose, 2002). A number of recent publications have seriously examined the coming importance of such memory stimulation, in terms of its ethics, its effect on schools and in the marketplace, and the social considerations to come. Considerable attention was attracted, for instance, to a recent study showing improved performance of pilots taking donepezil (Yesavage et al., 2002) and we can look forward to growing attention to any new therapies that purport to offer "Viagra for the brain" (Farah et al., 2004). The first section of this chapter focuses on drugs with the potential to produce symptomatic memory improvement, demonstrated after short-term trials.

Answer (b) We will treat to prevent development of cognitive decline and dementia that often comes with aging. The point here is that in many ways, the interest of certain investigators is in primary prevention of dementia. Primary prevention refers to the treatment of asymptomatic individuals to prevent later disease. Unfortunately, such clinical trials tend to be huge, long affairs which require almost unsustainable effort (Grundman & Thal, 1996). MCI represents a "high risk group" for development of dementia (Chertkow, 2002), and thus a study that would require 25 million dollars to carry out in the normal elderly can be undertaken for only 3 million dollars using individuals with MCI (Grundman & Thal, 1996). The bottom line is—treating MCI is in many instances a shorter and less expensive means of getting at prevention. Of course, MCI individuals are *not* asymptomatic, and many of them already have significant early AD pathology (Morris & Price 2001; Morris et al., 2001), and thus we are forfeiting expensive primary prevention studies in order to concentrate on more feasible secondary prevention of MCI subjects. As a result, when a prevention study in MCI fails, it is always possible that the problem was timing—perhaps the critical period for that particular intervention was years earlier before the cascade of AD was well-established. Furthermore, even when undertaken, a primary prevention study is not always sufficient. There is some suspicion (see the section "Estrogen") that the WHIMS Estrogen study, a huge primary prevention study in women, failed to show a benefit of estrogen in preventing Alzheimer disease because it limited itself to women of age 60 and over when in fact the critical period when estrogen is beneficial may be decades earlier (Fillit, 1995; Sherwin, 1999, 2000; Yaffe, Sawaya, Lieberburg, & Grady, 1998)!

Answer (c) We want to treat because in many cases MCI is the earliest detectable stage of Alzheimer disease. Essentially, we are treating MCI because, in many cases (most cases in some series), this, we believe, is the initial presentation of an individual who will evolve gradually into a patient with dementia, usually AD. Indeed, Morris and colleagues have suggested that all people with MCI go on to manifest AD, and that it should be called "MCI of the AD type" (Morris et al., 2001). If this is true, or even partially true, then we are not attempting treatment to prevent AD, so much as to modify and slow the disease. Thus, it is probably wrong to conceptualize MCI and dementia (i.e., AD) as a dichotomy, the way that we talk of treating hypertension in order to "prevent" stroke. Individuals do not actually "convert" from MCI to AD, so much as they progress from a state of pathological AD insufficiently severe to meet clinical criteria for dementia to a state of pathological AD *sufficiently* severe to meet clinical criteria for dementia. The corollary is that, in essence, pharma-sponsored drug studies have avoided "nonmemory single domain" MCI, have little to say about MCI individuals who do not progress, and the focus has been on amnestic MCI defined somewhat narrowly.

All of which brings us to a related point—MCI is heterogeneous, not all MCI individuals (at least in our experience and that of others) progress to AD (Bocti, Whitehead, Fellow, & Chertkow, 2005), and so in some cases one will be treating individuals to prevent progression, who would not in fact have progressed. Thus, the "risk/benefit" ratio in MCI differs from that in AD studies. The bar for acceptable medications must be set higher! Furthermore, the heterogeneous nature of MCI ensures that clinical trials will have to be bigger and longer, usually 3 years, if the goal is to demonstrate a significant decrease in the progression rate (Petersen, 2000; Petersen, Smith, Waring, Ivnik, Tangalos, & Kokmen, 1999).

Understanding causation of AD leads to preventative therapy strategies

Since the rest of the chapter concentrates on potential pharmacological strategies to prevent AD and dementia, it would be nice if we understood the pathophysiology of the disease itself. Sadly, our understanding of the complex cascade of molecular events leading to AD remains controversial, to say the least (LeBlanc, Liu, Goodyer, Bergeron, & Hammond, 1999; Selkoe, 2004). New evidence from population studies (risk factors), post-mortem studies of aging cohorts, cell biology, and molecular genetics is defining multiple molecular factors. At the same time, the clinician is faced with clinical trials that diverge, rather than converge, with our current understanding. For instance, the major proven effective symptomatic therapy for AD consists of cholinesterase inhibitor (CI) medications, which arose out of the "cholinergic hypothesis of AD" (Whitehouse, Price, Struble, Clark, Coyle, & Delon, 1982), a theory which has largely been abandoned by researchers. Recent evidence suggests an absence of cholinergic deficits in MCI or mild AD (DeKosky, Ikonomovic, Cochran, Kordower, & Mufson, 2002), and yet the medications are among the only molecules demonstrated to improve symptoms in MCI! At the same time, despite strong epidemiological evidence supporting protective effects of estrogen and anti-inflammatory medications (and claims from basic scientists that inflammatory molecules mediate early AD), clinical trials of these in AD, MCI, and normal aging have produced surprisingly strong NEGATIVE results!

Clearly there are genetic factors in many cases of AD, and the presence of a positive family history doubles the risk of developing AD in any single individual (Blacker & Tanzi, 1998; Mayeux et al., 1993). True autosomal dominant familial AD (with mutations in the amyloid precursor protein [APP], presenilin 1 and presenilin 2 genes) is rare in our experience, although devastating in its occurrence at an early age. As noted, apolipoprotein E-4 is a risk factor for occurrence of late onset sporadic AD.

Exactly how genes promote AD is largely speculative, but many of the mechanisms postulated to promote occurrence of AD are the same as those thought to promote "poor aging". That is to say, there are likely mechanisms that promote a higher threshold for disease and greater functional reserve, as well as mechanisms that protect against age-related processes such as free radical-mediated damage to neurons. Hence, antioxidants are a logical approach to preventing AD as well as preventing aging itself (Markesbery, 1997).

Fifteen years ago, publications stressed the dichotomy of vascular dementia and Alzheimer's disease. Recently, there has been a growing awareness of the importance of vascular factors in cognitive decline, dementia, and even the clinical expression of the dementia of AD (Snowdon, Greiner, Mortimer, Riley, Greiner, & Markesbery,1997). There is consistent, strong evidence from large studies such as the Honolulu Aging Study that hypertension in mid-life or later life is a risk factor for cognitive decline (Launer et al., 2000). Elevated serum homocysteine level is a newly identified risk factor both for stroke and for Alzheimer's disease (Miller, Green, Mungas, Reed, & Jagust, 2002). Moreover, in the Kentucky Nuns Study, a large number of women died with pathological evidence of senile plaques and neurofibrillary tangles in their brains. If there were no vascular lesions, then only 57% had been clinically demented during life. If there were even one or two lacunar infarcts found, then 93% had been demented during life (Snowdon et al., 1997). Interpretation of these findings remains controversial—does it mean that vascular lesions unmask AD, or that most cases of AD are actually a "mixed dementia"? The current suggestion, however, is that treatment of vascular risk factors might impact on the development of AD.

The dominant theories of AD causation revolve around amyloid and hyperphosphorylated tau proteins, the two major components, respectively, of senile plaques and neurofibrillary tangles, the characteristic histological hallmarks of AD (Selkoe, 1991, 2004). Amyloid is the major component of senile plaques evident in AD. In addition, the genetic abnormalities identified in familial AD all involve the amyloid-beta protein production pathway. It is important to remember, however, that evidence of association is not proof of causation, and it is still possible that extracellular amyloid plaques may be epiphenomenal to the disease process. Recently, amyloid, and the A-beta protein have been identified as a potential target for therapeutic intervention in AD. The dramatic occurrence of encephalitis in a small group of patients treated with passive immunization of amyloid-beta protein has slowed this approach to therapy (Hardy & Selkoe, 2002; Schenk, 2002), but there is still considerable hope that treating amyloid protein may treat and even prevent the disease. Current Phase III studies of GAG-mimetics to block amyloid fibril coalescence offer another plausible approach to antiamyloid therapy (Gervais, 2004).

There is, however, considerable evidence that abnormal phosphorylation of tau protein, a microtubule-associated protein critical for axonal function, may be more central or crucial in the pathophysiology of AD. Tau abnormalities produce neurofibrillary tangles in neurons, and these spread in a predictable and hierarchical manner in the aging brain. It has been shown (Braak & Braak, 1991; Delacourte et al., 1999) that neurofibrillary tangles begin to accumulate in transentorhinal and entorhinal cortex, and progressively involve hippocampus, and temporal lobe cortex as well (Figure 10.2, from Braak & Braak, 1991). The number of neurofibrillary tangles closely parallels the degree of clinical dementia, and this association is stronger than that for senile plaques full of amyloid. MCI brains generally have tau pathology, but those with tau as well as amyloid are thought to be more likely to progress to AD.

How are we then to conceptualize all these complex and inter-related factors? Development of AD may be expressed as a set of inter-related curves (Figure 10.3). Individuals with a low tau load will progress during aging, but are unlikely to develop a tau pathology load sufficient to cross the threshold for clinical development of dementia. Those with a heavy (++) load curve are more likely to express dementia at a late age. The presence of amyloid-beta protein in senile plaques serves to "drag" the trajectory of the curve downward, producing clinical dementia at an earlier age. The presence of additional vascular lesions shifts the entire curve downward, again increasing the likelihood that dementia will be clinically expressed at an even earlier age. Thus, the separate pathological factors interact to produce the clinical syndrome.

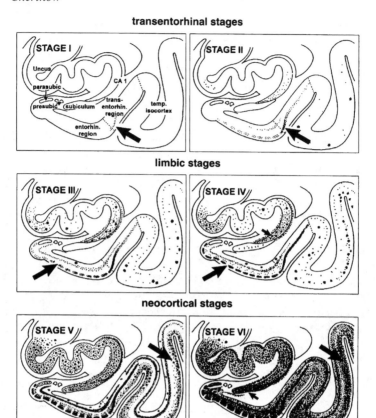

Figure 10.2 The pathological stages of AD (from Braak & Braak, 1991). The majority of MCI individuals show neurofibrillary tangles largely localized in the hippocampus (limbic stages), and rarely extending to the cortex (neocortical stages).

Symptomatic therapy

There is no current treatment for MCI sufficiently substantiated to have obtained government approval from FDA or Canadian government regulators. This contrasts with the situation in Europe, where medications such as Ginkgo and Hydergine have been approved broadly for "memory impairment". The three available CIs in North America are approved for treatment of Alzheimer's disease, not MCI. Symptomatic treatment of the memory complaints in MCI is, in fact, generally disappointing. Our own anecdotal experience with MCI patients using CIs, *Ginkgo biloba*, or stimulants such as ritalin, is that none of these usually make a significant clinical impact on their mild memory loss in the majority of patients. Occasionally however, MCI subjects may have a significant and even a dramatic benefit.

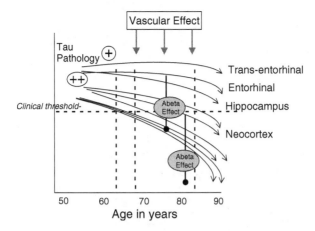

Figure 10.3 Interaction of multiple pathologies in cognitive decline. We can view the progression of cognitive decline (first to MCI, later to AD) in terms of the trajectory of tau pathology and the interacting additional loads of amyloid (Abeta) pathology, and vascular pathology. Depending on the cumulative factors, the clinical threshold for memory loss occurs at different ages. Adapted from Delacourte et al. (1999).

Symptomatic therapy with cholinesterase inhibitors

Symptomatic therapy for Alzheimer's disease has already come of age, with the availability in Canada of three CIs—donepezil (Aricept), rivastigmine (Exelon), and galantamine (Reminyl). These all produce modest improvement and stabilization in the majority of patients. A recent meta-analysis (Lanctôt et al., 2003) concluded that there is modest but significant therapeutic effect from all three, with insufficient evidence to demonstrate that one medication is superior to the others. The medications differ in terms of secondary pharmacological effects, dosing intervals, and side effect profiles. The numbers needed to treat for one additional patient to benefit were 7 for stabilization or better and 12 for at least minimal improvement. As a comparison, the number needed to treat for antidepressants for depression in medical illness is 4. All three medications can produce gastric side effects initially, but these are rarely intolerable. Starting doses are donepezil 5 mg daily, galantamine 4 mg bid, and rivastigmine 1.5 mg bid. Dose escalation for maximum efficacy is recommended in all three medications.

The Second Canadian Consensus Conference on dementia supported treatment of AD patients with CIs (Patterson et al., 1999). We often tell families that we hope to "roll back the decline by 6–12 months". Recent studies have reported good results with memantine, an NMDA antagonist available for many years in Germany (Reisberg, Doody, Stoffler, Schmitt, Ferris, & Mobius, 2003). Memantine appears most useful for the behavioural symptoms of moderate AD.

Regarding symptomatic treatment of MCI, the results to date have been much less impressive. Clinicians have anecdotally reported that certain MCI patients benefit from treatment with CIs in terms of memory and global function. Salloway et al. (2004) studied 270 patients across 20 centres meeting Petersen criteria for amnestic MCI. Half were treated with donepezil 10 mg for 6 months, and a series of cognitive and global tests were administered. Two thirds of the donepezil-treated cohort completed the study, and change in a paragraph recall test as well as the Clinical Global Impression of Change-MCI instrument were used as the primary outcome measures. Neither of these measures showed significant beneficial effects of therapy at the end of 6 months. A major secondary measure, the ADAS-Cog, did show a symptomatic benefit however. Subjectively, subjects treated with donepezil reported greater improvement in memory function than those given placebo. They reported feeling sharper mentally, more organized, and more confident of their memory. All of this suggests that at least some MCI individuals will have a significant clinical benefit from CIs, but overall the effects are mild.

Ginkgo biloba

Ginkgo biloba is commonly prescribed in Europe for all memory-impaired patients, with the idea that Ginkgo improves blood and oxygen flow to the brain and supports memory function, mental sharpness, and circulation. There are few if any well-designed clinical trials that support this conclusion (McDaniel, Maier, & Einstein, 2003). There was one placebo-controlled study of *Ginkgo biloba* in AD, with a high drop out rate. This showed a significant symptomatic benefit in AD, albeit approximately one fourth of the efficacy of CIs (Le Bars, Katz, Berman, Itil, Freedman, & Schatzberg, 1997)! It is notable that in some countries such as Germany, Ginkgo is routinely prescribed for AD because of its greater accessibility and lower cost to patients.

Recently, a large 24-week study, which was double-blind with placebo-controls, compared 123 patients on Ginkgo with 44 individuals on placebo (van Dongen, van Rossum, Kessels, Sielhorst, & Knipschild, 2003). The treated patients included one third with dementia, and two thirds defined as AAMI, a category with memory impairment compared to young control values (which approximates MCI, but is somewhat different). Neither treated group showed any benefit compared with placebo, and results did not support a role for Ginkgo in therapy.

There is an ongoing long-term study testing the hypothesis that *Ginkgo biloba*, as an antioxidant, might prevent onset or slow progression of AD. Data are not yet available.

Nootropics

There are a number of over-the-counter "dietary supplements" which have been suggested to have the effect of strengthening and protecting neurons of the brain involved in memory, serving as "memory nutrients". These "nootropics" have nonspecific mechanisms of action, with putative effects on energy metabolism, cholinergic mechanisms, excitatory amino acid receptor-mediated functions, as well as hormonal mechanisms (Riedel & Jolles, 1996). In this class one would list phosphatidyl-serine (PS), acetyl-L-carnitine, and piracetam. These are available through health food stores as diet supplements, not medications. Evidence for their efficacy is slim, but they have few if any side effects. Presumably these nootropics would have symptomatic rather than preventative effects in MCI.

PS plays a role in nerve cell membranes. The supplement version is obtained from cows, and more recently a form derived from soy lecithin is being sold. In the only scientific study (in 1991), subjects with mild memory loss similar to MCI who took 300 mg of PS for 3 months showed some modest improvement in their memory. The effects tended not to occur in everyone. There was no benefit in Alzheimer's disease (Crook, Tinklenberg, Yesavage, Petrie, Nunzi, & Massari, 1991). There have been no serious studies of PS in the past 10 years.

Acetyl-L-carnitine, choline (phosphatidylcholine, citicoline), and piracetam: Of these, the most tested has been piracetam, which was tested in a double-blind design in individuals who roughly speaking may have had MCI (Israel, Melac, Milinkevitch, & Dubos, 1994). There were mildly positive effects reported on delayed memory during the 3-month study, although groups were not distinguishable by the trial's end. In another multicentre cross-over study with nondemented individuals with memory impairment, there was a positive effect reported on tests of attention and memory as well (Fioravanti et al., 1991). Evidence for the other two compounds is quite thin in comparison.

Overall, despite lofty claims for dramatic effects of nootropics (generally from those involved in marketing of these agents), the proven benefit of each of these agents is modest. One broad review stated in conclusion, "All in all, we believe that the current data do not allow strong scientifically based recommendations for any of these memory nutrients (including PS and Ginkgo). However, the data also do not allow us to conclude that these nutrients are ineffective in boosting memory" (McDaniel et al., 2003).

Memory stimulants and future smart drugs

Wall Street and the media are abuzz about the "imminent" arrival of medications that will impact the neurochemical processes of memory itself. Such medications have the potential to compensate for the neurochemical deterioration thought to be part of MCI and even AD, without changing or retarding the underlying pathological processes. In addition, they have the remarkable potential to even impact on the putative changes we consider to be normal cognitive aging. The media are already speaking about potential "Viagra for the brain" (Tully, Bourtchouladze, Scott, & Tallman, 2003). While the clinical trials to come will certainly be aimed at MCI, the future potential for off-label use has been the subject already of a number of serious discussions (Farah et al., 2004). Bioethicists are contemplating the social effects and even dangers of memory enhancement, and potential use of these drugs in lifestyle enhancement.

Enhancement has largely been targeted at memory problems, inasmuch as these are the primary complaints of the elderly. In addition, enhancement of executive function has been achieved using methylphenidate in healthy volunteers (Farah et al., 2004; Pepeu, 2001). The candidate drugs directed at improving memory fall into one of two categories: those that target the initial induction of long-term potentiation, and those that target the later stages of memory consolidation (Squire & Kandel, 1999). The first category consists of (1) drugs that modulate NMDA receptors in their response to glutamate-induced depolarization, and (2) drugs that modulate AMPA (alpha-amino-3-hydroxy-5-methyl-4-isoxazole propionic acid) receptors to facilitate depolarization. NMDA receptors respond to repeated neuronal signalling by setting up a cascade of molecular events that strengthen the involved synaptic bond. Genetically engineered mice with genetically over-reactive NMDA receptors have enhanced memory performance! This represents one molecular approach to memory modification. Drugs using the AMPA mechanism would work through amplification of the AMPA receptor's response to glutamate. Drug candidates include the ampakines developed by Gary Lynch for Cortex Pharmaceuticals, among others (Lynch, 2002). Ampakines for MCI treatment are already beginning to enter Phase II clinical trials (Danysz, 2002). The efficacy and side effect profiles of these cognitive enhancers are unknown.

In the second category we find drugs aimed to increase CREB. CREB, discovered by Nobel Laureate Eric Kandel in snails, is the element-binding protein which in turn activates genes to produce proteins that strengthen the synapse in response to experience—the basis of long-term memory. A number of mechanisms are being explored that can impact on the CREB level (Squire & Kandel, 1999). One approach is via inhibiting the degradation of c-AMP (through blockade of phosphodiesterase), which acts to increase the CREB level in the cell. Memory Pharmaceuticals, co-founded by Kandel, is developing MEM1414 based on this CREB enhancer chemistry. Effects of CREB enhancement in animals have been dramatic—smart flies, mice, and mollusks. Human trials are still years away.

Prevention of AD by intervention at the MCI stage

The most critical interest from physicians, patients, and the pharma industry is in pharmacological interventions that can be instituted at the MCI stage to prevent progression to dementia, specifically AD. Slowing of progression to AD would have an enormous benefit to patients, and this has even been operationalized financially as a short-term benefit of US$5300 per year for each individual (Wimo, Jonsson, Karlsson, & Winblad, 1998). Most readers will be aware that no such effective medication currently exists, has been substantiated by multiple or convincing randomized placebo-controlled clinical trials, or is available in pharmacies.

Lacking this, we will focus on evidence for therapies derived from studies of risk factors for progression to Alzheimer's disease, as well as an overview of drugs that are "in the pipeline" at various stages. A number of agents (Table 10.1) could theoretically delay or prevent progression to Alzheimer's disease from the MCI state, and studies testing all of these inhibitors are currently underway. Such prevention studies are generally several years in duration, and results are beginning to reach the literature and will continue to be published over the coming years. Currently we have impressive epidemiological and natural history studies of risk factors in the development of cognitive decline and AD. It is important to point out, however, that retrospective observational

Table 10.1 Symptomatic and preventative therapies for MCI

Symptomatic therapy
Cholinesterase Inhibitors
Ginkgo biloba
Nootropic medications
Phosphatidyl-serine (PS)
Acetyl-L-carnitine
Choline (phosphatidylcholine, citicoline)
Piracetam
Memory stimulants
Ampakines
NMDA receptor modulation
CREB modulators
Preventative therapies
Antioxidants
Vitamin E
Other antioxidants (Selegiline, vitamin C)
Homocysteine
Omega fatty acids
Cholinesterase inhibitors
Anti-inflammatory agents
Estrogen
Statins
Antiamyloid therapies
Beta and gamma-secretase inhibitors
GAG-mimetics
Therapy for vascular risk factors

---

studies are not the same as carefully controlled randomized intervention studies. This has been brought harshly to the fore by the failure of a number of randomized clinical trials (RCTs) to confirm efficacy of interventions derived from epidemiological studies.

Why might population studies and RCTs diverge? It is always possible that the "critical period" for a pharmacological intervention occurs well before the occurrence of memory complaints in MCI, and MCI is simply too late a time to treat. Secondly, subjects in population studies who are taking some form of therapy are generally healthier and more motivated about their health than other people who are not taking anything. Why otherwise are they taking dietary supplements, for instance? Thirdly, we must consider the opposite bias—individuals with preclinical dementia might be more likely to stop taking medications, or forget to report their taking of supplements. Fourthly, there is a survival bias in population studies—we are, after all, measuring the survivors over time rather than ill individuals presenting to clinics. As one editorial points out, "these uncertainties highlight the great difficulty inherent in observational studies that depend on remembered information for estimation of risk factor exposures for illnesses that have long prodromal periods and that cause alterations in brain functions likely to influence behaviors, communications, memory, and other cognitive activity" (Foley & White, 2002). Nevertheless, in many cases we can only rely presently on intriguing population studies and await confirmatory RCTs.

Antioxidants and vitamin E—a case in point

What level of evidence is sufficient to advocate medications to prevent development of AD? Vitamin E is a case in point regarding the difficulties faced by clinicians. In a widely cited study of vitamin E in AD (Sano et al., 1997), patients on high dose vitamin E for up to 24 months reached the functional milestone of institutionalization more slowly than individuals on placebo. The treatment was regarded as safe; vitamin E was not associated with increased risk of death. Indeed, an identical number of subjects on vitamin E died during the course of the trial compared to patients on placebo. Based on this single study, and the theoretical benefits of antioxidants in preventing AD and cognitive decline as well as aging in general, a large number of AD and MCI subjects are currently prescribed vitamin E, or obtain it themselves from pharmacies.

The evidence for a benefit from vitamin E in preventing or delaying AD derives from a set of epidemiological studies. Individuals in the community eating a high level of dietary vitamin E have been found to have a 36% reduced risk of developing AD when compared to those consuming little dietary vitamin E (Morris, Evans, Bienias, Tangney, & Wilson, 2002). In the Rotterdam population study, individuals using supplements of vitamin E and vitamin C developed AD at a lower rate than subjects not using supplements (Engelhart et al., 2002a). The Cache County population study in Utah is currently examining risk factors for cognitive decline in a cohort of 5677 elderly subjects followed over 10 years.

While vitamin E supplementation alone was not found to have impressive results, this study suggests that healthy individuals using vitamin C or E supplements, as well as concurrent anti-inflammatory agents, are indeed at a lower risk of developing dementia (Fotuhi et al., 2005).

In contrast to this is new evidence from the "Memory Impairment Study", an important 3-year trial co-sponsored by the NIA, Alzheimer Disease Cooperative Study group (ADCS), and Pfizer. In this study, individuals with MCI were recruited and randomized into a vitamin E therapy arm, a donepezil therapy arm, or placebo. The study was large (240 subjects recruited into each arm), expensive, and elaborate. The investigators accepted only more "advanced" MCI individuals scoring below a memory cut-off score. The crucial primary endpoint was the number of subjects classified as progressing to dementia at the end of 3 years. This study assessed the effects of five daily capsules (2000 IU) of vitamin E and found no overall benefit in the vitamin E group in terms of prevention of progression to AD at the end of 3 years time (Petersen et al., 2005). One is flung back on the usual questions regarding RCT versus epidemiological evidence of efficacy.

Is vitamin E safe? A recent publication (Miller, Pastor-Barriuso, Dalal, Riemersma, Appel, & Guallar, 2005) examined the number of deaths in 19 clinical trials of vitamin E, including a total of 136,000 subjects. None of the individual studies showed an increase in risk of death for subjects on vitamin E alone. Similarly, when all 19 studies were examined together, there was no increase in the risk of death. However, when the studies were arranged by dose of vitamin E (above or below the 400 IU/day median dose), it appeared that individuals on low to moderate doses of vitamin E had a very slight protection against death while those on high dose vitamin E were at a very slightly higher risk of death. There are numerous methodological weaknesses of this study[1].

Nevertheless, it has led to confusion regarding the risk/benefit ratio for vitamin E in MCI. The Cache County population study failed to find any overall increase in mortality in subjects taking vitamin E. However, in subjects with previous cardiovascular incidents (stroke, coronary bypass, myocardial infarction), there might indeed be a small increased risk (Hayden et al., 2005). In the MCI "Memory Impairment Study", there was no increase in risk in the vitamin E group; the death rate was identical in individuals on placebo and vitamin E (Petersen et al., 2005).

Based on the pooled data in the recent publication, it is difficult to draw firm conclusions or make recommendations. The benefits of vitamin E supplements

---

[1] The majority of the deaths occurred in individuals who had known coronary artery disease. These trials varied in the characteristics of the subjects enrolled, the dose of vitamin E used, the duration of treatment, and the outcome measures studied. Many of the subjects enrolled in these trials had coronary artery disease or risk factors for cardiovascular disease. In about half of the studies, the active treatment under investigation was a combination of vitamin E plus other vitamins or minerals. Further, only 30% of the meta-analytical sample were in high dose studies and 12 studies with fewer than 10 deaths were not included in the analyses.

for AD prevention are unproven, and individuals with MCI have not shown benefit from vitamin E in terms of prevention of progression in a randomized controlled trial. Despite the meta-analysis, the risk of vitamin E also appears minimal. Might a single 400 IU vitamin E tablet be beneficially and safely prescribed for an MCI individual? They receive this in my own clinic, albeit with some hesitation.

Alternative antioxidants

The case for antioxidant therapy to prevent onset of AD (as well as other neurodegenerative diseases and aging in general) is relatively strong, and new evidence continues to accumulate. Oxidative damage can be found in a number of neurodegenerative conditions including AD (Markesbery, 1997; Perry et al., 2002). Oxidative damage in AD is indicated by the presence of elevated levels of nucleic acids, proteins, and oxidized lipids. This damage appears to occur early on in the course of the disease, and is most marked in those areas showing earliest AD pathology (Christen, 2000). In the brains of individuals suffering from MCI at the time of death, there are elevated protein carbonyls, malondialdehyde, and TBARS, all indicative of early oxidative damage (Keller et al., 2005).

Observational and population studies have largely focused on vitamin E (and vitamin C) as antioxidant (Engelhart et al., 2002a; Fotuhi et al., 2005; Morris et al., 2002). The evidence supporting vitamin E is reviewed above. What about other antioxidants? In fact, the objection has been raised that these studies used food questionnaires, and failed to find an effect of vitamin supplements. Furthermore, the interindividual dietary intake of antioxidants is actually quite narrow. High ascorbic acid and beta carotene plasma levels have been associated with better memory performance in the nondemented elderly (Perrig, Perrig, & Stahelin, 1997) but no such data exist in MCI. The protective effects of antioxidants may furthermore be overshadowed by the effect of smoking, which increases the load of free radicals, providing increased oxidative stress (Foley & White, 2002). Are there, therefore, RCTs that have tested the antioxidant hypothesis? *Ginkgo biloba*, vitamins A, C, and E all act as free radical scavengers. The failure of the Memory Impairment Study to show any effect whatsoever of vitamin E in MCI is thus a major blow to the antioxidant therapy lobbyists (Petersen et al., 2005).

Selegiline, an MAO inhibitor, reduces free radical formation and thus acts as an antioxidant through a different mechanism. Both vitamin E and selegiline produced a similar mild delay to institutionalization in AD patients (Sano et al., 1997). Selegiline has not been tested in MCI.

Homocysteine

Analysis of the Framingham study produced the somewhat surprising result that higher homocysteine levels were associated with increased risk of sporadic Alzheimer's disease (Seshadri et al., 2002). It is known that increased serum homocysteine is associated with histopathologic evidence of vascular endothelial injury, vascular smooth muscle proliferation, and progressive arterial stenosis. There has been substantial evidence that homocysteine levels correlate with arteriosclerotic vascular disease (Miller et al., 2002). What is surprising is the extension to AD as well. The factors in homocysteine levels are well known—vitamin supplements (folate, B6, B12) lower the levels, while caffeine, smoking, and lack of exercise increase levels. Current management of elevated homocysteine has been to increase folate in the diet or treat with supplements when increased homocysteine was greater than 15 μmol/L. Simple treatment with folate (3 mg daily), B6 (25 mg daily), and B12 (250–500 μg daily) keeps the homocysteine level low. Treatment of normal elderly as well as MCI individuals with folate, B6, and B12 found in multivitamins (even without following homocysteine levels) is likely to become the norm, even without controlled studies of this intervention (Hankey, 2002).

Omega fatty acids

Fats and oils in foods are made up of molecular components called fatty acids. Foods such as meat, butter, olive oil, or fish oil are composed of several different fatty acids, some of which are necessary or "essential" for human growth and development. Although the human body can synthesize most of the fatty acids it needs from what you eat, it cannot make certain fatty acids called essential fatty acids (EFAs), otherwise known as "omega" fatty acids. The most important of these is called DHA (docosahexaenoic acid). These must be consumed in the diet. They are highly concentrated in the human brain and are important for proper communication between nerve cells (Engelhart et al., 2002b; Kalmijn, Feskens, Launer, & Kromhout, 1997). Omega fatty acids, particularly DHA, can be obtained by eating cold water fatty fish such as salmon, sardines, mackerel, and bluefish. There is evidence from the Framingham study that those with the highest blood levels of DHA were half as likely as those with the lowest levels to develop dementia. Some doctors are now recommending that MCI patients eat such fish (or take two 200 mg DHA capsules) three times weekly (Engelhart et al., 2002b; Kalmijn et al., 1997).

Cholinesterase inhibitors to slow and prevent AD

The "Memory Impairment Study" described earlier was an important 3-year trial co-sponsored by the NIA, Alzheimer Disease Cooperative Study group (ADCS), and Pfizer. In this study, individuals with MCI were recruited and randomized into a vitamin E arm (2000 IU daily), a donepezil arm (10 mg daily), or placebo. The crucial primary endpoint was the number of subjects classified as progressing to dementia at the end of 3 years. The result was negative—no significant difference between the three groups was found at 3 years

(Petersen et al., 2005). This disappointing result seems to put to rest the possibility of CIs as effective therapies to prevent AD, but there are subanalyses that seem still to offer promise. For instance, it is clear that the group of individuals taking donepezil performed better than the others over the first 18 months, in terms of neuropsychological measures and global outcomes. It is also clear that the majority of individuals progressing to AD had an ApoE-4 allele, and if the analysis is restricted only to those individuals, they were indeed less "conversions to dementia" on donepezil at the end of 3 years. Currently, debate rages on whether this "negative study" might be reinterpreted as a positive result for a particular subgroup of patients. There are also the usual methodological concerns (heterogeneity of patients, weak outcome measure) that make it hard to achieve significant results even with large numbers of subjects.

The other main CIs are also being assessed for their potential to slow progression to AD. The Rivastigmine Trial (InDDEX) will be reported late in 2005. The galantamine trial was a 2-year study focusing on amnestic MCI patients with memory below a cut-off on paragraph recall. There was no difference in the primary analysis of conversion from amnestic MCI to AD. There did appear to be a reduced rate of whole-brain atrophy in the patients treated with galantamine (Scheltens, Fox, Barkhof, & Gold, 2004). However, therapy with this medication was associated with a small but statistically significant increased risk of dying. The sponsoring company discontinued the trial and has not recommended therapy for MCI with galantamine (Health Canada Advisory, 2005, January 21st).

The bottom line is that from the current evidence, if there is a benefit of CIs in slowing progression to AD, it appears to be transient as well as limited (Blacker, 2005).

Anti-inflammatory agents

There is clearly an inflammatory component to AD. There is now considerable evidence from observational studies that use of nonsteroidal anti-inflammatory drugs (NSAIDs) including ibuprofen and indomethacin as well as prednisone (a steroid) are associated with a decreased risk of Alzheimer's. These medications appear to protect against the development of AD through their anti-inflammatory action (Breitner & Zandi, 2001; Breitner et al., 1995; Zandi & Breitner 2001; Zandi, Anthony, Hayden, Mehta, Mayer, & Breitner, 2002). A meta-analysis of nine studies confirmed the fact that NSAIDs protect against development of AD in observational studies, with a pooled relative reduced risk of 0.72 (Etminan, Gill, & Samii, 2003). Those individuals with longer use of NSAIDs seemed to derive a greater protective effect. Nevertheless, a randomized, double-blind, placebo-controlled trial of rofecoxib in patients with MCI was negative, with no evidence of any protective effect (Aisen et al., 2003). Furthermore, results of a study that compared the effects of prednisone versus a placebo on people who had been diagnosed with Alzheimer's found no difference in cognitive decline between the prednisone and placebo treatment groups. Thus, a low-dose regimen of prednisone does not seem to be useful in treating Alzheimer's disease. Again this suggests that there is a (as yet unknown) critical period for treatment, and MCI is simply too late a stage to intervene with this medication.

Estrogen

There is considerable biological plausibility for the claim that estrogen has neuroprotective effects. Effects of estrogen can be seen on neuronal functioning in terms of neuronal organization, synaptogenesis, cerebral blood flow, and glucose utilization. Furthermore, there are interactions with neurotrophic factors, and a beneficial interaction with neurotoxic substances such as beta amyloid. In addition estrogen has antioxidant activity, and it produces inhibition of neuronal apoptosis. Estrogen clearly has a beneficial effect on verbal memory in postmenopausal estrogen-poor women (Sherwin, 2000). But can estrogen prevent Alzheimer's disease or prevent MCI?

Multiple observation studies have demonstrated a decreased risk of AD by 29–44% in hormone replacement therapy (HRT) users (Maki & Resnick, 2001; Yaffe et al., 1998). The optimal duration of therapy to produce this beneficial effect is uncertain, but the significant benefit may accrue only after more than 10 years of HRT use.

The Women's Health Initiative Memory Study (WHIMS), a large double-blind, placebo-controlled clinical trial of estrogen plus progesterone in healthy postmenopausal elderly women (Rapp et al., 2003; Shumaker et al., 2004)), failed to produce any change in the risk of developing MCI with estrogen treatment. Furthermore, the risk of dementia was actually elevated in the HRT group, with a hazard ratio of 2.05.

The discrepancies between the WHIMS RCT and observation studies of estrogen have received considerable attention. In the WHIMS, subjects were over 65 years in age, thus at least 15 years after menopause. In the observational studies, subjects are generally much younger. Thus, the possible critical period for neuroprotection might be soon after menopause. Furthermore, the oral treatment produced an increased risk of thromboembolism, vascular disease, and breast cancer. Thus the rationale for using HRT to prevent cognitive decline in elderly women is slim, and probably nonexistent.

Raloxifine is a SERMS (selective estrogen receptor modulator), which is more selective in its effects than estrogen. This family of medication has the ability to act in an estrogenic as well as an antiestrogenic compound in different tissues. In the "MORE" study, which focused on bone outcomes as well as cognition, a decreased risk of developing MCI was found (relative risk was decreased to 0.67) in those subjects taking raloxifine compared to placebo. This raises the possibility that the critical period for use of estrogens might be very early, earlier than when subjects already manifest MCI (Yaffe et al., 2005). Perhaps estrogen only helps if you start taking it at age 40.

As an argument against this view, the recently published results from the Nurses Health Study reported 13,807 nurses followed over 27 years. In this homogeneous group, use of HRT was not significantly associated with an alteration of cognitive decline. If anything, there was greater cognitive decline in long-term users or those who began estrogen intake at a later age (Kang, Weuve, & Grodstein, 2004). In our clinic, we do not prescribe estrogen pills specifically to prevent memory decline.

Statins

Statins are a group of drugs widely prescribed to reduce cholesterol. They lower levels of low-density lipoprotein (LDL) cholesterol—the type most strongly linked with coronary artery disease and stroke—by blocking a liver enzyme essential for cholesterol production. Statins are formally known as 3-hydroxy-3-methylglutaryl coenzyme A (HMG CoA) reductase inhibitors. Statins now marketed in the United States include atorvastatin (Lipitor), fluvastatin (Lescol), lovastatin (Mevacor), pravastatin (Pravachol), and simvastatin (Zocor). High LDL levels have been linked to Alzheimer's risk (Hartmann, 2001; Yaffe, Barrett-Connor, Lin, & Grady, 2002). In addition, high LDL levels also seem to favour deposition of beta-amyloid, the major component of the senile plaques characteristic of Alzheimer's. Reductions in cholesterol by statins might alter APP metabolism and thus reduce the production of A-beta (Das, 2002). Statins have also been shown to have immunomodulatory effects, blocking the ability of a cytokine called interferon-gamma (IFN-gamma) to activate T-cells. Statins might therefore have a neuroprotective effect by lowering inflammation.

An earlier multicentre analysis of over 60,000 patients indicated a decreased prevalence of AD in patients taking lovastatin and pravastatin, two statin drugs commonly used in lowering cholesterol (Jick, Zornberg, Jick, Seshadri, & Drachman, 2000; Wolozin, Kellman, Ruosseau, Celesia, & Siegel, 2000). A pilot study enrolling 63 individuals with normal cholesterol levels and mild to moderate Alzheimer's disease found preliminary evidence for some benefit with atorvastatin (Lipitor) (Sparks et al., 2005). There was a difference in the ADAS-Cog at the end of 1 year, and a suggestion that treated individuals had a change in the slope of their cognitive decline over that time. A large Phase II trial of Lipitor is currently underway for the treatment of AD. Clearly, the same logic in using statins applies to the MCI population. A large scale prevention trial of statins in MCI is warranted and necessary to establish whether these medications can prevent progression to AD.

Antiamyloid therapies

As noted above, amyloid is considered the most critical part of the pathophysiological cascade of AD. Reduction of A-beta production is theoretically possible through inhibition of two critical enzymes with a role in the cleavage that creates toxic A-beta fragments and its deposition in the form of plaques. Gamma-secretase inhibitors have been synthesized and are hopefully going to enter clinical testing (Moore, Leatherwood, Diehl, Selkoe, & Wolfe, 2000). An APP-specific beta secretase such as BACE (BACE stands for beta-site APP cleaving enzyme) could be another possible target for antiamyloid AD drugs (Selkoe, 2004). These are not yet in trials.

Prevention of amyloid deposition using inhibitors of A-beta aggregation such as GAG-mimetics (Alzhemed, from Neurochem Inc.) represents another approach. Alzhemed binds to soluble amyloid-beta protein to block the aggregation and hence the deposition of amyloid fibrils in the brain. This would hopefully reduce the toxic effect on neuronal and brain inflammatory cells associated with amyloid build-up. In a Phase II study, 19 mild-to-moderate AD patients received study medication for 20 months, and less decline was noted in the treated group. Approximately 70% of the mild AD patients had stabilized or improved cognitive function tests even after 20 months of enrollment in the Alzhemed open-label Phase II extension study (Gervais, 2004). Currently, a Phase III study of Alzhemed is underway in AD. In theory, such an approach should be even more effective at the MCI level.

Immunotherapy has been pursued in the treatment of AD, and potentially could be directed at individuals with MCI to prevent progression to AD (Schenk, 2002; Schenk et al., 1999). The dramatic occurrence of encephalitis in a small group of AD patients treated in a Phase II trial with passive immunization of amyloid-beta protein has slowed this approach to therapy. There is still considerable hope, however, that treating amyloid protein deposition via immunotherapy may eventually halt and even prevent the disease (Schenk, 2004).

In the future, there is also the possibility for development of interventions to prevent tau hyperphosphorylation. These have not yet reached the stage of clinical trials. It is hard at the present time to evaluate when these treatments might again arrive in clinical trials nor how effective they will be (Iqbal, 2004). One hopes that an effective and safe medication that directly blocks deposition and formation of amyloid protein and tau hyperphosphorylation will soon be found. This might become the ideal prevention treatment to institute at the MCI stage.

Therapy for vascular risk factors

As noted above in the section on causation, it is clear that vascular damage impacts on the occurrence of AD and mixed dementia. Risks for vascular disease (diabetes, hypertension, smoking, obesity, hyperlipidemia) are more and more being proven to be risk factors for development of dementia. In the Rotterdam Study in the Netherlands, individuals with diabetes had nearly double the risk of dementia (Ott, Stolk, van Harskamp, Pols,

Hofman, & Breteler, 1999). Presumably the microvascular damage from diabetes is the culprit, although it is possible that higher than normal levels of glucose in the blood might be toxic. The Framingham Heart Study demonstrated an impact of hypertension on cognition 6 years later (Elias, Elias, Sullivan, Wolf, & D'Agostino, 2003). The Cardiovascular Health Study showed that cognitive decline occurred even without frank stroke in individuals with vascular risk factors (Elkins, O'Meara, Longstreth, Carlson, Manolio, & Johnston, 2004).

These data give us important additional approaches to therapy of MCI, namely aggressively treating vascular risk factors. Note that this therapy is unproven in the sense that no one has yet mounted a long-term study that proves that intervention at the MCI stage will be effective in reducing or preventing occurrence of dementia or AD. However, treating these risks makes sense in their own right—a patient with uncontrolled hypertension should be treated *anytime!* Thus, in recommendations to family physicians, those working to prevent AD are now giving strong advice to "do what you already do"—namely aggressively treat any risk factors for vascular disease, in a patient with MCI. The risk of dementia thus represents an additional reason to treat the patient.

The MCI diet

Given the factors identified above, it is interesting to note that dietary and nutritional interventions are possible in the treatment of MCI/prevention of dementia. A healthy diet helps prevent hypertension (via reduced saturated fats and sodium), prediabetes (reduce sweets and caloric intake and consume more fibre), and stroke (dietary change to reduce cholesterol). Obesity is to be avoided by dietary limitation and exercise. One study from Chicago reported a higher risk of AD in seniors who ate more saturated and trans fat and less unsaturated fat (Morris et al., 2003) but another study did not find a link. Homocysteine levels (high or even normal) can in theory be reduced by a good intake of folic acid, B6, and B12 found in green leafy vegetables. Several multivitamins a day will also supply these amounts. There is evidence that an individual whose diet is high in omega-3 fatty acids, especially DHA, have a 50% reduction in their risk of developing dementia (Engelhart et al., 2002b; Kalmijn et al., 1997). About 180 mg of DHA daily intake is suggested and this amount can be achieved by eating cold water fatty fish such as salmon, sardines, mackerel, and bluefish, about three times a week. Thus, there is a theoretical basis for considerable dietary manipulation in MCI, none yet supported by RCTs.

Conclusion: current pharmacological management of MCI

Given the lack of clear prognostic markers, heterogeneity in the natural history of MCI individuals, and lack of proven therapies to prevent decline, the management of MCI patients remains largely nonspecific. The strongest evidence supports suggestions to "maintain a healthy lifestyle" with adequate exercise, avoidance of obesity, mental and physical stimulation, control of stress, treatment of medical illnesses and depression, and control of vascular risk factors such as diabetes, hypertension, and hypercholesterolemia.

Currently we lack proven pharmacological approaches to prevent cognitive decline or progression from MCI to dementia. Nevertheless, there are therapeutic interventions that the clinician can consider applying. With our increasing appreciation of the degree to which vascular factors interact with Alzheimer's disease in symptom onset, it makes good sense to aggressively treat vascular risk factors in MCI individuals using lifestyle interventions, diet, but also medications when necessary. Pharmacological treatment of depression is also indicated. Drugs with known anticholinergic activity, as well as sleeping pills and sedatives, should be avoided. Such treatment should be recommended to patients with MCI.

Physicians should inform patients that there is no current treatment for MCI sufficiently substantiated to have obtained government approval. Treating MCI individuals (or the healthy elderly) in order to prevent subsequent Alzheimer's disease using CIs, anti-inflammatories, estrogen, statins, various antioxidants, or even vitamin E represents prescription beyond proven therapies. It is advisable to refer the eager MCI patient to a research clinic where randomized controlled clinical trials of these and other preventative medications are currently underway. Only when the results of MCI drug studies begin to reach the literature will we be in a position to make informed scientific recommendations for such therapies (alone or in a cocktail) for the benefit of our patients.

The ADCS/NIA Donepezil study raises significant therapeutic issues. Since there was a delay in progression to AD in MCI individuals with a positive Apo E-4, then perhaps "a discussion of therapy" with donepezil is warranted. But what discussion? Should MCI patients be offered genetic testing with ApoE prior to a therapy decision? Should donepezil be offered with the hope that the symptomatic benefit will make up for our uncertainty regarding its long-term prevention role? Should its role in MCI (and the role of CIs in general) be downplayed as a major part of our therapeutic armamentarium, rather than using them up at the MCI stage? (This last is our own current thinking in the clinic.)

In our own clinic, we have exploited the dietary possibilities noted in the previous section as a way to maximize the potential beneficial effects of antioxidants and omega fatty acids, and to control homocysteine levels. Our patients generally are encouraged to take one or two multivitamins daily, which deliver adequate doses of vitamin E (400 IU), along with B6 and folate supplementation. And this is really all they are offered at the current time. The rest remains in the realm of current research and future possibilities.

Acknowledgments

This work was supported by a Chercheur-national award from the Fonds de la Recherche en Santé du Québec (FRSQ) to H. Chertkow, and funding from the CIHR (Canadian Institutes for Health Research).

References

Advisory, H. C. P. (2005, 21 January). *Health Canada Endorsed Important Safety Information on Reminyl (Galantamine)*. http://www.hc-sc.gc.ca/hpfb-dgpsa/tpd-dpt/index_advisories_public_e.html.

Aisen, P. S., Schafer, K. A., Grundman, M., Pfeiffer, E., Sano, M., Davis, K. L., et al. (2003). Effects of rofecoxib or naproxen vs. placebo on Alzheimer disease progression: A randomized controlled trial. *Journal of the American Medical Association, 289*(21), 2819–2826.

Blacker, D. (2005). Mild cognitive impairment—No benefit from vitamin E, little from donepezil. *New England Journal of Medicine, 352*(23), 2439–2441.

Blacker, D., & Tanzi, R. E. (1998). The genetics of Alzheimer's disease. Current status and future prospects. *Archives of Neurology, 55*(3), 294–296.

Bocti, C., Whitehead, V., Fellow, L., & Chertkow, H. (2005). Characteristics of patients with mild cognitive impairment who do not progress to dementia. *57th Annual Meeting American Academy of Neurology*. Miami Beach, FL.

Braak, H., & Braak, E. (1991). Neuropathological staging of Alzheimer-related changes. *Acta Neuropathologica, 82*(4), 239–259.

Breitner, J. C., Welsh, K. A., Helms, M. J., Gaskell, P. C., Gau, B. A., Roses, A. D., et al. (1995). Delayed onset of Alzheimer's disease with nonsteroidal anti-inflammatory and histamine H2 blocking drugs. *Neurobiology of Aging, 16*(4), 523–530.

Breitner, J. C., & Zandi, P. P. (2001). Do nonsteroidal antiinflammatory drugs reduce the risk of Alzheimer's disease? *New England Journal of Medicine, 345*(21), 1567–1568.

Chertkow, H. (2002). Mild cognitive impairment. *Current Opinion in Neurology, 15*(February 1999), 401–407.

Christen, Y. (2000). Oxidative stress and Alzheimer disease. *American Journal of Clinical Nutrition, 71*(2), 621S–629S.

Crook, T. H., Tinklenberg, J., Yesavage, J., Petrie, W., Nunzi, M. G., & Massari, D. C. (1991). Effects of phosphatidylserine in age-associated memory impairment. *Neurology, 41*(5), 644–649.

Danysz, W. (2002). CX-516 Cortex pharmaceuticals. *Current Opinion in Investigational Drugs, 3*(7), 1081–1088.

Das, U. N. (2002). Estrogen, statins, and polyunsaturated fatty acids: Similarities in their actions and benefits—Is there a common link? *Nutrition, 18*(2), 178–188.

DeKosky, S. T., Ikonomovic, M., Cochran, E. J., Kordower, J. H., & Mufson, E. J. (2002). Cholinergic upregulation in hippocampus in mild cognitive impairment—Relation to Alzheimer neuropathology. 54th Annual Meeting of the American Academy of Neurology, Denver, CO, USA; April 13–20, *Neurology, 58*, A239–A239.

Delacourte, A., David, J. P., Sergeant, N., Buee, L., Wattez, A., Vermersch, P., et al. (1999). The biochemical pathway of neurofibrillary degeneration in aging and Alzheimer's disease. *Neurology, 52*(6), 1158–1165.

Elias, M. F., Elias, P. K., Sullivan, L. M., Wolf, P. A., & D'Agostino, R. B. (2003). Lower cognitive function in the presence of obesity and hypertension: The Framingham heart study. *International Journal of Obesity and other Related Metabolic Disorders*, *27*(2), 260–268.

Elkins, J. S., O'Meara, E. S., Longstreth, W. T., Jr., Carlson, M. C., Manolio, T. A., & Johnston, S. C. (2004). Stroke risk factors and loss of high cognitive function. *Neurology*, *63*(5), 793–799.

Engelhart, M. J., Geerlings, M. I., Ruitenberg, A., Van Swieten, J. C., Hofman, A., Witteman, J. C., et al. (2002a). Dietary intake of antioxidants and risk of Alzheimer disease. *Journal of the American Medical Association*, *287*(24), 3223–3229.

Engelhart, M. J., Geerlings, M. I., Ruitenberg, A., Van Swieten, J. C., Hofman, A., Witteman, J. C., et al. (2002b). Diet and risk of dementia: Does fat matter? The Rotterdam Study. *Neurology*, *59*(12), 1915–1921.

Etminan, M., Gill, S., & Samii, A. (2003). Effect of non-steroidal anti-inflammatory drugs on risk of Alzheimer's disease: Systematic review and meta-analysis of observational studies. *British Medical Journal*, *327*(7407), 128–131.

Farah, M. J., Illes, J., Cook-Deegan, R., Gardner, H., Kandel, E., King, P., et al. (2004). Neurocognitive enhancement: What can we do and what should we do? *Nature Reviews Neuroscience*, *5*(5), 421–425.

Fillit, H. (1995). Future therapeutic developments of estrogen use. *Journal of Clinical Pharmacology*, *35*(Suppl. 9), 25S–28S.

Fioravanti, M., Bergamasco, B., Bocola, V., Martucci, N., Nappi, G., Neri, G., et al. (1991). A multi-centre, double-blind, controlled study of piracetam vs. placebo in geriatric patients with non-vascular mild-moderate impairment in cognition. *New Trends Clinical Neuropharmacology*, *5*(1), 27–34.

Foley, D. J., & White, L. R. (2002). Dietary intake of antioxidants and risk of Alzheimer disease: Food for thought. *Journal of the American Medical Association*, *287*(24), 3261–3263.

Fotuhi, M., Zandi, P., Hayden, K., Khachaturian, A., Wengreen, H. J., Munger, R., et al. (2005). Use of NSAIDs and antioxidant supplements in combination reduces the rate of cognitive decline: The Cache County Study (O2-02-05). Alzheimer's and Dementia, *Journal of the Alzheimer's Association*, *1*, S97–S98.

Gervais, F. (2004). GAG-mimetics: Potential to modify underlying disease process in AD. *Eighth International Montreal/Springfield Symposium on Advances in Alzheimer Therapy*, 23.

Grundman, M., & Thal, L. (1996). Clinical trials to prevent Alzheimer's disease in a population at-risk. In R. Becker & E. Giacobini (Eds.), *Alzheimer disease: From molecular biology to therapy* (pp. 375–379). Boston: Birkhauser.

Hankey, G. J. (2002). Is homocysteine a causal and treatable risk factor for vascular diseases of the brain (cognitive impairment and stroke)? [letter; comment]. *Annals of Neurology*, *51*(3), 279–281.

Hardy, J., & Selkoe, D. J. (2002). The amyloid hypothesis of Alzheimer's disease: Progress and problems on the road to therapeutics. *Science*, *297*(5580), 353–356.

Hartmann, T. (2001). Cholesterol, A beta and Alzheimer's disease. *Trends in Neurosciences*, *24*(Suppl. 11), S45–S48.

Hayden, K., Zandi, P., Wendgreen, H., Tschanz, J. T., Norton, M. C., Breitner, J., et al. (2005). Does Vitamin E use protect against dementia or increase the risk of mortality? (O2-01-07). Alzheimer's and Dementia, *Journal of the Alzheimer's Association*, *1*, S95–S96.

Iqbal, K. (2004). Pharmacological approaches of neurofibrillary degeneration. *Eighth International Montreal/Springfield Symposium on Advances in Alzheimer Therapy*, 22.

Israel, L., Melac, M., Milinkevitch, D., & Dubos, G. (1994). Drug therapy and memory training programs: A double-blind randomized trial of general practice patients with age-associated memory impairment. *International Psychogeriatrics*, *6*(2), 155–170.

Jick, H., Zornberg, G. L., Jick, S. S., Seshadri, S., & Drachman, D. A. (2000). Statins and the risk of dementia. *Lancet, 356*(9242), 1627–1631.

Kalmijn, S., Feskens, E. J., Launer, L. J., & Kromhout, D. (1997). Polyunsaturated fatty acids, antioxidants, and cognitive function in very old men. *American Journal of Epidemiology, 145*(1), 33–41.

Kang, J. H., Weuve, J., & Grodstein, F. (2004). Postmenopausal hormone therapy and risk of cognitive decline in community-dwelling aging women. *Neurology, 63*(1), 101–107.

Keller, J. N., Schmitt, F. A., Scheff, S. W., Ding, Q., Chen, Q., Butterfield, D. A., et al. (2005). Evidence of increased oxidative damage in subjects with mild cognitive impairment. *Neurology, 64*(7), 1152–1156.

Lanctôt, K. L., Herrmann, N., Yau, K. K., Khan, L. R., Liu, B. A., LouLou, M. M., et al. (2003). Efficacy and safety of cholinesterase inhibitors in Alzheimer's disease: A meta-analysis. *Canadian Medical Association Journal, 169*(6), 557–564.

Launer, L. J., Ross, G. W., Petrovitch, H., Masaki, K., Foley, D., White, L. R., et al. (2000). Midlife blood pressure and dementia: The Honolulu-Asia aging study. *Neurobiology of Aging, 21*(1), 49–55.

Le Bars, P. L., Katz, M. M., Berman, N., Itil, T. M., Freedman, A. M., & Schatzberg, A. F. (1997). A placebo-controlled, double-blind, randomized trial of an extract of Ginkgo biloba for dementia. North American EGb Study Group. *Journal of the American Medical Association, 278*(16), 1327–1332.

LeBlanc, A. C., Liu, H., Goodyer, C., Bergeron, C., & Hammond, J. (1999). Caspase-6 role in apoptosis of human neurons, amyloidogenesis and Alzheimer's disease. *Journal of Biological Chemistry, 274*, 23426–23436.

Lynch, G. (2002). Memory enhancement: The search for mechanism-based drugs. *Nature Neuroscience, 5*(Suppl.), 1035–1038.

Maki, P. M., & Resnick, S. M. (2001). Effects of estrogen on patterns of brain activity at rest and during cognitive activity: A review of neuroimaging studies. *NeuroImage, 14*(4), 789–801.

Markesbery, W. R. (1997). Oxidative stress hypothesis in Alzheimer's disease. *Free Radical Biology and Medicine, 23*(1), 134–147.

Mayeux, R., Ottman, R., Tang, M. X., Noboa-Bauza, L., Marder, K., Gurland, B., et al. (1993). Genetic susceptibility and head injury as risk factors for Alzheimer's disease among community-dwelling elderly persons and their first-degree relatives. *Annals of Neurology, 33*(5), 494–501.

McDaniel, M. A., Maier, S. F., & Einstein, G. O. (2003). Brain-specific nutrients: A memory cure? *Nutrition, 19*(11-12), 957–975.

Miller, E. R., 3rd, Pastor-Barriuso, R., Dalal, D., Riemersma, R. A., Appel, L. J., & Guallar, E. (2005). Meta-analysis: High-dosage vitamin E supplementation may increase all-cause mortality. *Annals of Internal Medicine, 142*(1), 37–46.

Miller, J. W., Green, R., Mungas, D. M., Reed, B. R., & Jagust, W. J. (2002). Homocysteine, vitamin B6, and vascular disease in AD patients. *Neurology, 58*(10), 1471–1475.

Moore, C. L., Leatherwood, D. D., Diehl, T. S., Selkoe, D. J., & Wolfe, M. S. (2000). Difluoro ketone peptidomimetics suggest a large S1 pocket for Alzheimer's gamma-secretase: Implications for inhibitor design. *Journal of Medicinal Chemistry, 43*(18), 3434–3442.

Morris, J. C., & Price, A. L. (2001). Pathologic correlates of nondemented aging, mild cognitive impairment, and early-stage Alzheimer's disease. *Journal of Molecular Neuroscience, 17*(2), 101–118.

Morris, J. C., Storandt, M., Miller, J. P., McKeel, D. W., Price, J. L., Rubin, E. H., et al. (2001). Mild cognitive impairment represents early-stage Alzheimer disease. *Archives of Neurology, 58*(3), 397–405.

Morris, M. C., Evans, D. A., Bienias, J. L., Tangney, C. C., Bennett, D. A., Aggarwal, N., et al. (2003). Dietary fats and the risk of incident Alzheimer disease. *Archives of Neurology, 60*(2), 194–200.

Morris, M. C., Evans, D. A., Bienias, J. L., Tangney, C. C., & Wilson, R. S. (2002). Vitamin E and cognitive decline in older persons. *Archives of Neurology, 59*(7), 1125–1132.

Ott, A., Stolk, R. P., van Harskamp, F., Pols, H. A., Hofman, A., & Breteler, M. M. (1999). Diabetes mellitus and the risk of dementia: The Rotterdam Study. *Neurology, 53*(9), 1937–1942.

Patterson, C., Gauthier, S., Bergman, H., Cohen, C., Feightner, J., Feldman, H., et al. (1999). The recognition, assessment and management of dementing disorders: Conclusions from the Canadian Consensus Conference on Dementia. *Canadian Medical Association Journal, 160*(Suppl. 12), S1–S15.

Pepeu, G. (2001). Overview and perspective on the therapy of Alzheimer's disease from a preclinical viewpoint. *Progress in Neuro-Psychopharmacology and Biological Psychiatry, 25*(1), 193–209.

Perrig, W. J., Perrig, P., & Stahelin, H. B. (1997). The relation between antioxidants and memory performance in the old and very old. *Journal of the American Geriatrics Society, 45*(6), 718–724.

Perry, G., Nunomura, A., Hirai, K., Zhu, X., Perez, M., Avila, J., et al. (2002). Is oxidative damage the fundamental pathogenic mechanism of Alzheimer's and other neurodegenerative diseases? *Free Radical Biology and Medicine, 33*(11), 1475–1479.

Petersen, R. C., Smith, G. E., Waring, S. C., Ivnik, R. J., Tangalos, E. G., & Kokmen, E. (1999). Mild cognitive impairment: Clinical characterization and outcome. *Archives of Neurology, 56*(3), 303–308.

Petersen, R. C., Thomas, R. G., Grundman, M., Bennett, D., Doody, R., Ferris, S., et al. (2005). Vitamin E and donepezil for the treatment of mild cognitive impairment. *New England Journal of Medicine, 352*(23), 2379–2388.

Petersen, R. C. (2000). Mild cognitive impairment: Transition from aging to Alzheimer's disease. *Neurobiology of Aging, 21*, S1–S1.

Rapp, S. R., Espeland, M. A., Shumaker, S. A., Henderson, V. W., Brunner, R. L., Manson, J. E., et al. (2003). Effect of estrogen plus progestin on global cognitive function in postmenopausal women: The Women's Health Initiative Memory Study: A randomized controlled trial. *Journal of the American Medical Association, 289*(20), 2663–2672.

Reisberg, B., & Doody, R., Stoffler, A., Schmitt, F., Ferris, S., & Mobius, H. J. (2003). Memantine in moderate-to-severe Alzheimer's disease. *New England Journal of Medicine, 348*(14), 1333–1341.

Riedel, W. J., & Jolles, J. (1996). Cognition enhancers in age-related cognitive decline. *Drug and Aging, 8*(4), 245–274.

Rose, S. P. (2002). "Smart drugs": Do they work? Are they ethical? Will they be legal? *Nature Reviews Neuroscience, 3*(12), 975–979.

Salloway, S., Ferris, S., Kluger, A., Goldman, R., Griesing, T., Kumar, D., et al. (2004). Efficacy of donepezil in mild cognitive impairment: A randomized placebo-controlled trial. *Neurology, 63*(4), 651–657.

Sano, M., Ernesto, C., Thomas, R. G., Klauber, M. R., Schafer, K., Grundman, M., et al. (1997). A controlled trial of selegiline, alpha-tocopherol, or both as treatment for Alzheimer's disease. The Alzheimer's Disease Cooperative Study. *New England Journal of Medicine, 336*(17), 1216–1222.

Scheltens, P., Fox, N. C., Barkhof, F., & Gold, M. (2004). Effect of galantamine treatment on brain atrophy as assessed by MRI in patients with mild cognitive impairment. *Neurobiology of Aging, 25*(Suppl. 2), S270–S271.

Schenk, D. (2002). Amyloid-beta immunotherapy for Alzheimer's disease: The end of the beginning. *Nature Reviews Neuroscience, 3*(10), 824–828.

Schenk, D. (2004). Advances in A-beta immunotherapy for potential treatment of AD. *Eighth International Montreal/Springfield Symposium on Advances in Alzheimer Therapy, 13*.

Schenk, D., Barbour, R., Dunn, W., Gordon, G., Grajeda, H., Guido, T., et al. (1999). Immunization with amyloid-beta attenuates Alzheimer-disease-like pathology in the PDAPP mouse [see comments]. *Nature, 400*(6740), 173–177.

Selkoe, D. J. (1991). Amyloid protein and Alzheimer's disease. *Scientific American, 265*(5), 68–71, 74–76, 78.

Selkoe, D. J. (2004). Alzheimer disease: Mechanistic understanding predicts novel therapies. *Annals of Internal Medicine, 140*(8), 627–638.

Seshadri, S., Beiser, A., Selhub, J., Jacques, P. F., Rosenberg, I. H., D'Agostino, R. B., et al. (2002). Plasma homocysteine as a risk factor for dementia and Alzheimer's disease. *New England Journal of Medicine, 346*(7), 476–483.

Sherwin, B. B. (1999). Can estrogen keep you smart? Evidence from clinical studies. *Journal of Psychiatry and Neuroscience, 24*(4), 315–321.

Sherwin, B. B. (2000). Mild cognitive impairment: Potential pharmacological treatment options. *Journal of the American Geriatrics Society, 48*(4), 431–441.

Shumaker, S. A., Legault, C., Kuller, L., Rapp, S. R., Thal, L., Lane, D. S., et al. (2004). Conjugated equine estrogens and incidence of probable dementia and mild cognitive impairment in postmenopausal women: Women's Health Initiative Memory Study. *Journal of the American Medical Association, 291*(24), 2947–2958.

Snowdon, D. A., Greiner, L. H., Mortimer, J. A., Riley, K. P., Greiner, P. A., & Markesbery, W. R. (1997). Brain infarction and the clinical expression of Alzheimer disease: The nun study. *Journal of the American Medical Association, 277*(10), 813–817.

Sparks, D. L., Sabbagh, M. N., Connor, D. J., Lopez, J., Launer, L. J., Browne, P., et al. (2005). Atorvastatin for the treatment of mild to moderate Alzheimer disease: Preliminary results. *Archives of Neurology, 62*(5), 753–757.

Squire, L. R., & Kandel, E. (1999). *Memory: From mind to molecules.* New York: W.H. Freeman & Co.

Tully, T., Bourtchouladze, R., Scott, R., & Tallman, J. (2003). Targeting the CREB pathway for memory enhancers. *Nature Reviews Drug Discovery, 2*(4), 267–277.

van Dongen, M., van Rossum, E., Kessels, A., Sielhorst, H., & Knipschild, P. (2003). Ginkgo for elderly people with dementia and age-associated memory impairment: A randomized clinical trial. *Journal of Clinical Epidemiology*, 56(4), 367–376.

Whitehouse, P. J., Price, D. L., Struble, R. G., Clark, A. W., Coyle, J. T., & Delon, M. R. (1982). Alzheimer,s disease and senile dementia: Loss of neurons in the basal forebrain. *Science*, 215(4537), 1237–1239.

Wimo, A., Jonsson, B., Karlsson, G., & Winblad, B. (1998). *Health economics of dementia*. Chichester: John Wiley & sons.

Wolozin, B., Kellman, W., Ruosseau, P., Celesia, G. G., & Siegel, G. (2000). Decreased prevalence of Alzheimer disease associated with 3-hydroxy-3-methyglutaryl coenzyme A reductase inhibitors. *Archives of Neurology*, 57(10), 1439–1443.

Yaffe, K., Barrett-Connor, E., Lin, F., & Grady, D. (2002). Serum lipoprotein levels, statin use, and cognitive function in older women. *Archives of Neurology*, 59(3), 378–384.

Yaffe, K., Krueger, K., Cummings, S., Blackwell, T., Henderson,V., Sarkar, S., et al. (2005). Effect of Raloxifene on prevention of dementia and cognitive impairment in older women: The multiple outcomes of Raloxifene evaluation (MORE) randomized trial. *American Journal of Psychiatry*, 162, 683–690.

Yaffe, K., Sawaya, G., Lieberburg, I., & Grady, D. (1998). Estrogen therapy in postmenopausal women: Effects on cognitive function and dementia. *Journal of the American Medical Association*, 279(9), 688–695.

Yesavage, J. A., Mumenthaler, M. S., Taylor, J. L., Friedman, L., O'Hara, R., Sheikh, J., et al. (2002). Donepezil and flight simulator performance: Effects on retention of complex skills. *Neurology*, 59(1), 123–125.

Zandi, P. P., Anthony, J. C., Hayden, K. M., Mehta, K., Mayer, L., & Breitner, J. C. (2002). Reduced incidence of AD with NSAID but not H2 receptor antagonists: The Cache County Study. *Neurology*, 59(6), 880–886.

Zandi, P. P., & Breitner, J. C. (2001). Do NSAIDs prevent Alzheimer's disease? And, if so, why? The epidemiological evidence. *Neurobiology of Aging*, 22(6), 811–817.

11 Cognition-based therapies and mild cognitive impairment

Robert T. Woods and Linda Clare

There has been increasing interest in recent years in the use of cognition-based therapies with people diagnosed as having Alzheimer's disease or other dementias (Clare, 2004; Woods, 2004). A Cochrane systematic review has been produced examining the effectiveness of such approaches in the context of early-stage Alzheimer's disease and vascular dementia (Clare, Woods, Moniz-Cook, Orrell, & Spector, 2003), which identified gaps in the outcome literature with people with dementia. However, the application of these approaches to individuals falling into the category of having a mild cognitive impairment (MCI) is even less well developed.

Clinical psychologists, who have been at the forefront of developing cognition-enhancing interventions in clinical areas, have tended to focus on those who meet the diagnostic criteria for dementia, rather than those who are in the hinterland between normal aging and dementia. This emphasis was reinforced by the promulgation of criteria for age-associated memory impairment, which appeared to pathologize normal aging (Deary, 1995), and did not fit readily with the realities of a clinical context already stretched in providing a service to those individuals and their families where a dementia diagnosis was currently supportable.

The continued development of Memory Clinics with the aim of early diagnosis and intervention (driven in part by the availability of acetylcholinesterase inhibitors) has brought many more people to clinical attention with concerns regarding their memory. A significant number of these individuals have objective memory difficulties on assessment, but do not meet diagnostic criteria for dementia, as other areas of cognitive function appear intact; others have several areas where it seems there may be cognitive decline, but not of the extent normally associated with a dementia. With the growing evidence that, over five years or so, a significant proportion of these people will go on to develop a dementia, there is now an added impetus to offer effective interventions for this group, rather than simply providing feedback that, whilst there is some impairment, this does not (yet) meet the criteria for dementia, and that their memory and other functions should be monitored periodically.

In this chapter, we will first examine what can be learned in relation to MCI from the application of cognition-based therapies with people with Alzheimer's and other dementias. We will then go on to consider issues of direct relevance to MCI, in terms of the therapeutic goals and outcomes required. Evidence supporting the role of cognitive activity in maintaining function will be considered, before examining the literature on cognitive interventions both for people with MCI and in relation to normal aging. Finally, we will consider clinical implications and future directions in this area.

Cognition-based therapies with people with dementia

In reviewing cognition-based therapies used with people with dementia, we have found it helpful to make a distinction between cognitive stimulation, cognitive training, and cognitive rehabilitation (Clare & Woods, 2004), although these terms have been used almost interchangeably in the literature.

Cognitive stimulation usually occurs in a group context. It offers engagement in a wide range of group activities and exercises aimed at general enhancement of cognitive and social functioning. The activities will have some cognitive component, but there will typically be an emphasis on enjoyment and social interaction. Reality orientation (RO), an approach developed in the 1950s in the USA, is now viewed as a type of cognitive stimulation (Woods, 2002).

Cognitive training may occur individually or in a group, or may be computer-based. It typically involves guided practice on a set of standard tasks designed to reflect particular cognitive functions, such as memory, attention, language, or executive function. The standard tasks may be available at several levels of difficulty to allow for individual differences in ability. The assumption is that regular or routine practice can potentially improve or at least maintain functioning in a given domain, and that any effects of practice will generalize to performance on other tasks and to everyday life. Thus, outcomes are most commonly assessed through performance on cognitive or neuropsychological tests, with an expectation of improvement or at least maintenance of performance. The aim of these approaches appears to be primarily to reduce underlying impairment or to arrest its progression.

Cognitive rehabilitation is a highly individualized approach. Here the person with dementia and the family caregiver work with a therapist to identify personally relevant goals and devise strategies for addressing these (Wilson, 2002). These strategies may involve, for example, the use of external memory aids to compensate for memory deficits, or training in specific skills to optimize procedural memory functioning, or working on optimizing residual memory performance. Spaced-retrieval has been shown, for example, to be an effective, if laborious, method of helping the person to learn new information (Camp, Bird, & Cherry, 2000). However, it can be remarkably effective; it is suggested that if the person with dementia is able to recall information within a training session for a critical interval (between 6 min and 1 hour, depending on the person and the study), then the information appears to be consolidated into long term memory and may be recalled days later.

The evidence base for the efficacy of these approaches is limited in early-stage dementia. Cognitive stimulation (especially in the guise of RO) has been evaluated in a number of randomized controlled trials (Spector, Davies, Woods, & Orrell, 2000), with positive findings in relation to cognition. This has been reinforced by findings from a recent large-scale study (Spector et al., 2003), where participation in cognitive stimulation groups was associated with improved cognition and quality of life. However, the majority of participants in this study were care-home residents with a moderate degree of dementia (with an average MMSE score of 14). The most relevant findings come from Breuil et al. (1994), where positive results from such groups were identified for people living at home in the early stages of dementia.

In relation to cognitive training, a Cochrane systematic review of randomized controlled trials (RCTs) of cognitive training (Clare et al., 2003) found six RCTs that could be included (Davis, Massman, & Doody, 2001; De Vreese et al., 1998b; Heiss, Kessler, Mielke, Szelies, & Herholz, 1994; Koltai, Welsh-Bohmer, & Schmechel, 2001; Quayhagen, Quayhagen, Corbeil, Roth, & Rodgers, 1995; Quayhagen et al., 2000). These used a diverse range of methods, measures, and comparison groups (Clare & Woods, 2004) limiting severely the meta-analyses that could be undertaken. It was possible to explore the impact on global measures of dementia severity (three studies), memory test scores (five studies), verbal fluency scores (three studies), self-ratings of depression (two studies), and behaviour ratings (two studies). There was no evidence from these analyses, or from conservative analyses of study data, that cognitive training was associated with positive outcomes. On the other hand, there was no evidence of increased depression, as was suggested by some earlier work, leading the American Psychiatric Association, in its 1997 Guidelines, to recommend that cognitive approaches not be used in the context of dementia. The lack of impact on cognition may be related to some studies being underpowered and the difficulty of showing change on standardized neuropsychological tests, rather than measures of everyday function, or areas of specific training. However, the dementia literature does not yet provide strong support for application of these approaches.

Cognitive rehabilitation has been reviewed comprehensively by De Vreese, Neri, Fioravanti, Belloi, and Zanetti (2001), who indicate its efficacy for people with early-stage Alzheimer's disease, emphasizing that interventions must be of sufficient duration and supported by caregiver involvement, and highlighting the importance of flexibility to allow for individual needs. However, most of the research studies are in the form of single-case experimental designs and controlled group studies, so that the Cochrane systematic review identified no randomized controlled trials of individualized cognitive rehabilitation for people with early-stage Alzheimer's disease (Clare et al., 2003). The available research has demonstrated that people with early-stage dementia can to some extent, given appropriate support, learn or relearn important and personally relevant information, maintain this learning over time, and apply it in the everyday context (Anderson, Arens, Johnson, & Coppens, 2001; Camp et al., 2000; Clare, Wilson, Breen, & Hodges, 1999; Clare, Wilson, Carter, Hodges, & Adams, 2001), that they can develop compensatory strategies such as using a memory aid (Clare, Wilson, Carter, Gosses, Breen, & Hodges, 2000), and that they can maintain or enhance their functional skills in activities of daily living (Josephsson, Bäckman, Borell, Bernspang, Nygard, & Ronnberg, 1993). The utility of techniques like spaced retrieval, cueing, and simple mnemonics has been demonstrated, and it has been suggested that reducing or eliminating errors during learning may be helpful when learning or relearning information and associations. Thus, there are some positive indications from this limited evidence base.

Therapeutic goals in MCI

In the context of MCI, what are the desired outcomes for cognitive interventions? On the one hand, the immediate impact might be considered. The aim might be to bring improvements in functional abilities, or to help the person with MCI to address their own specific concerns or perhaps to have an effect more generally on well-being and quality of life. On the other hand, the focus could be on having an impact on the progression from MCI to a diagnosable dementia. If cognitive interventions could even delay the progression to dementia, this would have a considerable impact on the prevalence of dementia, with benefits potentially for the individual, his/her family, and the health and social care systems.

From the outcome research on early-stage dementia, the first set of outcomes appear feasible and attainable, with cognitive stimulation approaches, appropriately modified, and cognitive rehabilitation methods, targeting the specific goals identified by the person with MCI and his/her family. Delaying the progression of MCI to dementia will inevitably be more challenging. Although prediction of those people with MCI who are most likely to progress will become more accurate, the multiple pathways to MCI will inevitably add uncertainty in the individual case as to whether the intervention has had any effect, especially when delay rather than absolute prevention is to be considered as a highly desirable outcome. The other challenge arises from the diagnostic criteria for a dementia, which specify an impairment in memory and at least one other area of cognitive function (American Psychiatric Association, 1994), with an impact on social or occupational functioning. Accordingly, a person with amnestic MCI may have significant memory and learning difficulties on objective assessment, but other areas of cognition may not show clear indications of impairment. The goal of cognitive intervention in such a case should then be to target areas of cognition other than memory, as it is decline in these areas that would lead to a conversion of the diagnosis from MCI to dementia. However, this focus will not address the person's current difficulties with memory, and so a combination approach would be more appropriate from a clinical perspective. This might combine cognitive stimulation as a general approach, incorporating cognitive training targeting unimpaired areas and cognitive rehabilitation addressing specific current goals, for example. The potential for cognitive stimulation to have an effect on progression to dementia finds support in a number of large-scale studies examining the relationship between the person's level of cognitive activity and the development of dementia, which are reviewed in the next section.

Cognitive activity and the development of dementia

Several studies have evaluated the role of cognitive activity in protecting against the onset of dementia. For example, Wilson et al. (2002a) report a longitudinal cohort study of 801 older people from Religious Orders (nuns, priests, and brothers from 40 Catholic groups across the USA), with an average follow-up of 4.5 years. At their initial interview they rated how often they participated in a range of cognitive activities, such as reading a newspaper or books, playing card games, crosswords and other puzzles, watching TV and visiting museums, as well as participation in physical activities (such as walking for exercise). They were also assessed on a number of cognitive tests. At follow-up, 111 were diagnosed as having Alzheimer's disease. Controlling for age, gender, and education, the risk of developing Alzheimer's was reduced by 33% for each point increase in cognitive-activity score at baseline. In contrast, number of hours of physical activity per week was not related to the risk of developing Alzheimer's disease. Greater cognitive activity was also related to reduced cognitive decline, particularly in working memory and perceptual speed, but not semantic memory or visuospatial ability. In a parallel study, sampling from a biracial community in Chicago, Wilson et al. (2002b) report a follow-up of 842 people judged to be free of Alzheimer's disease 4 years previously. Again at baseline, participation in cognitive and physical activity had been rated. In this sample, 139 people developed Alzheimer's disease. The risk of being given this diagnosis was reduced by 64% by a one-point increase in cognitive activity at baseline. Again, physical activity did not appear to predict the incidence of Alzheimer's disease.

An association between cognitive activity and reduced risk of developing Alzheimer's might be attributed to the effects of education. Better educated people might be expected to engage more in cognitive activities and it is well-established that people with higher levels of education are less likely to be diagnosed with a dementia. This has been attributed to educated people having either greater brain reserve (more neurones and connections can be lost before function is impaired) and/or greater cognitive reserve (able to use cognitive strategies to make more effective use of remaining brain systems). However, from their analyses of data on the incidence of dementia from the Canadian Study on Health and Aging, a study of over 10,000 older people, Tuokko, Garrett, McDowell, Silverberg, and Kristjansson (2003) conclude that the lower incidence of dementia for high functioning people primarily results from an ascertainment bias. The high functioning people who developed dementia were scoring less well on tests of memory initially than those who did not develop dementia, but not within the "impaired" range. If a single threshold for impairment is set, then less well educated people will reach it before those with a better education. In both these studies (Wilson et al., 2002a, 2002b), the effects of cognitive activity on risk of dementia were evident when the effects of educational level were controlled for, making this a less likely explanation of the findings, although the Religious Orders study includes participants with generally high educational levels.

Another possible explanation could be that in the period before Alzheimer's disease manifests itself, there is a prodromal period where subtle changes are occurring at a subclinical level. It is conceivable that these changes may predate the clinical onset of the condition by several years, and that they may have the effect of reducing cognitive and other activities. It is commonplace when reviewing the development of the dementia with someone in the early stages for the person to comment that they had withdrawn from previous activities (e.g., being an officer of a voluntary organization or church, or playing in a bridge club regularly) at least in part because they were aware they were not functioning as well as they had done previously.

A third large-scale prospective study reported by Verghese et al. (2003) addresses the possibility of the reduced activity being related to preclinical features of a dementia. Their sample comprised 469 people aged 75 and older, whose frequency of participation in leisure activities was assessed at baseline, with a median follow-up period of 5.1 years (maximum 21 years). Dementia was diagnosed in 124 participants (49% Alzheimer's disease; 25% vascular dementia; 20% mixed dementia). As in the Wilson et al. (2002a, 2002b) studies, cognitive activity was related to reduced risk of dementia, whereas physical activity was not. A reduced risk of dementia was related to specific activities: reading, playing board games, playing musical instruments, and dancing. Similar results were obtained for both Alzheimer's and vascular dementia. Excluding those thought at baseline to have possible preclinical dementia (by removing those who developed dementia within 7 years of the baseline) did not remove the association with the cognitive-activity score.

The superiority of cognitive activity to physical exercise reported by Wilson et al. (2002a, 2002b) and Verghese et al. (2003) needs to be examined carefully. Laurin, Verreault, Lindsay, MacPherson, and Rockwood (2001), analysing data from the Canadian Study on Health and Aging, report that regular exercise was associated with lower risks of dementia, for women. In the Verghese study, one form of physical exercise (dancing) was associated with lower risk of dementia, and the interaction between physical and cognitive activities must be acknowledged.

These three studies make a strong case for prospective intervention studies, which could target people with MCI as well as older people with no cognitive difficulties initially. Although the possibility that the link between cognitive activity and incidence of dementia may be related to level of education has been examined, it must be emphasized that "education" is a relatively insensitive variable, and more sophisticated examinations of life-long learning may be required, rather than years of education or school level attained.

In a similar vein, identification of "preclinical dementia" is no easy task, and even after 7 years, possible prodromal effects may still be operating. There is the possibility, for example, that depression may be either a prodrome for dementia, or a reaction to early cognitive impairment. Depression is, of course, linked to reduced activity levels, and may also be an important factor to take into account. Evidence regarding the effects of depressive symptoms on cognitive decline and the development of Alzheimer's disease is emerging from both the Religious Orders cohort and the Chicago biracial cohort. Wilson et al. (2002c) report that in the Religious Orders cohort, the greater the number of depressive symptoms at baseline, the greater the risk of developing Alzheimer's disease (with the risk increasing by 19% per depressive symptom). Depressive symptoms were also related to greater change on an index of global cognitive function. This finding was replicated in the Chicago cohort (Wilson, Mendes de Leon, Bennett, Bienias, & Evans, 2004) with number of depressive symptoms at baseline predicting cognitive decline in a group of 4392 older people followed up for an average period of 5.3 years, and controlling for education and initial level of cognition. Wilson et al. conclude that their findings do not reflect a depressive reaction to cognitive impairment but that "chronic experience of even relatively low levels of depressive symptoms may compromise the hippocampus and perhaps other neural systems...."

Depressive symptoms will, of course, fluctuate, in relation to external stresses and other factors, and so a one-off assessment at baseline may underestimate their impact. Wilson and colleagues have also used a brief measure of proneness to psychological distress, conceptualized as a stable personality trait indicator of susceptibility to negative emotional states across the lifespan, which may add to our understanding of the influence of mood on the development of dementia. In the Chicago cohort, following up 1064 people for between 3 and 6 years, persons prone to psychological distress were 2.4 times more likely to develop Alzheimer's disease than persons not distress prone, with the effect being weaker in African Americans (Wilson et al., 2005). In the Religious Orders study, at follow-up averaging 4.9 years, 140 people had developed Alzheimer's disease; in this cohort, high distress proneness was associated with twice the risk of developing Alzheimer's disease, compared with those having the lowest levels (Wilson, Evans, Bienias, Mendes de Leon, Schneider, & Bennett, 2003). High distress proneness was associated with a 10-fold increase in episodic memory decline. However, among those who died, distress proneness showed no relationship with the usual markers of Alzheimer's neuropathology at postmortem, suggesting that distress proneness may influence the expression of the disorder rather than the pathological basis.

The relationship between cognitive activity and subsequent cognitive decline or dementia appears consistent with the often quoted "Use it or lose it" hypothesis, with the exhortation to use the brain, engaging in activities with significant cognitive demands, to maintain brain function (Hultsch, Hertzog, Small, & Dixon, 1999). For example, in order to protect "brain health", Small (2002) recommends "Mental activity—do crosswords, puzzles, read, or challenge yourself intellectually" in addition to stress reduction, physical exercise, and a range of lifestyle measures. However, Salthouse, Berish, and Miles (2002) argue that "it may be premature to reach a definitive conclusion about the validity of the use it or lose it perspective". In a study involving 204 adults aged between 20 and 91 years of age, reported cognitive activity did not moderate age-related cognitive decline. The study was cross-sectional and the participants scored well above average on tests of cognitive ability, and perhaps cannot be generalized readily to those at immediate risk of developing a dementia. However, it does indicate the complexity of this area, and reinforces the need for prospective studies in at-risk populations.

Cognitive training and normal aging

There is a well-established literature on the effects of cognitive training in older people (Hill, Sheikh, & Yesavage, 1987; Scogin, 1992; Stigsdotter Neely, 2000; Yesavage & Jacob, 1984; Zarit, Cole, & Guider, 1981). A theme of this research has been the interplay between specific cognitive factors, such as encoding and retrieval processes, more general cognitive processes, such as attention, and noncognitive factors, such as anxiety levels and self-efficacy beliefs. For example, Yesavage and Jacob (1984) taught 25 normal older people (age 61–82 years) to use relaxation training and a mnemonic device to improve face–name recall. The mnemonic, in this and subsequent studies, includes identifying a prominent facial feature; developing a concrete image related to the person's name; linking in imagery the facial feature and name image. They concluded that relaxation training can reduce the cognitive component of anxiety, which otherwise interferes with performance on tasks involving memory and attention. Stigsdotter and Bäckman (1989, 1993) included relaxation training in their multifactorial memory training programme, which also involved practice of encoding skills and attentional training. Those participating in the programme showed a task-specific improvement on a memory task after 6 months that was maintained for 3.5 years. Similar improvements were obtained with the encoding skills training alone.

A meta-analysis of mnemonic training is reported by Verhaeghen, Marcoen, and Goossens (1992), including 31 studies in healthy older adults. Training was effective on episodic memory tasks. The effect size in terms of training gains was 0.73 (standard deviation units) compared with 0.38 for control groups. This indicates that simply retesting an older person on an episodic memory test results in an average improvement of almost two fifths of a standard deviation. Training gains were associated with younger age, pretraining designed to improve mnemonic learning, group format, and shorter duration of sessions. Neither the type of mnemonic taught nor the kind of pretraining used had an impact on outcomes.

Subjective confidence and self-efficacy in memory performance has also been examined. Fifty-nine older people (age 55–86 years) received 8 h of training in the use of a mnemonic, to assist in face–name learning (Hill et al., 1987). Compared with a waiting-list control group (comprising 17 older people), both face–name recall and perceived recall confidence improved in those receiving training. Thus, the training appeared to benefit confidence as well as performance. In a study which explored the benefits of an intervention specifically focused on developing more adaptive beliefs about memory, alongside memory training, Lachman, Weaver, Bandura, Elliott, and Lewkowicz (1992) randomly allocated 140 older adults (age 60–85 years) to one of five conditions. These comprised a cognitive restructuring condition, targeting beliefs about memory; a memory skills training condition; a combined cognitive restructuring and memory skills training condition; a condition involving extensive practice on memory tasks; and a no contact control group. Results indicated equal improvement across all groups (including the no contact control group) on the tests of memory function, where the primary effect appeared to be a practice effect with the same test materials being used on each occasion. Those in the memory skills training condition were more likely to report 3 months later that they had begun using new strategies in everyday life. The combined treatment was associated with the greatest increases in sense of control and perceived ability to improve memory.

Floyd and Scogin (1997) report a meta-analysis of the effects of memory training on subjective memory. Twenty-seven studies were included, with a small overall effect, but the effect size was lower for subjective memory (0.19) than that reported by Verhaeghen et al. (1992) for objective change (0.66). Memory training seemed to have more effect on subjective memory where it incorporated both mnemonic training and expectancy modification.

In a recent large-scale study, Ball et al. (2002) randomly assigned 2832 volunteers aged 65–94 to one of four groups (10 sessions of either verbal episodic memory, reasoning, or visual processing speed training and a no-contact control group). Sixty per cent in each of the active treatment groups was offered "booster" sessions 11 months later. The authors reported that each intervention successfully improved the targeted cognitive ability, with enhanced gains still apparent at 2-year follow-up in the reasoning and speed groups (but not the memory group) receiving booster training. No effects on everyday functioning were noted in a sample selected for independent functioning, many of whom scored close to the maximum possible score on the tests of everyday function used. The specific training effects were argued to be equivalent to the level of decline that might be expected over a 7–14 year period. Incident dementia was not formally examined in this study.

This large-scale study reinforces the earlier work in the field of normal aging, indicating that improvements following training and/or practice are achievable, but that they appear to be task or domain specific. Scogin (1992) sums this up well: "memory training...is not a powerful intervention. Most people do improve as a result of training, but the changes are neither extraordinary nor permanent" (p. 269). The challenge for MCI will be to both enhance the power of the intervention and select appropriate targets that will maximize the impact of the therapeutic effort expended.

Cognitive interventions in MCI

There have been relatively few studies as yet evaluating cognitive interventions in MCI. As would be expected, relevant studies have used a variety of labels to describe participants, reflecting changing definitions and practice. Sheikh, Hill, and Yesavage (1986) report a study in which the participants are described as having age-associated memory impairment (AAMI), although the study was similar to those from the same research group discussed above in the section Cognitive training and normal aging. They examined whether various forms of pretraining enhanced the effectiveness of training in the use of an imagery-based mnemonic to facilitate face–name recall. There were three types of specific pretraining used: training in developing and elaborating visual images; training in verbal judgement, to develop deeper processing; and relaxation training. The participants were 82 people with AAMI; average age was 67.4 years. The specific pretraining methods did appear to be associated with better performance in a face–name recall task at 6 month follow-up compared with the mnemonic training when it was preceded by a nonspecific pretraining condition.

Both Israel, Melac, Milinkevitch, and Dubos (1994) and Israel, Myslinski, and Kozarevic (1998) have reported an evaluation of a combined memory training programme with nootropic medication (praxilene), in a group of 162 patients (mean age 68.5 years) described as having AAMI, without dementia or depression. The memory training was delivered in a group format, with groups of 8–10 participants meeting for 90 min once a week. The best results after 3 months were reported for combined therapy with those who had the lowest memory scores at baseline, and where the memory training began 6 weeks after the person commenced on the medication, rather than at the same time.

Two distinct groups of older people were included in the evaluation of memory training programmes reported by De Vreese, Belloi, Iacono, Finelli, & Neri (1998a). All were described as being nondemented and nondepressed and residing in the community; they all had spontaneous memory complaints. For one group ($n = 39$), these subjective memory complaints were not evident on objective memory testing; the other, older group ($n = 20$) fulfilled the criteria for age-associated cognitive decline (AACD). The memory training programme was similar to that reported by Israel et al., in that groups of 8–10 participants met weekly for 90 min over a 3-month period. Mnemonic techniques and learning strategies were used, with exercises based around real life concerns such as remembering people's names, location of household objects, and prospective memory. In addition, efforts are made to develop new attitudes that help the person "to learn to forget in a more rational way with less distress" (p. 143). Both groups improved on objective measures of memory, but the improvement was greater in the AACD group, particularly on attention and short-term memory processing. The AACD group also showed an increase in their subjective appraisals of their current everyday memory ability.

One of the first cognitive intervention studies to use diagnostic criteria for MCI is reported by Rapp, Breenes, and Marsh (2002). Nineteen people (mean age 75.1) meeting the Petersen, Smith, Waring, Ivnik, Tangalos, and Kokmen (1999) criteria (subjective memory complaint with objective memory below 10th percentile; all other cognitive functions above 10th percentile; no ADL or IADL deficits) were randomized to either a memory training condition, delivered as six weekly group sessions of 2 hr duration, or to a no-treatment control condition. The intervention was multifaceted, including education on memory and dementia, relaxation training, mnemonic strategies, and cognitive restructuring to improve beliefs about memory control. The results on improved memory performance were disappointing, with no significant differences between trained and untrained participants at the end of the training or at 6 months follow-up. Conversely, trained participants reported their current memory ability to have improved, relative to controls, and this was still the case at follow-up. Immediately after treatment, trained participants reported a stronger belief in the potential for improvement in their memory, but this difference had been lost at follow-up. The control group reported greater use of mnemonic strategies at follow-up than the trained group (e.g. "to-do" lists and daily scheduling).

This study is small and underpowered, and further studies are needed before concluding that memory training in MCI is ineffective in improving objective memory performance. However, it does highlight some important issues. Does the dissociation between improved perceived memory ability and unchanged objective memory ability reflect a real improvement in self-efficacy or does it suggest that the participants are becoming less aware of real difficulties? Or is it that the objective memory tests are not able to tap into real improvements in everyday memory function? Does the lower use of mnemonics by trained participants reflect an overconfidence in their own ability to remember without external assistance? Rapp et al. highlight findings reported by Small, La Rue, Komo, and Kaplan (1997), indicating that greater self-reported mnemonic usage is associated with greater subsequent cognitive decline; however, this may represent a realistic attempt by those with early dementia to maintain function—in everyday life—as much as possible.

At least one study of cognitive and motor stimulation (Olazaran et al., 2004) has included people with MCI, alongside people with dementia.

However, the results of this small group ($n = 12$) were not presented separately, and so their contribution to the study's positive outcomes is unclear.

Finally, in relation to studies focusing on MCI, Fernández-Ballesteros, Zamarrón, and Tàrraga (2005) and Fernández-Ballesteros, Zamarrón, Tàrraga, Moya, and Iniguez (2003) have compared the learning ability of people with MCI, compared with normal older people and people with Alzheimer's disease. There were 200 participants, 50 having the diagnosis of MCI. All groups showed "cognitive plasticity" on learning tasks, which used visual, verbal, and executive function strategies. The MCI group's performance improved at an intermediate level, being rather better than that of the Alzheimer's group, but worse than the normal aging group.

Clinical implications

Having reviewed the evidence base for cognition-focused interventions in MCI, there would appear to be more guidance for the clinician from the dementia and normal aging literature than from the MCI-specific work, which is still in its infancy. In the clinical context, the focus must be on improving function and well-being, until research becomes available on what may influence the progression to dementia. It is becoming clear from the dementia literature that external memory aids and some learning strategies can be helpful; the normal aging literature reinforces the importance of self-efficacy, confidence, and control.

Emmerson and Frampton (1996) describe a psychological approach to working with people with memory impairment, but who did not at the time have a dementia diagnosis, in the context of a Memory Clinic. Their multiperspective model incorporates behavioural, cognitive, and systemic aspects. The behavioural component includes assisting the person in using appropriate internal and external memory aids, selecting aids that make most efficient use of the person's cognitive strengths, and using aids efficiently and effectively. Thus a person may have begun to use a diary to keep track of appointments etc., but be completing it in a disorganized way, which adds to confusion, or be leaving it in a drawer where it is forgotten about, rather than in a key place, such as by the telephone, where it will be readily used. The cognitive perspective focuses on the person's beliefs and negative automatic thoughts regarding their memory problems; these may catastrophize the problem, as indicating the onset of dementia or the person may blame themselves, calling themselves "stupid" for not being able to remember a name or find a misplaced object. The risk of going on to develop dementia is of course a real one, but the person is encouraged to focus on the current situation, and what they can do now to maintain their function and quality of life, rather than dwell on a future which is uncertain for all. Finally, the systemic perspective reflects the impact that memory problems may be having on the person's relationships; their partner or other relative may bear the brunt of the person repeating the same story over and over, or asking the same question repeatedly, or they may find the person does not seem to remember what they have asked them to do. The person's relatives and friends may also be worrying about the risk of dementia, or about how the balance of the relationship is changing. The need to involve significant others in any intervention is clear. The therapeutic work is always based on a detailed neuropsychological assessment profile, which assists in clarifying both the exact nature of the person's difficulties, and their strengths and preserved areas of function.

Our own clinical approach is broadly similar. To date, our practice has been to encourage people with MCI to continue to engage in cognitively stimulating activities of their preference, and to find ways of remaining involved in mainstream activities as far as possible, rather than establishing specific cognitive stimulation programmes for them. We offer individualized interventions, where appropriate, including the establishment or reinforcement of everyday memory strategies. We encourage the use of external memory aids, so that the person routinely uses them well before the onset of dementia, in those cases where progression is occurring. Input in relation to the person's mood is offered, where needed, with mood and cognition often interacting. Interventions involve other family members where appropriate. We present three brief case vignettes from the work we undertake in Memory Clinics to illustrate what might be involved; some details have been altered to protect the confidentiality of the patients concerned.

Case 1—Mrs A

This retired social worker was first seen 5 years ago when she was aged 70. She reported experiencing memory loss, following a hip replacement 6 months previously. At the initial assessment, she scored in the minimal depression range on the Beck Depression Inventory. On the CAMCOG-R (Roth, Huppert, Mountjoy, & Tym, 1998), a screening test of cognitive function, she scored above the 75th percentile for her age (Williams, Huppert, Matthews, Nickson, & MRC Cognitive Function and Aging Study, 2003). Most of the few points she lost were on new learning. Her scores on subtests of language, praxis, and executive function were excellent. Her Mini-Mental State score was 28/30. The presence of significant memory impairment was confirmed by her scores on the Doors and People test of memory and learning (Baddeley, Emslie, & Nimmo-Smith, 1994). She was at the 5th percentile for her age-group overall on this test, with no apparent discrepancies between verbal and visual modalities or recognition and free recall paradigms. The profile was consistent with MCI.

Mrs A was asked to keep a diary of her weekly activities, and to indicate instances where her memory had failed her. It was evident that, despite being retired, Mrs A had a very heavy and demanding workload, having positions of great responsibility in several charitable organizations and, at the same time, supporting several friends who were experiencing stress in their own lives. However, there were very few instances of memory failures recorded, in fact less than one per week, and these occurred when she was distracted or under time pressure. Mrs A used many memory strategies, including list-making, a diary, and taking notes at meetings. She spoke of being very concerned that she was developing Alzheimer's disease, and was worried about making a fool of herself in social situations, or losing control. Her major concern was that she would not be able to fulfil her pivotal role with the various organizations with which she worked, and that they would not be able to continue.

Initial therapeutic interventions focused on helping Mrs A reduce the pressure on herself, delegating some of her tasks, involving others, and assisting her in carving out some personal time in her hectic schedule. She found it difficult to practise relaxation techniques more than once a week, however. The negative automatic thoughts that she experienced in relation to the reaction of others to any mistakes that she made were discussed, and Mrs A was able to acknowledge that her friends and colleagues would be supportive, and that the expectation that she must never make mistakes was unreasonable.

Later, when Mrs A was reporting having difficulty remembering names, some work was carried out with her using the spaced retrieval learning method, to learn some face–name associations. Over several years, Mrs A was seen for monitoring and support; handing over her workload and the use of memory strategies continued to be constant themes. Four years after her initial assessment, she and her family reported a worsening of memory, with a number of examples of this being apparent in everyday life. A repeated neuropsychological assessment indicated that there were now difficulties with praxis (her score on the Block Design test was $1SD$ below average), in addition to her memory difficulties, and that her visual reasoning was at a lower level than expected for her predicted IQ and education level. Her anxiety and depression levels were within the normal range. The diagnosis of Alzheimer's disease was confirmed, and she commenced on an acetylcholinesterase inhibitor. She has attended a "Coping with Forgetting" group, with others in the early stages of a dementia, and has begun to speak to professional and lay groups regarding her experience of Alzheimer's.

Mrs A is perhaps an example of someone who had a surfeit of cognitive activity. Overload may be rarer than under-use, but the resulting pressure and stress was certainly debilitating for Mrs A. Her well-being in the phase between MCI diagnosis and Alzheimer's diagnosis was improved by the work on memory strategies, workload reduction, and cognitive restructuring that was carried out. By the time the diagnosis of Alzheimer's was finally made, she had been able to hand over all her responsibilities, and is able to take on new, manageable involvements in relation to her own condition. She has concerns about the future, and is making plans to address these; she has not been overwhelmed by the diagnosis, and talks of living with the condition.

Case 2—Mrs B

Mrs B, aged 79, was referred to the Memory Clinic following an incident where she had caused a flood by forgetting to turn off the taps in her bathroom and forgetting to turn off the gas on her stove. At initial assessment she seemed low, and in fact had had a history of depression since her husband died 20 years earlier. Her depression score on the Hospital Anxiety and Depression Scale (Kenn, Wood, Kucyj, Wattis, & Cunane, 1987) was in the clinical range (16; cut-off is 8). On the CAMCOG-R, she scored 86/105, which is just under the mean score for her age-group. Detailed assessment of her memory indicated that she scored below the 10th percentile on a list-learning task, and on immediate and delayed recall of a memory passage. Her verbal and performance IQ on the Wechsler Abbreviated Scale of Intelligence (WASI; Wechsler, 1999) were 99 and 100 respectively, confirming an average level of overall cognitive function. Following multidisciplinary assessment, the diagnosis of MCI was made. Mrs B was relieved to receive this diagnosis, as she had been concerned about the possibility of a dementia.

Low mood was viewed as a significant factor, and she was seen for 13 sessions of cognitive behaviour therapy, which focused on her low self-esteem and self-worth, and increasing her activity levels, within the constraints of physical limitations. Her Depression score fell to 7, within the normal range. Following the diagnostic feedback session she had no further concerns regarding her memory, although this will be monitored regularly in the Memory Clinic.

Case 3—Mr C

This 75-year-old former college lecturer has recently been diagnosed with MCI in the Memory Clinic. He and his wife had been very concerned about the possibility of Alzheimer's and so were relieved to have this diagnosis, even with its risk of progression. The everyday memory difficulties that he reports involve needing to check whether he has done something or not, such as locking the door. His mild memory difficulties appear to have triggered obsessional tendencies, which had never previously been problematic. He lacks confidence in his memory, and began to check several times. He has now been taught to carry out such tasks in a self-aware manner, so that he has a clear memory of having done so; when he does these tasks automatically without consciously thinking about it, he has no explicit memory of the task. Successful performance on this and other tasks is building his confidence. He is also engaging in life review work, as he is preoccupied with a number of thoughts from the past involving regrets; it is hypothesized that these distract him from attending to current tasks at times.

Clinical work with people with MCI will, by definition, involve work with a heterogeneous group of patients and difficulties, involving individualized interventions, as illustrated briefly here. Mood will often interact with the memory and other cognitive difficulties, as a reaction or as a factor in excess disability. Improving mood is a major factor in maintaining quality of life and maximizing function.

Future directions

The literature on cognitive interventions in MCI is clearly at an early stage, and there will undoubtedly be a rapid growth in this area. The use of widely recognized and accepted criteria for classifying MCI will assist in producing a more clinically applicable body of knowledge. Outcome studies in early-stage dementia provide some pointers, but this is also an underdeveloped area of research.

Large-scale, prospective, well-controlled studies examining the effects of cognitive interventions on progression to dementia will be needed to establish whether the findings on cognitive activity and the incidence of dementia reflect a controllable process, or are a marker of changes already in train. Widespread application of cognitive training, unless incorporated in activities enjoyed by the participants, is unlikely to offer a way forward.

The relationship of mood and proneness to distress to MCI and progression to dementia also merit further attention. There may be processes here, also, which may be amenable to interventions of various kinds.

References

American Psychiatric Association. (1994). *Diagnostic and Statistical Manual of mental disorders* (4th ed.). Washington, DC: American Psychiatric Association.

American Psychiatric Association. (1997). Practice guideline for the treatment of patients with Alzheimer's disease and other dementias of late life. *American Journal of Psychiatry*, *154*(Suppl. 5), 1–39.

Anderson, J., Arens, K., Johnson, R., & Coppens, P. (2001). Spaced retrieval vs. memory tape therapy in memory rehabilitation for dementia of the Alzheimer's type. *Clinical Gerontologist*, *24*, 123–139.

Baddeley, A., Emslie, H., & Nimmo-Smith, I. (1994). *Doors and people: A test of visual and verbal recall and recognition.* Bury St Edmunds: Thames Valley Test Company.

Ball, K., Berch, D. B., Helmers, K. F., Jobe, J. B., Leveck, M. D., Marsiske, M., et al. (2002). Effects of cognitive training interventions with older adults: A randomized controlled trial. *Journal of American Medical Association*, *288*, 2271–2281.

Breuil, V., Rotrou, J. d., Forette, F., Tortrat, D., Ganansia-Ganem, A., Frambourt, A., et al. (1994). Cognitive stimulation of patients with dementia: Preliminary results. *International Journal of Geriatric Psychiatry*, *9*, 211–217.

Camp, C. J., Bird, M., & Cherry, K. E. (2000). Retrieval strategies as a rehabilitation aid for cognitive loss in pathological aging. In R. D. Hill, L. Bäckman, & A. Stigsdotter Neely (Eds.), *Cognitive rehabilitation in old age* (pp. 224–248). Oxford: Oxford University Press.

Clare, L. (2004). Assessment and intervention in dementia of Alzheimer type. In A. Baddeley, M. D. Kopelman, & B. A. Wilson (Eds.), *The essential handbook of memory disorders for clinicians* (pp. 255–283). Chichester: Wiley.

Clare, L., Wilson, B. A., Breen, K., & Hodges, J. R. (1999). Errorless learning of face–name associations in early Alzheimer's disease. *Neurocase, 5*, 37–46.

Clare, L., Wilson, B. A., Carter, G., Gosses, A., Breen, K., & Hodges, J. R. (2000). Intervening with everyday memory problems in early Alzheimer's disease: An errorless learning approach. *Journal of Clinical & Experimental Neuropsychology, 22*, 132–146.

Clare, L., Wilson, B. A., Carter, G., Hodges, J. R., & Adams, M. (2001). Long-term maintenance of treatment gains following a cognitive rehabilitation intervention in early dementia of Alzheimer type: A single case study. *Neuropsychological Rehabilitation, 11*, 477–494.

Clare, L., Woods, B., Moniz-Cook, E., Orrell, M., & Spector, A. (2003). Cognitive rehabilitation and cognitive training interventions targeting memory functioning in early-stage Alzheimer's disease and vascular dementia (Cochrane Review). In *The Cochrane Library*, Issue 4. Chichester: Wiley.

Clare, L., & Woods, R. T. (2004). Cognitive training and cognitive rehabilitation for people with early-stage Alzheimer's disease: A review. *Neuropsychological Rehabilitation, 14*, 385–401.

Davis, R. N., Massman, P. J., & Doody, R. S. (2001). Cognitive intervention in Alzheimer's disease: A randomized placebo-controlled study. *Alzheimer Disease and Associated Disorders, 15*, 1–9.

Deary, I. J. (1995). Age-associated memory impairment: A suitable case for treatment? *Aging & Society, 15*, 393–406.

De Vreese, L. P., Belloi, L., Iacono, A., Finelli, C., & Neri, M. (1998a). Memory training programs in memory complainers: Efficacy on objective and subjective memory functioning. *Archives of Gerontology & Geriatrics, 26*(Suppl. 6), 141–154.

De Vreese, L. P., Verlato, C., Emiliani, S., Schioppa, S., Belloi, L., Salvioli, G., et al. (1998b). Effect size of a three-month drug treatment in AD when combined with individual cognitive retraining: Preliminary results of a pilot study (Abstract). *Neurobiology of Aging, 19*(4S), S213.

De Vreese, L. P., Neri, M., Fioravanti, M., Belloi, L., & Zanetti, O. (2001). Memory rehabilitation in Alzheimer's disease: A review of progress. *International Journal of Geriatric Psychiatry, 16*, 794–809.

Emmerson, C., & Frampton, I. (1996). A psychological treatment approach to memory problems. *Clinical Psychology Forum, 97*(November), 13–17.

Fernández-Ballesteros, R., Zamarrón, M. D., & Tàrraga, L. (2005). Learning potential: A new method for assessing cognitive impairment. *International Psychogeriatrics, 17*, 119–128.

Fernández-Ballesteros, R., Zamarrón, M. D., Tàrraga, L., Moya, R., & Iniguez, J. (2003). Cognitive plasticity in healthy, mild cognitive impairment (MCI) subjects and Alzheimer's disease patients: A research project in Spain. *European Psychologist, 8*, 148–159.

Floyd, M., & Scogin, F. (1997). Effects of memory training on the subjective memory functioning and mental health of older adults: A meta-analysis. *Psychology & Aging, 12*, 150–161.

Heiss, W. D., Kessler, J., Mielke, R., Szelies, B., & Herholz, K. (1994). Long-term effects of phosphatidylserine, pyritinol and cognitive training in Alzheimer's disease. *Dementia, 5*, 88–98.

Hill, R. D., Sheikh, J. I., & Yesavage, J. A. (1987). The effect of mnemonic training on perceived recall confidence in the elderly. *Experimental Aging Research, 13*, 185–188.

Hultsch, D. F., Hertzog, C., Small, B. J., & Dixon, R. A. (1999). Use it or lose it: Engaged lifestyle as a buffer of cognitive decline in aging? *Psychology & Aging, 14*, 245–263.

Israel, L., Melac, M., Milinkevitch, D., & Dubos, G. (1994). Drug therapy and memory training programs: A double-blind randomized trial of general practice patients with age-associated memory impairment. *International Psychogeriatrics, 6*, 155–170.

Israel, L., Myslinski, M., & Kozarevic, D. (1998). Nootropic treatment and combined therapy in age-associated memory impairment. *Archives of Gerontology & Geriatrics, 27*(Suppl. 6), 269–274.

Josephsson, S., Bäckman, L., Borell, L., Bernspang, B., Nygard, L., & Ronnberg, L. (1993). Supporting everyday activities in dementia: An intervention study. *International Journal of Geriatric Psychiatry, 8*, 395–400.

Kenn, C., Wood, H., Kucyj, M., Wattis, J. P., & Cunane, J. (1987). Validation of the Hospital Anxiety and Depression Rating Scale (HADS) in an elderly psychiatric population. *International Journal of Geriatric Psychiatry, 2*, 189–193.

Koltai, D. C., Welsh-Bohmer, K. A., & Schmechel, D. E. (2001). Influence of anosognosia on treatment outcome among dementia patients. *Neuropsychological Rehabilitation, 11*, 455–475.

Lachman, M. E., Weaver, S. L., Bandura, M., Elliott, E., & Lewkowicz, C. J. (1992). Improving memory and control beliefs through cognitive restructuring and self-generated strategies. *Journal of Gerontology: Psychological Sciences, 47*, 293–299.

Laurin, D., Verreault, R., Lindsay, J., MacPherson, K., & Rockwood, K. (2001). Physical activity and risk of cognitive impairment and dementia in elderly persons. *Archives of Neurology, 58*, 498–504.

Olazaran, J., Muniz, R., Reisberg, B., Pena-Casanova, J., del Ser, T., Cruz-Jentoft, A. J., et al. (2004). Benefits of cognitive-motor intervention in MCI and mild to moderate Alzheimer disease. *Neurology, 63*, 2348–2353.

Petersen, R. C., Smith, G. E., Waring, S. C., Ivnik, R. J., Tangalos, E. G., & Kokmen, E. (1999). Mild cognitive impairment: Clinical characterization and outcome. *Archives of Neurology, 56*, 303–308.

Quayhagen, M. P., Quayhagen, M., Corbeil, R. R., Hendrix, R. C., Jackson, J. E., Snyder, L., et al. (2000). Coping with dementia: Evaluation of four non-pharmacologic interventions. *International Psychogeriatrics, 12*, 249–265.

Quayhagen, M. P., Quayhagen, M., Corbeil, R. R., Roth, P. A., & Rodgers, J. A. (1995). A dyadic remediation program for care recipients with dementia. *Nursing Research, 44*, 153–159.

Rapp, S., Breenes, G., & Marsh, A. P. (2002). Memory enhancement training for older adults with mild cognitive impairment: A preliminary study. *Aging & Mental Health, 6*, 5–11.

Roth, M., Huppert, F. A., Mountjoy, C. Q., & Tym, E. (1998). *CAMDEX-R: The Cambridge examination for mental disorders of the elderly—Revised.* Cambridge: Cambridge University Press.

Salthouse, T. A., Berish, D. E., & Miles, J. D. (2002). The role of cognitive stimulation on the relations between age and cognitive functioning. *Psychology & Aging, 17*, 548–557.

Scogin, F. (1992). Memory training for older adults. In G. M. M. Jones & B. M. L. Miesen (Eds.), *Care-giving in dementia: Research and applications* (pp. 260–271). London: Routledge.
Sheikh, J. I., Hill, R. D., & Yesavage, J. A. (1986). Long-term efficacy of cognitive training for age-associated memory impairment: A six-month follow-up study. *Developmental Neuropsychology, 2*, 413–421.
Small, G. W. (2002). What we need to know about age related memory loss. *British Medical Journal, 324*, 1502–1505.
Small, G. W., La Rue, A., Komo, S., & Kaplan, A. (1997). Mnemonics usage and cognitive decline in age-associated memory impairment. *International Psychogeriatrics, 9*, 47–56.
Spector, A., Davies, S., Woods, B., & Orrell, M. (2000). Reality orientation for dementia: A systematic review of the evidence for its effectiveness. *Gerontologist, 40*(2), 206–212.
Spector, A., Thorgrimsen, L., Woods, B., Royan, L., Davies, S., Butterworth, M., et al. (2003). Efficacy of an evidence-based cognitive stimulation therapy programme for people with dementia: Randomized controlled trial. *British Journal of Psychiatry, 183*, 248–254.
Stigsdotter, A., & Bäckman, L. (1989). Multifactorial memory training with older adults: How to foster maintenance of improved performance. *Gerontology, 35*, 260–267.
Stigsdotter Neely, A. (2000). Multifactorial memory training in normal aging: In search of memory improvement beyond the ordinary. In R. D. Hill, L. Bäckman, & A. Stigsdotter Neely (Eds.), *Cognitive rehabilitation in old age* (pp. 63–80). Oxford: Oxford University Press.
Stigsdotter Neely, A., & Bäckman, L. (1993). Long-term maintenance of gains from memory training in older adults: Two 3.5 years follow-up studies. *Journal of Gerontology, 48*, P233–P237.
Tuokko, H., Garrett, D. D., McDowell, I., Silverberg, N., & Kristjansson, B. (2003). Cognitive decline in high-functioning older adults: Reserve or ascertainment bias? *Aging & Mental Health, 7*(4), 259–270.
Verghese, J., Lipton, R. B., Katz, M. J., Hall, C. B., Derby, C. A., Kuslansky, G., et al. (2003). Leisure activities and the risk of dementia in the elderly. *New England Journal of Medicine, 348*, 2508–2516.
Verhaeghen, P., Marcoen, A., & Goossens, L. (1992). Improving memory performance in the aged through mnemonic training: A meta-analytic study. *Psychology & Aging, 7*, 242–251.
Wechsler, D. (1999). *The Wechsler Abbreviated Scale of Intelligence.* London: Harcourt Assessment.
Williams, J. G., Huppert, F., Matthews, F. E., Nickson, J., & MRC Cognitive Function and Aging Study. (2003). Performance and normative values of a concise neuropsychological test (CAMCOG) in an elderly population sample. *International Journal of Geriatric Psychiatry, 18*, 631–644.
Wilson, B. A. (2002). Towards a comprehensive model of cognitive rehabilitation. *Neuropsychological Rehabilitation, 12*, 97–110.
Wilson, R. S., Barnes, L. L., Bennett, D. A., Li, Y., Bienias, J. L., Mendes de Leon, C. F., et al. (2005). Proneness to psychological distress and risk of Alzheimer disease in a biracial community. *Neurology, 64*, 380–382.
Wilson, R. S., Barnes, L. L., Mendes de Leon, C. F., Aggarwal, N. T., Schneider, J., Bach, J., et al. (2002a). Depressive symptoms, cognitive decline and risk of AD in older persons. *Neurology, 59*, 364–370.

Wilson, R. S., Bennett, D. A., Bienias, J. L., Aggarwal, N. T., Mendes de Leon, C. F., Morris, M. C., et al. (2002b). Cognitive activity and incident AD in a population-based sample of older persons. *Neurology, 59*, 1910–1914.

Wilson, R. S., Evans, D. A., Bienias, J. L., Mendes de Leon, C. F., Schneider, J. A., & Bennett, D. A. (2003). Proneness to psychological distress is associated with risk of Alzheimer's disease. *Neurology, 61*, 1479–1485.

Wilson, R. S., Mendes de Leon, C. F., Barnes, L. L., Schneider, J. A., Bienias, J. L., Evans, D. A., et al. (2002c). Participation in cognitively stimulating activities and risk of incident Alzheimer disease. *Journal of American Medical Association, 287*, 742–748.

Wilson, R. S., Mendes de Leon, C. F., Bennett, D. A., Bienias, J. L., & Evans, D. A. (2004). Depressive symptoms and cognitive decline in a community population of older persons. *Journal of Neurology, Neurosurgery & Psychiatry, 75*, 126–129.

Woods, B. (2002). Editorial: Reality Orientation: A welcome return? *Age & Ageing, 31*, 155–156.

Woods, B. (2004). Reducing the impact of cognitive impairment in dementia. In A. Baddeley, M. D. Kopelman, & B. A. Wilson (Eds.), *The essential handbook of memory disorders for clinicians* (pp. 285–299). Chichester: Wiley.

Yesavage, J. A., & Jacob, R. (1984). Effects of relaxation and mnemonics on memory, attention and anxiety in the elderly. *Experimental Aging Research, 10*, 211–214.

Zarit, S. H., Cole, K. D., & Guider, R. L. (1981). Memory training strategies and subjective complaints of memory in the aged. *Gerontologist, 21*, 158–164.

12 Combined therapies in mild cognitive impairment

Kevin Peters and Gordon Winocur

There are two main objectives of this chapter. The first is to provide an overview of the different treatment interventions that have been tested in, or might be potentially useful in treating, individuals with mild cognitive impairment (MCI). The second objective is to advocate for an approach to intervention for MCI that combines traditional pharmacological therapies with cognitive/behavioral techniques that emphasize the use of strategic processing abilities. To accomplish these objectives, the chapter is divided into five sections. We begin by describing the important conceptual and general methodological issues related to designing and implementing MCI treatment programs. One of the important themes developed in this section is the heterogeneity of MCI. Development of successful treatment programs for MCI will require consideration of the variability of cognitive profiles, etiology, and prognosis that characterizes this condition. We also emphasize the importance of recognizing and targeting noncognitive domains (e.g., psychosocial functioning) when developing treatment interventions for MCI. In the second section we summarize the major pharmacological therapies that have been tested in individuals with MCI and Alzheimer's disease (AD). The majority of this section focuses on the role and efficacy of the cholinesterase inhibitors (ChEIs) in treating AD and MCI. The third section is an overview of the different cognitive interventions that have been tested in individuals with normal cognitive functioning, MCI, AD, as well as individuals with memory impairment due to acquired brain damage. In this section we also describe a new cognitive rehabilitation program that is comprehensive in its approach and shown to be effective in improving cognitive performance in older adults who have experienced significant cognitive decline. Although not yet tested in individuals diagnosed with MCI, we think this program has potential to be usefully applied to this population. In the fourth section, we review the results of studies that have combined pharmacological and cognitive treatment interventions in individuals with mild AD and MCI. Despite the relatively few studies to date, the evidence favors combined approaches that include cognitive interventions that target more than just memory function. Finally, we end the chapter by summarizing the key points and highlighting areas for future research.

Treatment and MCI: Conceptual and methodological issues

Definition of MCI: Cognitive, etiological, and prognostic heterogeneity

An important issue with respect to MCI is how one defines this condition. A generic definition of MCI is impairment in any cognitive domain that falls short of meeting diagnostic criteria for dementia. A wide variety of labels[1] have been used to describe individuals with MCI and the reader is referred to excellent reviews by Collie and Maruff (2002) and Tuokko and Frerichs (2000). A critical point that needs to be emphasized is that MCI is a heterogeneous condition. Individuals with MCI are heterogeneous with respect to patterns of lost and spared cognitive function, the etiology of their condition, and their prognosis. Each of these types of heterogeneity and their implications for treatment are discussed below.

Regarding cognitive heterogeneity, despite the dominant focus on individuals with relatively isolated memory impairment, a consensus is emerging that MCI also encompasses individuals with impairment in cognitive domains other than memory. Petersen et al. (2001) have described three subgroups[2] of MCI: MCI-amnestic, MCI-multiple domain, and MCI-single nonmemory domain. These authors also suggest that the different MCI subgroups might be at increased risk for progressing to different types of dementia. For example, while an individual in the amnestic subgroup may develop AD, an individual in the single nonmemory domain subgroup is more likely to progress to another form of dementia (e.g., frontotemporal dementia or Lewy body dementia). Using a combination of factor and cluster analyses, Peters, Graf, Hayden, and Feldman (2005) identified five subgroups of cognitively impaired–not demented (CIND) individuals in two independent samples. Each subgroup was characterized by a distinct profile of cognitive abilities, and included: Verbal Dysfunction, Memory Dysfunction, Visuospatial Dysfunction, Memory/Verbal Dysfunction, and Verbal/Visuospatial Dysfunction. The results reported by Peters and colleagues provide empirical validation of the MCI subgroups proposed by Petersen et al. (2001).

The cognitive heterogeneity of MCI has important implications for the treatment of this condition in that different subgroups of MCI are likely to require different treatment interventions. For example, pharmacological and

---

[1] The term mild cognitive impairment (MCI) has been used as a general descriptive term to refer to older adults with deficits in any cognitive domain that fall short of meeting dementia criteria as well as a specific diagnostic label that refers to individuals with predominately memory impairment. Unless otherwise stated, the term MCI will be used in the general sense throughout this chapter.

[2] Although Petersen and colleagues used the term subtype, we prefer the term subgroup. As discussed by Fisher, Rourke, Bieliauskas, Giordani, Berent, and Foster (1996) and Jorm (1985), the term subtype is often applied to denote difference between groups of patients with respect to etiology. Accordingly, we feel that the term subgroup is more appropriate when describing groups of patients that differ with respect to neuropsychological test profiles.

cognitive interventions that target memory abilities might be helpful for individuals in the amnestic subgroup, but these forms of intervention would seem less appropriate for individuals with impaired visuospatial abilities. It is important, therefore, to keep in mind that individuals with MCI are diverse in their patterns of cognitive strengths and weaknesses, and that any treatment intervention should take into account, and build upon, the individual's particular cognitive profile.

A second source of heterogeneity in MCI concerns etiology. As pointed out by Petersen (2003), the memory deficit in amnestic MCI may be attributable to a variety of causes, such as neurodegeneration, depression, vascular factors, trauma, or substance abuse. In clinical settings, a good understanding of the nature and cause of cognitive impairment will influence the choice of treatment strategy. One problem in this regard is that the cause of cognitive impairment is not always known. In describing the etiological subtypes of CIND individuals from the Canadian Study of Health and Aging (CSHA), Graham et al. (1997) reported that the largest subtype (49.6%) was "unclassified other". Very little is known about the etiological heterogeneity of MCI because most studies employ stringent inclusion/exclusion criteria and therefore do not involve subjects that differ widely with respect to the causes of their cognitive impairments. One notable exception was the recent report by Tuokko et al. (2003) of no differences in the 5-year diagnostic outcomes among the following etiological subtypes of CIND individuals from the CSHA: delirium, alcohol or drug use, depression, psychiatric disorder, age-associated memory impairment, mental retardation, and other. Future research should examine the effect of etiological heterogeneity on treatment interventions and diagnostic outcomes in individuals with MCI.

A third type of heterogeneity in MCI is prognosis. There are at least three possible outcomes for individuals with MCI: their cognitive status may improve, it may remain stable, or it may deteriorate. Most research to date has focused on predicting deterioration. In this regard, individuals with amnestic MCI have been shown to convert to AD at rates between 10 and 15% per year (Petersen et al., 2001). Longer term follow-up of individuals with amnestic MCI has shown that approximately 80% convert to AD over a 6-year period (Petersen et al., 2001). Similarly, the Memory Dysfunction and the Memory/Verbal Dysfunction subgroups identified by Peters et al. (2005) had the highest rates of converting to dementia over a 5-year period (65 and 55%, respectively). These results clearly indicate that individuals with MCI who suffer some form of memory deficit are at relatively high risk for progressing to dementia. Accordingly, these individuals must be considered a priority subgroup for developing and implementing effective treatments.

Although it is critical to identify MCI subgroups that are at high risk for progressing to dementia, it is also important to identify lower-risk subgroups because treatment/management options will likely differ for higher- and lower-risk subgroups. Given the overburdened status of most health care systems, clinicians may choose not to re-evaluate lower-risk individuals every

6–12 months, as recommended for MCI. Rather, they may decide to wait for longer periods before bringing such individuals back into the clinic for reassessment. This practice would free up clinic resources so that higher-risk individuals may receive more attention but it could also result in the neglect of lower-risk individuals with potentially "reversible" causes of their cognitive impairment. For example, if depression were a factor in an individual's cognitive deficit, implementing treatment for depression may have the secondary effect of improving cognitive functioning. In one of the few studies to date that has documented the outcomes of lower-risk individuals, Peters et al. (2005) reported that, compared to other subgroups, the Verbal Dysfunction subgroup had a relatively low rate of converting to dementia (24%) and individuals in this subgroup were the most likely to improve (26%) over a period of 5 years. The relatively stable condition of such individuals makes them good candidates for therapy, which could lead to faster and longer-lasting recovery. Relatively little attention has been paid to developing treatment programs for MCI individuals at low risk for converting to dementia and there is a clear need for more research in this area.

General treatment-related issues

One obvious, but important, issue regarding treatment in MCI relates to the distinction over whether the goal of treatment is to cure the disease or to slow down its progression. Although there has been considerable progress in terms of understanding the etiology of AD and other dementias, current treatment options are restricted largely to symptomatic features. The focus on treatments that slow disease progression has important implications for the degree of success that one can realistically expect when treating AD or MCI. Nevertheless, it is important to stress that slowing disease progression even for limited periods is a desirable goal that could mean a significant improvement in the quality of life for the afflicted person and his/her family. As well, by maintaining a higher functional status and overall higher level of health, the individual stands to be a better candidate for new treatments as they become available.

A second important issue concerning treatment in MCI is which symptom domains should be targeted in interventions. Changes in cognition (especially memory) are commonly believed to be the earliest symptoms of AD (Zec, 1993). Other symptoms, however, also occur early in the course of AD and even MCI. Cummings (2003) has noted that neuropsychiatric symptoms such as depression, anxiety, psychosis, and agitation are commonly observed in early AD. Several recent studies have also reported that neuropsychiatric symptoms are present in 35–59% of individuals with MCI, with some of the more common symptoms being depression, anxiety, apathy, irritability, and problems with sleep (Feldman et al., 2004; Geda et al., 2004; Lyketsos, Lopez, Jones, Fitzpatrick, Breitner, & DeKosky, 2002). Accordingly, it is critical that treatment interventions attempt to target the entire range of symptoms that might be experienced by individuals with MCI or in the early stages of AD. In this respect, the goal of treatment should not be limited to only one symptom domain (e.g., memory), but rather it is desirable that beneficial effects of treatment interventions generalize to other aspects of functioning, such as improving quality of life and everyday activities. Indeed, this is the strategy adopted in comprehensive programs of cognitive rehabilitation (see below). Given the progressive nature of MCI, AD, and other neurodegenerative dementias, it is also important to keep in mind that symptoms change over time and that the treatment methods and goals for these populations be revised as needed over the course of treatment.

A third issue with respect to treatment interventions in individuals with MCI is to realize that there are a number of factors that affect treatment outcome over and above any underlying etiological processes. Level of premorbid functioning, financial and social support, motivation, and awareness have been identified as important variables to take into consideration when implementing treatment interventions (Anderson, Winocur, & Palmer, 2003; Prigatano, 1999). In addition, Dawson, Winocur, and Moscovitch (1999) provide a review of psychosocial factors that have been shown to influence cognitive functioning in the elderly. Locus of control, affect (e.g., depression), and beliefs about self-efficacy are important internal factors, while education, living situation, and lifestyle variables such as exercise and nutritional status are important external factors that can affect cognitive functioning. Dawson et al. (1999) pointed out that although these factors can negatively impact cognitive performance, some of them are amenable to change and should therefore be identified as targets themselves in treatment interventions. For example, Winocur, Moscovitch, and Freedman (1987) reported positive correlations between changes in cognitive performance and changes in psychosocial factors, such as locus of control and level of activity, in elderly individuals over time.

In the remainder of this chapter, we review some of the therapies that have been tested in individuals with MCI. We limit our focus to those therapies that may be of most benefit for individuals with the amnestic form of MCI. There are two reasons for this selective review. First, research has consistently shown that MCI individuals with memory impairment demonstrate relatively high rates of converting to dementia (Collie & Maruff, 2000; Tuokko & Frerichs, 2000). Second, the amnestic form of MCI is the most commonly used definition of MCI in the literature to date. Given that very little work has actually been done with respect to treatment of MCI individuals, we also review pharmacological and cognitive therapies that have been tested in normal aging, in individuals with acquired brain damage, and individuals with mild AD to get a sense of what might work with MCI individuals.

Pharmacological therapies

The use of pharmacological agents for treating individuals with MCI has been guided by the success of the various agents with AD. In this section, we review the most commonly used drugs for treating AD: the ChEIs. Only a few studies to date have examined pharmacological interventions in individuals with MCI, and these studies are included as appropriate. It should be noted that a number of noncholinergic pharmacological treatments are currently being tested in AD and other types of dementia (for reviews see Doraiswamy, 2002; Grundman & Thal, 2000; Knopman, 2003). These include antiamyloid agents, *N*-methyl-D-aspartate (NMDA) receptor antagonists (e.g., memantine), nerve regeneration approaches, estrogen and testosterone, vitamin E and other antioxidants (e.g., selenium, DHA fatty acids, *Ginkgo biloba*), anti-inflammatory drugs (e.g., nonsteroidal anti-inflammatory drugs [NSAIDs]), and calcium/calmodulin inhibitors. These approaches are based on different rationales and vary in terms of their treatment potential. A detailed description of noncholinergic approaches is beyond the scope of this chapter and the reader is referred to reviews noted above and to the chapter by Chertkow in this volume.

ChEIs and AD

The ChEIs represent a class of drugs that work by inhibiting the action of cholinesterase, an enzyme that breaks down the neurotransmitter acetylcholine at the level of the synapse. The rationale for targeting acetylcholine stems from the "cholinergic hypothesis" of AD (Coyle, Price, & DeLong, 1983; Davies & Maloney, 1976). The central feature of this hypothesis is that significant reductions of acetylcholine levels account for the memory loss and related cognitive deficits seen in the early stages of AD. The cholinergic hypothesis is based largely on findings from postmortem studies that have reported lower levels of the key enzyme for producing acetylcholine—choline acetyltransferase (ChAT)—in patients with AD (Grundman & Thal, 2000). It is believed that the low levels of acetylcholine in AD are due to damage in the basal forebrain area, one of the main sources of acetylcholine in the brain. This region contains many cholinergic neurons that project widely throughout the brain, especially to those brain regions that are known to be critical in memory and cognition—the hippocampus, amygdala, and frontal cortex (Grundman & Thal, 2000). Thus, ChEIs are intended to compensate for abnormally low levels of acetylcholine in the brains of patients with AD.

There has been some debate recently over the validity of the cholinergic hypothesis in early AD and MCI (Davis et al., 1999; DeKosky et al., 2002; Gilmor et al., 1999; Mesulam, Shaw, Mash, & Weintraub, 2004; Mufson et al., 2000). The argument is that cholinergic dysfunction likely accounts for some of the cognitive deficits observed in early AD and MCI, but the cholinergic hypothesis in its purest form is probably too simple an explanation for the full range of deficits, as well as those that develop as the disease progresses. With this caveat in mind, we review below the results of studies that have examined the effect of ChEIs in individuals with AD and MCI.

Several different types of ChEIs are used currently for treating AD, including donepezil (Aricept), rivastigmine (Excelon), and galantamine

(Reminyl). Considerable research into the efficacy and safety of ChEIs indicate that they are well tolerated and can lead to stabilized and even improved cognitive function in AD patients. The drugs are most effective in patients who are still in the relatively early stages of the disease with benefits observed for as long as 2–3 years (Farlow, Anand, Messina, Hartman, & Veach, 2000; Gauthier, 2002; Raskind, Peskind, Truyen, Kershaw, & Damaraju, 2004). The drugs, of course, are not a cure but, when effective, can slow down the progression of the disease, allowing for improved quality of life and reduced caregiver burden. Although donepezil is the most extensively studied of the three ChEIs, there seems to be little difference in terms of overall efficacy (Hogan, Goldlist, Naglie, & Patterson, 2004).

While some studies of the effects of ChEIs on cognitive change involved open label trials, others are based on randomized control trials. One such multicenter trial assessed the therapeutic value of donepezil, relative to placebo, using a prospective, randomized, double-blind design (Winblad et al., 2001). The results indicated a significant advantage of the donepezil group on several functional measures, including the MMSE, Gottfries–Bråne Scale, Progressive Deterioration Scale, and the Neuropsychiatric Inventory. Similar findings have been reported following treatment with rivastigmine (Rosler et al., 1999) and galantamine (Wilcock, Lilienfeld, & Gaens, 2000).

A recent review by Lanctôt et al. (2003) highlights the fact that not all AD patients respond to ChEIs. The authors identify a number of factors that may influence outcome and even predict the drug's effectiveness. These factors include Apoε4 status, post-treatment autonomic activity, disease stage, neuropsychiatric profile, and several biological markers, including CSF metabolites and the metabolic status of the amyloid precursor protein. Careful study of the individual and combined effects of these factors on the impact of ChEIs may help to identify subsets of AD patients who are most likely to benefit from this form of treatment.

The Cochrane Dementia and Cognitive Improvement Group recently published separate meta-analyses of double-blind, randomized, placebo-controlled trials for donepezil (Birks & Harvey, 2003), galantamine (Olin & Schneider, 2004), and rivastigmine (Birks, Grimley Evans, Iakovidou, & Tsolaki, 2004). The numbers of trials included in these reviews were 7, 8, and 16 for galantamine, rivastigmine, and donepezil. The trials reviewed ranged in duration from 12 to 52 weeks and included individuals with mild-to-moderate AD cases; only the trials in the donepezil review included severe cases. In terms of cognitive functioning, each of the three ChEIs was associated with a significant improvement relative to placebo. The magnitude of benefits on cognition corresponded to improvements of 2–4 points on the Cognitive component of the Alzheimer Disease Assessment Scale (ADAS-Cog; maximum = 70 points) and 1–2 points on the Mini-Mental State Exam (MMSE; maximum = 30). Significant benefits for each of the drugs were also observed on clinician-based ratings of global change (e.g., Clinician Interview-Based Impression and the AD Cooperative Study's Clinical Global Impression of Change) and measures of functional disability (e.g., the Lawton and Brody scale and the Disability Assessment for Dementia). Some evidence for improvement of behavioral symptoms (e.g., the Neuropsychiatric Inventory) was reported in the reviews on donepezil and galantamine, but not rivastigmine. While the drugs do not necessarily produce dramatic improvements in cognitive and related functions over baseline, it is important to emphasize that over the time periods that have been investigated, reduced rates of decline were reliably reported.

On balance, published reports indicate that ChEIs can impact positively on cognitive function in early AD patients. Studies of the effects of such treatment on other measures that reflect the quality of life of patients and their caregivers have produced mixed results. Some studies report that treatment with ChEIs, and donepezil in particular, extends to measures of global and daily function (Lanctôt et al., 2003; Mohs et al., 2001). Others underscore the need for caution in claiming benefits in a wide range of functional measures (Courtney et al., 2004). On the other hand, some investigators report substantial benefits following treatment with ChEIs. Recently, Trinh, Hoblyn, and Yaffe (2003) conducted a meta-analysis of 29 parallel-group or cross-over randomized, double-blind, placebo-controlled studies of patients diagnosed with probable mild-moderate AD and treated for at least 1 month with a ChEI. Sixteen studies included neuropsychiatric outcome measures and 18 included noncognitive functional measures (e.g., ADL). The results indicated statistically significant improvements in both domains. The authors concluded that, overall, there was reliable evidence of benefits of such treatment, although they are sometimes modest. They also noted the urgent need for more research into long-term outcome measures that include institutionalization and caregiver burden.

The common practice is to administer one of the ChEIs and, when benefits are no longer apparent, switch to one of the others. As a result, there are few studies of the combined effects of such drugs. Hogan et al. (2004) recently reviewed the results of three studies that directly compared the effectiveness of the ChEIs: two studies comparing donepezil and galantamine (Jones et al., 2004; Wilcock et al., 2003) and one study comparing donepezil and rivastigmine (Wilkinson et al., 2002). These authors concluded that due to methodological limitations in each of the comparison studies, it was not possible to make any definitive statements in favor of one ChEI over another. The question over which ChEI to use is important from a clinical standpoint, but future research involving better, more objective studies is needed.

Of relevance to the issue of combined pharmacological treatment, following several successful trials (Reisberg, Doody, Stoffler, Schmitt, Ferris, & Mobius, 2003), in October 2003 the FDA in the United States approved the use of memantine, an NMDA receptor antagonist, for the treatment of moderate to severe AD. A recent study (Tariot, Farlow, Grossberg, Graham, McDonald, & Gergel, 2004), using a randomized control design, examined the effects of administering memantine to AD patients who were already receiving donepezil. The efficacy of memantine was significantly better than placebo on all measures over the 6-month period of the trial. The combination of different medications represents a new and interesting approach to treating AD, and more study is clearly warranted.

In summary, the overall consensus is that ChEIs do offer benefits to individuals with AD, particularly with respect to cognitive function. While the gains are modest in some cases, overall, the results of outcome studies may be viewed as promising. Moreover, even when no improvements are observed, ChEIs reliably stabilize cognitive function for variable periods of time and that in itself represents a significant advance for treatment effectiveness compared to just 5 or 6 years ago.

ChEIs and MCI

Several studies examining the effectiveness of ChEIs in individuals with MCI are currently underway (for review, see Knopman, 2003). In terms of actual published studies, however, there have been a few reports involving donepezil use in MCI. Meyer, Li, Xu, Thornby, Chowdhury, and Quach (2002) followed a sample of 17 MCI patients for an average of 3.4 years and documented which patients used donepezil and which patients did not. These authors reported that seven of the 10 patients who remained stable or improved had received donepezil, and that none of the 7 patients who progressed to AD of vascular dementia were given donepezil. These findings must be interpreted cautiously as the study was not a formal randomized double-blind placebo-controlled clinical trial.

Salloway et al. (2004) recently conducted a 24-week randomized, double-blind clinical trial comparing donepezil to placebo in individuals with MCI. There were no significant differences between the two groups on either of the primary outcome measures for the study, which included a test of verbal delayed recall (New York University Paragraph Recall test) and a clinician-based measure of global change (the AD Cooperative Study Clinician's Global Impression of Change for MCI). In terms of secondary outcome measures, donepezil-treated patients did show improvements on some measures (e.g., ADAS-Cog total scores, Patient Global Assessment, Symbol Digits Modality Test), but not on others (e.g., Number Cancellation, Verbal Fluency). The authors suggested that the lack of any significant benefit due to donepezil on the primary outcome measures may have been due to the fact that decline in MCI is slower than in AD and that periods of 24 weeks are not sufficient to assess the effectiveness of treatment interventions in this population.

Petersen et al. (2005) recently reported the results of a longer duration study (3 years) comparing the efficacy of donepezil, vitamin E, and placebo in treating 769 individuals with amnestic MCI. Over the entire 3-year study, there were no differences among the three groups in the rate of progression to AD. More detailed analyses, however, revealed that individuals in the donepezil group had a lower rate of progression to AD relative to placebo during the first 12 months of the study. Individuals in the donepezil group also showed little evidence of decline on secondary cognitive (e.g., MMSE, ADAS-Cog, and other more detailed neuropsychological measures) and functional (e.g., activities of daily living, Clinical Dementia Rating scale, Global Deterioration Scale) measures during the first 6–18 months of the study, after which time they started declining at a rate similar to the placebo group. The vitamin E group did not differ from placebo at any point during the study in terms of rate of progression to AD or secondary measures. The results of this study showed that donepezil was effective in delaying progression to AD and decline on cognitive and functional measures. Clearly, additional clinical trials on the efficacy of donepezil in individuals with MCI are needed.

Two recent studies have examined the effect of ChEI administration on brain activity and cognitive performance in individuals with MCI. Saykin et al. (2004) used functional MRI to assess the effect of donepezil on brain activity of nine individuals with MCI and nine healthy controls while performing a working memory task (n-back). Goekoop et al. (2004) used functional MRI to examine the effect of galantamine on brain activity and performance on episodic (face encoding and recognition) and working memory (n-back) tasks in 28 individuals with MCI using a within subjects design. Both studies reported that ChEI administration was associated with improved working memory and with increased brain activation during the working memory task in several areas including the left frontal lobe (i.e., dorsolateral prefrontal and superior frontal gyrus following donepezil use, and middle frontal gyrus following galantamine use). These results suggest that functional neuroimaging in MCI may be useful in predicting conversion to dementia and for serving as an outcome variable in treatment intervention studies. These results are also particularly relevant to our rehabilitation program, part of which focuses on improving attentional control (see below).

Cognitive therapies

Little research to date has focused on cognitive rehabilitation approaches in individuals with MCI. This section provides an overview of the approaches that have been used to enhance or rehabilitate cognitive functioning in normal aging, MCI, AD, and in individuals with acquired brain damage. These approaches offer some useful clues for developing cognitive rehabilitation approaches in individuals with MCI, and the amnestic form of MCI in particular. Accordingly, the therapies described in this section involve memory interventions.

Anderson et al. (2003) described three general approaches to cognitive rehabilitation, including (1) cognitive retraining, (2) compensatory approaches, and (3) holistic approaches. The decision over which of these approaches to adopt is based on the clinician's preference, whether treatment goals are general or specific, and the degree of the individual's impairment (i.e., retraining and certain compensatory approaches are geared more towards higher functioning individuals than other compensatory strategies). Each of these approaches is described below (see Chapter 11 by Woods and Clare in this volume for a more detailed discussion of cognition-based therapies).

Cognitive retraining

One of the basic assumptions in the cognitive retraining approach is that strengthening more basic cognitive abilities will have an effect upstream on higher level cognitive abilities. In addition, it is also assumed that repeated practice of a specific cognitive ability will result in improvements in that cognitive ability by inducing changes in underlying neural processes (Glisky & Glisky, 2002). Although there is some evidence that direct training of various components of attention has been somewhat successful in individuals with acquired brain damage, studies on retraining memory ability by using practice drills have been largely unsuccessful (Glisky, 2004; Sohlberg & Mateer, 2001). Solhberg and Mateer (2001) have pointed out, however, that despite this lack of empirical evidence, many clinicians still use memory practice drills. These authors also suggest that any improvements that may be seen on an individual basis may be more related to improvements in attention rather than memory.

In terms of enhancing cognitive functioning in normal adults, Ball et al. (2002) conducted a large randomized controlled trial involving three different training interventions that targeted memory, speed of processing, and reasoning ability. Improvements were seen over a 2-year period on tasks that tapped the specific cognitive domains that were being trained. The training, however, had no effect on skills and abilities associated with day-to-day functioning. This rather disappointing result echoes a consistent finding within the cognitive rehabilitation literature: training-related benefits often do not generalize beyond the specific cognitive domain being targeted (Anderson et al., 2003). Extending the improvements of cognitive retraining to aspects of everyday functioning represents a major challenge for retraining intervention programs.

Compensatory approach

Compensatory approaches are those in which the individual uses internal (e.g., mnemonics) or external (e.g., calendars) strategies to help overcome the disabilities related to cognitive deficits. These approaches are realistic alternatives in cases where retraining or recovery of function is not likely to occur. In terms of underlying neural processes, compensatory approaches attempt to exploit residual abilities that are still intact or they may involve the substitution of neural processes that are normally used for different purposes (Glisky & Glisky, 2002).

With respect to memory performance, some examples of internal compensatory approaches have included the use of mnemonics (e.g., imagery, face–name associations) and spaced retrieval. The goal of each of these techniques is to facilitate whatever remaining neural and cognitive capacities may still be intact. Mnemonic strategies that help individuals organize information at encoding have been shown to be useful in normal older adults (Verhaeghen, Marcoen, & Goossens, 1992). One caveat to bear in mind is that certain mnemonic strategies may be more difficult to learn than others in older adults with even very subtle forms of cognitive impairment (Yesavage, Sheikh, Friedman, & Tanke, 1990).

Spaced retrieval is another example of an internal compensatory approach to memory rehabilitation that has been used with some success in individuals with acquired brain damage (Sohlberg & Mateer, 2001). This technique involves gradually increasing the duration of time over which the subject must retain information. There is some evidence that spaced retrieval can be used successfully in AD (Cherry & Simmons-D'Gerolamo, 2003; Hawley & Cherry, 2004; Hochhalter, Bakke, Holub, & Overmier, 2003). However, others have reported little or no beneficial effect of spaced retrieval and other compensatory approaches in AD (Cherry & Simmons-D'Gerolamo, 2003; Clare, Woods, Moniz-Cook, Orrell, & Spector, 2004; Davis, Massman, & Doody, 2003).

External compensatory approaches to memory interventions are generally reserved for individuals with severe memory impairments and for whom internal approaches are unlikely to be successful (Anderson et al., 2003). Because the memory deficits in most individuals with MCI are not as severe as those seen in amnesic or AD patients, external approaches will likely comprise only a single component of any cognitive intervention. At the most basic level, this approach involves restructuring the individual's environment in such a way that they do not have to rely on their own failing memory abilities. External aids such as memo pads, Post-It notes, calendars, alarm watches, and electronic organizers may also be of benefit to individuals who are able to use them (Glisky, 2004; Sohlberg & Mateer, 2001).

Vanishing cues and errorless learning are two other types of external compensatory techniques that have been used in individuals with acquired brain damage and AD. Vanishing cues involves initially presenting the individual with the entire word that is to be remembered and then successively presenting fragmented versions of that word (i.e., removing letters) until the individual is able to remember the entire word with no cues present (Glisky, Schacter, & Tulving, 1986). Errorless learning is similar to vanishing cues except that the task is set up in such a way as to prevent the individual from making errors early on in the process, which may interfere with subsequent learning of the correct word (Baddeley & Wilson, 1994).

These two techniques are believed to tap implicit memory systems that are generally intact in amnesic patients and individuals with early AD. Thus, the rationale here is to substitute a damaged memory system (explicit) with one that is intact (implicit). Although there has been some success with these approaches in AD (Clare, Wilson, Carter, Roth, & Hodges, 2002; Grandmaison & Simard, 2003; Winter & Hunkin, 1999), future research will need to address the applicability of these techniques in individuals with MCI.

Holistic approach

In contrast to retraining and compensatory approaches that focus primarily on specific cognitive processes, holistic programs attempt rehabilitation in the context of the full range of problems experienced by cognitively-impaired individuals. Holistic programs tend to be multidimensional in order to treat cognitive, emotional, and motivational consequences of brain injury in an integrated manner. Individuals participate in a variety of tasks, including simple drills, retraining exercises, as well as learning compensatory techniques. An important feature is to help patients gain insight into their strengths and weaknesses in order to achieve a realistic sense of their potential for improvement. The expectation is that, through heightened awareness and an appreciation of the practical limitations imposed by brain impairment, individuals will be better motivated and equipped to restructure their lives.

Two prominent holistic programs are those developed by Ben-Yishay (1978) and Prigatano (1986). Ben-Yishay's approach is characterized by the creation of a "therapeutic community" in which the patients, members of the therapeutic team, as well as family and significant others, work together to promote the rehabilitative process. Prigatano follows a similar approach but one that attaches great importance to the psychosocial consequences of neuropsychological disturbances. Prigatano's program focuses on residual function and is guided by the philosophy that optimal use of these functions can be achieved if the patient has psychologically adjusted to the injury-induced changes and is coping effectively.

Rapp, Brenes, and Marsh (2002) recently conducted one of the few studies involving a holistic approach to rehabilitating cognitive function in MCI. Using a randomized design, these investigators examined the effectiveness of a multifaceted memory training program that included educating subjects about memory loss, relaxation techniques, mnemonic strategies, and exercises aimed at changing the subjects' beliefs about their memory abilities. At the end of the study, subjects in the memory intervention group had more favorable views about their memory performance and their ability to control their memory in the future. However, the intervention did not yield improvement on objective memory tests. The authors suggested that shorter (i.e., less than 2 h) and more frequent training sessions might have produced more desirable outcomes.

The Rotman approach

For the most part, current rehabilitation programs target patients with traumatic brain injury or stroke, whose cognitive impairment is relatively stable. The programs often extend over long periods of time and, consequently, demand huge commitments of time and effort from the patients. As such, they are inappropriate for older adults or individuals with progressive disorders, whose cognitive abilities are likely to decline at an increasing rate over the course of such treatment.

Recently, a team of clinicians and scientists at the Rotman Research Institute in Toronto developed a new approach to cognitive rehabilitation that was designed for individuals who, for various reasons, suffer memory and related cognitive problems (see Anderson et al., 2003). The treatment protocol follows a general model of strategic processing which assumes that cognitive tasks, whether they involve straightforward aspects of learning and memory or complex problem solving, require strategic thought directed at achieving a particular goal. Normal young adults realize their objectives with relatively little awareness of the processes that were recruited to make this possible. Cognitively impaired individuals, because of limited resources, are less likely to apply strategies spontaneously and, in many cases, fail to adjust to the fact that conscious effort is now required. The Rotman program is based on the premise that, with insights gained from the program, participants' use of strategies would increase and their general cognitive performance would improve.

In line with the comprehensive approach advocated by proponents of holistic and related treatment (Rapp et al., 2002; Wilson, 2002) methods, a basic assumption of the Rotman program is that reduced cognitive function in cognitively impaired individuals is the combined effect of biological and nonbiological factors. Accordingly, the program incorporates a multidimensional approach that emphasizes attentional control, the use of internal and external aids to facilitate memory and executive function, the organization of goal-oriented strategies in solving practical problems, personal needs, and the relationship between psychological well-being and the realization of full cognitive potential.

An important feature of the program is that it is brief—12 weeks—and divides into three 4-week modules: (1) Memory Skills Training, where the emphasis is on the nature of memory loss and the use of various techniques that can be applied to the acquisition, retention, and recovery of information; (2) Practical Task Training, which focuses on developing strategies for managing goal-directed behavior in "real-life" situations; (3) Psychosocial Training, in which the aim is to enhance psychological well-being and to establish the link between overall functional status and cognitive performance. The program is administered to groups of six participants who meet once/week for 3-h sessions.

After piloting on a variety of cognitively impaired populations, the program was evaluated in a population of older adults who, despite being relatively healthy, had experienced considerable age-related cognitive decline. A multiple baseline, cross-over design with repeated measures of outcome, enabled between- and within-group assessments of the effects of rehabilitation training immediately and 6 months after the completion of training.

Neuropsychological testing assessed performance changes in three domains—memory, practical task planning, and psychosocial function. In all domains, significant benefits were observed following training. For example, in the psychosocial domain, a composite index, based on several correlated measures (e.g., personal control, optimism) and viewed as a measure of overall well-being, increased dramatically following training. Similar improvements were seen in tests of memory (e.g., Hopkins Verbal Learning Test, Paragraph Recall) and in practical task planning, which assessed people's ability to perform everyday, cognitively demanding tasks (e.g., cooking a meal, planning a trip). Of particular importance, improvement in the various outcome measures could be related to corresponding increases in the use of strategies that were appropriate to the respective tasks. The latter finding confirmed the utility of targeting attentional processes and strategy application in rehabilitation efforts aimed at achieving not only memory recovery, but also improvement in overall cognitive function.

The older adults who participated in this trial clearly exhibited significant improvement in cognitive function that extended at least 6 months beyond the completion of training. The results are also important in another sense. They suggest that individuals with mild-to-moderate cognitive impairment can benefit from a program of this nature. While the protocol used in the trial was oriented towards healthy older people, it was designed to be versatile and adaptable to other populations. Thus, with relatively minor adjustments it could be administered to individuals with MCI or even individuals diagnosed as being in the early stages of AD.

Combined therapies

In recognition of the need for improving treatment in AD and MCI, investigators have begun to examine the value of combining pharmacological and cognitive therapies in the treatment of AD and MCI. The rationale behind this approach is that treatment efficacy resulting from a combination of both pharmacological and cognitive therapies will be stronger than the response due to either of these approaches alone (i.e., the effect of the two approaches will be partially additive). In this section, we provide an overview of some of the recent studies that have examined the efficacy of combining pharmacological (i.e., ChEIs) and cognitive therapies.

The effect of combining ChEIs and memory training in individuals with mild AD has been examined in two recent series of studies. De Vreese and Neri (De Vreese & Neri, 1999; De Vreese, Neri, Fioravanti, Belloi, & Zanetti, 2001) followed three groups of individuals with mild AD: placebo, ChEI alone, and ChEI plus memory training. All subjects were taking ChEIs or placebo for a 3-month period before any memory training had started. Memory training sessions aimed at improving encoding and retrieval processes were carried out individually. Sessions lasting 30–40 min were held twice a week for 26 weeks. The combined group showed significant improvements on the ADAS-Cog, the MMSE, and on ratings of instrumental activities of daily living (IADL). Of particular importance, the combined group improved significantly over the ChEI alone group on all three of these outcome measures. Although this study did not include a proper memory training only control group, these preliminary results are promising.

In contrast to the positive results reported by De Vreese and Neri (1999; De Vreese et al., 2001), the results of a recent study (Cahn-Weiner, Malloy, Rebok, & Ott, 2003) that combined donepezil and memory training were not so favorable. In the study conducted by Cahn-Weiner et al., individuals with mild AD who were already taking donepezil were randomly assigned into two groups: memory training and control. Note that there was no donepezil-only group in this study. The memory training group received six sessions that involved instruction and practice on how to use mnemonic strategies such as organizing materials into categories and visualization to support memory performance. The control group received educational information on aging and dementia. A primary outcome measures battery that included comprehensive neuropsychological testing and caregiver ratings on ADL and everyday memory functioning was completed at baseline, immediately following the 6-week training period, and again at an 8-week follow-up session. The memory training group did show significant improvement on two process measures of memory performance (learning across trials and discrimination ability) over the study period. The memory training group did not differ from the control group on any of the primary outcome measures (including memory tests), indicating that there was no generalization of the memory training to performance in other cognitive domains or to measures of daily functioning.

More consistent positive findings have been reported in two recent studies that combined ChEIs and more comprehensive cognitive rehabilitation interventions that focused on improving memory and related cognitive functions. Loewenstein, Acevedo, Czaja, and Duara (2004) randomly assigned individuals with mild AD into a cognitive rehabilitation (CR) group or a mental stimulation (MS) group. All participants were already taking a ChEI for at least 2 months prior to entering the study. The CR training was multifaceted and involved the following: spaced retrieval training and dual cognitive support (assisting encoding and retrieval) to help learn face–name associations, use of external aids to practice time–place orientation, practice of a procedural motor skill without the object actually present, repeated use of a computerized sustained attention task, practicing how to make change, and practicing how to balance a check book and pay bills. The MS training involved several mental exercises that required the participants to become engaged cognitively and included the following: matching stimuli, the game "hangman", word find puzzles and word generation games, "topic of the day" discussions, and homework review and discussion. Over a 12-week period, participants completed two 45-min training sessions per week for a total of 24 sessions. Outcome measures were assessed three times: at baseline, after the last training session, and after a 3-month follow-up period. The results showed that improvements in the CR group were quite specific: The CR group improved significantly more than the MS group on outcome measures that were similar, but not identical, to those that were used during the CR training sessions. With the exception of a list-learning test, there were no significant improvements in either group on tests that were unrelated to those used in the CR training, indicating that there was no generalization to domains other than memory. From a practical standpoint, self- and informant-reported changes in memory ability were significantly greater in the CR group than in the MS group.

Consistent with the results reported by Loewenstein et al. (2004), Olazaran et al. (2004) also reported benefits due to a combined therapeutic approach in mild-to-moderate AD and MCI. A total of 84 participants (12 with MCI, 48 with mild AD, and 24 with moderate AD) who had been taking a ChEI for at least 1 month were randomly assigned into either the control or experimental group. Both groups received psychosocial support and the experimental group also received a comprehensive cognitive-motor intervention that consisted of reality orientation techniques as well as performing exercises in the areas of cognitive function, activities of daily living, and psychomotor ability. There were 103 cognitive-motor intervention sessions over a 1-year period. Each session involved groups of seven to ten participants and were 3.5 h in duration. In the experimental group, cognitive ability, as assessed by the ADAS-Cog and MMSE, was stable over the first 6 months, whereas the controls showed decline over this same period. Both groups declined at similar rates between the 6- and 12-month time points. Over the 12-month period, Geriatric Depression Scale scores improved in the experimental group but not in the control group. There was also some evidence for improvement on measures of behavior and quality of life in the experimental group.

In summary, although relatively few studies have examined the combined effects of pharmacological and cognitive interventions in mild AD and MCI, there is some evidence that such an approach will be promising. The evidence to date tends to favor combined approaches that include cognitive interventions that target more than just memory function. The ability to generalize gains to aspects of daily functioning will continue to be a major obstacle that needs to be overcome by any treatment intervention in the future. It will be essential for future studies on combined therapies in AD and MCI to include appropriate control and comparison groups (i.e., placebo, drug-only, cognitive-only, and drug-plus-cognitive groups) in order to determine which modality is contributing most to the treatment response and to determine whether the effects of these two treatment modalities are additive.

Summary and conclusions

MCI has been recognized as a distinct diagnostic entity for a relatively short time and so, not surprisingly, progress in developing effective treatment strategies is limited. Before that can happen, complicated issues need to be addressed satisfactorily including, for example, the fact of cognitive heterogeneity in MCI. The variation in identified symptoms has already presented significant challenges for accurate diagnosis, and underscores the need to devise interventions that are appropriate to the various clusters of symptoms. Given that MCI is not a unitary condition but rather a generic category that comprises several subtypes, etiology and prospects for rehabilitation are other important considerations in developing and selecting treatment programs.

The emergence of pharmacological therapies and, in particular, the reported efficacy of ChEIs in treating MCI and individuals in early stages of AD represent important developments. Following a different strategy, cognitive and clinical scientists have experimented with a variety of behaviorally oriented approaches that focus on specific cognitive processes or, more comprehensively, on improving function in the broader social context. To date, there has been relatively little work in evaluating cognitive rehabilitation programs in MCI but the initiative taken at the Rotman Research Institute offers a promising model. As this and related programs are developed and improved upon, it is important that they are evaluated in terms of long-term benefits, real-world generalization, and cost-effectiveness. As these issues are resolved, priority should be given to an assessment of the combined effects of behavioral and pharmacological therapies, in the hope that derived benefits would be greater than those associated with either treatment approach alone.

Acknowledgments

The Rotman Cognitive Rehabilitation Project (Coordinators: Gordon Winocur and Donald T. Stuss) and the preparation of this chapter were supported by a grant from the J.S. McDonnell Foundation.

References

Anderson, N. D., Winocur, G., & Palmer, H. (2003). Principles of cognitive rehabilitation. In P. W. Halligan, U. Kischka, & J. C. Marshall (Eds.), *Handbook of clinical neuropsychology* (pp. 48–69). Oxford: Oxford University Press.

Baddeley, A. D., & Wilson, B. A. (1994). When implicit memory fails: Amnesia and the problem of error elimination. *Neuropsychologia, 32*, 53–68.

Ball, K., Berch, D. B., Helmers, K. F., Jobe, J. B., Leveck, M. D., Marsiske, M., et al. (2002). Effects of cognitive training interventions with older adults: A randomized controlled trial. *Journal of the American Medical Association, 288*(18), 2271–2281.

Ben-Yishay, Y. (1978). Working approaches to remediation of cognitive deficits in brain damaged persons. *Rehabilitation Monograph No. 59*. New York: New York University Medical Center.

Birks, J., Grimley Evans, J., Iakovidou, V., & Tsolaki, M. (2004). Rivistigmine for Alzheimer's disease. *Cochrane Database of Systematic Reviews, 2*, 1–147.

Birks, J. S., & Harvey, R. (2003). Donepezil for dementia due to Alzheimer's disease. *Cochrane Database System Reviews, 3*, 1–107.

Cahn-Weiner, D. A., Malloy, P. F., Rebok, G. W., & Ott, B. R. (2003). Results of a randomized placebo-controlled study of memory training for mildly impaired Alzheimer's disease patients. *Applied Neuropsychology, 10*(4), 215–223.

Cherry, K. E., & Simmons-D'Gerolamo, S. S. (2003). Spaced-retrieval with probable Alzheimer's disease. *Clinical Gerontologist, 27*(1–2), 139–157.

Clare, L., Wilson, B. A., Carter, G., Roth, I., & Hodges, J. R. (2002). Relearning face-name associations in early Alzheimer's disease. *Neuropsychology, 16*(4), 538–547.

Clare, L., Woods, R. T., Moniz-Cook, E. D., Orrell, M., & Spector, A. (2004). Cognitive rehabilitation and cognitive training for early-stage Alzheimer's disease and vascular dementia. *The Cochrane Database of Systematic Reviews, 2*, 1–58.

Collie, A., & Maruff, P. (2000). The neuropsychology of preclinical Alzheimer's disease and mild cognitive impairment. *Neuroscience and Biobehavioral Reviews, 24*, 365–374.

Collie, A., & Maruff, P. (2002). An analysis of systems of classifying mild cognitive impairment in older people. *Australian and New Zealand Journal of Psychiatry, 36*, 133–140.

Courtney, C., Farrell, D., Gray, R., Hills, R., Lynch, L., Sellwood, E., et al. (2004). Long-term donepezil treatment in 565 patients with Alzheimer's disease (AD2000): Randomised double-blind trial. *Lancet, 363*(9427), 2105–2115.

Coyle, J. T., Price, D. L., & DeLong, M. R. (1983). Alzheimer's disease: A disorder of cortical cholinergic innervation. *Science, 219*, 1184–1190.

Cummings, J. L. (2003). Neuropsychiatric symptoms. In R. C. Petersen (Ed.), *Mild cognitive impairment: Aging to Alzheimer disease* (pp. 41–61). Oxford: Oxford University Press.

Davies, P., & Maloney, A. J. F. (1976). Selective loss of central cholinergic neurons in Alzheimer's disease. *Lancet, 2*, 1403.

Davis, K. L., Mohs, R. C., Marin, D., Purohit, D. P., Perl, D. P., Lantz, M., et al. (1999). Cholinergic markers in elderly patients with early signs of Alzheimer disease. *Journal of the American Medical Association, 281*(15), 1401–1406.

Davis, R. N., Massman, P. J., & Doody, R. S. (2003). Cognitive intervention in Alzheimer disease: A randomized placebo-controlled study. *Alzheimer Disease and Associated Disorders, 15*(1), 1–9.

Dawson, D., Winocur, G., & Moscovitch, M. (1999). The psychosocial environment and cognitive rehabilitation in the elderly. In D. T. Stuss, G. Winocur, & I. H. Roberston (Eds.), *Cognitive neurorehabilitation* (pp. 94–108). Cambridge: Cambridge University Press.

De Vreese, L. P., & Neri, M. (1999). Ecological impact of combined cognitive training program (CTP) and drug treatment (ChE-I) in AD. *International Psychogeriatrics, 11*(Suppl. 1), S91.

De Vreese, L. P., Neri, M., Fioravanti, M., Belloi, L., & Zanetti, O. (2001). Memory rehabilitation in Alzheimer's disease: A review of progress. *Journal of International Geriatric Psychiatry, 16*, 794–809.

DeKosky, S. T., Ikonomovic, M. D., Styren, S. D., Beckett, L., Wisniewski, S., Bennett, D. A., et al. (2002). Upregulation of choline acetyltransferase activity in hippocampus and frontal cortex of elderly subjects with mild cognitive impairment. *Annals of Neurology, 51*(2), 145–155.

Doraiswamy, P. M. (2002). Non-cholinergic strategies for treating and preventing Alzheimer's disease. *CNS Drugs, 16*(12), 811–824.

Farlow, M., Anand, R., Messina, J., Hartman, R., & Veach, J. (2000). A 52-week study of the efficacy of rivastigmine in patients with mild to moderately severe Alzheimer's disease. *European Neurology, 44*, 236–241.

Feldman, H., Scheltens, P., Scarpini, E., Hermann, N., Mesenbrink, P., Mancione, L., et al. (2004). Behavioral symptoms in mild cognitive impairment. *Neurology, 62*(7), 1199–1201.

Fisher, N. J., Rourke, B. P., Bieliauskas, L., Giordani, B., Berent, S., & Foster, N. L. (1996). Neuropsychological subgroups of patients with Alzheimer's disease. *Journal of Clinical and Experimental Neuropsychology, 18*(3), 349–370.

Gauthier, S. (2002). Advances in the pharmacotherapy of Alzheimer's disease. *Canadian Medical Association Journal, 166*(5), 616–623.

Geda, Y. E., Smith, G. E., Knopman, D. S., Boeve, B. F., Tangalos, E. G., Ivnik, R. J., et al. (2004). De novo genesis of neuropsychiatric symptoms in mild cognitive impairment (MCI). *International Psychogeriatrics, 16*(1), 51–60.

Gilmor, M. L., Erickson, J. D., Varoqui, H., Hersh, L. B., Bennett, D. A., Cochran, E. J., et al. (1999). Preservation of nucleus basalis neurons containing choline acetyltransferase and the vesicular acetylcholine transporter in the elderly with mild cognitive impairment and early Alzheimer's disease. *Journal of Comparative Neurology, 411*(4), 693–704.

Glisky, E. L. (2004). Disorders of memory. In J. Ponsford (Ed.), *Cognitive and behavioral rehabilitation* (pp. 100–128). New York: The Guilford Press.

Glisky, E. L., & Glisky, M. L. (2002). Learning and memory impairments. In P. J. Eslinger (Ed.), *Neuropsychological interventions: Clinical research and practice* (pp. 137–162). New York: The Guilford Press.

Glisky, E. L., Schacter, D. L., & Tulving, E. (1986). Learning and retention of computer-related vocabulary in memory-impaired patients: Method of vanishing cues. *Journal of Clinical and Experimental Neuropsychology, 8*, 292–312.

Goekoop, R., Rombouts, S. A., Jonker, C., Hibbel, A., Knol, D. L., Truyen, L., et al. (2004). Challenging the cholinergic system in mild cognitive impairment: A pharmacological fMRI study. *Neuroimage, 23*(4), 1450–1459.

Graham, J. E., Rockwood, K., Beattie, B. L., Eastwood, R., Gauthier, S., Tuokko, H., et al. (1997). Prevalence and severity of cognitive impairment with and without dementia in an elderly population. *Lancet, 349*, 1793–1796.

Grandmaison, E., & Simard, M. (2003). A critical review of memory stimulation programs in Alzheimer's disease. *Journal of Neuropsychiatry and Clinical Neurosciences, 15*(2), 130–144.

Grundman, M., & Thal, L. J. (2000). Treatment of Alzheimer's disease. *Neurologic Clinics, 18*(4), 807–828.

Hawley, K. S., & Cherry, K. E. (2004). Spaced-retrieval effects on name-face recognition in older adults with probable Alzheimer's disease. *Behavior Modification, 28*(2), 276–296.

Hochhalter, A. K., Bakke, B. L., Holub, R. J., & Overmier, J. B. (2003). Adjusted spaced retrieval training: A demonstration and initial test of why it is effective. *Clinical Gerontologist, 27*(1–2), 159–168.

Hogan, D. B., Goldlist, B., Naglie, G., & Patterson, C. (2004). Comparison studies of cholinesterase inhibitors for Alzheimer's disease. *Lancet Neurology, 3*(10), 622–626.

Jones, R. W., Soininen, H., Hager, K., Aarsland, D., Passmore, P., Murthy, A., et al. (2004). A multinational, randomised, 12-week study comparing the effects of

donepezil and galantamine in patients with mild to moderate Alzheimer's disease. *International Journal of Geriatric Psychiatry, 19*(1), 58–67.
Jorm, A. F. (1985). Subtypes of Alzheimer's dementia: A conceptual analysis and critical review. *Psychological Medicine, 15*, 543–553.
Knopman, D. S. (2003). Treatment of mild cognitive impairment and prospects for prevention of Alzheimer's disease. In R. C. Petersen (Ed.), *Mild cognitive impairment: Aging to Alzheimer's disease* (pp. 243–258). Oxford: Oxford University Press.
Lanctôt, K. L., Herrman, N., Yau, K. K., Khan, L. R., Liu, B. A., LouLou, M. M., et al. (2003). Efficacy and safety of cholinesterase inhibitors in Alzheimer's disease: A meta-analysis. *Canadian Medical Association Journal, 169*, 557–564.
Loewenstein, D. A., Acevedo, A., Czaja, S. J., & Duara, R. (2004). Cognitive rehabilitation of mildly impaired Alzheimer disease patients on cholinesterase inhibitors. *American Journal of Geriatric Psychiatry, 12*(4), 395–402.
Lyketsos, C. G., Lopez, O., Jones, B., Fitzpatrick, A. L., Breitner, J., & DeKosky, S. (2002). Prevalence of neuropsychiatric symptoms in dementia and mild cognitive impairment: Results from the cardiovascular health study. *Journal of the American Medical Association, 288*(12), 1475–1483.
Mesulam, M., Shaw, P., Mash, D., & Weintraub, S. (2004). Cholinergic nucleus basalis tauopathy emerges early in the aging-MCI-AD continuum. *Annals of Neurology, 55*(6), 815–828.
Meyer, J. S., Li, Y., Xu, G., Thornby, J., Chowdhury, M., & Quach, M. (2002). Feasibility of treating mild cognitive impairment with cholinesterase inhibitors. *International Journal of Geriatric Psychiatry, 17*(6), 586–588.
Mohs, R. C., Doody, R. S., Morris, J. C., Ieni, J. R., Rogers, S. L., Perdomo, C. A., et al. (2001). A 1-year placebo-controlled preservation of function survival study of donepezil in AD patients. *Neurology, 57*, 481–489.
Mufson, E. J., Ma, S. Y., Cochran, E. J., Bennett, D. A., Beckett, L. A., Jaffar, S., et al. (2000). Loss of nucleus Basalis neurons containing trkA immunoreactivity in individuals with mild cognitive impairment and early Alzheimer's disease. *The Journal of Comparative Neurology, 427*, 19–30.
Olazaran, J., Muniz, R., Reisberg, B., Pena-Casanova, J., del Ser, T., Cruz-Jentoft, A. J., et al. (2004). Benefits of cognitive-motor intervention in MCI and mild to moderate Alzheimer disease. *Neurology, 63*(12), 2348–2353.
Olin, J., & Schneider, L. (2004). Galantamine for dementia due to Alzheimer's disease. *Cochrane Database of Systematic Reviews, 2*, 1–84.
Peters, K. R., Graf, P., Hayden, S., & Feldman, H. (2005). Neuropsychological subgroups of cognitively-impaired-not-demented (CIND) individuals: Delineation, reliability, and predictive validity. *Journal of Clinical and Experimental Neuropsychology, 27*(2), 164–188.
Petersen, R. C. (2003). Conceptual overview. In R. C. Petersen (Ed.), *Mild cognitive impairment: From aging to Alzheimer's disease* (pp. 1–14). Oxford: Oxford University Press.
Petersen, R. C., Doody, R., Kurz, A., Mohs, R. C., Morris, J. C., Rabins, P. V., et al. (2001). Current concepts in mild cognitive impairment. *Archives of Neurology, 58*, 1985–1992.
Petersen, R. C., Thomas, R. G., Grundman, M., Bennett, D., Doody, R., Ferris, S., et al. (2005). Vitamin E and donepezil for the treatment of mild cognitive impairment. *New England Journal of Medicine, 352*(23), 2379–2388.

Prigatano, G. P. (1999). Motivation and awareness in cognitive neurorehabilitation. In D. T. Stuss, G. Winocur, & I. H. Roberston (Eds.), *Cognitive neurorehabilitation* (pp. 240–251). Cambridge: Cambridge University Press.

Prigatano, G. P. (Ed.). (1986). *Personality and psychosocial consequences of brain injury*. Baltimore: Johns Hopkins University Press.

Rapp, S., Brenes, G., & Marsh, A. P. (2002). Memory enhancement training for older adults with mild cognitive impairment: A preliminary study. *Aging and Mental Health*, 6(1), 5–11.

Raskind, M. A., Peskind, E. R., Truyen, L., Kershaw, P., & Damaraju, C. V. (2004). The cognitive benefits of galantamine are sustained for at least 36 months: A long-term extension trial. *Archives of Neurology*, 61, 252–256.

Reisberg, B., Doody, R., Stoffler, A., Schmitt, F., Ferris, S., & Mobius, H. J. (2003). Memantine in moderate-to-severe Alzheimer's disease. *New England Journal of Medicine*, 348(14), 1333–1341.

Rosler, M., Anand, R., Cicin-Sain, A., Gauthier, S., Agid, Y., Dal-Bianco, P., et al. (1999). Efficacy and safety of rivastigmine in patients with Alzheimer's disease: International randomised controlled trial. *British Medical Journal*, 318, 633–638.

Salloway, S., Ferris, S., Kluger, A., Goldman, R., Griesing, T., Kumar, D., et al. (2004). Efficacy of donepezil in mild cognitive impairment: A randomized placebo-controlled trial. *Neurology*, 63(4), 651–657.

Saykin, A. J., Wishart, H. A., Rabin, L. A., Flashman, L. A., McHugh, T. L., Mamourian, A. C., et al. (2004). Cholinergic enhancement of frontal lobe activity in mild cognitive impairment. *Brain*, 127(Pt 7), 1574–1583.

Sohlberg, M. M., & Mateer, C. A. (2001). *Cognitive rehabilitation: An integrative neuropsychological approach*. New York: The Guildford Press.

Tariot, P. N., Farlow, M. R., Grossberg, G. T., Graham, S. M., McDonald, S., & Gergel, I. (2004). Memantine treatment in patients with moderate to severe Alzheimer disease already receiving donepezil. *Journal of the American Medical Association*, 291(3), 317–324.

Trinh, N. H., Hoblyn, J., & Yaffe, K. (2003). Efficacy of cholinesterase inhibitors in the treatment of neuropsychiatric symptoms and functional impairment in Alzheimer disease. *Journal of the American Medical Association*, 289(2), 210–216.

Tuokko, H., Frerichs, R., Graham, J., Rockwood, K., Kristjansson, B., Fisk, J., et al. (2003). Five-year follow-up of cognitive impairment with no dementia. *Archives of Neurology*, 60(4), 577–582.

Tuokko, H., & Frerichs, R. J. (2000). Cognitive impairment with no dementia (CIND): Longitudinal studies, the findings, and the issues. *The Clinical Neuropsychologist*, 14(4), 504–525.

Verhaeghen, P., Marcoen, A., & Goossens, L. (1992). Improving memory performance in the aged through mnemonic training: A meta-analytic study. *Psychology and Aging*, 7(2), 242–251.

Wilcock, G., Howe, I., Coles, H., Lilienfeld, S., Truyen, L., Zhu, Y., et al. (2003). A long-term comparison of galantamine and donepezil in the treatment of Alzheimer's disease. *Drugs and Aging*, 20(10), 777–789.

Wilcock, G. K., Lilienfeld, S., & Gaens, E. (2000). Efficacy and safety of galantamine in patients with mild to moderate Alzheimer's disease: Multicentre randomise controlled trial. *British Medical Journal*, 321, 1445–1449.

Wilkinson, D. G., Passmore, A. P., Bullock, R., Hopker, S. W., Smith, R., Potocnik, F. C., et al. (2002). A multinational, randomised, 12-week, comparative study of

donezepil and rivastigmine in patients with mild to moderate Alzheimer's disease. *International Journal of Clinical Practice, 56*(6), 441–446.
Wilson, B. A. (2002). Memory rehabilitation. In L. R. Squire & D. L. Schacter (Eds.), *Neuropsychology of memory* (3rd ed., pp. 263–272). New York: The Guilford Press.
Winblad, B., Engedal, K., Soininen, H., Verhey, F., Waldemar, G., Wimo, A., et al. (2001). A 1-year, randomized, placebo-controlled study of donepezil in patients with mild to moderate AD. *Neurology, 57*(7), 489–495.
Winocur, G., Moscovitch, M., & Freedman, J. (1987). An investigation of cognitive function in relation to psychosocial variables in institutionalized old people. *Canadian Journal of Psychology, 41*(2), 257–269.
Winter, J., & Hunkin, N. M. (1999). Re-learning in Alzheimer disease. *International Journal of Geriatric Psychiatry, 14*, 983–990.
Yesavage, J. A., Sheikh, J. I., Friedman, L., & Tanke, E. (1990). Learning mnemonics: Roles of aging and subtle cognitive impairment. *Psychology and Aging, 5*(1), 133–137.
Zec, R. F. (1993). Neuropsychological functioning in Alzheimer's disease. In R. W. Parks, R. F. Zec, & R. S. Wilson (Eds.), *Neuropsychology of Alzheimer's disease and other dementias* (pp. 3–80). New York: Oxford University Press.

Part V

Summary and Future Directions

13 The future of mild cognitive impairment

Holly A. Tuokko and David F. Hultsch

The aim of this chapter is to provide a summary of the multiple perspectives on mild cognitive impairment (MCI) presented in the preceding chapters of this book. In these chapters, the authors have provided information about MCI derived from multiple studies involving different samples from a variety of countries. The introductory chapter discussed the epidemiology of MCI and related constructs (e.g., CIND, AD, dementias) and base rate differences among different samples (e.g., population-based studies, studies involving various samples of convenience). In this introductory chapter, challenges confronting researchers studying MCI were identified. The next three sections described the findings from different perspectives and from different parts of the world. To facilitate comparisons between chapters, each chapter described the types of information collected in the study, how MCI was defined, and the important information concerning MCI emerging from that study. The final section of this book described the status of intervention research for persons with MCI (e.g., pharmacologic and behavioral). Our intent in bringing together this information was to provide a comprehensive examination of the concept of MCI that would offer a composite picture of the current understanding of MCI and suggest future directions for research.

Current understanding of MCI

As a prodrome to dementia

Perhaps the most striking consistency from all perspectives is that MCI is a heterogeneous construct that captures a mix of people, some of whom show progressive cognitive decline over time and some who do not. The term MCI implies a descriptive, quantified, behavioral classification. Some definitions, but not all, implicitly assume the notion of decline or change in function but few (see Collie, Maruff, Darby, Masters, & Currie, this volume; Wilson, Aggarwal, & Bennett, this volume) require objective evidence of cognitive decline. Instead, they rely on the identification of cognitive impairment at a single point in time, an approach that implies a specific, common threshold for inclusion. Both the prevalence (number of MCI cases in the population at any one time) and incidence (number of new cases in a year) of MCI vary widely between studies, and many of the sources for this variability are discussed in Tuokko and McDowell (this volume). Smith, Machulda, and Kantarci (this volume), using their own data and the assumption that dementia incidence = MCI prevalence × Annual progression rate × Cumulative progression rate, arrive at an estimated MCI prevalence of 9–18%. Where progression to dementia has been the outcome of interest (i.e., incidence of dementia), the exact rates of conversion from MCI to dementia observed across studies differ as a function of MCI *definition* and the *sample* studied.

The observation that MCI is a heterogeneous classification, regardless of how it is *defined* (i.e., narrow to broad definitions), has led some researchers to question the use of MCI as a clinical construct because research, to date, does not support the often-held global etiological assumption that MCI necessarily reflects early-stage AD (Wolf & Gertz, this volume). Instead, some researchers have chosen to make no assumptions about the relation between behavioral presentation and underlying pathology; rather, they identify MCI only as a given level of cognitive impairment in the absence of dementia as evidenced by performance on measures of cognitive functioning (e.g., Palmer, Bäckman, Small, & Fratiglioni, this volume; Wilson et al., this volume). This approach also makes no assumptions about the relative importance of particular types of cognitive impairments and allows for empirical determination of risk factors and the most relevant features in relation to specific outcomes. Broad definitions, as discussed in Chapter 1, result in higher prevalence rates, with lower rates of conversion, but may yield some different types of information than that derived from studies using highly selective diagnostic MCI criteria. For example, in Tuokko, Frerichs, Graham, Rockwood, Kristjansson, Fisk, et al.'s (2003a) study of people identified with cognitive dementia–no dementia (CIND) from the Canadian Study of Health and Aging, all subgroups identified on the basis of presumed etiology declined at similar rates. Fabrigoule, Barberger-Gateau, and Dartigues (this volume) and Palmer et al. (this volume) demonstrate that it may be important to include people with impairments in activities of daily living within the construct of MCI, rather than excluding them.

Others have suggested that subcategories within the construct of MCI can be identified in a number of ways that may enhance the utility of the overall construct. In particular, attention has been directed toward examining patterns of impairment across cognitive domains (e.g., memory, nonmemory; single, multiple); relationships to underlying pathology (e.g., AD, vascular dementia); and prognostic outcomes (e.g., decline, no change, remission) (see Winblad et al., 2004). Palmer et al. (this volume) note that one third of their cognitively impaired sample developed dementia within 3 years whereas one third reverted to normality. Those with significant nonmemory MCI did not have an increased risk for developing AD, whereas three fourths of the multidomain MCI progressed to AD. Peters and Winocur (this volume) make a distinction between subtypes (differing in etiology) and subgroups that differ with respect to neuropsychological or cognitive profile. Smith et al. (this volume), in describing their work at the Mayo Clinic, combine types (amnestic, nonamnestic) and degrees (single or multiple domains) of cognitive impairment with presumed etiologies in their proposed model on MCI. This approach may result in higher conversion rates to AD (at least for some subgroups) but is likely to do so at the risk of missing large numbers of eventual cases of AD (increasing specificity at the expense of sensitivity, see Chapter 1). However, some encouraging work has begun linking subtypes to subgroups using neuroimaging techniques and genetic markers (e.g., Smith et al., this volume; Wilson et al., this volume; Wolf & Gertz, this volume).

A third issue related to the definition is how the criteria are operationalized. In Chapter 1 (Tuokko & McDowell), three approaches were identified: norm-based, criterion-based, and clinical judgment. Both Smith et al. (this volume) and Tierney (this volume) note that cases identified using clinical judgment show a higher conversion rate than those identified using norm-based cut-off scores. Wilson et al. (this volume) also rely on clinical judgment to identify people with MCI. If we fully understood the factors that clinicians are taking into consideration when making their judgments, it may be possible to design computer algorithms to assist in and improve on this process. To date, very few studies have examined this decision-making process (e.g., Tuokko, Gabriel, & the CSHA Neuropsychology Working Group, 2006).

The *sample* under investigation is another source of variability in the prevalence and incidence of MCI across studies. For example, samples derived from memory clinics or referred by concerned physicians are likely to show high rates of conversion, presumably because they are further along the spectrum from normality to dementia when defined as MCI. On the other hand, representative, population samples capture a wide range of types, degrees, and causes of cognitive impairment and tend to show high rates of remission from MCI to normality (Petersen, 2004). Moreover, representativeness is relative and biases may emerge dependent on sampling characteristics such as a healthy volunteer effect in population studies or a vigilant consumer effect in clinical studies (Tuokko & McDowell, this volume). This speaks of the importance of examining a phenomenon such as MCI from a variety of different perspectives and of taking these sampling differences into consideration when interpreting study findings.

Measurement of predictors and outcomes

Initially, in studies of MCI, memory was considered to be the central cognitive domain of interest. This is because of the presumed association between MCI and AD, where memory plays a prominent role in the diagnosis of dementia (DSM-IV; American Psychiatric Association, 1994). Repeatedly, it has been shown that measures of memory are very good predictors of decline to AD or dementia (e.g., Tierney, this volume; Tuokko & Frerichs, 2000).

In many ways this is not surprising; present memory impairment is highly predictive of future, more severe, memory impairment, even when different specific memory tests are used for predictive and diagnostic purposes (Tierney, this volume). Because all measures of memory are intercorrelated to some extent (often highly), this apparent circularity is inherent in the study of MCI and is rarely seen as a limitation. Of greater concern, particularly to neuropsychologists, is the clear articulation of the magnitude and type(s) of memory impairment most sensitive to decline. Certainly, it appears that simple measures (e.g., three-word recall on MMSE) are not adequate (Wolf & Gertz, this volume) and that more demanding neuropsychological measures of memory functions are more useful in this regard (Tierney, this volume). Since different types of memory may relate to different neural substrates, the choice of memory tasks (sometimes beyond those typically employed in clinical practice) is of particular concern. Smith et al. (this volume) and Tierney (this volume) note that delayed recall (retrieval) measures, especially those expressed as saving or retention, are particularly useful predictors of dementia, whereas Collie et al. (this volume) identified tasks requiring associative learning as most useful in this regard. Wilson et al. (this volume) note that rates of decline in semantic memory, perceptual speed and, most notably, episodic memory were accelerated in MCI but rates of decline in working memory and visuospatial ability were not.

Not only which memory measures but also how memory measures are to be used in defining MCI differs among research groups. Some suggest that performance on memory measures be used to inform clinical decision-making concerning the diagnosis on MCI by neuropsychologists (e.g., Wilson et al., this volume) or clinical teams (e.g., Smith et al., this volume), whereas others have used norm-based criteria (e.g., 1*SD* below age- and education-based norms) within specific memory domains (e.g., Palmer et al., this volume) to define MCI. In either circumstance, the types of memory domains assessed may engender very different samples (Smith et al., this volume). Although variations in publications by the researchers at the Mayo Clinic have led to some confusion about their use of a strict psychometric cut-off on measures of memory function, Smith et al. (this volume) argue against rigorous norm-based cut-offs, citing the performances of premorbidly high and/or low functioning individuals as requiring clinical judgment to overcome the possibility of identifying cases falsely. When they examined longitudinal data for cases who were both clinically and psychometrically defined, the clinically defined MCI cases were more likely to convert to dementia (likelihood ratio = 5.2) than those psychometrically defined (likelihood ratio = 2.1) (Smith et al., this volume).

Collie et al. (this volume), like others (e.g., Tuokko & Frerichs, 2000; Zaudig, 2002), have called into question the adequacy of identifying memory *deficit or impairment*, psychometrically or clinically at one point in time, if the intent is really to identify those people likely to *progress or decline* over time. Single test scores are influenced by many factors inherent to the measure itself and the test-taking environment (e.g., participant anxiety, fatigue) and can fluctuate over time (i.e., measurement error) resulting in, potentially, considerable misclassification. Instead, decline in cognitive functions through serial cognitive assessments (e.g., every 6–12 months) may be a better predictor for AD or dementia. In the Melbourne Aging Study, Collie et al. (this volume) focused on the development of brief tests designed specifically for serial assessment of older adults in the context of predicting AD as an outcome. In developing this series of "cognitive screening" tests, they have overcome the limitations of most conventional neuropsychological tests such as limited alternative forms, the presence of practice effects, or the presence of floor and ceiling effects. This break from the use of traditional clinical neuropsychological measures comes with the realization that measures designed for one purpose (i.e., identification of brain dysfunction) may not be particularly relevant for other purposes (i.e., assessment of change in brain function).

Another break from the conventional is the position taken by Fabrigoule et al. (this volume). They propose that, in addition to memory, other cognitive processes are important to the concept of MCI, most notably components of executive control. Their findings suggest that the more effortful and executive aspects within any task domain (e.g., visuospatial, language, or memory) may be associated with the risk of dementia and AD. They argue that combining memory and executive control deficits is likely to improve the sensitivity of the syndrome. This may serve to identify people who are further along the spectrum of normality to dementia, increasing the conversion rate, but perhaps at the cost of missed cases. They also argue for the inclusion of slight deterioration of highly cognitively loaded IADL in the MCI construct as these tasks demand executive control processes, and executive control is at the heart of the ability to use compensatory strategies to perform everyday tasks.

It has also been suggested that other noncognitive domains (e.g., neuropsychiatric symptoms) may be useful for identifying those likely to develop MCI (Palmer et al., this volume) or those likely to decline to dementia (e.g., Peters & Winocur, this volume; Woods & Clare, this volume). Depressive symptoms, anxiety, personality changes, and psychotic states all have been implicated as manifestations of early AD (Cummings, 2003) but only recently have these features been examined in relation to MCI (e.g., Balsis, Carpenter, & Storandt, 2005).

Other recommendations for improving the prediction of conversion to dementia from MCI include the addition of biological measures (e.g., Smith et al., this volume; Tierney, this volume; Wilson et al., this volume; Wolf & Gertz, this volume) such as genetic measures and measures of brain structure or function obtained through neuroimaging techniques. As was illustrated in these chapters, several biological variables including baseline hippocampal volume, medial temporal lobe atrophy rating, corpus callosum size, and brain volume are associated with MCI and its progression to dementia. Typically, these measures show moderate predictive accuracies in nondemented subjects and so cannot yet be considered to be "biological markers" for cognitive decline. The work of Tierney (this volume) and Wolf and Gertz (this volume) suggests that the added clinical value of biological parameters, over and above the prognostic and diagnostic value of clinical tools and personal expertise of a clinician, has not been adequately demonstrated as yet. Tierney (this volume) noted that the contribution of a genetic marker (ApoE) was greater when measured well before the diagnosis of AD. Closer to the diagnosis, neuropsychological measures emerged as better predictors (at least in part because the change in cognition is how AD is expressed). In contrast, Smith et al. (this volume) report greater optimism concerning the independent contributions of their biological and cognitive measures to the prediction of progression from MCI to dementia.

Finally, in terms of outcome measures, most researchers argue that change in diagnostic status to dementia, or specific forms of dementia, is only one important outcome. Other outcomes of concern include death, behavioral indices (e.g., cognitive functions, quality of life indicators, independence in everyday functioning, prolonged time to admission to facility care), as well as biological measures (e.g., genetic, biochemical, or neuroimages). The behavioral and biological outcome measures are relevant both for monitoring the evolution of the condition over time (e.g., Fleming, Matthews, Chatfield, & Brayne, this volume; Palmer et al., this volume) as well as the effects of interventions, whether pharmacological or behavioral (e.g., Chertkow, this volume; Peters & Winocur, this volume; Woods & Clare, this volume). The primary reason why such an array of outcome measures is required is the observation that the link between underlying pathology and the manifest behavioral symptoms (e.g., cognitive impairment) is not always clear (e.g., Wolf & Gertz, this volume). It has been demonstrated by many research groups that specific forms of neuropathology may or may not be associated with particular cognitive or behavioral impairments. Yet pharmacological interventions, designed to slow, stop, or even reverse underlying pathological changes, are undertaken with heterogeneous samples (i.e., not all progress to dementia) defined with behavioral criteria and typically evaluated on change (or lack thereof) on behavioral outcome measures. Determining this all-important connection between brain and behavior is likely to be one important focus for future MCI research (see below).

Methods

To date, two types of MCI studies have dominated the research literature: (1) cross-sectional studies characterizing the behavioral and/or biological functioning of people with MCI, and (2) longitudinal studies of large samples with a focus on evaluating MCI's utility as an early indicator of dementia or specific forms of dementia over intervals of 1–5 years. These two types of studies have been conducted with various samples around the world and have highlighted the complexities inherent in the study of MCI raised in this book.

Another type of design option has been proposed and employed by Collie et al. (this volume). This involves the intensive study of groups of participants (with and without objective evidence of memory decline) with serial assessments conducted at relatively short time intervals (e.g., 6 months). Their findings support the use of this shorter time interval in monitoring for change in cognitive functions and are in keeping with the time frames often employed in the context intervention studies (e.g., Peters & Winocur, this volume). In addition, their studies have revealed that many of the traditional forms of cognitive assessment used in research with MCI are inappropriate for use in serial assessments and this has led them to develop new measures with very different psychometric properties from conventions measures.

Other investigators have suggested that measurement of within-person variability in performance over short intervals (e.g., trial-to-trial within a testing session or day-to-day or week-to-week across different testing sessions) may be a useful indicator of MCI (Lindenberger & von Oertzen, 2006; Hultsch, Hunter, MacDonald, & Strauss, 2005; Rabbitt, 2000; Stuss, Pogue, Buckle, & Bondar, 1994). Indeed, two recent studies suggest that individuals classified as MCI show greater within-person inconsistency in response time on reaction time tasks than individuals classified as intact (Christensen, Dear, Anstey, Parslow, Sachdev, & Jorm, 2005; Dixon, Garrett, Lentz, MacDonald, Strauss, & Hultsch, 2005). Both studies found measures of variability distinguished among different classifications of MCI. Dixon et al. reported that inconsistency was exacerbated in individuals with deficits in multiple as compared with single domains. Christensen et al. found greater inconsistency in participants classified as MCI as defined by Petersen, Smith, Waring, Ivnik, Tangalos, and Kokmen (1999) and age-associated cognitive decline as defined by Levy (1994), but not for those classified with age-associated memory impairment (Crook, Bartus, Ferris, Whitehouse, Cohen, & Gershon, 1986). Importantly, Dixon et al. (2005) demonstrated that although both mean level and inconsistency of response speed were useful in differentiating MCI from intact individuals, inconsistency was arguably the better predictor of cognitive status, particularly when more complex reaction time tasks were evaluated.

What we still need to know

As a prodrome to AD and related dementias

It is clear that the MCI construct, as presently defined and employed, does not fulfill its promise to successfully identify those individuals destined to develop AD or a related dementia. Should the concept be abandoned or are there directions for future research that may enhance our understanding? In our opinion, the term MCI, as a descriptive label, is useful and should be retained, but it will be important that future studies address the intent of their research, describe their samples clearly, and provide a reasoned, clearly articulated approach to defining the condition under investigation.

The findings in the field to date suggest a number of possible fruitful areas for future research, some of which embrace the broad construct of MCI as a behavioral descriptor, and some that specifically seek to elucidate the natural history of neurodegenerative brain disorders associated with cognitive decline. These two approaches differ with respect to the underlying assumptions and may be viewed as complementary. As with behavioral and pharmacological interventions, the intent of studying MCI as a behavioral descriptor is different from the intent of studying MCI to elucidate the natural history of a disease process. Both approaches are likely to yield important information relevant to the lives of the individuals with MCI, their families, health care practitioners, and the society in which they live.

MCI as a behavioral descriptor

Studies focusing on the first approach would concern themselves with the manner in which cognitive impairment, insufficient to be diagnosed as dementia, is defined and the implications of this impairment for the afflicted individual. These studies may choose to examine the behavioral definition of MCI and its functional correlates to clearly characterize this population and elucidate the social and health care needs of this group. For example, the inclusion of other specific cognitive domains beyond memory, such as executive functions, in the definition of MCI may yield another socially important group (Fabriougle et al., this volume). Those with disorders of executive function may show a breakdown in social conduct that may include disinhibited behavior (e.g., violent behavior), misdemeanors (e.g., shoplifting), lack of initiative (e.g., social withdrawal), or stereotyped, perseverative behaviors (e.g., ritualistic preoccupations such as hoarding). Individuals with these types of socially disabling behaviors are likely to be overlooked unless executive functions are specifically addressed in the MCI definition. In a similar fashion, the observation of many research groups that MCI may be associated with impairment in other noncognitive domains (e.g., neuropsychiatric symptoms) and/or cognitively demanding activities of daily living (Fabriougle et al., this volume) is of importance with respect to understanding the social needs of those with MCI. The identification of MCI, then, may prompt further evaluation to identify those having difficulty with important, high-risk everyday tasks such as driving or handling finances. In addition, it will be important to examine various neuropsychiatric symptoms to determine their prevalence and impact. Examining these features in relation to MCI and their relations with other observed cognitive, behavioral, and neuropathological factors may yield important new insights.

Longitudinal studies focusing on MCI as a behavioral descriptor may be equally interested in many different outcomes, and not only be concerned with those who progress to dementia. For example, study of those with MCI who do not progress to dementia may prove very informative. It may be that those who do not decline are engaging in some behaviors (e.g., physical exercise, mentally stimulating hobbies) that either slow the progression of the underlying disease process or facilitate brain compensation (e.g., Woods & Clare, this volume). This information would be particularly relevant with respect to planning and evaluating intervention studies. Similarly, studying those who "revert" to normal cognitive functioning over time may yield important information about the nature of variability in cognitive functions in later life. It will be important to determine the proportion of the cases where there are clear explanations for the variations in cognitive functions (e.g., illness; change in lifestyle) and those where there are not. These studies may include more information about the individual from across the lifespan. In this way, it may be possible to distinguish those who have had life-long weakness in a cognitive domain or may help to identify risk factors for relatively stable forms of MCI as well as dementia.

MCI and the natural history of a disease process

To study the natural history of a disease process requires longitudinal studies. To date, few studies of MCI have been concerned with the identification of risk factors for MCI, as an entity apart from AD, and few have adopted a lifespan perspective. The primary difficulty in studying MCI as part of the natural history of AD, as noted earlier, has been that the link between underlying pathology and the manifest behavioral symptoms (e.g., cognitive impairment) is not always clear. If brain pathology defines the disease process, then the focus of future research must be on the use of neuroimaging and other biological markers when identifying an abnormal condition and to demonstrate improvement following interventions.

However, as indicated in Chapter 1 (Tuokko & McDowell), it can be debated whether cases in which pathological changes do not result in changes in behavioral presentation represent disease. It is in response to this quandary that some theoretical discussion has begun, not only to explain observations, but also to stimulate a theory-driven, hypothesis-testing approach to research in this area. The theoretical models most frequently raised for discussion in relation to MCI and AD include the brain reserve capacity model (Roth, 1971; Roth, Tomlinson, & Blessed, 1967; Satz, 1993), the cognitive reserve model (Stern, 2002), and brain area compensation, a distinct change in the brain area used in performance of a task induced by brain damage (Stern, 2002; see Tuokko & McDowell, this volume; Wolf & Gertz, this volume). It is possible that various factors inherent in the individual or resulting from the interaction of the individual with their environment may influence the development and function of neural substrates, positively or negatively. Researchers are only beginning to search for these factors, generate models, and then "test" these in relation to MCI (e.g., Tuokko, Garrett, Silverberg, Kristjansson, & McDowell, 2003b). Smith et al.'s (this volume) two-dimensional graphical representation of the relation between MCI and AD, Tuokko and McDowell's (this volume) use of the rain analogy to characterize the potential relations between underlying pathology and behavioral change, and Chertkow's (this volume) sets of inter-related curves (Figure 10.3) are examples of starting points in conceptualizing these relations for model development. Full enquiry will require the simultaneous collection of behavioral and biological measures (as predictors and/or outcomes).

Some longitudinal studies have focused on objectively defined cognitive *decline* as opposed to MCI (e.g., Wilson et al., this volume). For example, some researchers (Frerichs & Tuokko, 2005, 2006) have compared different methods for measuring cognitive decline such as reliable change indices (RCIs), standardized regression-based methods, clinician identified change, or decline reported by knowledgeable informants (i.e., friends of family members of the person with MCI). The findings from these studies suggest that RCIs, in particular, can be useful when making diagnostic discriminations in older adults but that the strength of the association is dependent on the nature of the psychometric instrument under examination and the length of test–retest interval.

Another type of longitudinal study that addresses the natural history issue more directly than most previous MCI studies is that proposed by Collie et al. (this volume). They intensively studied groups of participants with serial assessments conducted at relatively short time intervals (e.g., 6 months). Unlike other studies using serial assessments (e.g., pharmacological interventions), they have developed new theoretically grounded cognitive measures with very different psychometric properties from conventional cognitive assessment measures. Linking this approach to the assessment of cognitive *decline* with biological studies may prove more fruitful than the MCI/biological studies done to date that focus on cognitive impairment as opposed to decline. Future studies need to combine theoretically grounded, psychometrically sound cognitive tools and the use of cutting-edge imaging studies.

Intervention studies are in the early stages and are beginning to yield additional important information about MCI. At this point in time, efficacy studies are those being conducted with only narrowly defined clinical samples where the base rate for conversion is quite high. Findings from these studies are only beginning to emerge. To date, these have been limited by the complexity of the MCI construct and so there is little clear evidence to guide practice (Chertkow, this volume). However, it is important to note that pharmacological and behavioral intervention approaches differ markedly in their intent. The intent of the pharmacological approaches is to slow, stop, or even reverse the underlying pathological condition and rests heavily on the assumption of a direct link between underlying pathology and behavioral presentation. As noted earlier, this link is not clearly understood. Only when such a connection is made will it be possible to clearly evaluate the effects of intervention studies on the underlying pathological process. To date, no pharmacological treatment of MCI is approved in North America, and medical management of people with MCI remains nonspecific. Even so, Chertkow (this volume) notes that talk of potential "Viagra for the brain" is prompting serious discussion of social effects and the possible dangers of cognitive enhancers.

In contrast, behavioral interventions for MCI are intended to optimize functioning and well-being, minimize the risk of disability, and prevent the development of dysfunctional family or social functioning (Woods & Clare, this volume). Here the importance of humanism, or personhood, and social context are paramount. Although behavioral approaches may relate to, or bring about, changes in neural functioning (e.g., brain area compensation), that is not their primary intent. The rationale for instituting such interventions for people with MCI is clear and there is a substantial cognitive rehabilitation from the head injury literature on which to build. In addition, from the three chapters on intervention strategies (Chertkow, this volume; Peters & Winocur, this volume; Woods & Clare, this volume), it is apparent that there are many psychosocial influences that affect the outcomes of intervention (whether pharmacological or behavioral) and these need to be considered carefully (Peters & Winocur, this volume).

Conclusion

In this chapter, we have briefly summarized the current perspectives on MCI from around the world as presented in this book. Not all research groups studying MCI were included. Instead, those contributing came from different disciplines and backgrounds, studied samples derived in different ways, employed different study methods, and/or focused on different features associated with MCI. The fact that so much research has been stimulated around the MCI construct speaks of its importance to clinicians and researchers. It is also important to the individual with some form of MCI and the society in which s/he lives. If, as has been suggested, those with MCI manifest difficulties that place them at risk with respect to present capacities of everyday functioning or with respect to future vulnerabilities, they and those who would support them need to know how and when support is to be provided. Of equal importance is making clear the links between the behavioral symptomatic manifestations and the presumed underlying neurodegenerative process(es).

Although early interest in the construct was voiced over 40 years ago (Kral, 1962), it has only been in the last decade, with the emergence of possible pharmacological interventions for AD, that MCI has generated substantial research interest. The plethora of approaches taken and the resulting proliferation of terms used to define similar, yet distinct, constructs have made very complex that which appeared quite simple in 1962 (benign vs. malignant senescent forgetfulness). As this book illustrates, it is only after much research, conducted by many researchers from a variety of perspectives, that a composite picture begins to emerge to inform an area. We have identified avenues for future research that build on this broad foundation. It will be only through the continued efforts of many researchers worldwide that the complexities inherent in the MCI construct will be mastered.

References

American Psychiatric Association. (1994). *Diagnostic and statistical manual of mental disorders* (4th ed.). Washington, DC: American Psychiatric Association.

Balsis, S., Carpenter, B. D., & Storandt, M. (2005). Personality change precedes clinical diagnosis of dementia of the Alzheimer Type. *Journals of Gerontology: Psychological Sciences, 60B*, P98–P101.

Chertkow, H. (2006) Emerging pharmacological therapies for mild cognitive impairment. In H. A. Tuokko & D. F. Hultsch (Eds.), *Mild cognitive impairment*. New York: Taylor & Francis.

Christensen, H., Dear, K. B. G., Anstey, K. J., Parslow, R. A., Sachdev, P., & Jorm, A. F. (2005). Within occasion intra-individual variability and pre-clinical diagnostic status: Is intra-individual variability an indicator of mild cognitive impairment? *Neuropsychology, 19*, 309–317.

Collie, A., Maruff, P., Darby, D. G., Masters, C., & Currie, J. (2006). The Melbourne Aging Study. In H. A. Tuokko & D. F. Hultsch (Eds.), *Mild cognitive impairment*. New York: Taylor & Francis.

Crook, T., Bartus, R. T., Ferris, S. H., Whitehouse, P., Cohen, G. D., & Gershon, S. (1986). Age associated memory impairment: Proposed diagnostic criteria and measures of clinical change: Report of a National Institute of Mental Health Work Group. *Developmental Neuropsychology, 2*, 261–276.

Cummings, J. L. (2003). Neuropsychiatric symptoms. In R. C. Petersen (Ed.), *Mild cognitive impairment: Aging to Alzheimer's disease* (pp. 41–62). New York: Oxford University Press.

Dixon, R. A., Garrett, D. D., Lentz, T. L., MacDonald, S. W. S., Strauss, E., & Hultsch, D. F. (2005). *Neurocognitive resources in mild cognitive impairment: Exploring markers of speed and inconsistency*. Manuscript submitted for publication.

Fabrigoule, C., Barberger-Gateau, P., & Dartigues, J.-F. (2006). The PAQUID study. In H. A. Tuokko & D. F. Hultsch (Eds.), *Mild cognitive impairment*. New York: Taylor & Francis.

Fleming, J., Matthews, F. E., Chatfield, M., & Brayne, C. (2006). Population levels of mild cognitive impairment in England and Wales. In H. A. Tuokko & D. F. Hultsch (Eds.), *Mild cognitive impairment*. New York: Taylor & Francis.

Frerichs, R. J., & Tuokko, H. (2005). A comparison of methods for measuring cognitive change in older adults. *Archives of Clinical Neuropsychology, 20*, 321–333.

Frerichs, R. J., & Tuokko, H. (2006). Reliable change scores and their relation to perceived change in memory: Implications for the diagnosis of mild cognitive impairment. *Archives of Clinical Neuropsychology, 21*, 109–115.

Hultsch, D. F., Hunter, M. A., MacDonald, S. W. S., & Strauss, E. (2005). Inconsistency in response time as an indicator of cognitive aging. In J. Duncan, L. Phillips, & P. McLeod (Eds.), *Measuring the mind* (pp. 33–58). Oxford, UK: Oxford University Press.

Kral, V. A. (1962). Senescent forgetfulness: Benign and malignant. *Canadian Medical Association Journal, 86*, 257–260.

Levy, R. (1994). Aging-associated cognitive decline. Working Party of the International Psychogeriatric Association in collaboration with the World Health Organization. *International Psychogeriatrics, 6*, 63–68.

Lindenberger, U., & von Oertzen, T. (2006). Variability in cognitive aging: From taxonomy to theory. In F. I. M. Craik & E. Bialystok (Eds.), *Lifespan cognition: Mechanisms of change* (pp. 297–314). Oxford, UK: Oxford University Press.

Palmer, K., Bäckman, L., Small, B. J., & Fratiglioni, L. (2006). Cognitive impairment in elderly persons without dementia: Findings from the Kungsholmen Project. In H. A. Tuokko & D. F. Hultsch (Eds.), *Mild cognitive impairment*. New York: Taylor & Francis.

Peters, K., & Winocur, G. (2006). Combined therapies in mild cognitive impairment. In H. A. Tuokko & D. F. Hultsch (Eds.), *Mild cognitive impairment*. New York: Taylor & Francis.

Petersen, R. C. (2004). Mild cognitive impairment as a diagnostic entity. *Journal of Internal Medicine, 256,* 183–194.

Petersen, R. C., Smith, G. E., Waring, S. C., Ivnik, R. J., Tangalos, E. G., & Kokmen, E. (1999). Mild cognitive impairment: Clinical characterization and outcome. *Archives of Neurology, 56,* 303–308.

Rabbitt, P. M. A. (2000). Measurement indices, functional characteristics, and psychometric constructs in cognitive aging. In T. J. Perfect & E. A. Maylor (Eds.), *Models of cognitive aging* (pp. 160–187). New York: Oxford University Press.

Roth, M. (1971). Classification and etiology in mental disorders of old age: Some recent developments. *British Journal of Psychiatry, Special Publication No. 6,* 1–18.

Roth, M., Tomlinson, B. E., & Blessed, G. (1967). The relationship between quantitative measures of dementia and of degenerative changes in the cerebral grey matter of elderly subjects. *Proceedings of the Society of Medicine, 60,* 254–259.

Satz, P. (1993). Brain reserve capacity on symptom onset after brain injury: A formulation and review of evidence for threshold theory. *Neuropsychology, 7,* 273–295.

Smith, G., Machulda, M., & Kantarci, K. (2006). In H. A. Tuokko & D. F. Hultsch (Eds.), *Mild cognitive impairment*. New York: Taylor & Francis.

Stern, Y. (2002). What is cognitive reserve? Theory and research application of the reserve concept. *Journal of the International Neuropsychological Society, 8,* 448–460.

Stuss, D. T., Pogue, J., Buckle, L., & Bondar, J. (1994). Characterization of stability of performance in patients with traumatic brain injury: Variability and consistency on reaction time tests. *Neuropsychology, 8,* 316–324.

Tierney, M. C. (2006). Prediction of probable Alzheimer's disease: The Sunnybrook Memory Study. In H. A. Tuokko & D. F. Hultsch (Eds.), *Mild cognitive impairment*. New York: Taylor & Francis.

Tuokko, H., & Frerichs, R. J. (2000). Cognitive impairment with no dementia (CIND): Longitudinal studies, the findings, and the issues. *The Clinical Neuropsychologist, 14,* 504–525.

Tuokko, H., Frerichs, R., Graham, J., Rockwood, K., Kristjansson, E., Fisk, J., et al. (2003). Five year follow-up of cognitive impairment with no dementia. *Archives of Neurology, 60*(April), 577–582.

Tuokko, H., Gabriel, G., & the CSHA Neuropsychology Working Group. (2006). Neuropsychological detection of cognitive impairment: Inter-rater reliability, factors affecting decision-making and relations to other classification methods. *Journal of the International Neuropsychological Society, 12*(1), 72–79.

Tuokko, H., Garrett, D. D., Silverberg, N., Kristjansson, E., & McDowell, I. (2003). Cognitive decline in high-functioning older adults: Reserve or ascertainment bias? *Aging and Mental Health, 7*(4), 259–270.

Tuokko, H. A., & McDowell, I. (2006). An overview of mild cognitive impairment. In H. A. Tuokko & D. F. Hultsch (Eds.), *Mild cognitive impairment*. New York: Taylor & Francis.

Wilson, R. S., Aggarwal, N. T., & Bennett, D. A. (2006). Mild cognitive impairment in the Religious Orders Study. In H. A. Tuokko & D. F. Hultsch (Eds.), *Mild cognitive impairment*. New York: Taylor & Francis.

Winblad, B., Palmer, K., Kivipelto, M., Jelic, V., Fratiglioni, L., Wahlund, L.-O., et al. (2004). Mild cognitive impairment—beyond controversies towards consensus. A report of the International Working Group on Mild Cognitive Impairment. *Journal of Internal Medicine, 256,* 240–246.

Wolf, H., & Gertz, H.-J. (2006). Studies in the Leipzig Memory Clinic: Contribution to the concept of MCI. In H. A. Tuokko & D. F. Hultsch (Eds.), *Mild cognitive impairment*. New York: Taylor & Francis.

Woods, R. T., & Clare, L. (2006). Cognition-based therapies and mild cognitive impairment. In H. A. Tuokko & D. F. Hultsch (Eds.), *Mild cognitive impairment*. New York: Taylor & Francis.

Zaudig, M. (2002). Mild cognitive impairment in the elderly. *Current Opinions in Psychiatry, 15,* 387–393.

Author Index

Adams 248
Adroer 100
Aggarwal 117, 121–123, 291
Agostino 93, 231, 236
Aguero-Torres 57
Ahmed 87
Aisen 232
Akhtar 34
Albert 118, 148, 151, 201, 205
Allison 123
Almkvist 61, 103
Amieva 9(t), 43, 44
Anand 17, 271
Anderson 247, 269, 274, 275, 276, 278
Andrews 205
Angermeyer 7, 185, 189, 198
Anstey 297
Anthony 232
Arendt 192, 193, 197
Arens 248
Arnold 124
Artero 8(t), 39, 50, 153, 170, 171, 174
Asis 177, 201
Aurich 185, 198

Bäckman 45, 46, 57, 59, 61–65, 71, 248, 252
Baddeley 257, 276
Bakke 276
Ball 253, 275
Balsis 295
Bandura 253
Barberger-Gateau 13, 38, 46–49, 292
Barker 7, 78
Barkhof 202, 232
Barnetson 185, 202
Baron 145
Barrett-Connor 234

Bartus 4, 297
Baty 152
Baxter 144
Bayon 123
Beard 132
Beardsall 79
Beattie 14
Beck 121
Beckett 120
Beig 46
Beiser 93
Beksinska 98
Bell 41, 100
Belle 62
Belloi 247, 254, 279
Benedict 106
Bennett 7, 10(t), 117–122, 124–131, 150, 251, 291
Benton 34, 199, 135, 165, 167
Ben-Yishay 277
Berent 16, 71, 102, 148, 266
Berg 184, 206, 207
Berger 45, 71
Bergeron 220
Beringer 184
Berish 252
Berman 242
Bernspang 248
Berry-Kravis 121
Bettin 71, 194(t)
Bieliauskas 266
Bienias 118–121, 124, 228, 251
Bird 246
Birks 271
Bischkopf 7, 72, 198
Bitsch 143
Blacker 220, 232
Blackford 5
Blair 118

Author Index

Blau 41, 100
Blennow 177
Blesa 100
Blessed 19, 79, 203, 299
Blumenthal 4
Bobinski 200
Bocti 219
Boeve 140, 152
Bogdanovic 202
Bolzani 165
Bondar 297
Bondi 152
Borell 248
Borenstein 105
Bosma 205
Bourtchouladze 225
Bouter 39
Bowen 9(t), 93, 102, 103, 148, 151, 205
Bozoki 9(t), 16, 71, 148
Braak 124, 203, 204(f), 221, 222
Braekhus 71
Brand 143
Brayne 4, 78–79, 82–87, 296
Breen 248
Breenes 255
Breitner 232
Brenes 277
Breteler 202, 236
Breuil 247
Brines 108
Brodaty 202
Brody 34, 46, 272
Broekhoven, van 123
Bronge 202
Bronisch 184
Brown 94
Bruscoli 40
Buck 105
Buckle 297
Burgess 105
Burian 46
Buschke 135
Busse 7, 9(t), 10(t), 74, 185, 188, 191, 192, 197, 198
Butters 154, 165

Cabelli 80
Cahn 183
Cahn-Weiner 280
Caine 4, 6(t)
Callahan 10(t)
Calloway 4, 78
Camp 246, 248

Carlson 236
Carpenter 295
Carr 152
Carroll 123
Carter 248, 277
Caselli 145
Cash 34
Catani 143
Cauley 62
Celesia 234
Cerhan 154
Cha 150
Chadwick 80
Chatfield 296
Chen 62, 124
Cherry 246, 276
Chertkow 218–219, 296, 300–301
Chetelat 145
Chi 84
Chiodo 50
Chowdhury 10(t), 273
Christen 230
Christensen 297
Chu 125
Cipolli 167
Clare 18–19, 245, 248, 276–277, 295–296, 299, 301
Clark 220
Clarke 84
Clayton 87
Coben 184
Cochran 124–125, 220
Cohen 4, 297
Cole 252
Collie 12, 93–94, 99, 102–105, 107, 266, 294–296, 300
Convit 177, 201
Cooper 84, 119
Copeland 5, 80, 148
Coppens 248
Corbeil 247
Corder 12
Coria 122
Correa 16, 20
Court 119
Courtney 272
Coyle 143, 220, 270
Craik 119
Crain 141
Crook 4, 100(t), 184, 225, 297
Cruts 123
Crystal 41, 100
Cullum 87– 88
Cummings 7, 17, 268, 295

Cunane 259
Currie 94, 104, 291
Cutler 17

Dalal 229
Daly 148
Damaraju 271
Danysz 226
Danziger 184
Darby 93, 104, 106–107, 291
Dartigues 13, 32, 36, 38, 41–44, 47, 292
Davey 21
Davies 247, 270
Davis 247, 270
Dawson 269
Dean 5
Deary 245
DeCarli 9(t), 14, 202
Degenhardt 184
DeKosky 7, 9(t), 62, 72, 125, 174, 220, 268, 270
Delacourte 221, 223
De La Paz 145
de la Sayette 145
Delis 152, 165
Delon 220
DeLong 270
De Ronchi 64
De Santi 177
Desgranges 145
Desrosiers 18
De Vreese 167, 247, 254, 279, 280
Dewey 80, 84
DiCarlo 8(t), 13, 50
Dickerson 145
Dickson 124
Diehl 235
Dietrich 71, 194(t)
Dixon 252, 297
Dodge 9(t), 72, 174, 205
Doody 223, 247, 272, 276
Dooneief 41, 100
Doraiswamy 270
Downs 34
Drachman 35, 60, 94, 120, 136, 165, 200, 234
Drzezga 145
Duara 7, 78, 280,
Dubos 225, 254
Duff 106
Dufouil 87
Duncan 46
Dunn 173

Eastwood 14
Ebly 64, 71
Ecke 71, 194(t)
Edland 150
Eichenbaum 105
Einstein 224
Ekstrom 118–119
Elby 121
Elias 93, 100, 236
Elkins 236
Elliott 253
Elton 134
Emmerson 256
Emslie 257
Engedal 71
Engelhart 228, 230–231, 236
Ericsson 57
Esiri 202
Espino 11(t)
Etminan 232
Eustache 145
Evans 118–120, 124, 228, 251

Fabrigoule 13, 40–41, 43–44, 47–48, 292, 295, 298
Fahn 134
Falleti 106
Farah 218, 226
Farlow 17, 271, 272
Fastbom 11(t), 50, 57, 121
Feldman 266, 268
Fellgiebel 144
Fellows 83, 219
Ferman 133, 140
Fernández-Ballesteros 256
Ferris 4, 7, 31, 135, 138, 148, 184, 223, 272, 297
Feskens 231
Fillenbaum 94
Fillit 219
Finelli 254
Fioravanti 225, 247, 279
Fischl 201
Fisher 266
Fisk 9(t), 12, 14, 71–72, 292
Fitzpatrick 268
Fleming 298
Flicker 7, 31, 138, 148
Flier 71
Floyd 253
Foley 228, 230
Folstein 34–35, 58, 60, 79, 94, 97, 118, 120, 134, 136, 200

Foster 16, 71, 148, 266
Fotuhi 229, 230
Fox 71, 232
Framingham 41, 230, 231
Frampton 256
Fratiglioni 7, 11(t), 50, 57, 58, 61–65, 69, 121, 292
Freedman 224, 269
Frerichs 8(t), 16, 20, 121, 266, 269, 292, 293, 294
Friedman 276
Frisoni 11(t), 50, 121
Fuld 94
Funkenstein 118

Gabriel 14, 293
Gadian 143
Gaens 271
Gagnon 46
Galasko 152
Gale 84, 205
Ganguli 7, 9(t), 62, 72, 174–175, 205
Garcia-Sierra 128
Garrett 249, 297, 299
Gauthier 14, 46, 271
Gearing 141
Geda 268
Geerlings 7, 39
Gelinas 46
Gergel 272
Gershon 4, 297
Gertz 71, 181, 184, 189, 192, 193, 194(t), 196(t), 197, 292–296, 299
Gervais 221, 235
Geslani 173, 174
Geula 17
Ghoshal 125
Gill 78, 79, 232
Gilleard 79
Gilleron 36
Gilmor 270
Giordani 16, 71, 148, 266
Glisky 275, 276
Goekoop 145, 274
Gold 232
Golden 5
Goldlist 271
Goldman 62, 152
Golomb 148
Goodglass 97, 118, 135, 165
Goodwin 84
Goodyer 220
Goossens 252, 276

Gosche 200, 201
Gosses 248
Gould 205
Grady 46, 219, 234
Graf 266
Graham 8(t), 14, 21, 267, 272, 292
Grandmaison 277
Graves 205
Gray 152
Green 220
Greger 184
Greiner 18, 220
Griffiths-Jones 80
Grimley Evans 271
Grober 118
Grodstein 234
Grossberg 272
Grotz 34
Grundman 218, 270
Grunwald 194(t)
Grut 58
Guallar 229
Guider 252
Gunther 148
Guo 11(t), 50
Gurland 5
Gussekloo 121
Guyatt 164, 169

Hachinski 35, 79, 134, 186
Hallikainen 7, 93
Hamilton 152
Hammond 220
Hampel 177
Hamsher 119, 135
Hankey 231
Hänninen 7, 10(t), 13, 93, 103, 104(f)
Hansen 141
Haque 11(t)
Hara 7
Hardy 221
Harman 118
Hartman 271
Hartmann 234
Harvey 271
Hasher 44
Hasselmo 105
Haug 206
Hawley 276
Hayden 229, 232, 266
Haynes 169
Heaton 20
Hebert 50

Hedreen 141
Heeren 121
Heidebrink 16, 71, 148
Heiss 247
Helmers 36, 47
Henderson 78
Hendrie 10(t)
Henke 105
Hensel 192, 193, 194(t)–196(t), 197, 202
Herholz 247
Herlitz 61, 62
Herrmann 173, 174
Hertzog 252
Heyman 94, 141
Hickie 202
Hill 252–254
Hiller 181
Hoblyn 272
Hochhalter 276
Hodges 248
Hodkinson 79, 85
Hofman 202, 236
Hogan 64, 71, 121, 271, 272
Holub 276
Horton 108
Huber 183, 184
Hughes 184, 185, 198
Hultsch 252, 292, 297
Hunkin 277
Hunter 297
Huppert 78–80, 170, 257
Hyde 83

Iacono 254
Iakovidou 271
Ihara 71
Ikonomovic 125, 220
Iniguez 256
Isaacs 34
Israel 225, 254
Itil 224
Ivnik 4, 31, 39, 67, 102, 133, 146, 147, 150, 152–154, 174, 199, 219, 255, 297

Jack 11(t), 105, 106, 123, 141, 142, 148, 200, 201, 203
Jacobs 41, 100, 252
Jacobson 152
Jacoby 45
Jaeschke 164, 169, 173
Jagust 220

Jastak 135
Jayashree 17
Jelic 189
Jick 234
Jobst 185
Johnson 85, 123, 145, 248
Johnston 205, 236
Joles 123,
Jolles 205, 225
Jones 45, 63, 71, 83, 151, 268, 272
Jonker 7, 12, 16, 39
Jonsson 226
Jonsson Laukka 63
Jorm 44, 266, 297
Josephsson 248
Julin 189, 197

Kalmijn 231, 236
Kandel 226
Kang 234
Kaplan 97, 118, 135, 149, 165, 255
Karlsson 226
Karp 57
Katz 33, 34, 224
Katzman 35, 60, 94, 120, 136, 165, 184, 200, 205
Keightley 46
Keller 230
Kellman 234
Kemper 18
Kenn 259
Kermen 118
Kershaw 271
Kessels 224
Kessler 247
Kiefer 181
Kiss 171
Kittner 84
Kitwood 19
Kivipelto 196(t), 197
Kluger 148
Klunk 143
Kneifel 105
Knight 105, 106
Knipschild 224
Knook 121
Knopman 270, 273
Koivisto 93, 103
Kokmen 4, 31, 39, 67, 102, 103, 132, 134, 149, 150, 152, 174, 184, 199, 219, 255, 297
Koltai 247
Komo 255

Kordower 124, 125, 220
Korf 9(t)
Koudstaal 202
Kozarevic 254
Kraemer 7
Kral 3, 5, 183, 301
Kratz 8(t)
Kristjansson 167, 249, 292, 299
Kromhout 231
Kruggel 193
Kucyj 259
Kukull 9(t), 93, 148
Kumamoto 8(t)
Kuriansky 100
Kurland 146

La Rue 5, 100(t), 255
Laake 71
Lachman 253
LaCroix 84
Lafont 41
Lagaay 121
Lanctôt 223, 271, 272
Lane 104(f)
Larrabee 8(t)
Larrieu 8(t), 25, 38(t), 71, 150
Larson 9(t), 93, 148, 205
Lasek 181
Laukka 45, 63, 71
Launer 220, 231
Laurin 250
Lautenschlager 134, 135
Lawton 33, 46, 272
Le Bars 224
Leatherwood 235
LeBlanc 220
Ledesert 10(t), 170
Leeuw 202
Lehr 8(t)
Leibfritz 143
Leigh 98
Lentz 297
Letenneur 13, 36, 38, 39, 41, 43, 46, 47
Levin 8(t)
Lewkowicz 253
Li 273
Lieberburg 219
Liebowitz 20
Lilienfeld 271
Lin 234
Lindeboom 39
Lindenberger 297
Lindsay 250

Linn 41
Lipton 41, 100
Liu 84, 220
Loewenstein 7, 78, 280, 281
Logroscino 205
Longstreth 202, 236
Lopez 10(t), 50, 140, 150, 151, 202, 268
Lovestone 40
Lucas 133
Luis 7, 78
Lund 136
Lyketsos 268
Lynch 226

MacDonald 297
Machulda 144, 292
MacPherson 250
Maguire 105, 106
Maier 224
Maki 233
Malec 103, 133, 146, 148, 153
Mallison 184
Malloy 280
Maloney 270
Manolio 236
Marcoen 252, 276
Marder 41, 100
Marie 143
Markesbery 18, 200, 202, 203, 205, 220, 230
Markides 11(t)
Marsden 98
Marsh 255, 277
Martin 184
Martyn 84, 205
Maruff 12, 93, 94, 98, 99, 102, 104–107, 266, 269, 291
Mash 270
Massari 225
Massman 166, 247, 276
Masters 104, 291
Masur 41, 100
Mateer 18, 275, 276
Matschinger 185, 189
Matthews 80, 257, 296
Mattis 135, 147(f), 165
Mayer 232
Mayeux 145
Maytan 57
McCaffrey 106, 107
McClure 143
McCormick 93, 148, 205
McCurry 9(t), 93, 148

McDaniel 224, 225
McDonald 272
McDowell 14, 171, 173, 292, 293, 299
McHugh 34, 58, 79, 94, 118, 134, 165
McIntosh 46
McKeil 141
McKeith 136
McKhann 200
Meara 236
Meguro 9(t)
Mehta 232
Melac 225, 254
Mendes de Leon 119, 185, 201, 251
Merry 12, 71
Messina 271
Mesulam 270
Meyer 10(t), 11(t), 273
Mielke 247
Miles 252
Milinkevitch 225, 254
Miller 83, 152, 167, 220, 229, 231
Minnemann 8(t)
Mirra 124, 141
Mitchell 125
Mittelhammer 181
Mittelman 148
Mobius 223, 272
Mohs 94, 272
Monastero 69
Moniz-Cook 245, 276
Monsch 135, 152
Moore 235
Moossy 143
Morris 3, 11(t), 12, 17, 50, 62, 93, 94, 97, 118, 135, 141, 148, 150, 152, 206, 219, 228, 230, 236
Mortimer 18, 200, 202, 203, 205, 220
Moscovitch 44, 269
Moss 151
Mountjoy 257
Moya 256
Mueller 183
Mufson 124, 125, 141, 220, 270
Muir 78
Muller 181, 197
Müller-Oerlinghausen 181
Mungas 220
Myers 98
Mykkanen 103
Myslinski 254

Nagaraja 17
Naglie 271

Nagy 200, 202
Nargeot 170
Neale 85
Nelson 118
Neri 167, 247, 254, 279, 280
Nguyen 11(t)
Nickson 257
Nilsson 197
Nimmo-Smith 257
Noble 143
Noda 7
Nordberg 189
Nunzi 225
Nygard 13, 50, 248

O'Brien 132, 149–150
Oertzen 297
Ogawa 71
Okazaki 184
O'Keefe 105
Olazaran 255, 281
Olin 271
Oliva 100
Orgogozo 36
Orrell 245, 247, 276
Orsillo 106
Ortega 106
Oshima 71
Ott 235, 280
Overmier 276
Owen 46, 98
Ozsarfati 132

Palmer 7, 50, 64, 65, 67–69, 269, 292, 294–296
Panchalingam 143
Pantel 8(t)
Parhad 121
Parisi 4, 184
Parslow 297
Pastor-Barriuso 229
Patterson 223, 271
Paykel 79, 86, 87
Peck 94
Pepeu 226
Perrault 16
Perrig 230
Perry 230
Peskind 271
Peters 266–268, 292, 295–297, 301
Petersen 13, 174, 183
Petrie 225

Pettegrew 143
Pettie 79
Pickett 169
Pinek 169
Piracetam 225
Pogue 297
Polk 50
Pollitt 83, 84
Pols 235
Ponds 123
Price 35, 60, 93, 94, 120, 136, 165, 200, 219, 220, 270
Prigatano 269, 277

Qiu 9(t), 57, 69
Quach 10(t), 273

Rabbitt 297
Rao 134, 135
Rapp 233, 255, 277, 278
Raskind 271
Ratcliff 62
Rauch 11(t)
Raven 119
Ray 11(t)
Rebok 280
Rediess 4, 6(t)
Reed 93, 220
Reinikainen 103
Reisberg 7, 30, 135, 138, 148, 184, 223, 272
Reitan 166, 167
Remarque 121
Resnick 233
Rey 134, 147, 167
Reynolds 205
Richards 78
Richter-Landsberg 143
Riedel 225
Riedel-Heller 7, 72, 185, 189, 198
Riekkinen 103
Riemersma 229
Riley 18, 200, 202, 203, 204(f), 220
Ritchie 8(t), 10(t), 11(t), 39, 46, 50, 52, 151, 153, 170, 175
Rocca 132, 150
Rockwood 9(t), 12, 14, 71, 250, 292
Rodgers 247
Rodriquez-Artalejo 123
Rogers 94
Roman 136
Ronnberg 248

Rosen 186
Rosler 271
Rossor 71
Roth 19, 78, 79, 83, 167, 186, 203, 247, 257, 299
Rothschild 203
Rouch 13
Rouch-Leroyer 43, 44
Rourke 266
Royall 50, 51
Rubichi 167
Rubio 122
Rudorfer 20
Ruosseau 234
Rusinek 177, 201

Sabat 19
Sabbagh 145
Sachdev 297
Sackett 164, 169
Sager 119
Salloway 224, 273
Salmon 152, 165
Salthouse 252
Samet 84
Samii 232
Sano 41, 100, 228, 230
Santaengracia 123
Satz 19, 299
Sauer 8(t)
Saunders 122
Sauvel 46
Sawaya 219
Saykin 224
Saz 84
Schacter 277
Schatzberg 224
Schechter 94
Scheltens 9(t), 17, 202, 232
Schenk 221, 235
Scherr 118
Schimmel 94
Schipper 125
Schmahmann 148
Schmand 7, 39
Schmechel 247
Schmitt 223, 272
Schneider 44, 119, 251, 271
Schnirman 98
Schoenberg 184
Schofield 111, 205
Schork 189
Schroder 8(t)

Author Index 313

Scogin 252, 253
Scott 202, 225
Selkoe 220, 221, 235
Seshadri 231, 234
Severson 149
Shafiq-Antonacci 94
Shaw 270
Sheikh 252, 254, 276
Sheldon 21
Shen 9(t), 72, 174
Shepstone 185
Sherwin 219, 233
Shiffrin 44
Shumaker 233
Siegel 234
Sielhorst 224
Silbert 106
Silverberg 249, 299
Silverman 71
Simard 277
Simmons-D'Gerolamo 276
Sivan 119
Sliwinski 41, 100, 118
Smith 4, 21, 31, 39, 67, 93, 102, 103, 118, 119, 133, 134, 137(t), 146, 148–150, 152–154, 174, 184, 199, 200, 202, 219, 255, 292–297, 299
Snowdon 18, 104, 200, 202, 203, 205, 220, 221
Sohlberg 18, 275, 276
Soininen 7, 103
Song 21
Sparks 234
Spector 245, 247, 276
Spielmeyer 183
Spreen 118, 119, 135, 165, 167
Squire 105, 226
Sramek 17
Stadlan 35, 60, 94, 120, 136, 165, 200
Stahelin 230
Stern 19, 22, 41, 100, 145, 205, 299
Stevens 7
Stieler 196(t)
Stigsdotter 252, 260
Stoffler 223, 272
Stolk 235
Stollery 98
Stone 165, 167
Storandt 295
Strauss 297
Struble 220
Stump 10(t)
Stuss 297
Sugihara 71

Sullivan 236
Sumi 141
Summers 98
Susskind-Wilder 145
Swets 169
Szalai 170, 173, 174, 176
Szelies 247

Tallman 225
Tangalos 4, 7, 31, 39, 67, 102, 103, 133, 134, 146, 150, 152, 153, 174, 199, 219, 255, 297
Tangney 228
Tanke 276
Tanzi 151, 220
Tariot 272
Tàrraga 256
Tarshish 176, 201
Teri 9(t), 93, 148
Tervo 10(t)
Thal 218, 270
Theisen 108
Thornby 10(t), 273
Tierney 123, 148, 151, 152, 168, 170–174, 176, 293–296
Tinklenberg 152, 225
Tisserand 205
Tittgemeyer 200
Todd 84
Tomlinson 19, 79, 203, 299
Touchon 8(t), 10(t), 39, 50, 151, 153, 170, 174
Trinh 272
Truyen 271
Tsai 143
Tsolaki 271
Tugwell 169
Tulving 276
Tuokko 8(t), 14, 16, 21, 50, 64, 71, 121, 167, 199, 249, 266, 267, 269, 292–294, 299, 300
Tuomainen 7
Tyler 94
Tym 257

van Amerongen 202
van Boxtel 205
van Dongen 224
van Harskamp 235
van Rossum 224
Vanhanen 7
Varney 119, 135

Veach 271
Verghese 250
Verhaeghen 252, 253, 276
Verhey 123
Vermeer 202
Veroff 17
Verreault 250
Viader 145
Viitanene 121
Visser 9(t), 123
Von Dras 4
von Strauss 57

Wahlin 62
Wahlund 9(t), 189, 193, 197, 202
Wallenstein 105
Walton 205
Wang 57, 64, 124
Warring 4, 33, 39, 67, 102, 152, 174, 184, 199, 219, 255, 297
Warrington 71
Wattis 259
Weaver 253
Weaver-Cargin 104
Weber 105
Wechsler 34, 41, 60, 118, 134, 147, 165, 166(f), 167, 259
Weintraub 97, 118, 134, 135, 165, 270
Wekstein 18
Welles 106
Welsh 97
Welsh-Bohmer 247
Wenzlow 205
Weschler 98
Westrdorp 121
Westervelt 106
Weuve 234
Whelihan 13
Whitehead 219
Whitehouse 4, 197, 220
Wieck 183, 184
Wieser 105
Wilcock 271, 272

Wilhelm 202
Wilkinson 135, 272
Williams 143, 257
Wilson 117–121, 124, 228, 246, 248–251, 278, 291–295, 299
Wimo 250, 267, 313
Winblad 20, 24, 37, 39, 64, 67, 69, 72, 73, 77, 79, 80, 84, 88–90, 94, 218, 219, 233–235
Wingblad 127, 128
Winocur 269, 292, 295–297, 301
Wolf 71, 84, 93, 181, 189, 192, 193, 194(t)–196(t), 197, 198, 200, 201, 204, 236, 292–296, 299
Wolfe 235
Wolfson 16
Wolozin 234
Woods 18, 19, 245–247, 275, 276, 295, 299, 301
Wurtman 143

Xu 10(t), 142, 273

Yaffe 219, 233, 234, 272
Yamaguchi 71
Yao 171
Yesavage 20, 218, 225, 252, 254, 276

Zacks 447
Zaitchik 148
Zamarrón 256
Zandi 232
Zanetti 247, 279
Zarit 252
Zarow 200, 203
Zaudig 4, 5, 17, 181, 185–189, 197, 294
Zec 268
Zgaljardic 106
Zola-Morgan 105
Zornberg 234

Subject Index

AACD *see* Age-associated cognitive decline
AAMI *see* Age-associated memory impairment
ACMI (Age-consistent memory impairment) 100(t)
Activities of daily living (ADL) 13, 14, 33, 36, 37, 46, 137, 255, 272, 280
Activities of daily living, Instrumental (IADL) 13, 14, 32, 33, 40, 46–51, 280
Activities, physical 208, 249, 250
Age-associated cognitive decline (AACD) 4, 8(t), 11(t), 100(t), 137, 191, 192, 195(t), 198, 255
Age-associated memory impairment (AAMI) 4, 6(t), 7, 89(t), 11(t), 100(t), 103, 137, 224, 254
Alzheimer('s) disease
 diagnosis of 60, 62, 63, 69, 168, 189, 258
 early-stage 245, 247
 mild 17, 196(t), 220, 265, 269, 279–281
 pathology 124–126, 143, 188, 200, 201, 219
 risk of 40–42, 122, 123
 treating 265, 268–270, 273
Alzheimer Predictive Index (API) 170, 172–174
Amnestic Mild Cognitive Impairment *see* Mild Cognitive Impairment, amnestic form
Amyloid 221, 223, 234
Annual progression rate *see* Mild Cognitive Impairment annual progression rate
Antioxidants 220, 224, 227, 228, 230, 238, 270

Anxiety 95, 98, 102, 103, 252, 258, 268
Apolipoprotein (APOE) 59, 93, 95, 101, 122, 126, 145, 146, 172, 177, 189, 190(t)
Assessments
 multiple 107, 108
 serial 106, 107, 295, 297, 300
Atrophy 185, 188, 193, 194(t), 195(t), 201, 205
Attention, selective 43, 44, 48
Auditory Verbal Learning Test (AVLT) 134, 135, 147, 148, 154
 delayed recall 169, 170, 172, 173

Biological markers 18, 189, 190(t), 206, 207, 271, 295, 299
Blessed Dementia Scale 79, 87
Brain
 activity 274
 autopsy 117, 120, 124
 damage, acquired 18, 19, 265, 269, 274–276
 pathology 23, 143, 144, 152
 regions 142, 201, 270
 volume 192, 193, 195(t), 201, 202, 205, 206, 295
Brain Reserve Capacity (BRC) 19
Benton Visual Retention Test (BVRT) 34, 36, 41, 43(t), 43, 45, 49(t)

Cambridge City over-75 Cohort (CC75C) 77, 79–87
Cambridge Mental Disorders of the Elderly Examination (CAMDEX) 78, 79, 81(t), 81, 83, 85, 87, 167, 173, 186, 199

316 Subject Index

Cambridge Cognitive examination (CAMCOG) 79, 80, 83, 88
Cambridge Neuropsychological Test Automated Battery (CANTAB) 97, 98
Canadian Study of Health and Aging (CSHA) 9(t), 171, 172, 176, 267
CDR *see* Clinical Dementia Rating scale
CERAD *see* Consortium to Establish a Registry for Alzheimer's Disease
Cerebral infarctions 120, 124–127
Cerebrovascular disease (CVD) 33, 192, 202, 203
Cholesterol 21, 25, 181, 190, 195(t), 196(t), 197, 234, 236
Cholinergic system 125, 126
Cholinesterase inhibitors (ChEI or CI) 145, 146, 220, 222–224, 227(t), 231, 232, 237, 265, 269–273, 279–282
CIND *see* Cognitive Impairment, no dementia
Clinical Dementia Rating (CDR) 9(t), 11(t), 17, 95, 101, 102, 135, 136, 137(t), 181, 189, 192, 193, 194(t), 195(t), 198, 206, 274
Clinical judgment 12–14, 120, 136, 147, 154, 293, 294
Clinical
 samples 14–16, 70, 151, 152
 studies 14–17, 70, 88, 182, 202, 217, 293
 symptoms 18, 21, 190, 199, 202, 203, 207, 208
 trials 151, 176, 218–220, 225, 226, 229, 235, 273, 274
Cognition-based therapies *see* Interventions, cognitive
Cognitive *see also* Mild Cognitive Imapirment, Interventions, cognitive
 change 3, 87, 133, 184, 199–201, 271
 complaints 4, 32, 135, 136, 137(t)
 continuum 86, 88, 142, 185, 191, 192, 194(t), 195(t), 197, 199
 performance 18, 32, 36, 40, 47, 61–64, 77, 80, 102, 109, 147, 198, 200, 205, 269, 274, 278
 rehabilitation 18, 19, 246, 247, 249, 252–255, 260, 269, 274–276, 278–280, 301
Cognitive Failures Questionnaire 99, 102
Cognitive Impairment, no dementia (CIND) 8(t), 11(t), 21, 63–72, 137, 155, 266, 291

Cognitive Reserve (CR) 19
Combined therapies *see* Intervention, combined
Consortium to Establish a Registry for Alzheimer's Disease (CERAD) 94, 95, 97, 101, 103, 124, 141, 181
Conversion *see* Mild Cognitive Impairment, conversion to dementia, including AD
Cortex, entorhinal 124, 142, 221
CSHA *see* Canadian Study of Health and Aging
Computerized Tomography (CT) 181, 188–190, 193, 202
CVD *see* Cerebrovascular disease

Dementia
 conversions to *see* Mild Cognitive Impairment, conversion to dementia, including AD
 criteria 31, 34, 138
 defined 14, 77, 187, 198, 207
 development of 4, 16, 36, 42, 61, 64–66, 87, 88, 90, 134, 138, 139, 154, 159, 201, 205, 218, 223, 227, 229, 234–236, 242, 249–251, 292
 diagnosis 4, 34, 35, 36, 46, 57, 60, 62, 63, 66, 72, 118, 138, 139, 142, 186, 199, 245, 256, 293
 early-stage 247, 248
 frontotemporal 136, 140, 266
 incident 35, 49, 58, 87, 151, 253
 mixed 221, 235, 250
 multi-infarct 181, 186
 preclinical 58, 61, 228, 250, 251
 risk of 41, 42, 45, 122, 197, 233, 235, 236, 250, 257, 295
Dementia Rating Scale 11(t), 135, 147, 147(f), 148, 163, 165, 168(t), 169
Depression 12, 32, 33, 78, 95, 102, 103, 155, 223, 237, 247, 251, 254, 259, 267, 268, 269
Depressive symptoms 70, 251, 295
Diabetes 33, 94, 235–237
Diagnostic and Statistical Manual-III-Revised (DSM-III-R) 34–37, 81
Digit Symbol Substitution Test (DSST) 34, 43(t), 43, 45, 48(t), 49(t)
Distress, psychological 251
Donepezil 145, 218, 223, 224, 232, 237, 270–274, 280, 285, 286
DRS *see* Dementia Rating Scale

Subject Index   317

Education 7, 33, 36, 39, 40, 42, 47, 48(t), 64, 65, 70, 85(f), 87, 94, 95(t), 118, 120–123, 132, 168, 168(t), 169, 170, 171(t), 171–173, 182, 191, 193, 206, 249, 250–252, 255, 269
Encoding 52, 152, 252, 274, 276, 280
Epidemiological studies 31, 40, 52, 132, 175, 228, 229
Episodic memory 41, 45, 46, 59, 62–67, 69, 71, 98, 100, 102, 105, 118, 119, 122, 123, 152, 251, 294
Estrogen 219, 220, 227(t), 233, 237, 270
Executive control 44, 46, 50, 52, 295

Finances, handling 13, 47, 49, 50, 298

Galantamine 145, 223, 232, 270–274, 285
Genes and genetic studies 93, 122, 123, 126, 145, 146, 146(t), 164, 168, 169, 171–173, 189, 190, 271
Ginkgo biloba 222, 224, 225, 227(t), 230, 270

Hippocampal
 atrophy 141, 142, 193, 194(t), 197, 200, 203, 204(f)
 formation 105, 106
 volume 142(f), 142, 144, 144(f), 190(t), 192, 201, 201(f), 206, 207
Hippocampus 125, 142, 144, 200, 205, 221, 222(f), 251, 270
Homocysteine levels 230, 231, 236
Hormone Replacement Therapy (HRT) 233, 234

IADL *see* Activities of Daily Living, Instrumental
Intracranial Volume 193, 195(t), 196, 197, 205, 206
Imaging 52, 133, 141, 184
 Magnetic resonance imaging (MRI or MR) 11(t), 32, 132, 143, 181, 189, 192(t), 193, 201, 202
 Flurodeoxyglucouse Positron Emission Tomography 145
 Functional MRI (FMRI or ƒMRI) 144, 145
Immediate recall *see* Memory, immediate recall

Incidence
 of AD 37, 38
 of dementia 86, 150, 188, 249, 251, 260, 292
 of MCI 36
Informant Rating Scale 173, 174
Instrumental activities of daily living *see* Activities of Daily Living, Instrumental
Interventions (also referred to as therapies)
 behavioral 18, 21, 296
 cognitive 245–249, 252–255, 260, 265, 267, 269, 274–276, 279, 281
 combined 254, 279, 281
 evaluation of 17, 18, 20, 245
 pharmacological 17, 18, 20, 21, 125, 215, 217, 226, 228, 265, 266, 269, 279, 281, 282, 296, 298, 300, 301

Kungsholmen Project (KP) 50, 57, 58(f), 58, 60, 61(f), 61, 63, 64, 66–71

Leipzig
 Longitudinal Study of the Aged (LEILA) 185, 188, 189, 191, 192, 196, 198, 200
 Memory Clinic 163, 181, 185, 194(t)
Lewy body dementia 12, 136, 140, 177, 266

Magnetic resonance imaging (MRI) *see* Imaging
Mayo Clinic 4, 131, 132, 155, 174, 293, 294
Melbourne Aging Study 93, 94, 95(t), 99, 109, 110, 295
Memantine 223, 270, 272
Memory
 complaints, subjective 31, 63, 66, 67, 72, 151, 152, 154, 198, 199, 220, 222, 228, 229
 delayed recall 41, 43, 45, 47, 48, 62, 107, 118, 146, 152, 154, 165, 167, 169, 171(t), 259, 294
 immediate recall 146, 152, 167, 186
 impairment
  episodic 66, 105, 123, 124, 126
  isolated 187, 204(f), 266
  objective 36, 37, 145
  semantic 118, 119, 122, 123, 249, 294

Subject Index

Mild cognitive disorder 5, 100(t), 183, 184
Mild Cognitive Impairment (MCI)
  amnestic form (MCI-A or a-MCI or aMCI) 8(t), 9(t), 10(t), 12, 13, 14, 27, 67–69, 68(f), 71, 140–148, 146(t), 191, 192, 195(t), 198, 207, 219, 224, 232, 248, 266, 267, 273, 293
  annual progression rate 149, 150, 292
  conversion to dementia, including AD 7, 8(t), 12, 14, 15, 19, 31, 32, 38–40, 51, 93, 102, 148, 174, 175, 199, 232, 248, 292, 293, 295, 300
  criteria 32, 40, 67, 72, 103, 136, 188, 199
  defined 12, 13, 39, 67, 82, 121, 154, 174, 197, 292, 294
  diagnoses 36, 136, 146–148, 153, 258, 259
  multiple domain (MCI-MD or md-MCI or multidomain) 12, 68, 68(f), 69, 140, 146, 151, 292
  progression to dementia (also referred to as evolution) 16, 17, 22, 31, 32, 35, 39(t), 58, 63, 64 65(f), 69, 70, 71, 131, 137(t), 140, 141, 143, 148, 150, 153, 174, 175, 274
  single nonmemory domain (MCI-SD or sd-MCI) 12, 67–69, 68(f)
  subgroups 266, 267
  subtypes 12, 68–71
Mini-Mental State Examination (MMSE) 11(t), 17, 20, 34–37, 41, 43(t), 46, 47, 58, 59, 62–66, 68–71, 79–85, 82(t), 86(f), 87, 88, 94, 97, 101, 118, 119, 121, 163–165, 168, 168(t), 169(t), 172–175, 186, 198(t), 207, 271, 274, 280, 281, 294
MRI *see* Imaging

Neurofibrillary tangles 120, 204(f), 220–222
Neuropsychiatric symptoms 150, 268, 295, 298
Neuropsychological tests 22, 41, 42, 43(t), 45, 47, 51, 96–98, 107, 164, 167, 171, 172, 174–177, 189, 246
Normal aging 46, 72, 131, 132, 142, 174, 197, 207, 220, 225, 245, 246, 252, 254, 269, 274
Nun Study 18, 204(t)

Outcome measures 18, 20, 163, 183, 193, 199, 229, 279–281, 296
Oxidative
  damage 230
  stress 125, 126

PAQUID *see* Personnes Agées QUID: What about the Elderly?
Parkinson's
  dementia 42, 140
  disease 117, 163, 165, 182
Personality changes 5(t), 184, 295
Pharmacological therapies *see* Interventions, pharmacological
Personnes Agées QUID: What about the Elderly? (PAQUID) 32, 35, 39–41, 46, 47, 49(t), 51
Population-based
  samples 3, 16, 17, 35, 50, 70, 80, 82(t), 86, 198, 199, 293
  studies 14–17, 41, 77, 78, 82, 131, 176, 220, 228, 230, 291, 292
Practice effects 106, 107, 109, 200, 246, 253, 295
Preclinical dementia 44, 52, 61–63, 66(f), 70–72, 109, 147
Predictive
  value 32, 33, 39, 40, 47, 50, 51
Prevalence
  of dementia 248
  estimates 7, 12, 16, 82, 150
  of Mild Cognitive Impairment 7, 13, 16, 68, 72, 81, 82, 151, 174, 191, 192
Progession *see* Mild Cognitive Impairment, progession to dementia

Religious Orders Study 6, 117–125
Retrieval, spaced 248, 276

Serial assessments *see* Assessments, serial
State-Trait Anxiety Inventory (STAI) 95, 98, 102
Statins 227(t), 234, 237
Structured Interview for Diagnosis of Alzheimer type, Mutli-infarct and dementia of other aetilogies according to the ICD-10 and DSM-III-R (SIDAM) 181, 186–189, 191, 192, 197, 206

Sunnybrook Memory Study 163, 164, 172, 173, 175, 176, 177
Symptomatic therapy *see* Interventions, pharmacological
Symptoms, neuropsychiatric *see* Neuropsychiatric symptoms

Therapies *see* Interventions

Vascular dementia 3, 10(t), 21, 42, 57, 61–63, 136, 167, 177, 182, 186, 189, 190(t), 195(t), 220, 221, 27(t), 233, 235–237, 245, 250, 273, 292
Verbal fluency 41, 65–68, 273
Visuospatial 43–46, 60, 67–69, 119, 120, 122–124, 170, 186, 249, 294, 295

Volume
 intracranial 193, 196
 reduction 192, 194(t), 195(t), 200
 white matter 190, 192, 193, 202

Wechsler Adult Intelligence Test Similarities (WST) 34, 41, 43(t), 47, 48(t), 49(t)
Wechsler Memory Scale (WMS and subtests) 41, 43(t), 44–47, 48(t), 49, 49(t), 165, 167, 169, 170, 172, 173
Wechsler Memory Scale-Revised (WMS-R) 118, 134, 147
White Matter Lesions (WML) 188, 194(t), 195(t), 202
Women's Health Initiative Memory Study 233
Working memory 43, 44, 98, 107, 118, 119, 122, 123, 249, 274, 294

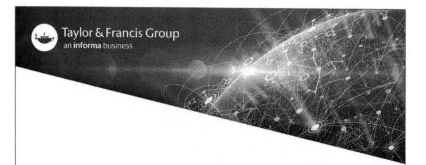